PRACTICAL DEEP LEARNING

A Python-Based Introduction

by Ronald T. Kneusel

no starch press

San Francisco

First printing

25 24 23 22 21   1 2 3 4 5 6 7 8 9

ISBN-13: 978-1-7185-0074-7 (print)
ISBN-13: 978-1-7185-0075-4 (ebook)

Publisher: William Pollock
Executive Editor: Barbara Yien
Production Editor: Dapinder Dosanjh
Developmental Editor: Alex Freed
Cover Illustration: Gina Redman
Interior Design: Octopod Studios
Technical Reviewer: Paul Nord
Copyeditor: Chris Cartwright
Proofreader: Sharon Wilkey

The following images are reproduced with permission. Figure 4-2: the middle image is licensed under the Creative Commons Attribution 2.0 Generic license (*https://commons.wikimedia.org/wiki/File:Border_Collie_liver_portrait.jpg*) and the right image is licensed under the Creative Commons Attribution-Share Alike 3.0 Unported license (*https://commons.wikimedia.org/wiki/File:Lynn-red_merle_Aussie_12_Months.jpg*)

For information on book distributors or translations, please contact No Starch Press, Inc. directly:
No Starch Press, Inc.
245 8th Street, San Francisco, CA 94103
phone: 415.863.9900; fax: 415.863.9950; info@nostarch.com; www.nostarch.com

Library of Congress Cataloging-in-Publication Data
Names: Kneusel, Ronald T., author.
Title: Practical deep learning : a python-based introduction / Ronald T. Kneusel.
Description: First edition. | San Francisco, CA : No Starch Press, Inc.,
   [2021] | Includes index.
Identifiers: LCCN 2020035097 (print) | LCCN 2020035098 (ebook) | ISBN
   9781718500747 (paperback) | ISBN 9781718500754 (ebook)
Subjects: LCSH: Machine learning. | Python (Computer program language)
Classification: LCC Q325.5 .K55 2021 (print) | LCC Q325.5 (ebook) | DDC 006.3/1-dc23
LC record available at https://lccn.loc.gov/2020035097
LC ebook record available at https://lccn.loc.gov/2020035098

For my children: David, Peter, Paul, Monica, Joseph, and Francis.

About the Author

Ron Kneusel has been working with machine learning in industry since 2003 and completed a PhD in machine learning from the University of Colorado, Boulder, in 2016. He currently works for L3Harris Technologies, Inc. Ron has two other books, both available from Springer: *Numbers and Computers*, and *Random Numbers and Computers*.

About the Technical Reviewer

Paul Nord works for the Valparaiso University Department of Physics and Astronomy as a technical specialist and research assistant. He is a 1991 graduate from Valparaiso University with a degree in physics. He also earned a master's degree in analytics and modeling from VU in 2017. Paul has worked on numerous machine learning projects, including the Disk Detective Collaboration, a Faculty Learning Community discussion group, and an art show using Google Deep Dream. Paul's other activities include science outreach programs for kids of all ages.

BRIEF CONTENTS

CONTENTS IN DETAIL

7
EXPERIMENTS WITH CLASSICAL MODELS
129

8
INTRODUCTION TO NEURAL NETWORKS
169

9
TRAINING A NEURAL NETWORK   189

10
EXPERIMENTS WITH NEURAL NETWORKS   221

16
GOING FURTHER   411

INDEX   417

FOREWORD

Since the dawn of the modern digital era, scientists and engineers have taken inspiration from the human brain to imagine how massively parallel networks of simple neuron-like processors might learn and adapt from experience. There have been waves of excitement in this topic as new mathematical methods were developed. In 1958, Frank Rosenblatt proposed a learning device called the Perceptron, which had the amazing property that it could learn any task that one could program it by hand to perform. The enthusiasm for this device vanished when Marvin Minsky and Seymour Papert performed a careful analysis showing limitations on what the device could be programmed to do, both in principle and in practice.

In the late 1980s, cognitive scientist David Rumelhart, along with Geoffrey Hinton and Ronald Williams, proposed a learning algorithm called back propagation that had the potential to overcome the limitations identified by Minsky and Papert. Impressive demonstrations of the algorithm, such as a text-to-speech system called NetTalk, led to another surge of interest in neural networks. This time, enthusiasm in the field was dampened when the algorithm did not seem to scale up to handle larger problems.

Over the next 20 years, computers got faster, datasets got larger, and new software tools made it easier to build neural networks. With these developments, much larger models became feasible. The field was rechristened *deep learning*, and a new generation of practitioners were able to tackle problems on a scale that was previously unimaginable.

Although history suggests that we will once again hit a wall with modern deep learning, the field has proven that it can solve difficult, practical, high-impact problems. From voice-controlled assistants to human-expert-level diagnosis of medical images to autonomous vehicles to myriad other behind-the-scenes applications, our lives have been transformed. The deep learning revolution is upon us, and the future holds untold promises of capabilities yet to come.

One might think that such advanced technology is beyond the understanding of most of us, but the underlying principles are quite understandable and accessible. Indeed, the academic grandparents of the deep learning revolution were psychologists by training. A standard desktop computer with open source software tools is adequate to explore the ideas and concepts in this textbook. With a modest investment in hardware upgrades (notably, a graphics processing unit, or GPU), the computer becomes what would have been considered a supercomputer a decade ago, enabling sophisticated research and implementation.

Dr. Kneusel is an expert in image processing and has over 15 years of industry experience with machine learning. He wrote *Practical Deep Learning* to make the field approachable to novices and hobbyists. With no assumption of background knowledge, it starts at the beginning. It shows how to build a dataset that will be useful for training a successful deep learning model. It then explores classical machine learning algorithms with the intent of grounding the methods that led to the deep learning revolution.

Practical Deep Learning provides not only a solid conceptual foundation but also the practical guidance readers will appreciate to design their own projects and solutions. It addresses how to tune and evaluate the performance of a machine learning model via the standards of current practice. Throughout the book, intuition is emphasized. Practical knowledge builds on intuition.

Practical Deep Learning also serves as a springboard to help launch you on to more advanced treatments of the methods and algorithms. The last four chapters dive into convolutional neural networks, a workhorse of supervised deep learning. The experiments in these chapters use standard datasets familiar to all those who work in the field. These chapters culminate in a case study, an example of how to approach a problem, from a dataset to evaluating a predictive model.

No book is complete. *Practical Deep Learning* is an introduction. The final chapter of the book points you toward what you may want to investigate next as you continue your journey into the deep learning revolution. Enjoy the exploration.

Michael C. Mozer, PhD
Professor, Department of Computer Science and
Institute of Cognitive Science
University of Colorado, Boulder

Research Scientist
Google Research
Mountain View, California

ACKNOWLEDGMENTS

"I am not I in myself alone, but only in all others."

As this quote from David Bentley Hart states, we are only ourselves in relation to all others. This is true in every area of our lives, including, even, in the writing of books.

First, I'd like to thank my family for their patience and encouragement to help me see this project through.

Next, I want to thank my editor, No Starch's very excellent and easy-to-work-with Ms. Alex Freed, who turned a mass of rough text into a flowing and coherent book. The same is to be said of Mr. Paul Nord, who saved me from my foolish errors and ensured that what I claim is true, is true. Any remaining errors are on me for not listening to Paul's suggestions.

Finally, I want to thank all the good folks at No Starch Press for believing in the book and helping it to become a reality.

INTRODUCTION

When I was in high school, I wanted to write a tic-tac-toe program that the user would play against a computer. At the time, I was blissfully unaware of how real computer scientists approached such a problem. I had only my own thoughts, and those were to implement a lot of rules using the crude if-then statements and gotos supported by unstructured Applesoft BASIC. It was a lot of rules—a few hundred lines' worth.

In the end, the program worked well enough, until I found the sequence of moves that my rules didn't cover and was able to win every time. I felt certain that there must be a way to teach a computer how to do things by showing it examples instead of brute-force code and rules—a way to make the computer learn on its own.

As an undergraduate student in the later 1980s, I was excited to sign up for a course in artificial intelligence. The course finally answered my question about how to write a tic-tac-toe playing program, but the computer wasn't learning; it was still just using a clever algorithm. Incidentally, the same course assured us that while it was expected that someday a computer would beat the world's best chess player, which happened in 1997, it was impossible for a computer to beat the best human at a game like Go. In March 2016, the AlphaGo deep learning program did just that.

In 2003, while working as a consultant for a scientific computing company, I was assigned to a project with a major medical device manufacturer. The goal was to classify, in real time, intravascular ultrasound images of coronary arteries by using *machine learning*: a subfield of artificial intelligence that learns from data on its own, developing models that were not explicitly programmed by a human. This was what I was waiting for!

I was vaguely aware of machine learning and that there were strange beasts called neural networks that could do some interesting things, but for the most part, machine learning was simply a small research area and not something the average computer science person paid much attention to. However, during the project, I fell in love with the idea of training a machine to do something useful without explicitly writing a lot of code. I kept learning on my own, even after the project ended.

Circa 2010, I was involved with another machine learning project, and the timing was perfect. People were just beginning to discuss a new approach to machine learning called *deep learning*, which revived the old neural networks. When 2012 rolled around, the flood-gates opened. I was fortunate enough to be in the room at the ICML 2012 conference in Edinburgh, Scotland when Google presented its initial breakthrough deep learning results that responded to cats in YouTube videos. The room was crowded. After all, there were a whopping 800 people at the conference.

It's now 2020, and the machine learning conference I recently went to had over 13,000 attendees. Machine learning has exploded: it's not a fad that will disappear. Machine learning has profoundly affected our lives and will continue to do so. It would be nice to know something about it, to get past the oftentimes hyped-up presentations down to the essential core, which is interesting enough, no hype needed. That is why this book exists, to help you learn the essentials of machine learning. Specifically, we'll be focusing on the approach known as deep learning.

Who Is This Book For?

I wrote this book for readers who have no background in machine learning, but who are curious and willing to experiment with things. I've kept the math to a minimum. My goal is to help you understand core concepts and build intuition you can use going forward.

At the same time, I didn't want to write a book that simply instructed you on *how* to use existing toolkits but was devoid of any real substance as to the *why* of things. It's true that if all you care about is the *how*, you can build useful models. But without the *why*, you'll only be parroting, not understanding, let alone eventually moving the field forward with your own contributions.

As far as assumptions on my part, I assume you have some familiarity with computer programming, in any language. The language of choice for machine learning, whether you are a student or a major corporation, is

Python, so that's the language we'll use. I'll also assume you're familiar with high school math but not calculus. A little calculus will creep in anyway, but you should be able to follow the ideas, even if the technique is unfamiliar. I'll also assume you know a bit of statistics and basic probability. If you've forgotten those topics since high school, don't worry—you'll find relevant sections in Chapter 1 that give you enough of a background to follow the narrative.

What Can You Expect to Learn?

If you work through this book in its entirety, you can expect to learn about the following:

- How to build a good training dataset. This is a dataset that will let your model be successful when used "in the wild."
- How to work with two of the leading machine learning toolkits: scikit-learn and Keras.
- How to evaluate the performance of a model once you've trained and tested it.
- How to use several classical machine learning models like k-Nearest Neighbors, Random Forests, or Support Vector Machines.
- How neural networks work and are trained.
- How to develop models using convolutional neural networks.
- How to start with a given set of data and develop a successful model from scratch.

About This Book

This book is about machine learning. Machine learning is about building models that take input data and arrive at some conclusion from that data. That conclusion might be a label placing the object into a particular class of objects, like a certain kind of dog, or a continuous output value, say the price one should ask for a house with the given set of amenities. The key here is that the model learns from the data on its own. In effect, the model learns by example.

You can think of the model as a mathematical function, $y = f(x)$, where y is the output, the class label, or the continuous value, and x is the set of *features* representing the unknown input. Features are measurements or information about the input that the model can use to learn what output to generate. For example, x might be a vector representing the length, width, and weight of a fish, where each of those measurements is a feature. Our goal is to find f, a mapping between x and y that we'll be able to use on new instances of x, for which we do not know y.

The standard way to learn f is to give our model (or algorithm) known data, and have the model learn the parameters it needs to make f a useful mapping. This is why it's called *machine learning*: the machine is learning the parameters of the model. We're not thinking of the rules ourselves and cementing them in code. Indeed, for some model types like neural networks, it's not even clear *what* the model has learned, only that the model is now performing at a useful level.

There are three main branches to machine learning: *supervised learning*, *unsupervised learning*, and *reinforcement learning*. The process we just described falls under supervised learning. We supervised the training of the model with a set of known *x* and *y* values, the *training set*. We call a dataset like this a *labeled* dataset because we know the *y* that goes with each *x*. Unsupervised learning attempts to learn the parameters used by the model using only *x*. We won't discuss unsupervised learning here, but you can transfer a lot of our discussion of supervised learning if you want to explore that area on your own later.

Reinforcement learning trains models to perform tasks, like playing chess or Go. The model learns a set of actions to take given the current state of its world. This is an important area of machine learning, and it has recently achieved a high level of success on tasks previously thought to be solely the domain of humans. Sadly, compromises had to be made to make this book manageable, so we'll ignore reinforcement learning altogether.

One quick note on terminology. In the media, a lot of what we're talking about in this book is referred to as *artificial intelligence*, or *AI*. While this is not wrong, it's somewhat misleading: machine learning is one subfield of the broader field of artificial intelligence. Another term you'll often hear is *deep learning*. This term is a bit nebulous, but for our purposes, we'll use it to mean machine learning with neural networks, in particular, neural networks with many layers (hence *deep*). Figure 1 shows the relationship between these terms.

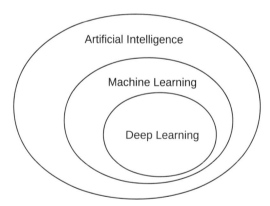

Figure 1: The relationship between artificial intelligence, machine learning, and deep learning

Of course, within the fields of machine learning and deep learning, there's considerable variety. We'll encounter a number of models throughout this book. We could arrange them in what we'll call "the tree of machine learning," pictured in Figure 2.

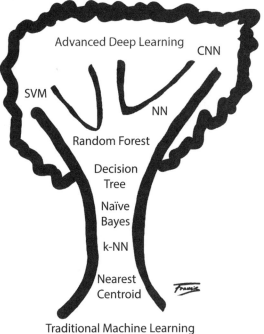

Traditional Machine Learning

Figure 2: The tree of machine learning

The tree shows the growth from traditional machine learning at the root to modern deep learning at the top of the tree. Consider this a preview of what's to come: we'll look at each of these models in this book.

Along those same lines, we'll end this introduction with a quick synopsis of each chapter.

Chapter 1: Getting Started   This chapter tells you how to set up our assumed working environment. It also includes sections about vectors, matrices, probability, and statistics that you can use as refreshers or for background.

Chapter 2: Using Python   This chapter will get you started on Python.

Chapter 3: Using NumPy   NumPy is an extension to Python. It's what makes Python useful for machine learning. If you are not familiar with it, peruse this chapter.

Chapter 4: Working with Data   Bad datasets lead to bad models; we'll teach you what makes a good one.

Chapter 5: Building Datasets   We'll build the datasets used through-out the book. You'll also learn how to augment datasets.

Chapter 6: Classical Machine Learning   To understand where you are going, sometimes it's good to know where you came from. Here we'll cover some of the original machine learning models.

Chapter 7: Experiments with Classical Models   This chapter shows the strengths and weaknesses of the old-school approach to machine learning. We'll refer to these results for comparison purposes throughout the book.

Chapter 8: Introduction to Neural Networks   Modern deep learning is all about neural networks; we'll introduce them here.

Chapter 9: Training a Neural Network   This challenging chapter gives you the knowledge you need to understand how neural networks are trained. Some basic calculus slipped into this chapter, but don't panic—it's discussed at a high level to give you intuition, and the notation isn't as frightening as it might seem at first.

Chapter 10: Experiments with Neural Networks   Here we run experiments to build intuition and get a feel for actually working with data.

Chapter 11: Evaluating Models   To understand the results presented in machine learning papers, talks, and lectures, we need to understand how to evaluate models. This chapter will take you through the process.

Chapter 12: Introduction to Convolutional Neural Networks   The deep learning we will focus on in this book is embodied in the idea of a convolutional neural network, or CNN. This chapter discusses the basic building blocks of these networks.

Chapter 13: Experiments with Keras and MNIST   Here we'll explore how CNNs work by experimenting with the MNIST dataset, the workhorse of deep learning.

Chapter 14: Experiments with CIFAR-10   The MNIST dataset, useful as it is, is a simple one for CNNs to master. Here we explore another workhorse dataset, CIFAR-10, which consists of actual images and will challenge our models.

Chapter 15: A Case Study: Classifying Audio Samples   We'll conclude with a case study. We start with a new dataset, one not in widespread use, and work through the process of building a good model for it. This chapter uses everything we studied in the book, from building and augmenting data to classical models, traditional neural networks, CNNs, and ensembles of models.

Chapter 16: Going Further   No book is complete. This one won't even try to be. This chapter points out some of what we've neglected and helps you sift through the mountains of resources around you related to machine learning so you can focus on what you should study next.

All the code in the book, organized by chapter, can be found here: *https://nostarch.com/practical-deep-learning-python/*. Let's now take a look at setting up our operating environment.

1

GETTING STARTED

This chapter introduces our operating environment and details how to set it up. It also includes a primer on some of the math we will encounter. We'll end with a brief note about graphics processors, or GPUs, which you may have heard are essential for deep learning. For our purposes, they're not, so don't worry—this book won't suddenly cost you a lot of money.

The Operating Environment

In this section, we'll detail the environment we'll assume throughout the remainder of the book. Our underlying assumption is that we're using a 64-bit Linux system. The exact distribution is not critical, but to make things simpler in the presentation, we'll also assume that we're using Ubuntu 20.04. Given the excellent support behind the Ubuntu distribution, we trust that any newer distributions will also work similarly. The Python language is our *lingua franca*, the common language of machine learning. Specifically, we'll use Python 3.8.2; that's the version used by Ubuntu 20.04.

Let's look at a quick overview of the Python toolkits that we'll be using.

NumPy

NumPy is a Python library that adds array processing abilities to Python. While Python lists can be used like one-dimensional arrays, in practice they are too slow and inflexible. The NumPy library adds the array features missing from Python—features that are necessary for many scientific applications. NumPy is a base library required by all the other libraries we'll use.

scikit-learn

All of the traditional machine learning models we'll explore in this book are found in the superb scikit-learn library, or *sklearn*, as it's usually called when loaded into Python. Note also that we're writing *scikit-learn* without caps as this is how the authors consistently refer to it in their documentation. This library uses NumPy arrays. It implements a standardized interface to many different machine learning models as well as an entire host of other functionality that we won't even have time to touch. I strongly encourage you to review the official sklearn documentation (*https://scikit-learn.org/stable/documentation.html*) as you become more and more familiar with machine learning and the tools behind it.

Keras with TensorFlow

Deep learning is hard enough to understand, let alone implement efficiently and correctly, so instead of attempting to write convolutional neural networks from scratch, we'll use one of the popular toolkits already in active development. From its inception, the deep learning community has supported the development of toolkits to make deep networks easier to use and has made the toolkits open source with very generous licenses. At the time of this writing, there are many popular toolkits we could have used in Python. Among many others, these include the following:

- Keras
- PyTorch
- Caffe
- Caffe2
- Apache MXnet

Some of these toolkits are waxing, and others appear to be waning. But the one that has probably the most active following at present is Keras with the TensorFlow backend, so that's the one we'll use here.

Keras (*https://keras.io/*) is a Python deep learning toolkit that uses the TensorFlow toolkit (*https://www.tensorflow.org/*) under the hood. *TensorFlow* is an open source Google product that implements the core functionality of deep neural networks for many different platforms. We selected Keras not only because it's popular and in active development, but also because it's straightforward to use. Our goal is to become familiar with deep learning to the point where we can implement models and use them with a minimum of programming overhead.

Installing the Toolkits

We can't reasonably give an exhaustive guide for installing the toolkits on all systems and hardware. Instead, we'll provide step-by-step instructions for the specific operating system we'll use as the reference system. These steps, along with the minimum version numbers of the libraries, should be enough for most readers to get a working system in place.

Remember, we're assuming that we're working in a Linux environment, specifically Ubuntu 20.04. Ubuntu is a widely used Linux distribution, and it runs on almost any modern computer system. Other Linux distributions will work, as will macOS, but the instructions here are specific to Ubuntu. For the most part, the machine learning community has left the Windows operating system. Still, individuals have ported toolkits to Windows; therefore, an adventurous reader might give Windows a try.

A freshly installed Ubuntu 20.04 base desktop system gives us Python 3.8.2 for free. To install the remaining packages, we need to go into a shell and execute the sequence of steps below in the order given:

```
$ sudo apt-get update
$ sudo apt-get install python3-pip
$ sudo apt-get install build-essential python3-dev
$ sudo apt-get install python3-setuptools python3-numpy
$ sudo apt-get install python3-scipy libatlas-base-dev
$ sudo apt-get install python3-matplotlib
$ pip3 install scikit-learn
$ pip3 install tensorflow
$ pip3 install pillow
$ pip3 install h5py
$ pip3 install keras
```

Once the installation is complete, we'll have installed the following versions of the libraries and toolkits:

```
NumPy 1.17.4
sklearn 0.23.2
keras 2.4.3
tensorflow 2.2.0
pillow 7.0.0
h5py 2.10.0
matplotlib 3.1.2
```

The `pillow` library is an image processing library, `h5py` is a library for working with HDF5 format data files, and `matplotlib` is for plotting. *HDF5* is a generic, hierarchical file format for storing scientific data. Keras uses it to store model parameters.

The following two sections are light introductions to some of the math that will creep into the book.

Basic Linear Algebra

We're about to look at vectors and matrices. The math that deals with these concepts falls under the general heading of *linear algebra*, or matrix theory. As you might imagine, linear algebra is a complex field. All we need to know for this book is what a vector is, what a matrix is, and how we can multiply two vectors, or two matrices, or vectors and matrices together. We'll see later on that this gives us a powerful way to implement specific models, particularly neural networks.

Let's begin by looking at vectors.

Vectors

A *vector* is a one-dimensional list of numbers. Mathematically, a vector might appear as

$$a = [0, 1, 2, 3, 4]$$

with the third element given as $a_2 = 2$. Notice we're following the programming convention of indexing from zero, so a_2 gives us the third element in the vector.

The vector above was written horizontally and therefore is known as a *row vector*. When used in mathematical expressions, however, vectors are usually assumed to be written vertically:

$$a = \begin{bmatrix} 0 \\ 1 \\ 2 \\ 3 \\ 4 \end{bmatrix}$$

When written vertically, a vector is known as a *column vector*. This vector has five elements and is denoted as a five-element column vector. In this book, we'll typically use vectors to represent one *sample*: one set of features that we'll input to a model.

Mathematically, vectors are used to represent points in space. If we're talking about the two-dimensional (2D) Cartesian plane, we locate a point with a vector of two numbers, (x, y), where x is the distance along the x-axis and y is the distance along the y-axis. That vector represents a point in two dimensions, even though the vector itself has only one dimension. If we have three dimensions, we need a vector with three elements, (x, y, z).

In machine learning, since we often use vectors to represent the inputs to our models, we'll be working with dozens to hundreds of dimensions. Of course, we can't plot them as points in a space, but mathematically, that's what they are. As we'll see, some models, such as the *k*-Nearest Neighbors model, use the feature vectors as just that—points in a high-dimensional space.

Matrices

A *matrix* is a two-dimensional array of numbers where we index a particular entry by its row number and column number. For example, this is a matrix:

$$a = \begin{bmatrix} 1 & 2 & 3 \\ 4 & 5 & 6 \\ 7 & 8 & 9 \end{bmatrix}$$

If we want to refer to the 6, we write $a_{1,2} = 6$. Again, we're indexing from zero. Because this matrix a has three rows and three columns, we call it a 3×3 matrix.

Multiplying Vectors and Matrices

The simplest way to think of multiplying two vectors together is to multiply their corresponding elements. For example:

$$[1, 2, 3] \times [4, 5, 6] = [4, 10, 18]$$

This is the most common way to multiply an array when using a toolkit like NumPy, and we'll make heavy use of this in the chapters that follow. However, in mathematics, this is seldom actually done.

When multiplying vectors together mathematically, we need to know if they are row or column vectors. We'll work with two vectors, $A = (a, b, c)$, and $B = (d, e, f)$, which, following mathematical convention, are assumed to be column vectors. Adding a superscript T turns a column vector into a row vector. The mathematically allowed ways to multiply A and B are

$$AB^T = \begin{bmatrix} a \\ b \\ c \end{bmatrix} \begin{bmatrix} d & e & f \end{bmatrix} = \begin{bmatrix} ad & ae & af \\ bd & be & bf \\ cd & ce & cf \end{bmatrix}$$

which is called the *outer product* and

$$A^T B = \begin{bmatrix} a & b & c \end{bmatrix} \begin{bmatrix} d \\ e \\ f \end{bmatrix} = ad + be + ef$$

which is called the *inner product*, or *dot product*. Notice that the outer product becomes a matrix, and the inner product becomes a single number, a *scalar*.

When multiplying a matrix and a vector, the vector is typically on the right side of the matrix. The multiplication can proceed if the number of columns in the matrix matches the number of elements in the vector, again assumed to be a column vector. The result is also a vector with as many elements as there are rows in the matrix (read $ax + by + cz$ as a single element).

For example:

$$\begin{bmatrix} a & b & c \\ d & e & f \end{bmatrix} \begin{bmatrix} x \\ y \\ z \end{bmatrix} = \begin{bmatrix} ax + by + cz \\ dx + ey + fz \end{bmatrix}$$

Here we've multiplied a 2×3 matrix by a 3×1 column vector to get a 2×1 output vector. Notice that the number of columns of the matrix and the number of rows of the vector match. If they do not, then the multiplication is not defined. Also, notice that the values in the output vector are sums of products of the matrix and vector. This same rule applies when multiplying two matrices:

$$\begin{bmatrix} a & b & c \\ d & e & f \end{bmatrix} \begin{bmatrix} A & B \\ C & D \\ E & F \end{bmatrix} = \begin{bmatrix} aA + bC + cE & aB + bD + cF \\ dA + eC + fE & dB + eD + fF \end{bmatrix}$$

Here multiplying a 2×3 matrix by a 3×2 matrix has given us a 2×2 answer.

When we get to convolutional neural networks, we'll work with arrays that have three and even four dimensions. Generically, these are referred to as *tensors*. If we imagine a stack of matrices, all the same size, we get a three-dimensional tensor, and we can use the first index to refer to any one of the matrices and the remaining two indices to refer to a particular element of that matrix. Similarly, if we have a stack of three-dimensional tensors, we have a four-dimensional tensor, and we can use the first index of that to refer to any one of the three-dimensional tensors.

The main points of this section are that vectors have one dimension, matrices have two dimensions, there are rules for multiplying these objects together, and our toolkits will work with four-dimensional tensors in the end. We'll review some of these points as we encounter them later in the book.

Statistics and Probability

The topics of statistics and probability are so broad that often it's better to either say almost nothing or to write a book or two. Therefore, I'll mention only key ideas that we'll use throughout the book and leave the rest to you to pick up as you see fit. I'll assume you know some basic things about probability from flipping coins and rolling dice.

Descriptive Statistics

When we do experiments, we need to report the results in some meaningful way. Typically, for us, we'll report results as the mean (arithmetic average) plus or minus a quantity known as the *standard error of the mean (SE)*. Let's define the standard error of the mean through an example.

If we have many measurements x, say the length of a part of a flower, then we can calculate the mean ($\bar{x}$) by adding all the values together and dividing by the number of values we added. Then, once we have the mean, we can calculate the average spread of the individual values around the mean by subtracting each value from the mean, squaring the result, and adding all these squared values together before dividing by the number of values we added minus one. This number is the *variance*. If we take the square root of this value, we get the *standard deviation* (σ), which we'll see again below. With the standard deviation, we can calculate the standard error of the mean as $SE = \sigma/\sqrt{n}$, where n is the number of values that we used to calculate the mean. The smaller the SE is, the more tightly the values are clustered around the mean. We can interpret this value as the uncertainty we have about the mean value. This means we expect the actual mean, which we don't really know, to be between $\bar{x} - SE$ and $\bar{x} + SE$.

Sometimes, we'll talk about the median instead of the mean. The *median* is the middle value, the value that half of our samples are below and half are above. To find the median for a set of values, we first sort the values numerically and then find the middle value. This is the exact middle value if we have an odd number of samples, or the mean of the two middle values if we have an even number of samples. The median is sometimes more useful than the mean if the samples do not have a good, even spread around the mean. The classic example is income. A few very rich people move the mean income up to the point where it does not have much meaning. Instead, the median, the value where half the people make less and half make more, is more representative.

In later chapters, we'll talk about *descriptive statistics*. These are values derived from a dataset that can be used to understand the dataset. We just mentioned three of them: the mean, the median, and the standard deviation. We'll see how to use these and how they can be plotted to help us understand a dataset.

Probability Distributions

In this book, we'll talk about something known as a *probability distribution*. You can think of it as an oracle of sorts—something that, when asked, will give us a number or set of numbers. For example, when we train a model, we use numbers, or sets of numbers, that we measure; we can think of those numbers as coming from a probability distribution. We'll refer to that distribution as the *parent distribution*. Think of it as the thing that generates the data we'll feed our model; another, more Platonic, way to think about it is as the ideal set of data that our data is approximating.

Probability distributions come in many different forms; some even have names. The two that we'll encounter are the two most common: uniform and normal distributions. You've already encountered a uniform distribution: it's what we get if we roll a fair die. If the die has six sides, we know that the likelihood of getting any value, 1 through 6, is the same. If we roll the die 100 times and tally the numbers that come up, we know that the tally will be roughly equal for each number and that in the long run, we can easily convince ourselves that the number will even out.

A *uniform distribution* is an oracle that is equally likely to give us any of its allowed responses. Mathematically, we'll write uniform distributions as $U(a, b)$ where U means uniform and a and b are the range of values it will use to bracket its response. Unless we specify the distribution gives only integers, any real number is allowed as the response. Notationally, we write $x \sim U(0, 1)$ to mean that x is a value returned by the oracle that gives real numbers in the range $(0, 1)$ with equal likelihood. Also, note that using "(" and ")" to bracket a range excludes the associated bound, while using "[" and "]" includes it. Thus $U[0, 1)$ returns values from 0 to 1, including 0 but excluding 1.

A *normal distribution*, also called a *Gaussian* distribution, is visually a bell curve—a shape where one value is most likely, and then the likelihood of the other values decreases as one gets further from the most likely value. The most likely value is the mean, $\bar{x}$, and the parameter that controls how quickly the likelihood drops to zero (without ever really reaching it) is the standard deviation, σ (sigma). For our purposes, if we want a sample from a normal distribution, we'll write $x \sim N(\bar{x}, \sigma)$ to mean x is drawn from a normal distribution with a mean of $\bar{x}$ and a standard deviation of σ.

Statistical Tests

Another topic that will pop up from time to time is the idea of a *statistical test*, a measurement used to decide if a particular hypothesis is likely true or not. Typically, the hypothesis relates to two sets of measurements, and the hypothesis is that the two sets of measurements came from the same parent distribution. If the statistic calculated by the test is outside of a certain range, we reject the hypothesis and claim we have evidence that the two sets of measurements are *not* from the same parent distribution.

Here, we'll usually use the *t-test*, a common statistical test that assumes our data is normally distributed. Because we assumed that our data is normally distributed, which may or may not be true, the t-test is known as a *parametric test*.

Sometimes, we'll use another test, the *Mann−Whitney U test*, which is like a t-test in that it helps us decide if two samples are from the same parent distribution, but it makes no assumption about how the data values in the sample are themselves distributed. Tests like these are known as *nonparametric tests*.

Whether the test is parametric or nonparametric, the value we ultimately get from the test is called a *p-value*. It represents the probability that we would see the test statistic value we calculated if the hypothesis that the samples come from the same parent distribution is true. If the *p*-value is low, we have evidence that the hypothesis is not true.

The usual *p*-value cutoff is 0.05, indicating a 1 in 20 chance that we'd measure the test statistic value (t-test or Mann−Whitney U) even if the samples came from the same parent distribution. However, in recent years, it has become clear that this threshold is too generous. When *p*-values are near 0.05, but not above, we begin to think there is some evidence against the hypothesis. If the *p*-value is, say, 0.001 or even less, then we have strong evidence that the samples are not from the same parent distribution. In this case, we say that the difference is *statistically significant*.

Graphics Processing Units

One of the enabling technologies for modern deep learning was the development of powerful *graphics processing units (GPUs)*. These are co-computers implemented on graphics cards. Originally designed for video gaming, the highly parallel nature of GPUs has been adapted to the extreme computational demands of deep neural network models. Many of the advances of recent years would not have been possible without the supercomputer-like abilities GPUs provide to even basic desktop computers. NVIDIA is the leader in the creation of GPUs for deep learning, and via its Compute Unified Device Architecture (CUDA), NVIDIA has been foundational to the success of deep learning. It's not an understatement to say that without GPUs, deep learning would not have happened, or at least not been so widely used.

That said, we're not expecting GPUs to be present for the models we'll work with in this book. We'll use small enough datasets and models so that we can train in a reasonable amount of time using just a CPU. We've already enforced this decision in the packages we've installed, since the version of TensorFlow we installed is a CPU-only version.

If you do have a CUDA-capable GPU and you want to use it for the deep learning portion of this book, please do so, but don't think that you need to purchase one to run the examples. If you're using a GPU, be sure to have CUDA properly installed before installing the packages indicated previously and be sure to install a GPU-enabled version of TensorFlow. The sklearn toolkit is CPU only.

Summary

In this chapter, we summarized our operating environment. Next, we described the essential Python toolkits we'll use throughout the book and gave detailed instructions for installing the toolkits assuming an Ubuntu 20.04 Linux distribution. As mentioned, the toolkits will work just as nicely on many other Linux distributions as well as macOS. We then briefly reviewed some of the math we'll encounter later and ended with an explanation of why we do not need GPUs for our models.

In the next chapter, we'll review the fundamentals of Python.

2

USING PYTHON

If you're already familiar with Python, you can skip this chapter. This summary is for those who are comfortable with programming but who aren't familiar with Python. We'll cover only enough of the language to be able to read and understand the code examples in this book. If you have little to no experience with computer programming, you should first read a more complete text like *Python Crash Course*, 2nd Edition, by Eric Matthes (No Starch Press, 2019).

Python is, at its simplest, sequential statements grouped into blocks via indentation; data structures like numbers, strings, tuples, lists, and dictionaries; control structures including if-elif-else, for loops, while loops, with statements, and try-except blocks; functions with optional nested functions; and a large library of importable modules. We'll cover each of these features.

The Python Interpreter

On a Linux system, Python is typically used in one of two ways. You can run the Python interpreter from the command line and enter commands interactively, or you can run a script of Python commands. Simply enter **python3** in your console to use Python interactively:

```
$ python3
Python 3.6.7 (default, Oct 22 2018, 11:32:17)
[GCC 8.2.0] on linux
Type "help", "copyright", "credits" or "license" for more information.
>>>
```

As you can see, Python opens a prompt for you to enter commands into, beginning with >>>. Type an expression like 1+2 and hit ENTER. Python will respond immediately by evaluating the equation and passing you the result. When you want to exit the console, use CTRL-D.

Statements and Whitespace

As in almost every other programming language, unless modified by a control flow structure, statements in Python are executed one after the other in the order in which they appear in the code. Consider, for example, this code:

```
statement1
statement2
statement3
```

Here statement1 will be executed first, followed by statement2, and then, finally, statement3.

Multiple statements can be grouped into units called *blocks*. For example, the condition of an if statement evaluating to True could trigger a block to run. Syntactically, the statements that go with the if need to be marked in some way so that the computer knows which statements to execute. Classic languages like Pascal used bulky BEGIN and END keywords. The C family of languages, which includes most of the languages in current widespread use, uses curly brackets: "{" and "}".

In Python, we use indentation. This makes reading Python code somewhat elegant as it follows the format of a traditional outline. It also makes the code more visually consistent across authors and leaves less room for confusion. In Python, when we use an if else statement, we can easily see which statements should run with which part of the condition, even if we have not yet understood the format of the if statement. For example:

```
if condition1:
    statement1
    statement2
else:
    statement3
```

The indentation makes it clear that `statement1` and `statement2` are executed when `condition1` (whatever it is) is true. Similarly, we see that `statement3` is executed when `condition1` is not true.

Notice the colons in the preceding `if` example. Python uses these to designate blocks of code. You must place a colon after any control statement, and then the next line should always be indented one level. If you try to use a control structure but don't provide any statements in the body of the control structure, Python will throw an error.

For example, the `else:` clause cannot be present without at least one statement in the block. If there is no need for the `else`, just don't include it. (If you really want to include it, use the `pass` keyword to indicate to Python that you know a statement needs to be there, but you really don't want that condition to do anything.)

Indentation can seem intimidating to people new to Python, but you can make it easier on yourself by properly configuring your text editor. Python convention says that you should tell your text editor to do the following:

1. Insert spaces in place of tab characters. Shun tab characters like the plague.

2. Insert four spaces every time you hit the TAB key.

3. Automatically indent when you hit the ENTER key.

With these settings, when you enter the ":" of a control statement, just hit ENTER, and Python will indent the block automatically.

The way to configure these settings depends on the text editor used, of course, but any text editor worth its salt will be able to do all of these, and many have automatic indentation set as standard. If you use integrated development environments (IDEs), then it's probable that once the IDE recognizes that you're coding in Python, most of these conventions will just happen.

Variables and Basic Data Structures

Python's native data structures are simple and elegant. In this section, we'll cover number representation, variables, strings, lists, and dictionaries.

Representing Numbers

Numbers in Python are of two kinds: integers or floating-point. *Integers* are whole numbers like 42 and 66. *Floating-point numbers* are those with a decimal point like 3.1415 and 2.718. We'll ignore complex numbers in this book, although Python supports them.

If you don't include a decimal point, Python will assume you mean an integer; otherwise, it will use floating-point numbers. Floating-point numbers can also be specified using scientific notation, where `6.022e23` means 6.023×10^{23}.

Most programming languages can represent only numbers in a certain range, but Python does not have this restriction for integers, which can be as large as there is memory to hold them. For fun, enter **2**2001** and see what happens. The many ways in which computers store and operate on numbers is quite fascinating. Those who are curious might want to look further.[1]

Variables

Variables provide a useful place to store data for reuse. Fortunately, using Python variables is straightforward. Python is *dynamically typed*, which means we don't need to declare the type of data a variable will store in advance. We simply assign data to a variable, and Python figures out the type for us.

We can even change the type of data stored in a variable by assigning a new value, regardless of its type. For example, all of these are valid assignments in Python:

```
❶ >>> v = 123
❷ >>> n = 3.141592
❸ >>> v = 6.022e23
```

The code assigns integer 123 to v ❶, the floating-point value 3.141592 to n ❷, and then reassigns a floating-point value to v: 6.022×10^{23} ❸.

Python variable names are case-sensitive, must start with a letter, and can include letters, numbers, and "_" (underscore) characters. Many Python programmers follow the camel-case convention of Java, shown here, but this is not strictly required:

```
>>> myVariableName=123
```

Strings

Python supports textual data with strings. You mark the beginning and end of *strings* with quotes, either single ('), double (''), or triple ('''), as long as you use the same for both opening and closing. The triple-quoted string is special: it can span multiple lines of text, and you would often use it immediately after defining a function to implement a simple documentation string. All of these are valid Python strings:

```
>>> thing1 = 'how now brown cow?'
>>> thing2 = "I don't think; therefore I am not."
>>> thing3 = """
one
two
three
"""
```

Here, thing1 is a simple string; thing2 is also a simple string, but note that it has a single quote embedded in it to act as an apostrophe. We can do this

---

1. See *Numbers and Computers* by Ronald T. Kneusel (Springer-Verlag, 2017).

because we started the string with a double quote character; if we wanted to use double quotes inside the string, then we would have to enclose it with single quotes.

The last string, thing3, spans multiple lines. The newline characters typed to move from one to two are also part of the string, and when printed, they will be shown. Note, if you actually enter the assignment to thing3 in the Python interpreter, you will see that the interpreter inserts an ellipsis (...). We ignored those in the example as they would be confusing and are not really part of the string.

Lists

Strings and numbers are *primitive data types*, meaning they are not made up of grouped collections of data. Think of them as atoms. They can be combined into more sophisticated data structures by using tuples and lists. A *list* is an ordered collection of other data, which could be primitive data or any other collection of data. A list can hold lists, for example.

Basic List Operations

Unlike with some other data types, the order in which items are appended to a list matters. Let's just jump in with some examples of lists and then talk about what's happening:

❶ ```
>>> t = ["Quednoe","Biggles",39]
>>> t
    ['Quednoe', 'Biggles', 39]
```
❷ ```
>>> t[0]
    'Quednoe'
>>> t[1]
    'Biggles'
>>> t[2]
    39
```

First, we define a list ❶. We use a "[" character to start the list, enter the items, and end with a "]" character. Items in the list are separated by commas (,). This list has three items, as we see when we ask Python to evaluate the expression t, which is the list itself.

We can index into lists by using a number and square brackets, just as we would an array. Here we ask for the first item in the list using bracket notation ❷. We do the same for the second and the third.

We can add to a list by using the append method:

```
>>> t.append(3.14)
>>> t
    ['Quednoe', 'Biggles', 39, 3.14]
```

Here we see that the list, t, now has a fourth member, 3.14. Note that appending an item to a list adds it to the *end* of the list.

Let's look at a few more examples with lists.

❶
```
>>> t[-1]
    3.14
```
❷
```
>>> t[0:2]
    ['Quednoe', 'Biggles']
```
❸
```
>>> t[1] = 'Melvin'
>>> t
    ['Quednoe', 'Melvin', 39, 3.14]
```
❹
```
>>> t.index("Melvin")
    1
```

These examples show us how to use a negative index ❶, which will start at the *end* of the list and count backward, so that -1 will always return the last item in the list. We also see how to use a range to select a subset of the list ❷.

To use Python ranges, follow the format [a:b] to return all items from index a to *one less than* b. Mathematically this is $[a, b)$, where the *b*-th item is not included. So, asking for t[0:2] will return items 0 and 1 only. Note, if you skip the beginning part or ending part of the range, it defaults to the first item (if the beginning is skipped) or the last item (if the ending is skipped).

If you use an index on the left side of an assignment statement, that element of the list is modified ❸. We now see that the second element of the list has changed.

Finally, we use the index method to search the list for an item ❹. If the item is found, index returns the index of the item. If the item is not in the list, Python will raise an error.

If you want to know if an item is in the list but do not care *where* it is, use in, like so:

```
>>> b = [1,2,3,4]
>>> 2 in b
    True
>>> 5 in b
    False
```

Here the returned values are Booleans, True and False. Note the uppercase on True and False. Booleans can be assigned to variables as well. We should also mention None, which is Python's version of NULL as found in other languages (at least to a first approximation). We'll see a good use for None when we talk about Python functions in "Functions" on page 24.

Copying Lists

One last thing to note about lists is that Python does not copy lists when you assign them to new variables; instead, it points the new variable to the location in memory where the list already exists. For example:

```
>>> a = [0,1,2,3,4]
>>> a
    [0, 1, 2, 3, 4]
```

```
>>> b = a
>>> b
    [0, 1, 2, 3, 4]
```

Here we define a as a list of five numbers. We then assign that list to a new variable, b, and see that b is, indeed, the same as a.

So far, so good. However, what if we decide to change an element of a like so:

```
>>> a[2] = 3
>>> a
    [0, 1, 3, 3, 4]
>>> b
    [0, 1, 3, 3, 4]
```

We see that a has updated as we desired, but, perhaps surprisingly, so has b. This is because assigning a to b points b to the same place in memory as a. It does not actually copy the contents of a.

If we want to copy a when we assign it to b, we need to explicitly select all the elements of a like this:

```
❶ >>> b = a[:]
>>> a
    [0, 1, 3, 3, 4]
>>> b
    [0, 1, 3, 3, 4]
>>> a[2] = 2
>>> a
    [0, 1, 2, 3, 4]
>>> b
    [0, 1, 3, 3, 4]
```

Here we define a list, a, and then assign a to b by selecting all of the elements of a ❶. We see that b now looks like a. Next, we update the *third* item in a and see that a now looks as we expect, with its third item now 2 instead of 3. However, b has not been altered in this case because the original assignment created a new list in memory by selecting all the elements of a.

The reason Python doesn't automatically copy lists is that lists can be large, so copying them unnecessarily would waste a lot of memory. Completely copying a list made up of other, nested, lists can be nontrivial. The selecting everything method ❶ makes only a shallow copy—nested elements are still aliased. Use the deepcopy function of the copy module to recursively copy all levels of a list with nested elements.

Python has another data type similar to a list called a *tuple*. Tuples, defined with parentheses rather than square brackets, are just like lists except that once defined, they cannot be modified. In general, we will stick with lists, but NumPy uses tuples from time to time (see Chapter 3).

Dictionaries

The last data type we'll look at is the *dictionary*. A dictionary is made up of a set of keys, each associated with a value. You define dictionaries with "{" and "}" characters. As with a list, the value can be anything, including another dictionary. They key is typically a string but can be a number or other object as well. You define a dictionary like so:

```
>>> d = {"a":1, "b":2, "c":3}
>>> d.keys()
    dict_keys(['a', 'b', 'c'])
```

This example shows how to define the dictionary by directly listing its contents. The elements of the dictionary are given as key:value pairs. Here, the keys are all strings, and the value associated with each key is an integer. The keys method returns all the keys in the dictionary.

The syntax above is useful when the contents of the dictionary are already known. Typically, this isn't the case. Most of the time, the dictionary is defined, and we add elements individually:

```
>>> d = {}
>>> d["a"] = 1
>>> d["b"] = 2
>>> d["c"] = 3
```

Here we define an empty dictionary d, and individually assign values for a new set of keys. If the key already exists in the dictionary d, its value is updated.

To get the value associated with a particular key, just index the dictionary with the key:

```
>>> d["b"]
    2
```

If the key doesn't exist in that dictionary, Python will raise an error. To test if a key is in the dictionary, use in, like so:

```
>>> "c" in d
    True
```

Between lists and dictionaries, you can conveniently store almost any data. This is one of the benefits of a language like Python: programmers can devote energy to completing the task at hand instead of implementing complicated data structures. Lists and dictionaries are fast to use and generally all you'll need unless you're doing scientific programming, in which case we have NumPy, as discussed in Chapter 3.

Control Structures

Python implements several *control structures* to allow you to alter program flow using syntax. We'll look at these:

- if-elif-else
- for loops
- while loops
- with statements
- try-except blocks

if-elif-else Statements

An if statement makes a decision. You give it a condition that must result in a Boolean value, True or False. If the condition is true, the first block of the if statement is executed. If the condition is false, nothing happens and the code moves past the if statement, unless you include an else, in which case the body of the else will be executed. You can test multiple conditions in one statement by using the elif keyword, which adds additional conditions with their own blocks of code to run. For example:

```
❶ >>> disc = b**2 - 4*a*c
❷ >>> if (disc < 0):
        print("imaginary")
❸ elif (disc == 0):
        print("single real")
    else:
      ❹ print("two real")
```

This checks the discriminant of a quadratic polynomial, $ax^2 + bx + c$, to identify the number and type of solution: a real number, a pair of real numbers, or imaginary numbers. The solutions are the values of x that make the polynomial equal to zero.

First, the code calculates the discriminant value (disc) ❶. It then asks if the value is less than zero ❷. If it is, it means there are two imaginary solutions. If the discriminant is exactly zero ❸, there's only one solution, a real number. Finally, the else executes if neither of the conditions is true; in this case, it means there are two real-number solutions ❹. The parentheses around the conditions are not required but can help with readability. Also note that Python uses "**" for exponentiation so that b**2-4*a*c = $b^2 - 4ac$. You can use as many elif clauses as needed, including none, followed by an optional final else. Python lacks the case or switch statements found in other common programming languages.

for Loops

Almost all structured programming languages have loops to run a particular block of code repeatedly. In this section, we'll cover a few kinds in Python.

Python's primary looping construct is the for loop. In other languages, typically for loops are counted loops from some starting value to an ending value that increments by some fixed amount. In Python, loops run over objects that can be iterated through, things that have a next method. This includes the characters of a string, the elements of a list or tuple, or the elements of a dictionary.

Python has two built-in functions that are quite handy with loops. The first is range, which creates a generator object that produces integers in order, starting with 0 unless otherwise specified:

❶ >>> for i in range(6):
        print(i)
0
1
2
3
4
5

The range function ❶ returns the values 0...5, and the for statement assigns the values one at a time to i for each iteration of the loop. Here we simply print the current value of i using the built-in Python function, print.

Another useful function to use with for loops is enumerate. This function returns two values. The first is the index of the current element of its argument and the second is the element itself. An example will clarify:

>>> x = ["how","now","brown","cow"]
>>> for i in x: ❶
        print(i)
how
now
brown
cow
>>> for i,v in enumerate(x): ❷
        print(i,v)
0 how
1 now
2 brown
3 cow

In the first loop over just the list x ❶, we get each element of x assigned to i for each iteration. The second loop uses enumerate and gives us *two* values for each iteration: the current index, stored in i, and the current element of the list x, stored in v ❷. Python is capable of assigning multiple parts to multiple variables at the same time. In this case, the loop body prints the index followed by the element at that index.

What happens when we use a for loop with a dictionary? Let's see:

```
❶ >>> d = {"a":1, "b":2, "c":2.718}
❷ >>> for i in d:
        print(i)
   a
   b
   c
❸ >>> for i in d:
        print(i, d[i])
   a 1
   b 2
   c 2.718
```

Here we first define a dictionary, d, with three keys ❶. If we simply loop over the dictionary variable, we will be given the keys ❷. However, if we then use the key to return the associated value, as in the second loop ❸, we'll iterate over the entire dictionary, accessing each value exactly once.

One particularly attractive feature of Python is that we can combine a for loop with a list in a *list comprehension*. A list comprehension starts out as a list with a leading "[", but instead of listing the individual elements, the body of the list is actually code that generates the list. This shorthand takes a bit of getting used to, but once you're familiar with it, you'll see that it's an efficient replacement for many for loops. For example:

```
❶ >>> import random
   >>> a = []
   >>> for i in range(10000):
❷          a.append(random.random())
❸ >>> b = [random.random() for i in range(10000)]
❹ >>> m3 = [i for i in range(10000) if (i % 3) == 0]
```

We first import the standard random number library ❶ and then fill the list a with 10,000 random numbers in the range [0, 1) (meaning 0 is included, 1 is not) ❷. Next, we also fill b with 10,000 random numbers but do so using a list comprehension ❸. Note that the syntax is the same as when we define a list with values, but here the body of the list is something that *returns* a value. In this case, it's a call to random.random() and a for loop over 10,000 elements.

The last example creates a list, m3, of all multiples of 3, including 0, less than 10,000 ❹. The if clause is the test that decides whether a particular i value will be in the list. The percent operator is *modulo*, which gives the remainder after division. In this case, it's asking if the remainder after dividing i by 3, using integer division, is zero. If it is, there is no remainder, which means i is a multiple of 3 (or 0).

while Loops

Many programming languages include both top-tested and bottom-tested loops. A *top-tested loop* tests the loop condition at the beginning, before executing any of the body, and if the test is not true, the body is never executed. A *bottom-tested loop* executes the body at least once and *then* tests to see if the loop should execute again. The `while` loop in C is a top-tested loop and the `do...while` loop is a bottom-tested loop. Python has only a top-tested `while` loop with the following syntax:

```
❶ >>> i = 0
❷ >>> while (i < 4):
        print(i)
      ❸ i += 1
0
1
2
3
```

We have to initialize the loop control variable (`i`) with a 0 *before* we start the loop ❶ so that the condition `i < 4` is true to begin with ❷. Also note that we explicitly increment `i` at the end of the body of the loop ❸. The expression `i += 1` is shorthand for `i = i + 1` and increments `i` by 1. Python doesn't support C-style increment and decrement such as `i ++`. If you try it, Python will kindly let you know with a `SyntaxError`.

The `while` loop repeats as long as the condition evaluates to `True`. It's up to the programmer to do things in the loop body that will eventually make the condition `False` so the loop will end. You can also manually exit the loop, as you'll see in the following section.

break and continue Statements

The `for` and `while` loops work with two other Python statements: to immediately exit the loop, use the `break` statement; to immediately move to the next iteration, use `continue`. One common use of `break` is to leave an infinite loop:

```
>>> i = 0
>>> while True:
        print(i)
        i += 1
        if (i == 4):
          ❶ break
0
1
2
3
```

This produces the same output as the earlier while loop example, but exits the loop explicitly via break when the termination condition is met ❶; here, that's when i is incremented up to 4. Using break for this toy example does not really make sense since there are other, clearer ways to do this, but often the loop might need to execute until the program ends or until some other rare situation or error occurs. For example, the command line interpreter will keep checking for keyboard input. As each character comes in, it is added to a buffer. However, if the character is a "newline," it breaks out of the loop and interprets the contents of the buffer.

The continue statement iterates the loop without executing any body statements after it. For example:

```
>>> for i in range(4):
        print(i)
❶   continue
        print("xyzzy")
0
1
2
3
```

Here the presence of continue ❶ ensures that the second print statement is never executed.

with Statement

The Python with statement is useful when dealing with files. For example, the following code uses a with statement to open a file on disk and read its contents into a string:

```
>>> with open("sesame") as f:
        s = f.read()
>>> s
'this is a file\n'
```

The with statement opens a file called *sesame* and assigns the file object to f. We then use the read method to read the entire file as a string and assign it to s. Evaluating s shows us that the file contains the string "this is a file" with a newline character at the end.

Note that the example above uses open and read but doesn't explicitly close the file when done. This is because when the with statement exits, the close method is called automatically as f leaves scope (meaning f is defined only within the body of the with statement).

Handling Errors with try-except Blocks

Finally, let's take a quick look at Python's ability to trap and process errors, rather than let errors halt our programs. Again, we'll just look at a quick skeleton of Python's error-control abilities as an aid to debugging.

To capture an error instead of letting it stop program execution, we can encapsulate the statements that might cause the error with a try...except block. If an error is raised by any of the statements after the try and before the except, it will be caught and execution will pass to the statements of the except clause. The example here shows how to catch *any* error that happens within the statements enclosed by the try block; though it's useful to know that Python has a rich set of error types, and users can define their own:

```
>>> x = 1.0/0.0
Traceback (most recent call last):
  File "<stdin>", line 1, in <module>
ZeroDivisionError: float division by zero
>>> try:
        x = 1.0/0.0
    except:
        x = 0
>>> x
0
```

Here we first attempt to assign the result of a division by zero to x. This fails with the given error message from Python. However, if we wrap the assignment in a try block, Python will move to the x = 0 line of the except block and assign x = 0 as shown.

If you're not using a sophisticated Python programming environment that supports breaks while executing code, the following construct is useful, as it halts execution when encountered. Here it halts execution immediately after the divide-by-zero error occurs:

```
>>> try:
        x = 1.0/0.0
    except:
        import pdb; pdb.set_trace()
```

When an error occurs, the pdb module will be imported, if it hasn't been already, and the set_trace function will be called to enter into a debugging environment. Of course, pdb.set_trace() can be called at any point in the code—it need not be inside of a try...except block.

Functions

You define a function in Python with the def keyword followed by the function name and a list of arguments the function will take in parentheses. Even if you include no arguments, you must include a pair of parentheses. Since Python is dynamically typed, you list the parameters of the function but no type information. You can, if necessary, also include default values. Again, we are ignoring Python's object-oriented abilities and just focusing on a small section of what we can do with functions. Let's define a simple function:

```
>>> def product(a,b):
        return a*b
>>> product(4,5)
    20
```

This function is called product and it accepts two arguments that we will refer to in the function as a and b. The body of this function consists of a single statement—a return statement, which returns to the point in the code where product was called with the given value, here the product of the two arguments. If we test this function, then we see that it does indeed multiply its arguments.

Next, let's redefine product and supply a default value for the second argument using the following code:

```
>>> def product(a,b=3):
        return a*b
>>> product(4,5)
    20
>>> product(3)
    9
```

We supply default values in the argument list of the function. If we use two arguments, Python will assign the value of the second argument inside the function as before. However, if we do not supply a second argument, Python will use the given default value of 3, giving us a meaningful return value of $3 \times 3 = 9$. Supplying a default value to a function argument makes it a keyword parameter, and, as we see above, we do not need to supply a value for that argument when we invoke the function. This technique is particularly handy, and we will see it in our code examples from time to time.

Our final example below shows how to define a function that accepts no arguments:

```
>>> def pp():
        print("plugh")
>>> pp()
    plugh
```

The function pp has an empty argument list. The only statement in the body of the function prints the word *plugh*. There is no return value.

Python allows you to nest function definitions so that a function can itself have functions defined within it. The inner functions are accessible to only the outer function. There is seldom a need to do this, and if you find yourself doing it often, you might want to think about refactoring to an object-oriented design; but, on occasion, it makes sense, so we mention it here.

Finally, one helpful thing to do is to make the default value None, enabling us inside the function to check whether the value was given by testing if the argument is None. Any variable holding any type of data can be tested against None.

Modules

We conclude our whirlwind review of Python with a look at the module system. This is akin to the C standard library, and it provides Python with a rich set of tools out of the box, all defined as modules. Naturally, users can create their own modules as well. A *module*, then, is a collection of functions that can be imported into your program. You can also import specific functions from a specific module into your own program, rather than the whole module, as long as you're aware of the possibility that the imported function might have the same name as a function from another namespace.

By *namespace*, we mean a bag of functions, sort of like a family, where the functions are the names of the individuals in the family. All the functions that our program knows about are in our namespace. If we import a function from a module, that function is now also in our namespace. If we import the entire module and refer to the function by prefixing the module name, we get to use the function, but it's not in our namespace. We'll see shortly why this distinction matters.

Let's see some examples using the modules of the Python library:

```
>>> import time
>>> time.time()
    1524693601.402852
```

We first import the time module. This means that we now have access to all the functions in the time module as long as we prefix the function name with time.. The time function of the time module returns the current time as the number of seconds since January 1, 1970. Known as the *epoch time*, this is useful for timing how long code takes to execute. Because the value returned only increases, the difference in epoch time at the start of the code to the end of the code indicates the length of time for code execution.

Let's look at another example:

```
>>> from time import ctime, localtime
>>> ctime()
    'Wed Apr 25 16:00:21 2020'
>>> localtime().tm_year
    2018
```

Here, instead of importing the entire time module, we import only two functions from it. Doing this puts the functions in our namespace so that we can call them directly. The ctime function returns a string showing the current date and time, while the localtime function returns the sections of the current time broken down by date and time part. Here we show the year at the time of this writing.

Our last example shows us why it is often best to import a module directly instead of importing functions from it:

```
>>> def sqrt(x):
        return 4
>>> sqrt(2)
    4
>>> from math import *
>>> sqrt(2)
    1.4142135623730951
```

First, we define a function we call `sqrt`. This function always returns 4 no matter what the argument is. Not particularly useful, of course, but still a valid Python function.

Next, let's import the entire `math` library of functions. This syntax takes all the functions in the module and places them in our namespace so we can refer to them without using the module name as well. After doing this, we see that `sqrt` now returns the actual square root.

What happened to our dubious implementation of `sqrt`? It was masked when we imported the entire `math` library because the `math` library also contains a function called `sqrt` and, since the `math` library was imported after our `sqrt` was defined, the `math` library's version of `sqrt` takes precedence.

Python's module library is one of the key strengths of the language in terms of utility. The standard library has extensive documentation. For a quick look at the list of available Python 3.X modules, see *https://docs.python.org/3/py-modindex.htm*. The main Python site is here: *http://www.python.org/*. I strongly recommend that you spend some time at these links and really learn all that Python has to offer.

Summary

In this chapter, we reviewed the fundamentals of Python to give us the background we need to understand the code examples in the remainder of this book. We learned about Python syntax and statements. We also examined Python variables and data structures, and then explored Python's suite of control structures and functions, ending with a look at Python's module library.

In the next chapter, we'll dive into NumPy to see how to make Python even more useful to us. NumPy is a core piece of the machine learning toolkit used by virtually all machine learning libraries, including the ones we will use in this book.

3

USING NUMPY

NumPy is foundational to all of the machine learning we'll explore in this book. If you're already comfortable with NumPy, you can skip this chapter. If you're not, don't be shy; consider this chapter a refresher and dive in.

A full tutorial of NumPy is beyond what we can cover here, so if you're interested, you can look further at *https://docs.scipy.org/doc/numpy/user/quickstart.html*.

Why NumPy?

Python is an elegant programming language but it lacks an important data structure that's fundamental to scientific and mathematical programming: the array. Yes, you could use a dictionary as an array, or a sizeable predefined list, but this would be an abuse of those data structures—and, more practically, it would be slow. Let's look at the difference in implementation between an array and a list. Python lists are more advanced than the notion of a list we're using here, but in essence they're the same.

Arrays vs. Lists

The *array* is simply a fixed-size block of *contiguous* memory, a single block of RAM with no gaps, used to represent a set of *n* elements, each of which uses exactly *m* bytes. For example, an IEEE 754 double precision floating-point number occupies 64 bits of memory, 8 bytes, and is what Python uses under the hood for its float data type. Therefore, an array of *n* = 100 Python floats would occupy, at a minimum, *nm* = 100(8) = 800 bytes of memory. If Python had arrays as a data structure, it would allocate 800 bytes of memory and point the array variable name, A, to the memory as in Figure 3-1.

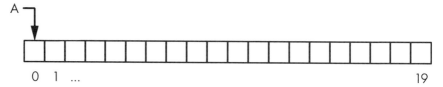

Figure 3-1: An array stored in contiguous memory

Whenever we want to access an element of the array, say x[3], we can very quickly calculate the exact location in memory by adding 3(8) = 24 to the memory address of the base of the array. This is the indexing operation for an array.

Multidimensional arrays are also stored in memory as contiguous blocks, and the indexing operation is only slightly more complicated. A *multi-dimensional array* uses two or more numbers to index the elements. Think of a chess board; two numbers are needed to determine the location of a piece: the row and the column. Therefore, the chess board is a two-dimensional array. If we add one more dimension to turn the chess board into a stack of chess boards, we need three numbers to locate a piece: the row, the column, and the board number. Therefore, we have a three-dimensional array.

We will use arrays with one, two, and three dimensions throughout the book. All of these are stored in memory as a single block of RAM. The point is, an array is quick to index, and therefore operations on array elements can be performed very quickly.

Contrast this with a list. Figure 3-2 shows the basic structure of a list, B, in memory. In this case, the elements in the list are not in contiguous memory, but are scattered throughout RAM with pointers linking one element to the next, like a chain. Each link in the chain contains the data value we want to store and a pointer to the memory of the next link in the chain.

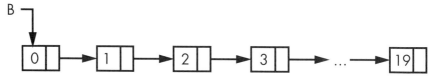

Figure 3-2: A list stored as a collection of linked nodes scattered throughout memory

We can't index into a list by just adding an offset to a base memory address. Instead, if we want the fourth element of the list, then we need to start at the head of the list, use the link there to the next element, and the next, and the next, to reach the memory associated with the fourth element, the 3 in Figure 3-2. This isn't too bad until we want to index the 1,000,000th element and have to repeat the process 1 million times instead of adding 8 million once to a base address.

Most machine learning involves arrays. If the array has a single dimension, we call it a *vector*; vectors are the inputs to many of our models. If the array has two dimensions, it's a *matrix*. A matrix can be thought of as a chess board or an image where each pixel of the image is one of the board locations. Matrices can also be an input to our models, or used internally by the model; for example, the weight matrices of a neural network, or the convolution kernels and filter outputs of a convolutional neural network are matrices.

Therefore, it's critically important to be able to quickly operate on array data. This is where the numpy library comes in. It adds the missing array data type to Python so that we can perform calculations rapidly. Frankly, without it, Python would be unsuitable for implementing anything but the simplest of machine learning algorithms. However, with NumPy, Python immediately becomes the premier environment for machine learning research.

Testing Array and List Speed

Let's see a quick example of how much speed NumPy gives us over pure Python. The code we'll execute is in Listing 3-1.

```
❶ import numpy as np
  import time
  import random

  n = 1000000
  a = [random.random() for i in range(n)]
  b = [random.random() for i in range(n)]

  s = time.time()
❷ c = [a[i]*b[i] for i in range(n)]
  print("comprehension:", time.time()-s)

  s = time.time()
  c = []
❸ for i in range(n):
      c.append(a[i]*b[i])
  print("for loop:", time.time()-s)

  s = time.time()
❹ c = [0]*n
  for i in range(n):
```

```
    c[i] = a[i]*b[i]
print("existing list:", time.time()-s)

❺ x = np.array(a)
y = np.array(b)
s = time.time()
c = x*y
print("NumPy time", time.time()-s)
```

Listing 3-1: Comparing NumPy to pure Python. See numpy_speed_test.py.

In Listing 3-1, we first import the numpy library ❶ and then create two lists of random numbers using a list comprehension. These lists include 1,000,000 elements each. Our goal is to multiply the two lists together, element by element, as quickly as possible.

We can measure the time the program takes to run by logging our starting time in s and subtracting it from our ending time when we print. The time function of the time module returns the number of seconds, including fractions of a second, since a set origin time (January 1, 1970). We print time.time()-s after each operation we run.

In our first attempt to multiply a and b, we use a list comprehension ❷. Next, we use a loop ❸ to select each element from a and b and append their product to the list c. Note that this approach starts with an empty list and appends each new product to it so that the list needs to grow in memory.

As a third approach, we pre-allocate the output list so that instead of appending each output to c, we update the corresponding element of c ❹. This approach might be a bit faster—we'll see.

Finally, we use NumPy to do the calculation ❺. We exclude the time it takes to make the two lists into NumPy arrays (lines 25–26) since we could have easily created the random arrays (vectors since they are 1D) with a call to the NumPy random number module. The entire operation with NumPy vectors is c = x*y. Notice that there's no explicit looping. NumPy is an array-processing library, and it will automatically iterate over all the elements of the arrays for you.

If we run the code in Listing 3-1 ten times to get an average runtime for each of the four approaches, we find the following:

Approach	Runtime (seconds, mean ± SE)
List comprehension	0.158855 ± 0.000426
for loop	0.226371 ± 0.000823
for loop w/existing list	0.201825 ± 0.000409
NumPy	0.009253 ± 0.000027

This table shows that NumPy is on average just under 25× faster than pure Python with a naïve implementation. This is why we want to use NumPy for machine learning in Python! Here, *SE* means *standard error of the mean*, which is the standard deviation divided by the square root of the number of values that went into the mean, 10 in this case. The *standard deviation* is a measure of how the values differ from the mean. A large standard deviation means that the values are spread over a broad range. These standard deviations are small, meaning the times are consistent from run to run.

Listing 3-1 shows us the true power of NumPy. Operations are immediately broadcast across compatible dimensions without requiring explicit loops. The normal linear algebra operations on vectors and matrices are also present, but in general, operations on NumPy arrays are performed automatically element-wise, without looping.

Now that you've seen why we're using NumPy, let's take a look at some of its features.

Basic Arrays

NumPy is all about arrays, so we'll start there. Let's dive right in with some basic examples and then explain what they do and why they look the way they do.

Defining an Array with np.array

Let's start with some basic array creation:

```
>>> import numpy as np
>>> a = np.array([1,2,3,4])
>>> a
    array([1, 2, 3, 4])
>>> a.size
    4
>>> a.shape
    (4,)
>>> a.dtype
    dtype('int64')
```

Here we define an array, a, using the array function. The argument to the array function needs to be something that NumPy can turn into an array. A list is something that NumPy can turn into an array, as is a tuple, so these are most often the arguments to the array function.

If we ask Python to show us what's in a, we're told it's an array and given the values. NumPy will display the contents of an array, but if the array has many elements, it will show us only the first and last few.

We next ask for the three most common properties of a NumPy array: the size, the shape, and the data type (dtype). The array a has four elements, so its size is 4. The size of an array is the number of elements it contains. The array a is a vector, meaning it's only one-dimensional, so the shape is returned as a tuple, always, where the first and only dimension is 4, meaning there are four elements along the first dimension.

The data type is new in that Python normally doesn't care about data types. But to be memory efficient, the numpy library has to care about them. When we created a using array, we didn't specify a data type, so NumPy defaulted to 64-bit integers because all the values in the list we gave to array were integers. If even one of them had been a float, NumPy would have instead defaulted to 64-bit floating-point numbers, the same as the double type in languages like C, C++, and Java.

Now let's be explicit about the type of data that we want the NumPy array to hold:

```
>>> b = np.array([1,2,3,4], dtype="uint8")
>>> b.dtype
    dtype('uint8')
>>> c = np.array([1,2,3,4], dtype="float64")
>>> c.dtype
    dtype('float64')
```

Here we define two arrays, b and c. Both arrays contain the same elements from the list [1,2,3,4]. However, notice the dtype keyword argument to array. This tells NumPy the data type to use for the array. For b, we are telling NumPy to use an unsigned 8-bit integer (uint8). This is a byte or a single ASCII character. If we ask for the dtype property, we are told that the array b is, indeed, of data type unsigned 8-bit integer.

The array c contains the same elements as b, but here we tell NumPy to make the array hold 64-bit floating-point numbers. Again, asking for the data type tells us that the array c is of the requested type. When working with NumPy, we must be aware of the type of data our arrays will hold.

The most commonly used NumPy data types, and their C equivalents, are given in Table 3-1. When defining arrays, specify the NumPy data type as a string with the data type name. We will see examples of this next.

Table 3-1: NumPy Data Type Names, C Equivalents, and Range

NumPy name	Equivalent C type	Range
float64	double	$\pm [2.225 \times 10^{-308}, 1.798 \times 10^{308}]$
float32	float	$\pm [1.175 \times 10^{-38}, 3.403 \times 10^{38}]$
int64	long long	$[-2^{63}, 2^{63}-1]$
uint64	unsigned long long	$[0, 2^{64}-1]$
int32	long	$[-2^{31}, 2^{31}-1$
uint32	unsigned long	$[0, 2^{32}-1]$
uint8	unsigned char	$[0, 255 = 2^{8}-1]$

So far, we've created only vectors with NumPy. Let's look at how to create a matrix, a two-dimensional array:

```
>>> d = np.array([[1,2,3],[4,5,6],[7,8,9]])
>>> d.shape
    (3, 3)
>>> d.size
```

```
         9
>>> d
    array([[1, 2, 3],
           [4, 5, 6],
           [7, 8, 9]])
```

We use the `array` function as before, but instead of a single list, we pass in a list of lists. Each element of the supplied list is itself a list of three elements, and there are three such lists. Therefore, the resulting NumPy array will be a 3×3 matrix. The first row of the matrix is the first list of three elements ([1,2,3]), the second row is the second list ([4,5,6]), and the third row is the third list ([7,8,9]).

If we ask for the shape of d, we're told that it's (3, 3). This tuple says that there are two dimensions to the array, since there are two elements in the tuple, and that the first dimension has length 3 (three rows) and that the second dimension also has length 3 (three columns). Asking for the size of d tells us that there are nine elements. The size of a NumPy array is equal to the product of all the values in the tuple returned by shape, here $3 \times 3 = 9$.

Asking for the array itself causes NumPy to print it. As the array is small, NumPy shows us the entire array as a two-dimensional matrix:

$$\begin{bmatrix} 1 & 2 & 3 \\ 4 & 5 & 6 \\ 7 & 8 & 9 \end{bmatrix}$$

NumPy is not limited to two-dimensional arrays. For example, here's a three-dimensional array:

```
>>> d = np.array([[[1,11,111],[2,22,222]],
                  [[3,33,333],[4,44,444]]])
>>> d.shape
    (2, 2, 3)
>>> d
    array([[[  1,  11, 111],
            [  2,  22, 222]],

           [[  3,  33, 333],
            [  4,  44, 444]]])
```

We know that d is three-dimensional because shape returns a tuple with three elements. We also know that d is three-dimensional because the list we passed to array contains two sublists, each of which contains two sublists with three elements each, hence a shape of (2, 2, 3). NumPy displays d using a blank line between the two 2×2 subarrays. We can think of a three-dimensional array as a vector where each element of the vector is a matrix. We will use three-dimensional NumPy arrays to hold collections of images. For this example, d can be thought of as holding two images, each of two rows by three columns.

Defining Arrays with 0s and 1s

Defining NumPy arrays with the array function would be very tedious if we wanted a large array since we need to supply the elements of the array. Fortunately, NumPy is not so cruel. Let's look now at two NumPy workhorse functions that we'll use often in this book. The first builds arrays where every element is initialized to 0:

```
>>> x = np.zeros((2,3,4))
>>> x.shape
    (2, 3, 4)
>>> x.dtype
    dtype('float64')
>>> b = np.zeros((10,10),dtype="uint32")
>>> b.shape
    (10, 10)
>>> b.dtype
    dtype('uint32')
```

The zeros function returns new arrays with every element set to 0. The example defines x to be a three-dimensional array since the argument to zeros is the shape of the new array—in this case, the tuple (2,3,4). This array can be thought of as a pair of tiny images, each 3×4 pixels. Notice that the default type for an array created with zeros is a 64-bit float (dtype). This means each element of the array uses 8 bytes in memory.

The array b has two dimensions, 10×10 elements, and we've explicitly declared it to be of 32-bit unsigned integers. This means that each element uses only 4 bytes in memory. When using NumPy, we need to be aware of how much memory an array might be using to avoid allocating arrays that are exceptionally large or of a large data type, such as float64, that wastes memory.

Our second workhorse function is similar to zeros but instead initializes each element to 1:

```
>>> y = np.ones((3,3))
>>> y
    array([[1., 1., 1.],
           [1., 1., 1.],
           [1., 1., 1.]])
>>> y = 10*np.ones((3,3))
>>> y
    array([[10., 10., 10.],
           [10., 10., 10.],
           [10., 10., 10.]])
>>> y.dtype
    dtype('float64')
>>> y.astype("uint8")
    array([[10, 10, 10],
```

```
           [10, 10, 10],
           [10, 10, 10]], dtype=uint8)
```

Just like zeros, ones takes a tuple specifying the number of elements along each dimension of the array, here a 3×3 matrix. We can also optionally specify a dtype to make the array hold something other than 64-bit floats.

The real utility of ones is creating arrays initialized to any value. We do this by multiplying the ones array by the value we want, here 10. Notice how NumPy realizes that we're multiplying by a scalar value and performs the operation on every element of the array automatically—no loops required.

We slipped in something new, the astype method. This method on an array returns a copy of the array, casting each element to the given data type. Note, casting to a data type that cannot hold the original values, like casting 64-bit floats to unsigned bytes, will result in data being lost. NumPy will do its best, but this is also something to be aware of when using NumPy.

Finally, in Python, a list or dictionary object is passed by reference so that assigning one to a new variable doesn't make a copy; it simply creates an alias that points back to the original memory. This saves time and space but can lead to unintended consequences if we get careless. The same is true with NumPy arrays. They can be very large, so it doesn't make sense to copy them every time they are passed to a function. If you want to actually create a new copy of a NumPy array, use the copy method or an array slice that represents all the elements of the array. Unlike Python lists, NumPy arrays are flat: the value in a particular place in the array cannot be another array.

So, all the following statements, except the second, create a copy of the array a:

```
>>> a = np.arange(10)
>>> b = a
>>> c = a.copy()
>>> d = a[:]
```

Changing an element of a will change the corresponding element of b since b is pointing to the same memory as a, but the elements of c and d will be unaffected.

Accessing Elements in an Array

In this section, we'll look at two different ways to access elements in an array.

Indexing into an Array

Arrays aren't much use if we can't refer to the elements within them and update them when necessary. This is called *array indexing*. Understanding array indexing is critical to making good use of NumPy. Let's jump in with some examples:

```
>>> b = np.zeros((3,4),dtype='uint8')
>>> b
```

```
      array([[0, 0, 0, 0],
             [0, 0, 0, 0],
             [0, 0, 0, 0]], dtype=uint8)
❶ >>> b[0,1] = 1
  >>> b[1,0] = 2
  >>> b
      array([[0, 1, 0, 0],
             [2, 0, 0, 0],
             [0, 0, 0, 0]], dtype=uint8)
```

We index arrays in the same way that we index lists, with square brackets: [begins the index and] ends it. In between the square brackets goes an expression that tells NumPy which elements of the array to return or assign—this is the *subscript*. A subscript is appended to an array name to specify one or more elements of the array.

In the example above, b is a matrix of three rows and four columns with each element initialized to 0. We see this when we evaluate b.

Next, we do something new: we set up an assignment statement ❶ where the left-hand side of the statement is not a single variable name but a variable name with a subscript, the text [0,1]. This subscript tells NumPy that the value of the right-hand side of the statement, here just 1, should be put into the element of b at row 0 and column 1. Likewise, NumPy should put a 2 into the element at row 1, column 0. We see that NumPy did as we asked when we look at b and see that the second column of row 0 is now 1, and the first column of row 1 is now 2.

If we continue working with b as defined previously, we see how to ask NumPy for elements from the array:

```
>>> b[1,0]
    2
>>> b[1]
    array([2, 0, 0, 0], dtype=uint8)
>>> b[1][0]
    2
```

Since b is a matrix, we need subscripts to select a specific element of it, one for the row, another for the column. Therefore, b[1,0] should return the value in the second row and first column, as we see it does.

The next line uses a single subscript, b[1], and returns the entire second row of b. This is a very useful feature that we'll see in our own code throughout the book.

Lastly, if b[1] returns the entire second row of the matrix, b, then we can use b[1][0] to ask for the first element of that row. We see that it matches the result of the b[1,0] syntax we started with.

Slicing an Array

Accessing individual elements of an array, or an entire subarray, with a single index is useful, but NumPy is far more flexible than that. It's possible to specify parts of the array by using *slicing*, which returns subarrays carved out of the larger array as if with a knife. Let's look at how it works:

```
>>> a = np.arange(10)
>>> a
    array([0, 1, 2, 3, 4, 5, 6, 7, 8, 9])
>>> a[1:4]
    array([1, 2, 3])
>>> a[3:7]
    array([3, 4, 5, 6])
```

Here we use arange, which is the NumPy analogue of the Python range function, to set a to a vector of the digits $[0, 9]$. We then ask for a slice of this vector, a[1:4], and see that it returns [1, 2, 3]. The slice was specified with two values: the first is the starting index, 1, and the second is the ending index, 4.

Wait—if the ending index is 4,then shouldn't the slice have returned [1, 2, 3, 4] instead? NumPy follows the Python convention for lists, so the ending index is never included in the returned subarray. We can read the slice as asking for all the elements of a starting at index 1 and up to *but not including* index 4. Mathematically, a slice given as a[x:y] means all elements, i, of a such that $x \leq i < y$. Therefore, the second example, a[3:7], now makes sense as it's asking for all elements of a starting with index 3 up to but not including index 7.

The slices selected all elements in the given range. NumPy allows for an optional third slice argument that specifies a step size. If not given, the step size is 1. Therefore, with a as a vector of the digits as before, we get this:

```
>>> a[0:8:2]
    array([0, 2, 4, 6])
>>> a[3:7:2]
    array([3, 5])
```

The first slice starts at the beginning of the array, index 0, and goes to index 8 (but not including index 8) returning every second element. The second example does the same starting with index 3.

Any part of the full slice syntax, [x:y:z], may be omitted, but at least one colon must remain. If so, the default value is the first index (for x), the last index (for y), and 1 (for z). For example:

```
>>> a[:6]
    array([0, 1, 2, 3, 4, 5])
>>> a[6:]
    array([6, 7, 8, 9])
```

In the first example, the starting index is omitted so it defaults to 0 and we're given the first six elements of a. In the second example, the ending index is omitted so it defaults to the last index, meaning "return everything from index 6 to the end." In both cases, the increment was omitted and defaulted to 1.

Array slicing leads to some handy shortcuts. Two are given here:

```
>>> a[-1]
    9
>>> a[::-1]
    array([9, 8, 7, 6, 5, 4, 3, 2, 1, 0])
```

The first example shows us that like Python lists, NumPy arrays can be indexed with negative values to count from the end of an axis. So, asking for index −1 will always return the last element.

The second example is a bit mysterious at first. We know that a is a vector of the digits from 0 through 9. The example returns the vector in reverse order. How? Let's break down the meaning of ::-1. We said that any part of the array slice notation can be omitted, and if it is, the default is either the first index, the last index, or the increment. In this case, the first index is omitted so it defaults to 0. The required colon (:) is present, and then the last index is omitted so it defaults to the last index. Then there's a : for the increment, which is given as −1, to count backward from the ending index to the starting index. This is what counts backward and reverses the elements of the array.

Naturally, array slicing works with NumPy arrays with any number of dimensions. Let's look at slicing a two-dimensional matrix:

```
>>> b = np.arange(20).reshape((4,5))
>>> b
    array([[ 0,  1,  2,  3,  4],
           [ 5,  6,  7,  8,  9],
           [10, 11, 12, 13, 14],
           [15, 16, 17, 18, 19]])
>>> b[1:3,:]
    array([[ 5,  6,  7,  8,  9],
           [10, 11, 12, 13, 14]])
>>> b[2:,2:]
    array([[12, 13, 14],
           [17, 18, 19]])
```

We define b to be a vector of the numbers [0, 19] by using arange and then immediately use reshape to change the vector into a matrix of four rows and five columns. The argument to reshape is a tuple specifying the new shape for the array. There must be exactly as many elements in the array as the new shape. The vector had 20 elements, and the new shape has 4×5 = 20 elements, so we are okay in this case.

Array slicing applies per dimension, so the second example, b[1:3,:] is asking for rows 1 and 2 and all the columns in those rows. That is what : by itself means—all the elements along that axis.

The next example asks for all the rows and columns starting with row 2 and column 2. This is the submatrix pulled from the lower-right corner of the full matrix b.

The Ellipsis

NumPy supports a shorthand notation for slicing that's sometimes useful. Let's show it and then discuss what it's doing. First, however, we need to define some arrays to work with:

```
>>> c = np.arange(27).reshape((3,3,3))
>>> c
    array([[[ 0,  1,  2],
            [ 3,  4,  5],
            [ 6,  7,  8]],
           [[ 9, 10, 11],
            [12, 13, 14],
            [15, 16, 17]],
           [[18, 19, 20],
            [21, 22, 23],
            [24, 25, 26]]])
>>> a = np.ones((3,3))
>>> a
    array([[1., 1., 1.],
           [1., 1., 1.],
           [1., 1., 1.]])
```

First we define c to be a three-dimensional array with three elements along each dimension. We use the same reshape trick that we used previously, and we know it will work because 3 × 3 × 3 = 27 and there are 27 elements in the initial vector produced by arange. Again, we can think of c as three 3×3 images stacked together. Next we use ones to define a simple 3×3 matrix with every value set to 1.

From our discussion of array slicing so far, we know that we can replace the 3×3 subarray in c for any particular "image" by using the colon notation. For example, let's replace the second "image" of c by a:

```
>>> c[1,:,:] = a
>>> c
array([[[ 0,  1,  2],
        [ 3,  4,  5],
        [ 6,  7,  8]],
       [[ 1,  1,  1],
        [ 1,  1,  1],
        [ 1,  1,  1]],
```

```
    [[18, 19, 20],
     [21, 22, 23],
     [24, 25, 26]]]])
```

Here we tell NumPy to replace the second subarray, which is 3×3, with the 3×3 array in a. It's the second subarray because the first index is given as 1. When we print c, we see that the second 3×3 subarray is now all 1s.

Now for the shorthand notation. This time, we want to replace the first 3×3 subarray of c with a. We could do this with a syntax of c[0,:,:] but instead we'll use the shorthand notation:

```
>>> c[0,...] = a
>>> c
    array([[[ 1,   1,   1],
            [ 1,   1,   1],
            [ 1,   1,   1]],
           [[ 1,   1,   1],
            [ 1,   1,   1],
            [ 1,   1,   1]],
           [[18, 19, 20],
            [21, 22, 23],
            [24, 25, 26]]]])
```

Notice that instead of c[0,:,:], where we specified all the indices of all the remaining dimensions of c, we used c[0,...] which NumPy interprets as meaning "and as many colons as necessary to cover all the remaining dimensions." Of course, the shape of a must match the shape of the subarray specified by all the remaining dimensions. In this example, there are two remaining dimensions and a is a two-dimensional array, so we do match. The ellipsis notation (...) is commonly used in Python code related to machine learning, so that's why I mention it here. You could argue that from a readability standpoint, using ... is not a good idea because it requires the reader of the code to remember how many dimensions a particular array has.

Operators and Broadcasting

NumPy uses all the standard math operators as well as a heap of other methods and functions that implement more advanced operations. NumPy also uses a concept called *broadcasting* to decide how to apply an operator to arrays. Let's look at some simple operators and broadcasting:

```
>>> a = np.arange(5)
>>> a
    array([ 0, 1, 2, 3, 4])
>>> c = np.arange(5)[::-1]
>>> c
    array([ 4, 3, 2, 1, 0])
>>> a*3.14
    array([ 0., 3.14, 6.28, 9.42, 12.56])
```

```
>>> a*a
    array([ 0,  1,  4,  9, 16])
>>> a*c
    array([0, 3, 4, 3, 0])
>>> a//(c+1)
    array([0, 0, 0, 1, 4])
```

From earlier examples, we know that a is a vector of the digits 0 through 4. And, we know because of our discussion of array slicing, that c is a vector of the digits 4 down to 0, the reverse of a.

With that in mind, we see that multiplying a by 3.14 multiplies each element by 3.14. NumPy has broadcast the scalar 3.14 across all the elements of the array a. NumPy would do this no matter what shape a has. Operating on an array with a scalar performs the operation on all elements of the array, regardless of its shape.

The expression a*a multiplies a by itself. In this case, NumPy sees that the two arrays have the same shape, so it multiplies corresponding elements, thereby squaring each element of a. Multiplying a by c is also straightforward because c has the same shape as a.

The last example uses broadcasting twice. First, it broadcasts the scalar 1 across c to add one to each element of c. This operation does not change the shape of c, so dividing a by using integer division (// not /), by the expression (c+1), works since each has the same shape.

Let's look at some more examples. There's no end to the number of examples we could give, but one more small set should cement the concepts for us. First a more complex broadcasting example:

```
>>> a
    array([0, 1, 2, 3, 4])
>>> b=np.arange(25).reshape((5,5))
>>> b
    array([[ 0,  1,  2,  3,  4],
           [ 5,  6,  7,  8,  9],
           [10, 11, 12, 13, 14],
           [15, 16, 17, 18, 19],
           [20, 21, 22, 23, 24]])
>>> a*b
    array([[ 0,  1,  4,  9, 16],
           [ 0,  6, 14, 24, 36],
           [ 0, 11, 24, 39, 56],
           [ 0, 16, 34, 54, 76],
           [ 0, 21, 44, 69, 96]])
```

Remember that a is a vector of digits. We then define b to be a 5×5 matrix of the numbers 0 through 24. Next, we multiply a and b.

At this point, you should object. How can we multiply these two arrays when their shapes don't match? The array a has only 5 elements, while b has 25. This is where broadcasting comes into play. NumPy recognizes that the five-element vector in a matches the size of each *row* of b so it multiplies each row of b by a to return a new 5×5 matrix. This sort of broadcasting is actually quite handy. We'll be storing our datasets primarily as two-dimensional NumPy arrays, where each row is a sample and the columns correspond to input values for that sample.

NumPy also supports matrix math operations. These are the operations on vectors and matrices that we find in linear algebra. For example:

```
>>> x = np.arange(5)
>>> x
    array([0, 1, 2, 3, 4])
>>> np.dot(x,x)
    30
```

Here we define x to be a simple vector of five elements. We then introduce NumPy's primary vector and matrix product function, dot, to multiply x by itself. We already know that if we multiply x by itself in the standard way, using x*x, we'll get each element times itself, giving [0,1,4,9,16], but that's not what we get here. Instead we get the scalar value, 30. Why?

The answer has to do with what dot does. It doesn't implement element-wise multiplication but instead implements linear algebra multiplication. Specifically, because both arguments to dot are vectors, it implements vector times vector, which is known as the *dot product*, hence the name of the NumPy function. The dot product for vectors multiplies each element of the first vector by the corresponding element of the second vector and then adds all those products together. So, for dot(x,x) NumPy is calculating as follows:

$$[0, 1, 2, 3, 4] \times [0, 1, 2, 3, 4] = [0, 1, 4, 9, 16]; 0 + 1 + 4 + 9 + 16 = 30$$

The dot function can be used to multiply two vectors, a vector and a matrix, or two matrices, all following the rules of linear algebra, which are beyond the scope of this book to explore in detail. That said, the dot function is of great importance to us because it is the workhorse function of machine learning with NumPy. In the end, most of modern machine learning boils down to math with vectors and matrices.

Let's look at an example using dot with two matrices:

```
>>> a = np.arange(9).reshape((3,3))
>>> b = np.arange(9).reshape((3,3))
>>> a
    array([[0, 1, 2],
           [3, 4, 5],
           [6, 7, 8]])
>>> np.dot(a,b)
    array([[ 15,  18,  21],
           [ 42,  54,  66],
           [ 69,  90, 111]])
>>> a*b
```

```
array([[ 0,  1,  4],
       [ 9, 16, 25],
       [36, 49, 64]])
```

Here we define both a and b to be the same 3×3 matrix of the digits 0 through 9. We then use dot with these two matrices. For comparison purposes, we also show normal multiplication of the two matrices.

The two results are not the same. The first uses linear algebra rules for multiplying two 3×3 matrices, which says that the first element of the 3×3 output will be the first column of b, [0, 3, 6], multiplied element by element with the first row of a, [0, 1, 2], with each product summed:

$$[0, 3, 6] \times [0, 1, 2] = [0, 3, 12];\ 0 + 3 + 12 = 15$$

A similar process creates each of the other entries. For the simple multiplication, the first element of the 3×3 output is simply $0 \times 0 = 0$.

If the inputs to dot are matrices, then dot acts as we expect: it's matrix multiplication. It's when one of the inputs is a vector and the other a matrix that things get a little sloppy. NumPy is somewhat careless about whether the vector is a row or column vector—it produces the correct result regardless, though the shape of the result might not follow linear algebra rules precisely.

We trudged through the linear algebra examples because as you continue to explore machine learning, you'll encounter code using dot quite frequently. It's good to know what it does, but because of its tolerance of the shape of its inputs, you might need to work through the code paying careful attention to the actual shapes of your arrays to avoid getting lost.

Array Input and Output

NumPy would be difficult to use if it didn't provide the means for storing arrays on disk and reading arrays from disk. Sure, we could use a standard Python module like pickle, but that's inefficient and makes interchange between software packages difficult. Fortunately for us, the creators of NumPy were thorough and included input/output functions.

In the following, we'll refer to several disk files. The first is *abc.txt*, which looks like this:

```
1 2 3
4 5 6
7 8 9
```

It's a file of three lines with three numbers per line separated by a space. The second is *abc_tab.txt*, which is identical to *abc.txt*, but the spaces have been replaced by a tab character, \t in Python. Tab-delimited files are commonly used to store data in files. The last file is *abc.csv*, which is a comma-separated values (CSV) file often used by spreadsheet programs. It's also the same as *abc.txt*, but the spaces have been replaced by commas. Now, let's look at NumPy's basic input/output capabilities.

```
>>> a = np.loadtxt("abc.txt")
>>> a
    array([[1., 2., 3.],
           [4., 5., 6.],
           [7., 8., 9.]])
>>> a = np.loadtxt("abc_tab.txt")
>>> a
    array([[1., 2., 3.],
           [4., 5., 6.],
           [7., 8., 9.]])
❶ >>> a = np.loadtxt("abc.csv", delimiter=",")
>>> a
    array([[1., 2., 3.],
           [4., 5., 6.],
           [7., 8., 9.]])
❷ >>> np.save("abc.npy", a)
❸ >>> b = np.load("abc.npy")
>>> b
    array([[1., 2., 3.],
           [4., 5., 6.],
           [7., 8., 9.]])
❹ >>> np.savetxt("ABC.txt", b)
>>> np.savetxt("ABC.csv", b, delimiter=",")
```

The first three examples use loadtxt, which reads text files and produces NumPy arrays from them. The first two examples show that loadtxt knows how to parse files with values separated by spaces and tab characters. The function uses the rows of the text file as rows of the matrix, and the values on each line as the elements in each row.

The third example explicitly states that the delimiter (separator) between values in the text file is the comma character (,) ❶. This is how to read a *.csv* file in NumPy.

NumPy uses the save function to write arrays to disk ❷. This function writes a single array to the given filename. NumPy uses a *.npy* file extension to identify the file as containing a NumPy array. We'll make extensive use of *.npy* files throughout this book.

To read an array back into memory from disk, use load ❸. Note that the data in the array is loaded, but you must assign it to a new variable name. The *.npy* file doesn't store the original name of the array.

Sometimes we'll want to write arrays in a format that will be readable by other programs or humans. On those occasions, we'll use the savetxt function ❹. These examples write text files, first using spaces between values and then using a comma between values.

What if we want to write multiple arrays to disk? Are we forced to use a single file for each array? Fortunately, no, we can use savez and read them with load.

For example:

```
>>> a
array([[1., 2., 3.],
       [4., 5., 6.],
       [7., 8., 9.]])
>>> b
array([[1., 2., 3.],
       [4., 5., 6.],
       [7., 8., 9.]])
```
❶ `>>> np.savez("arrays.npz", a=a, b=b)`
```
>>> q = np.load("arrays.npz")
```
❷ `>>> list(q.keys())`
```
['a', 'b']
>>> q['a']
array([[1., 2., 3.],
       [4., 5., 6.],
       [7., 8., 9.]])
>>> q['b']
array([[1., 2., 3.],
       [4., 5., 6.],
       [7., 8., 9.]])
```

Here we store the two arrays, a and b, to a single file, *arrays.npz* ❶. We still read the file with load, but instead of the arrays, q is more like a dictionary so that if we ask for the keys as a list ❷, we get a list of the names of the arrays read from the file. Referencing an array by its name returns it.

Look again at the call to savez ❶. Notice how we specified the arrays? This is the keyword approach, and it gives the arrays the keyword name, which we made the same as the variable name so that when we asked for the keys after opening the file, we got back the names we expect. We could have dispensed with the keyword names and simply used the following:

```
>>> np.savez("arrays.npz", a, b)
```

This would write the arrays to the file by using default names of arr_0 and arr_1. Lastly, since arrays can be quite large, we might want to compress them (losslessly!), and for that, we'd have used savez_compressed in place of savez.

Compression might be worth it, but it does slow reading and writing. For example, a 64-bit floating-point array of 10 million element requires at a minimum 80,000,000 bytes of memory. Using savez to write such an array to disk uses 80,000,244 bytes and takes only a fraction of a second. The extra 244 bytes are overhead for the structure of the dictionary. Writing the compressed file to disk takes a second or two but results in a file of 11,960,115 bytes, considerably smaller. Since this example was made using arange, each element of the output array was unique so the compression is not the result of storing an array of 10 million zeros. For the curious, storing 10 million zeros uncompressed still uses 80,000,244 bytes but compressed uses only

77,959 bytes on disk. So, the more redundant the array, the more the savings when compressed.

Random Numbers

NumPy has extensive support for pseudorandom number generation. We'll be sloppy and simply call them *random numbers*, understanding that computers are not capable by any algorithmic process of producing actual random numbers—if you're curious about pseudorandom number generation, you can read my book, *Random Numbers and Computers* (Springer 2018). The NumPy random number library is under `random` and can generate samples from many different distributions, the most common being a uniform distribution, [0, 1). This means that any (representable) floating-point number in that range is equally likely. Usually, this is what we want. At other times we might want to use a normal distribution that looks like the classic bell-shaped curve. Many physical processes follow this curve. NumPy can generate such samples as well.

The random number functions we'll use in this book are `random.random` to generate random numbers from [0, 1), `random.normal` to generate random numbers drawn from a bell-shaped curve, and `random.seed` to set the seed of the generator so we can produce the same sequence of random numbers over and over. We'll leave it to the philosophers to decide if such a sequence still deserves the label *random* or, for that matter, if it ever did, regardless of the seed value.

NumPy and Images

Some of the datasets we'll use are image based. We'll want to work with the datasets in NumPy, so we need to know something about how to work with images in Python and how to get images into and out of NumPy arrays. Fortunately, it's pretty straightforward. Besides NumPy, we'll need to work with the Pillow module (`PIL`) to read and write images. We have Pillow installed already—it comes with the installation of our main toolkits. We also have some sample images as part of `sklearn`.

We need to think in terms of two worlds when working with images. There's the "NumPy" world, where the image has been converted into a NumPy array, and there's the `PIL` world that reads and writes images in common graphics formats like JPEG and PNG. The distinction really isn't so black-and-white—we can do image processing in `PIL` too, and sometimes that is more convenient; but for now, we'll use `PIL` only as a way to read and write image files.

Images are two-dimensional arrays of numbers, but if the image is color, we will have three or even four numbers for each pixel, each a byte value representing the intensity of the red, green, blue, and sometimes, alpha, channels of the image. We'll assume that all of our images are either one-channel grayscale or three-channel RGB. We'll eliminate any alpha channel when we encounter one. The alpha channel determines how transparent the pixel is.

First, let's see how to get at the example images sklearn provides and how to turn them into `PIL` images, store them on disk, and display them:

```
❶ >>> from PIL import Image
   >>> from sklearn.datasets import load_sample_images
❷ >>> china = load_sample_images().images[0]
   >>> flower = load_sample_images().images[1]
   >>> china.shape, china.dtype
       ((427, 640, 3), dtype('uint8'))
   >>> flower.shape, flower.dtype
       ((427, 640, 3), dtype('uint8'))
❸ >>> imChina = Image.fromarray(china)
   >>> imFlower = Image.fromarray(flower)
   >>> imChina.show()
   >>> imFlower.show()
❹ >>> imChina.save("china.png")
   >>> imFlower.save("flower.png")
❺ >>> im = Image.open("china.png")
   >>> im.show()
```

First, we need to import `PIL` ❶ and the sample images function from sklearn. Once we have those, we can get at the actual images as NumPy arrays ❷. We see that the *china* and *flower* images are three-dimensional arrays, meaning they are RGB images. The images are 427×640 pixels. The third dimension is 3, corresponding to the red, green, and blue channels. If the images were grayscale, they would have only two dimensions.

We can convert the NumPy arrays to `PIL` image objects ❸ by using the `fromarray` function. The argument is assumed to be a NumPy array of the proper format for conversion. Usually this means that the array must have a data type of `uint8`. Once we have the `PIL` image objects, we can view the images with the `show` method.

To write the images to disk as actual graphics files, not NumPy arrays, we use the save method on the `PIL` objects ❹. The format of the output file is determined by the file extension. Here we're using PNG.

To read an image file from disk, we use the `open` function ❺. Note that open returns a `PIL` image object, not a NumPy array.

Let's see how to turn the `PIL` image object into a NumPy array. Also, let's see how to use `PIL` to make a color image grayscale before turning it into a NumPy array. We'll use each of these steps later in the book:

```
   >>> im = Image.open("china.png")
❶ >>> img = np.array(im)
   >>> img.shape, img.dtype
       ((427, 640, 3), dtype('uint8'))
❷ >>> gray = im.convert("L")
   >>> gray.show()
```

```
>>> g = np.array(gray)
>>> g.shape, g.dtype
    ((427, 640), dtype('uint8'))
```

We first load the image from disk into a `PIL` image object, `im`. We then pass the image object to NumPy via the `array` function ❶. This function is savvy enough to recognize a `PIL` image object and make the proper conversion to a NumPy array.

We can also turn the `PIL` RGB image into a grayscale image using the `convert` method. Note that `PIL` uses `L` for *luminance* to refer to grayscale images ❷. Again, `array` converts the now grayscale image into a NumPy array. We see that the image has only two dimensions, as we would expect from a grayscale image, where each pixel value is just a shade of gray, not a color.

The `PIL` module has many other abilities. It's a good idea to look at the Pillow website, *https://pillow.readthedocs.io/en/5.1.x/*, to see the other things you can do with PIL.

Summary

In this chapter, we reviewed how to work with NumPy, the foundational toolkit used by both `sklearn` and Keras. This gives us the background we need to understand the code examples we'll see later in the book. It's essential to understand how to use NumPy, at least at a basic level. The examples in this chapter should help.

Now that we're familiar with NumPy, we are ready to dive into working with data.

4

WORKING WITH DATA

Developing a proper dataset is the single most important part of building a successful machine learning model. Machine learning models live and die by the phrase "garbage in, garbage out." As you saw in Chapter 1, the model uses the training data to configure itself to the problem. If the training data is not a good representation of the data the model will receive when it is used, we can't expect our model to perform well. In this chapter, we'll learn how to create a good dataset that represents the data the model will encounter in the wild.

Classes and Labels

In this book, we're exploring *classification*: we're building models that put things into discrete categories, or *classes*, like dog breed, flower type, digit, and so on. To represent classes, we give each input in our training set an identifier called a *label*. A label could be the string "Border Collie" or, better still, a number like 0 or 1.

Models don't know what their inputs represent. They don't care whether the input is a picture of a border collie or the value of Google stock. To the model, it's all numbers. The same is true of labels. Because the label for the input has no intrinsic meaning to the model, we can represent classes however we choose. In practice, class labels are usually integers starting with 0. So, if there are 10 classes, the class labels are 0, 1, 2, ..., 9. In Chapter 5, we'll work with a dataset that has 10 classes representing images of different real-world things. We'll simply map them to the integers as in Table 4-1.

Table 4-1: Label Classes with Integers: 0, 1, 2, . . .

Label	Actual class
0	airplanes
1	cars
2	birds
3	cats
4	deer
5	dogs
6	frogs
7	horses
8	ships
9	trucks

With that labeling, every training input that is a dog is labeled 5, while every input that is a truck is labeled 9. But what exactly is it that we're labeling? In the next section, we'll cover features and feature vectors, the very lifeblood of machine learning.

Features and Feature Vectors

Machine learning models take *features* as inputs and deliver, in the case of a classifier, a label as output. So what are these features and where do they come from?

For most models, features are numbers. What the numbers represent depends upon the task at hand. If we're interested in identifying flowers based on measurements of their physical properties, our features are those measurements. If we're interested in using the dimensions of cells in a medical sample to predict whether a tumor is breast cancer or not, the features are those dimensions. With modern techniques, the features might be the pixels of an image (numbers), or a sound's frequency (numbers) or even how many foxes were counted by a camera trap over a two-week period (numbers).

Features, then, are whatever numbers we want to use as inputs. The goal of training the model is to get it to learn a relationship between the input features and the output label. We assume that a relationship exists between the input features and output label before training the model. If the model fails to train, it might be that there is no relationship to learn.

After training, feature vectors with unknown class labels are given to the model, and the model's output predicts the class label based on the relationships it discovered during training. If the model is repeatedly making poor predictions, one possibility is that the selected features are not sufficiently capturing that relationship. Before we go into what makes a good feature, let's take a closer look at the features themselves.

Types of Features

To recap, features are numbers representing something that is measured or known, and *feature vectors* are sets of these numbers used as inputs to the model. There are different kinds of numbers you could use as features, and as you'll see, they're not all created equal. Sometimes you'll have to manipulate them before you can input them into your model.

Floating-Point Numbers

In Chapter 5, we'll be building a historic flower dataset. The features of that dataset are actual measurements of things like a flower's sepal width and height (in centimeters). A typical measurement might be 2.33 cm. This is a *floating-point* number—a number with a decimal point, or, if you remember your high school math courses, a *real* number. Most models want to work with floating-point numbers, so you can just use the measurements as they are. Floating-point numbers are *continuous*, meaning there are an infinite number of values between one integer and the next, so we have a smooth transition between them. As we'll see later on, some models expect continuous values.

Interval Values

Floating-point numbers don't work for everything, however. Clearly, flowers cannot have 10.14 petals, though they might have 9, 10, or 11. These numbers are *integers*: whole numbers without a fractional part or a decimal point. Unlike floating-point numbers, they are *discrete*, which means they pick out only certain values, leaving gaps in between. Fortunately for us, integers are just special real numbers, so models can use them as they are.

In our petal example, the difference between 9, 10, and 11 is meaningful in that 11 is bigger than 10, and 10 is bigger than 9. Not only that, but 11 is bigger than 10 in exactly the same way that 10 is bigger than 9. The difference, or interval, between the values is the same: 1. This value is called an *interval* value.

The pixels in an image are interval values, because they represent the (assumed linear) response of some measurement device, like a camera or an MRI machine, to some physical process like intensity and color of visible light or the number of hydrogen protons in free water in tissue. The key point is that if value x is the next number in the sequence after value y, and value *z* is the number before value *y*, then the difference between *x* and *y* is the same difference as between *y* and *z*.

Ordinal Values

Sometimes the interval between the values is not the same. For example, some models include someone's educational level to predict whether or not they will default on a loan. If we encode someone's educational level by counting their years of schooling, we could use that safely since the difference between 10 years of schooling and 8 is the same as the difference between 8 years of schooling and 6. However, if we simply assign 1 for "completed high school," 2 for "has an undergraduate degree," and 3 for "has a doctorate or other professional degree," we'd probably be in trouble; while $3 > 2 > 1$ is true, whether or not meaningful for our model, the difference between the values represented by 3 and 2 and 2 and 1 is not the same. Features like these are called *ordinal* because they express an ordering, but the differences between the values are not necessarily always the same.

Categorical Values

Sometimes we use numbers as codes. We might encode sex as 0 for male and 1 for female, for example. In this case, 1 is not understood to be greater than 0 or less than 0, so these are not interval or ordinal values. Instead, these are *categorical* values. They express a category but say nothing about any relationship between the categories.

Another common example, perhaps relevant to classifying flowers, is color. We might use 0 for red, 1 for green, and 2 for blue. Again, no relationship exists between 0, 1, or 2 in this case. This doesn't mean we can't use categorical features with our models, but it does mean that we usually can't use them as they are since most types of machine learning models expect at least ordinal, if not interval numbers.

We can make categorical values at least ordinal by using the following trick. If we wanted to use a person's sex as an input, instead of saying 0 for male and 1 for female, we would create a two-element vector, one element for each possibility. The first digit in the vector will indicate whether the input is male by signaling either 0 (meaning they're not male) or 1 (meaning they are). The second digit will indicate whether or not they are female. We map the categorical values to a binary vector, as shown in Table 4-2.

Table 4-2: Representing Categories as Vectors

Categorical value		Vector representation
0	→	1 0
1	→	0 1

Here a 0 in the "is male" feature is meaningfully less than a 1 in that feature, which fits the definition of an ordinal value. The price we pay is to expand the number of features in our feature vector, as we need one feature for each of the possible categorical values. With five colors, for example, we would need a five-element vector; with five thousand, a five-thousand-element vector.

To use this scheme, the categories must be mutually exclusive, meaning there will be only one 1 in each row. Because there's always only one nonzero value per row, this approach is sometimes called a *one-hot encoding*.

Feature Selection and the Curse of Dimensionality

This section is about *feature selection*, the process of selecting which features to use in your feature vectors, and why you shouldn't include features you don't need. Here's a good rule of thumb: the feature vector should contain only features that capture aspects of the data that allow the model to generalize to new data.

In other words, features should capture aspects of the data that help the model separate the classes. It's impossible to be more explicit, since the set of best features are always dataset specific, unknowable in advance. But that doesn't mean we can't say things that might be helpful in guiding us toward a useful set of features for whatever dataset we're working with.

Like many things in machine learning, selecting features comes with trade-offs. We need enough features to capture all the relevant parts of the data so that the model has something to learn from, but if we have too many features, we fall victim to the *curse of dimensionality*.

To explain what this means, let's look at an example. Suppose our features are all restricted to the range [0, 1). That's not a typo; we're using interval notation, where a square bracket means the bound is included in the range, and a parenthesis means the bound is excluded. So here 0 is allowed but 1 isn't. We'll also assume our feature vectors are either two-dimensional or three-dimensional. That way, we can plot each feature vector as a point in a 2D or 3D space. Finally, we'll simulate datasets by selecting feature vectors, 2D or 3D, uniformly at random so that each element of the vector is in [0, 1).

Let's fix the number of samples at 100. If we have two features, or a 2D space, we can represent 100 randomly selected 2D vectors as in the top of Figure 4-1. Now, if we have three features, or a 3D space, those same 100 features look like the bottom of Figure 4-1.

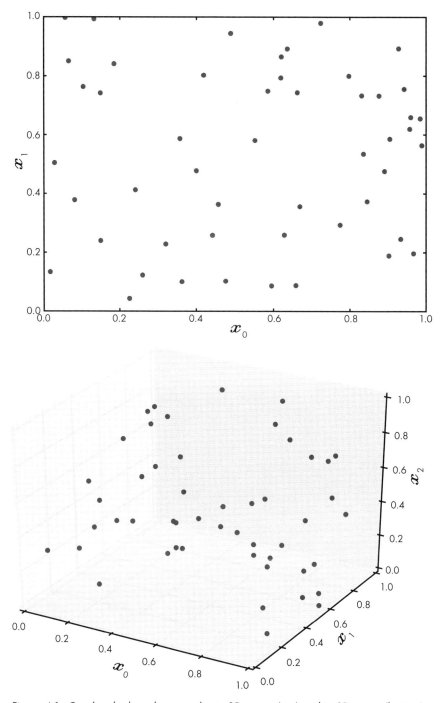

Figure 4-1: One hundred random samples in 2D space (top) and in 3D space (bottom)

Since we're assuming our feature vectors can come from anywhere in the 2D or 3D space, we want our dataset to sample as much of that space as possible so that it represents the space well. We can get a measure of how well the 100 points are filling the space by splitting each axis into 10 equal sections. Let's call these sections *bins*. We'll end up with 100 bins in the 2D space, because it has two axes (10×10), and 1,000 in the 3D space, because it has three axes ($10 \times 10 \times 10$). Now, if we count the number of bins occupied by at least one point and divide that number by the total number of bins, we'll get the fraction of bins that are occupied.

Doing this gives us 0.410 (out of a maximum of 1.0) for the 2D space and 0.048 for the 3D space. This means that 100 samples were able to sample about half of the 2D feature space. Not bad! But 100 samples in the 3D feature space sampled only about 5 percent of the space. To fill the 3D space to the same fraction as the 2D space, we'd need about 1,000—or 10 times as many as we have. This general rule applies as the dimensionality increases: a 4D feature space would need about 10,000 samples, while a 10D feature space would need about 10,000,000,000! As the number of features increases, the amount of training data we need to get a representative sampling of the possible feature space increases dramatically, approximately as 10^d, where d is the number of dimensions. This is the *curse of dimensionality*, and it was the bane of machine learning for decades. Fortunately for us, modern deep learning has overcome this curse, but it's still relevant when working with traditional models like the ones we will explore in Chapter 6.

For example, a typical color image on your computer might have 1,024 pixels on a side where each pixel requires 3 bytes to specify the color as a mix of red, green, and blue. If we wanted to use this image as input to a model, we'd need a feature vector with $d = 1024 \times 1024 \times 3 = 3,145,728$ elements. This means we'd need some $10^{3,145,728}$ samples to populate our feature space. Clearly, this is not possible. We'll see in Chapter 12 how to overcome this curse by using a convolutional neural network.

Now that we know about classes, features, and feature vectors, let's describe what it means to have a good dataset.

Features of a Good Dataset

The dataset is everything. This is no exaggeration, since we build the model from the dataset. The model has parameters—be they the weights and biases of a neural network, the probabilities of each feature occurring in a Naïve Bayes model, or the training data itself in the case of Nearest Neighbors. The parameters are what we use the training data to find out: they encode the knowledge of the model and are learned by the training algorithm.

Let's back up a little bit and define the term *dataset* as we we'll use it in this book. Intuitively, we understand what a dataset is, but let's be more scientific and define it as a collection of pairs of values, $\{X, Y\}$, where X is an *input* to the model and Y is a label. Here X is some set of values that we've measured and grouped together, like length and width of flower parts, and Y is the thing we want to teach the model to tell us, such as which flower or which animal the data best represents.

For *supervised* learning, we act as the teacher, and the model acts as the student. We are teaching the student by presenting example after example, saying things like "this is a cat" and "this is a dog," much as we would teach a small child with a picture book. In this case, the *dataset* is a collection of examples, and *training* consists of showing the examples to the model repeatedly, until the model "gets it"—that is, until the parameters of the model are conditioned and adjusted to minimize the error made by the model for this particular dataset. This is the learning part of machine learning.

Interpolation and Extrapolation

Interpolation is the process of estimating within a certain known range. And *extrapolation* occurs when we use the data we have to estimate outside the known range. Generally speaking, our models are more accurate when they in some sense interpolate, which means we need a dataset that is a comprehensive representation of the range of values that could be used as inputs to the model.

As an example, let's look at world population, in billions, from 1910 to 1960 (Table 4-3). We have data for every 10 years in our known range, 1910 to 1960.

Table 4-3: The World Population by Decade

Year	Population (billions)
1910	1.750
1920	1.860
1930	2.070
1940	2.300
1950	2.557
1960	3.042

If we find the "best fitting" line to plot through this data, we can use it as a model to predict values. This is called *linear regression*, and it allows us to estimate the population for any year we choose. We'll skip the actual fitting process, which you can do simply with online tools, and jump to the model:

$$p = 0.02509y - 46.28$$

For any year, y, we can get an estimate of the population, p. What was the world population in 1952? We don't have actual data for 1952 in our table, but using the model, we can estimate it like so:

$$p = 0.02509(1952) - 46.28 = 2.696 \text{ billion}$$

By checking the actual world population data for 1952, we know that it was 2.637 billion, so our estimate of 2.696 billion was only some 60 million off. The model seems to be pretty good!

In using the model to estimate the world population in 1952, we performed interpolation. We made an estimate for a value that was between data points we had, and the model gave us a good result. Extrapolation, on the other hand, is measuring beyond what is known, outside the range of our data.

Let's use our model to estimate world population in 2000, 40 years after the data we used to build our model ends:

$$p = 0.02509(2000) - 46.28 = 3.900 \text{ billion}$$

According to the model, it should be close to 3.9 billion, but we know from actual data that the world population in 2000 was 6.089 billion. Our model is off by over 2 billion people. What happened here is that we applied the model to input it wasn't suited for. If we remain in the range of inputs that the model is "trained" to know about, namely, dates from 1910 through 1960, then the model performs well enough. Once we went beyond the model's training, however, it fell apart because it assumed knowledge we didn't possess.

When we interpolate, the model will see examples that are similar to the set of examples it saw during training. Perhaps unsurprisingly, it will do better on these examples than when we extrapolate and ask the model to go beyond its training.

When it comes to classification, it's essential we have comprehensive training data. Let's assume we're training a model to identify dog breeds. In our dataset, we have hundreds of images of classic black-and-white border collies like the one on the left in Figure 4-2. If we then give the model a new image of a classic border collie, we will, hopefully, get back a correct label: "Border Collie." This is akin to asking the model to interpolate: it's working with something is has already seen before because the "Border Collie" label in the training data included many examples of classic border collies.

Figure 4-2: A border collie with classic markings (left), a border collie with liver-colored markings (middle), an Australian shepherd (right)

However, not every border collie has the classic border collie markings. Some are marked like the collie in the middle of Figure 4-2. Since we didn't include images like this in the training set, the model must now try to go beyond what it was trained to do and give a correct output label for an instance of a class it was trained on but of a type it was not trained with. It will likely fail, giving a false output like "Australian Shepherd," a breed similar to a border collie, as seen on the right of Figure 4-2.

The key concept to remember, however, is that the dataset must cover the full range of variation *within* the classes the model will see when the model is predicting labels for unknown inputs.

The Parent Distribution

The dataset must be representative of the classes it's modeling. Buried in this idea is the assumption that our data has a *parent distribution*, an unknown data generator that created the particular dataset we're using.

Consider this parallel from philosophy. The ancient Greek philosopher Plato uses the concept of ideals. In his view, there was an ideal chair somewhere "out there," and all existing chairs were more or less perfect copies of that ideal chair. This is what we mean by the relationship between the dataset we are using, the copy, and the parent distribution, the ideal generator. We want the dataset to be a representation of the ideal.

We can think of a dataset as a sample from some unknown process that produces data according to the parent distribution. The type of data it produces—the values and ranges of the features—will follow some unknown, statistical rule. For example, when you roll a die, each of the six values is equally likely in the long run. We call this a *uniform parent distribution*. If you make a bar graph of the number of times each value appears as you roll the die many times, then you will get a (more or less) horizontal line since each value is equally likely to happen. We see a different distribution when we measure the height of adults. The distribution of heights will have a form with two humps, one around mean male height and the other around mean female height.

The parent distribution is what generates this overall shape. The training data, the test data, and the data you give the model to make decisions must all come from the same parent distribution. This is a fundamental assumption models make, and one that shouldn't seem too surprising to us. Still, sometimes it's easy to mix things up and train with data from one parent distribution while testing or using the model with data from a different parent distribution. (How to train with one parent distribution and use that model with data from a different distribution is a very active research area at the moment. Search for "domain adaptation.")

Prior Class Probabilities

The *prior class probability* is the probability with which each class in the dataset appears in the wild.

In general, we want our dataset to match the prior probabilities of the classes. If class A appears 85 percent of the time and class B only 15 percent of the time, then we want class A to appear 85 percent of the time and class B to appear 15 percent of the time in our training set.

There are exceptions, however. Say one of the classes we want the model to learn is rare, showing up only once for every 10,000 inputs. If we make the dataset strictly follow the actual prior probabilities, the model might not see enough examples of the rare class to learn anything helpful about it. And, worse yet, what if the rare class is the class we are most interested in?

For example, let's pretend we're building a robot that locates four-leaf clovers. We'll assume that we already know that the input to the model is a clover; we just want to know whether it has three or four leaves. We know that an estimated 1 in every 5,000 clovers is a four-leaf clover. Building a dataset with 5,000 three-leaf clovers for every instance of a four-leaf clover seems reasonable until we realize that a model that simply says every input is a three-leaf clover will be right, on average, 4,999 times out of 5,000! It will be an extremely accurate but completely useless model because it never finds the class we're interested in.

Instead, we might use a 10:1 ratio of three-leaf to four-leaf clovers. Or, when training the model, we might start with an even number of three- and four-leaf clovers, and then, after training for a time, change to a mix that is increasingly closer to the actual prior probability. This trick doesn't work for all model types, but it does work for neural networks. Why this trick works is poorly understood but, intuitively, we can imagine the network learning first about the visual difference between a three-leaf and four-leaf clover and then learning something about the actual likelihood of encountering a four-leaf clover as the mix changes to be closer to the actual prior probabilities.

In reality, the trick is used because it often results in better-performing models. For much of machine learning, especially deep learning, empirical tricks and techniques are well in advance of any theory to back them up. "It just works better; that's why" is still a valid, though ultimately unsatisfying, answer to many questions about why a particular approach works well.

How to work with imbalanced data is something the research community is still actively investigating. Some choose to start with a more balanced ratio of classes; others use data augmentation (see Chapter 5) to boost the number of samples from the underrepresented class.

Confusers

We said that we need to include examples in our dataset that reflect all the natural variation in the classes we want to learn. This is definitely true, but at times it is particularly important to include training samples that are similar to one or more of our classes but really are not examples of that class.

Consider two models. The first learns the difference between images of dogs and images of cats. The second learns the difference between images of dogs and images that are not dogs. The first model has it easy. The input is either a dog or a cat, and the model is trained using images of dogs and images of cats. The second model, however, has it rougher. It's obvious that we need images of dogs for training. But, what should the "not dog" images be? Given the preceding discussion, we should be starting to intuit that we'll need images that cover the space of images the model will see in the wild.

We can take this one step further. If we want to tell the difference between dogs and not dogs, we should be sure to include wolves in the "not a dog" class when training. If we don't, the model might not learn enough to tell the difference when it encounters a wolf and will return a "dog" classification. If we build the dataset by using hundreds of "not dog" images that are all pictures of penguins and parrots, should we be surprised if the model decides to call a wolf a dog?

In general, we need to make sure the dataset includes *confusers*, or *hard negatives*—examples that are similar enough to other classes to be mistaken for them, but don't belong in the class. Confusers give the model a chance to learn the more precise features of a class. Hard negatives are particularly useful when distinguishing between something and everything else, as in "dog" versus "not dog."

Dataset Size

So far we've talked about what kind of data to include in a dataset, but how much of it do we need? "All of it" is a temptingly cheeky answer. For our model to be as precise as possible, we should use as many examples as possible. But it's rarely possible to get all of the data.

Choosing the size of your dataset means considering a trade-off between accuracy and the time and energy it takes to acquire the data. Acquiring data can be expensive or slow, or, as we saw with our clover example, sometimes the key class of the dataset is rare and seldom encountered. Because labeled data is generally expensive and slow to acquire, we should have some idea of how much we need before we get started.

Unfortunately, the truth is that there is no formula that answers the question of how much data is enough data. After a certain point, there are diminishing returns on the benefit of additional data. Moving from 100 examples to 1,000 examples might boost the accuracy of the model dramatically, but moving from 1,000 to 10,000 examples might offer only a small increase in accuracy. The increased accuracy needs to be balanced against the effort and expense of acquiring an additional 9,000 training examples.

Another factor to consider is the model itself. Models have a *capacity*, which determines the complexity they can support relative to the amount of training data available. The capacity of a model is directly related to its number of parameters. A larger model with more parameters will require a lot of training data to be able to find the proper parameter settings. And though it's often a good idea to have more training examples than model parameters, deep learning can work well when there is less training data than parameters. For example, if the classes are very different from each other—think buildings versus oranges—and it's easy for us to tell the difference, the model likely will also learn the difference quickly, so we can get away with fewer training examples. On the other hand, if we're trying to separate wolves from huskies, we might need a lot more data. We will discuss what to do when you don't have a lot of training data in Chapter 5, but none of those tricks are a good substitute for simply getting more data.

The only correct answer to the question of how much data is needed is "all of it." Get as much as is *practical*, given the constraints of the problem: expense, time, rarity, and so forth.

Data Preparation

Before we move on to building actual datasets, we're going to cover two situations you'll likely encounter before you can feed your dataset to a model: how to scale features, and what to do if a feature value is missing.

Scaling Features

A feature vector built from a set of different features might have a variety of ranges. One feature might take on a wide range of values, say, −1000 to 1000, while another might be restricted to a range of 0 to 1. Some models will not work well when this happens, as one feature dominates the others because of its range. Also, some model types are happiest when features have a mean value that is close to 0.

The solution to these issues is scaling. We'll assume for the time being that every feature in the feature vector is continuous. We'll work with a fake dataset consisting of five features and 15 samples. This means that our dataset has 15 samples—feature vectors and their labels—and each of the feature vectors has five elements. We'll assume there are three classes. The dataset looks like Table 4-4.

Table 4-4: A Hypothetical Dataset

Sample	x_0	x_1	x_2	x_3	x_4	Label
0	6998	0.1361	0.3408	0.00007350	78596048	0
1	6580	0.4908	3.0150	0.00004484	38462706	1
2	7563	0.9349	4.3465	0.00001003	6700340	2
3	8355	0.6529	2.1271	0.00002966	51430391	0
4	2393	0.4605	2.7561	0.00003395	27284192	0
5	9498	0.0244	2.7887	0.00008880	78543394	2
6	4030	0.6467	4.8231	0.00000403	19101443	2
7	5275	0.3560	0.0705	0.00000899	96029352	0
8	8094	0.7979	3.9897	0.00006691	7307156	1
9	843	0.7892	0.9804	0.00005798	10179751	1
10	1221	0.9564	2.3944	0.00007815	14241835	0
11	5879	0.0329	2.0085	0.00009564	34243070	2
12	923	0.4159	1.7821	0.00002467	52404615	1
13	5882	0.0002	1.5362	0.00005066	18728752	2
14	1796	0.7247	2.3190	0.00001332	96703562	1

As this is the first dataset covered in the book, let's go over it thoroughly to introduce some notation and see what is what. The first column in Table 4-4 is the sample number. The sample is an input, in this case a collection of five features representing a feature vector. Notice that the numbering starts at 0. As we'll be using Python arrays (NumPy arrays) for data, we'll start counting at 0 in all cases.

The next five columns are the features in each sample, labeled x_0 to x_4, again starting indices at 0. The final column is the class label. Since there are three classes, the labels run from 0 through 2. There are five samples from class 0, five from class 1, and five from class 2. Therefore, this is a small but balanced dataset; the prior probability of each class is 33 percent, which should, ideally, be close to the actual prior probability of the classes appearing in the wild.

If we had a model, then each row would be its own input. Writing $\{x_0, x_1, x_2, x_3, x_4\}$ to refer to these is tedious, so instead, when we are referring to a full feature vector, we'll use an uppercase letter. For example, we'd refer to Sample 2 as X_2 for dataset X. We'll also sometimes use matrices—2D arrays of numbers—that are also labeled with uppercase letters, for clarity. When we want to refer to a single feature, we'll use a lowercase letter with subscript, for example, x_3.

Let's look at the ranges of the features. The minimum, maximum, and range (the difference between the maximum and minimum) of each feature are shown in Table 4-5.

Table 4-5: The Minimum, Maximum, and Range of the Features in Table 4-4

Feature	Minimum	Maximum	Range
x_0	843.0	9498.0	8655.0
x_1	0.0002	0.9564	0.9562
x_2	0.0705	4.8231	4.7526
x_3	4.03e-06	9.564e-05	9.161e-05
x_4	6700340.0	96703562.0	90003222.0

Note the use of computer notation like 9.161e-05. This how computers represent scientific notation: $9.161 \times 10^{-5} = 0.00009161$. Notice, also, that each feature covers a very different range. Because of this, we'll want to scale the features so their ranges are more similar. Scaling is a valid thing to do prior to training a model as long as you scale all new inputs the same way.

Mean Centering

The simplest form of scaling is *mean centering*. This is easy to do: from each feature, simply subtract the mean (average) value of the feature over the entire dataset. The mean over a set of values, x_i $i = 0, 1, 2, \ldots$ is simply the sum of each value divided by the number of values:

$$\bar{x} = \frac{1}{N} \sum_{i=0}^{N} x_i$$

The mean value for feature x_0 is 5022, so to center x_0, we replace each value like so:

$$x_i \leftarrow x_i - 5022, \; i = 0, 1, 2, \ldots$$

where in this case the i index is across the samples, not the other elements of the feature vector.

Repeating the preceding steps for the mean value of all the other features will center the entire dataset. The result is that the mean value of each feature, over the dataset, is now 0, meaning the feature values themselves are all above and below 0. For deep learning, mean centering is often done by subtracting a mean image from each input image.

Changing the Standard Deviation to 1

Mean centering helps, but the distribution of values around 0 remains the same as before the mean was subtracted. All we did was shift the data down toward 0. The spread of values around the mean has a formal name: it's called the *standard deviation*, and it's computed as the average difference of the data values and the mean:

$$\sigma = \sqrt{\frac{\sum_{i=0}^{N}(x_i - \bar{x})^2}{N - 1}}$$

The letter σ (sigma) is the usual name for the standard deviation in mathematics. You don't need to memorize this formula. It's there to show us how to calculate a measure of the spread, or range, of the data relative to the mean value of the data.

Mean centering changes $\bar{x}$ to 0, but it does not change σ. Sometimes we want to go further and, along with mean centering, change the spread of the data so that the ranges are the same, meaning the standard deviation for each feature is 1. Fortunately, doing this is straightforward. We replace each feature value, x, with

$$x \leftarrow \frac{x - \bar{x}}{\sigma}$$

where $\bar{x}$ and σ are the mean and standard deviation of each feature across the dataset. For example, the preceding toy dataset can be stored as a 2D NumPy array

```
x = [
 [6998, 0.1361, 0.3408, 0.00007350, 78596048],
 [6580, 0.4908, 3.0150, 0.00004484, 38462706],
 [7563, 0.9349, 4.3465, 0.00001003,  6700340],
 [8355, 0.6529, 2.1271, 0.00002966, 51430391],
 [2393, 0.4605, 2.7561, 0.00003395, 27284192],
 [9498, 0.0244, 2.7887, 0.00008880, 78543394],
 [4030, 0.6467, 4.8231, 0.00000403, 19101443],
```

```
[5275, 0.3560, 0.0705, 0.00000899, 96029352],
[8094, 0.7979, 3.9897, 0.00006691,  7307156],
[ 843, 0.7892, 0.9804, 0.00005798, 10179751],
[1221, 0.9564, 2.3944, 0.00007815, 14241835],
[5879, 0.0329, 2.0085, 0.00009564, 34243070],
[ 923, 0.4159, 1.7821, 0.00002467, 52404615],
[5882, 0.0002, 1.5362, 0.00005066, 18728752],
[1796, 0.7247, 2.3190, 0.00001332, 96703562],
]
```

so that the entire dataset can be processed in one line of code:

```
x = (x - x.mean(axis=0)) / x.std(axis=0)
```

This approach is called *standardization* or *normalizing*, and you should do it to most datasets, especially when using one of the traditional models discussed in Chapter 6. Whenever possible, standardize your dataset so that the features have 0 mean and a standard deviation of 1.

If we standardize the preceding dataset, what will it look like? Subtracting, per feature, the mean value of that feature and dividing by the standard deviation gives us a new dataset (Table 4-6). Here, we've shortened the numbers to four decimal digits for display and have dropped the label.

Table 4-6: The Data in Table 4-4 Standardized

Sample	x_0	x_1	x_2	x_3	x_4
0	0.6930	-1.1259	-1.5318	0.9525	1.1824
1	0.5464	-0.0120	0.5051	-0.0192	-0.1141
2	0.8912	1.3826	1.5193	-1.1996	-1.1403
3	1.1690	0.4970	-0.1712	-0.5340	0.3047
4	-0.9221	-0.1071	0.3079	-0.3885	-0.4753
5	1.5699	-1.4767	0.3327	1.4714	1.1807
6	-0.3479	0.4775	1.8823	-1.4031	-0.7396
7	0.0887	-0.4353	-1.7377	-1.2349	1.7456
8	1.0775	0.9524	1.2475	0.7291	-1.1207
9	-1.4657	0.9250	-1.0446	0.4262	-1.0279
10	-1.3332	1.4501	0.0323	1.1102	-0.8966
11	0.3005	-1.4500	-0.2615	1.7033	-0.2505
12	-1.4377	-0.2472	-0.4340	-0.7032	0.3362
13	0.3016	-1.5527	-0.6213	0.1780	-0.7517
14	-1.1315	0.7225	-0.0250	-1.0881	1.7674

If you compare the two tables, you'll see that after our manipulations, the features are more similar than they were in the original set. If we look at x_3, we'll see that the mean of the values is $-1.33e - 16 = -1.33 \times 10^{-16} = -0.000000000000000133$, which is virtually 0. Good! This is what we want. If you do the calculations, you'd see that the means of the other features are similarly close to 0. What about the standard deviation? For x_3 it's

0.99999999, which is virtually 1—again, this is what we'd like. We'll use this new, transformed, dataset to train the model.

Therefore, we must apply the per feature means and standard deviations, as measured on the training set, to any new inputs we're giving to the model:

$$x_{\text{new}} \leftarrow \frac{x_{\text{new}} - \bar{x}_{\text{train}}}{\sigma_{\text{train}}}$$

Here, x_{new} is the new feature vector we want to apply to the model, and $\bar{x}_{\text{train}}$ and σ_{train} are the mean and standard deviation, per feature, from the training set.

Missing Features

Sometimes we don't have all the features we need for a sample. We might have forgotten to make a measurement, for example. These are *missing features*, and we need to find a way to correct them, since most models don't have the ability to accept missing data.

One solution is to fill in the missing values with values that are outside of the feature's range, in the hopes that the model will learn to ignore those values or make more use of other features. Indeed, some more advanced deep learning models intentionally zero some of the input as a form of regularization (we'll see what that means in later chapters).

For now, we'll learn the second most obvious solution: replacing missing features with the mean value of features over the dataset. Let's look again at our practice dataset from earlier. This time, we'll have some missing data to deal with (Table 4-7).

Table 4-7: Our Sample Dataset (Table 4-4) with Some Holes

Sample	x_0	x_1	x_2	x_3	x_4	Label
0	6998	0.1361	0.3408	0.00007350	78596048	0
1		0.4908		0.00004484	38462706	1
2	7563	0.9349	4.3465		6700340	2
3	8355	0.6529	2.1271	0.00002966	51430391	0
4	2393	0.4605	2.7561	0.00003395	27284192	0
5	9498		2.7887	0.00008880	78543394	2
6	4030	0.6467	4.8231	0.00000403		2
7	5275	0.3560	0.0705	0.00000899	96029352	0
8	8094	0.7979	3.9897	0.00006691	7307156	1
9			0.9804		10179751	1
10	1221	0.9564	2.3944	0.00007815	14241835	0
11	5879	0.0329	2.0085	0.00009564	34243070	2
12	923			0.00002467		1
13	5882	0.0002	1.5362	0.00005066	18728752	2
14	1796	0.7247	2.3190	0.00001332	96703562	1

The blank spaces indicate missing values. The means of each feature, ignoring missing values, are shown in Table 4-8.

Table 4-8: The Means for Features in Table 4-7

x_0	x_1	x_2	x_3	x_4
5223.6	0.5158	2.345	4.71e-05	42957735.0

If we replace each missing value with the mean, we'll get a dataset we can standardize and use to train a model.

Of course, real data is better, but the mean is the simplest substitute we can reasonably use. If the dataset is large enough, we might instead generate a histogram of the values of each feature and select the mode—the most common value—but using the mean should work out just fine, especially if your dataset has a lot of samples and the number of missing features is fairly small.

Training, Validation, and Test Data

Now that we have a dataset—a collection of feature vectors—we're ready to start training a model, right? Well, actually, no. That's because we don't want to use the entire dataset for training. We'll need to use some of the data for other purposes, and so we need to split it into at least two subsets, although ideally we'd have three. We call these subsets the training data, validation data, and test data.

The Three Subsets

The *training data* is the subset we use to train the model. The important thing here is selecting feature vectors that well represent the parent distribution of the data.

The *test data* is the subset used to evaluate how well the trained model is doing. We *never* use the test data when training the model; that would be cheating, because we'd be testing the model on data it has seen before. Put the test dataset aside, resist the temptation to touch it until the model is complete, and then use it to evaluate the model.

The third dataset is the *validation data*. Not every model needs a validation dataset, but for deep learning models, having one is helpful. We use the validation dataset during training as though it's test data to get an idea of how well the training is working. It can help us decide things like when to stop training and whether we're using the proper model.

For example, a neural network has some number of layers, each with some number of nodes. We call this the *architecture* of the model. During training, we can test the performance of the neural network with the validation data to figure out whether we should continue training or stop and try a different architecture. We don't train the model with the validation set, and we don't use the validation set to modify model parameters. We also can't use validation data when reporting actual model performance, since we used results based on the validation data to select the model in the first place. Again, this would make it seem like the model is doing better than it is.

Figure 4-3 illustrates the three subsets and their relationships to one another. On the left is the whole dataset. This is the entire collection of feature vectors and associated labels. On the right are the three subsets. The training data and the validation data work together to train and develop the model, while the test data is held back until the model is ready for it. The size of the cylinders reflects the relative amount of data that should fall into each subset, though in practice the validation and test subsets might be even smaller.

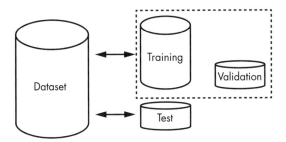

Figure 4-3: Relationships among training, validation, and test subsets

To recap: use the training and validation sets to build the model and the test set to evaluate it.

Partitioning the Dataset

How much data should go into each dataset?

A typical split is 90 percent for training, 5 percent for validation, and 5 percent for testing. For deep learning models, this is fairly standard. If you're working with a very large dataset, you could go as low as 1 percent each for validation and testing. For classic models, which might not learn as well, we might want to make the test dataset larger to ensure we are able to generalize to a wide variety of possible inputs. In those cases, you might try something like 80 percent for training and 10 percent each for validation and test. If you're not using validation data, the full 20 percent might go to testing. These larger test sets might be appropriate for multiclass models that have classes with low prior probabilities. Or, since the test set is not used to define the model, you might increase the number of rare classes in the test set. This might be of particular value should missing the rare class be a costly event (think missing a tumor in a medical image).

Now that we've determined how much data to put into each set, let's use sklearn to generate a dummy dataset that we can partition:

```
>>> import numpy as np
>>> from sklearn.datasets import make_classification
>>> x,y = make_classification(n_samples=10000, weights=(0.9,0.1))
```

```
>>> x.shape
    (10000, 20)
>>> len(np.where(y == 0)[0])
    8969
>>> len(np.where(y == 1)[0])
    1031
```

Here, we've used two classes and 20 features to generate 10,000 samples. The dataset is imbalanced, with 90 percent of the samples in class 0 and 10 percent in class 1. The output is a 2D array of samples (x) and associated 0 or 1 labels (y). The dataset is generated from multidimensional Gaussians that are the analogs of the normal bell curve in more than one dimension, but that doesn't matter to us right now. The useful part for us is that we have a collection of feature vectors and labels, so that we can look at ways in which the dataset might be split into subsets.

The key to the preceding code is the call to make_classification, which accepts the number of samples requested and the fraction for each class. The np.where calls simply find all the class 0 and class 1 instances so that len can count them.

Earlier, we talked about the importance of preserving—or at least approaching—the actual prior probabilities of the different classes in our dataset. If one class makes up 10 percent of real world cases, it would ideally make up 10 percent of our dataset. Now we need to find a way to preserve this prior class probability in the subsets we make for training, validation, and test. There are two main ways to do this: partitioning by class and random sampling.

Partitioning by Class

The exact approach, which is suitable when the dataset is small or perhaps when one class is rare, is to determine the number of samples representing each class, and then set aside selected percentages of each, by class, before merging them together. So, if there are 9,000 samples from class 0, and 1,000 samples from class 1, and we want to put 90 percent of the data into training and 5 percent each into validation and test, we would select 8,100 samples, *at random*, from the class 0 collection and 900 samples, *at random*, from the class 1 collection to make up the training set. Similarly, we would randomly select 450 of the remaining 900 unused class 0 samples for the validation set along with 50 of the remaining unused class 1 data. The remaining class 0 and class 1 samples become the test set.

Listing 4-1 shows the code to construct the subsets using a 90/5/5 split of the original data.

```
import numpy as np
from sklearn.datasets import make_classification

❶ a,b = make_classification(n_samples=10000, weights=(0.9,0.1))
  idx = np.where(b == 0)[0]
  x0 = a[idx,:]
```

```
  y0 = b[idx]
  idx = np.where(b == 1)[0]
  x1 = a[idx,:]
  y1 = b[idx]

❷ idx = np.argsort(np.random.random(y0.shape))
  y0 = y0[idx]
  x0 = x0[idx]
  idx = np.argsort(np.random.random(y1.shape))
  y1 = y1[idx]
  x1 = x1[idx]

❸ ntrn0 = int(0.9*x0.shape[0])
  ntrn1 = int(0.9*x1.shape[0])
  xtrn = np.zeros((int(ntrn0+ntrn1),20))
  ytrn = np.zeros(int(ntrn0+ntrn1))
  xtrn[:ntrn0] = x0[:ntrn0]
  xtrn[ntrn0:] = x1[:ntrn1]
  ytrn[:ntrn0] = y0[:ntrn0]
  ytrn[ntrn0:] = y1[:ntrn1]

❹ n0 = int(x0.shape[0]-ntrn0)
  n1 = int(x1.shape[0]-ntrn1)
  xval = np.zeros((int(n0/2+n1/2),20))
  yval = np.zeros(int(n0/2+n1/2))
  xval[:(n0//2)] = x0[ntrn0:(ntrn0+n0//2)]
  xval[(n0//2):] = x1[ntrn1:(ntrn1+n1//2)]
  yval[:(n0//2)] = y0[ntrn0:(ntrn0+n0//2)]
  yval[(n0//2):] = y1[ntrn1:(ntrn1+n1//2)]

❺ xtst = np.concatenate((x0[(ntrn0+n0//2):],x1[(ntrn1+n1//2):]))
  ytst = np.concatenate((y0[(ntrn0+n0//2):],y1[(ntrn1+n1//2):]))
```

Listing 4-1: Exact construction of training, validation, and test datasets

There's a lot of bookkeeping in this code. First, we create the dummy dataset ❶ and split it into class 0 and class 1 collections, stored in x0,y0 and x1,y1, respectively. We then randomize the ordering ❷. This will let us pull off the first *n* samples for the subsets without worrying that we might be introducing a bias because of ordering in the data. Because of how sklearn generates the dummy dataset, this step isn't required, but it's always a good idea to ensure randomness in the ordering of samples.

We use a trick that's helpful when reordering samples. Because we store the feature vectors in one array and the labels in another, the NumPy shuffle methods will not work. Instead, we generate a random vector of the same length as our number of samples and then use argsort to return the indices of the vector that would put it in sorted order. Since the values in the vector are random, the ordering of the indices used to sort it will also be random.

These indices then reorder the samples and labels so that the each label is still associated with the correct feature vector.

Next, we extract the first 90 percent of samples for the two classes and build the training subset with samples in xtrn and labels in ytrn ❸. We do the same for the 5 percent validation set ❹ and the remaining 5 percent for the test set ❺.

Partitioning by class is tedious, to say the least. We do know, however, that the class 0 to class 1 ratio in each of the subsets is exactly the same.

Random Sampling

Must we be so precise? In general, no. The second common method for partitioning the full dataset is via random sampling. If we have enough data— and 10,000 samples is enough data—we can build our subsets by randomizing the full dataset and then extracting the first 90 percent of samples as the training set, the next 5 percent as the validation set, and the last 5 percent as the test set. This is what we show in Listing 4-2.

```
❶ x,y = make_classification(n_samples=10000, weights=(0.9,0.1))
   idx = np.argsort(np.random.random(y.shape[0]))
   x = x[idx]
   y = y[idx]

❷ ntrn = int(0.9*y.shape[0])
   nval = int(0.05*y.shape[0])

❸ xtrn = x[:ntrn]
   ytrn = y[:ntrn]
   xval = x[ntrn:(ntrn+nval)]
   yval = y[ntrn:(ntrn+nval)]
   xtst = x[(ntrn+nval):]
   ytst = y[(ntrn+nval):]
```

Listing 4-2: Random construction of training, validation, and test datasets

We randomize the dummy dataset stored in x and y ❶. We need to know how many samples to include in each of the subsets. First, the number of samples for the training set is 90 percent of the total in the dataset ❷, while the number in the validation set is 5 percent of the total. The remainder, also 5 percent, is the test set ❸.

This method is so much simpler than the one shown in Listing 4-1. What's the downside of using it? The possible downside is that the mix of classes in each of these subsets might not quite be the fractions we want. For example, imagine we want a training set of 9,000 samples, or 90 percent of the original 10,000 samples, with 8,100 of them from class 0, and 900 of them from class 1. Running the Listing 4-2 code 10 times gives the splits between class 0 and class 1 in the training set that are shown in Table 4-9.

Table 4-9: Ten Training Splits Generated by Random Sampling

Run	Class 0	Class 1
1	8058 (89.5)	942 (10.5)
2	8093 (89.9)	907 (10.1)
3	8065 (89.6)	935 (10.4)
4	8081 (89.8)	919 (10.2)
5	8045 (89.4)	955 (10.6)
6	8045 (89.4)	955 (10.6)
7	8066 (89.6)	934 (10.4)
8	8064 (89.6)	936 (10.4)
9	8071 (89.7)	929 (10.3)
10	8063 (89.6)	937 (10.4)

The number of samples in class 1 ranges from as few as 907 samples to as many as 955 samples. As the number of samples of a particular class in the full dataset decreases, the number in the subsets will start to vary more. This is especially true of smaller subsets, like the validation and test sets. Let's do a separate run, this time looking at the number of samples from each class in the *test* set (Table 4-10).

Table 4-10: Ten Test Splits Generated by Random Sampling

Run	Class 0	Class 1
1	446 (89.2)	54 (10.8)
2	450 (90.0)	50 (10.0)
3	444 (88.8)	56 (11.2)
4	450 (90.0)	50 (10.0)
5	451 (90.2)	49 (9.8)
6	462 (92.4)	38 (7.6)
7	441 (88.2)	59 (11.8)
8	449 (89.8)	51 (10.2)
9	449 (89.8)	51 (10.2)
10	438 (87.6)	62 (12.4)

In the test set, the number of samples from class 1 ranges from 38 to 62.

Will these differences influence how the model learns? Probably not, but they might make the test results look better than they are, as most models struggle to identify the classes that are least common in the training set. The possibility exists of a pathological split that results in having no examples from a particular class, but in practice, it's not really that likely unless your pseudorandom number generator is particularly poor. Still, it's worth keeping the possibility in mind. If concerned, use the exact split approach in Listing 4-1. In truth, the better solution is, as always, to get more data.

Algorithmically, the steps to produce the training, validation, and test splits are as follows:

1. Randomize the order of the full dataset so that classes are evenly mixed.

2. Calculate the number of samples in the training (ntrn) and validation (nval) sets by multiplying the number of samples in the full dataset by the desired fraction. The remaining samples will fall into the test set.

3. Assign the first ntrn samples to the training set.

4. Assign the next nval samples to the validation set.

5. Finally, assign the remaining samples to the test set.

At all times, ensure that the order of the samples is truly random, and that when reordering the feature vectors, you're sure to reorder the labels in the exact same sequence. If this is done, this simple splitting process will give a good split unless the dataset is very small or some classes are very rare.

We neglected to discuss one consequence of this approach. If the full dataset is small to begin with, partitioning it will make the training set even smaller. In Chapter 7, we'll see a powerful approach to dealing with a small dataset, one that's used heavily in deep learning. But first, let's look at a principled way to work with a small dataset to get an idea of how well it will perform on new data.

k-Fold Cross Validation

Modern deep learning models typically need very large datasets, and therefore, you're able to use a single training/validation/test split as described previously. More traditional machine learning models, like those in Chapter 6, however, often work with datasets that are too small (in general) for deep learning models. If we use a single training/validation/test split on those datasets, we might be holding too much data back for testing, or else have too few samples in the test set to get a meaningful measurement of how well the model is working.

One way to address this issue is to use *k-fold cross validation*, a technique that ensures each sample in the dataset is used at some point for training and testing. Use this technique for small datasets intended for traditional machine learning models. It can also be helpful as a way to decide between different models.

To do *k*-fold cross validation, first partition the full, randomized dataset into *k* non-overlapping groups, $x_0, x_1, x_2, \ldots, x_{k-1}$. Your *k* value is arbitrary, though it typically ranges from 5 to 10. Figure 4-4a shows this split, imagining the entire dataset laid out horizontally.

We can train a model by holding x_0 back as test data and using the other groups, $x_1, x_2, \ldots, x_{k-1}$ as training data. We'll ignore validation data for the time being; after building the current training data, we can always hold some of it back as validation data if we want. Call this trained model m_0. You can then start over from scratch, this time holding back x_1 as test data and training with all the other groups, including x_0. We'll get a new trained model. Call it m_1. By design, m_0 and m_1 are the same *type* of model. What we are interested in here is multiple instances of the same type of model trained with different subsets of the full dataset.

Repeat this process for each of the groups, as in Figure 4-4b, and we'll have k models trained with $(k-1)/k$ of the data each, holding $1/k$ of the data back for testing. What k should be depends upon how much data is in the full dataset. Larger k means more training data but less test data. If the per model training time is low, tend toward a larger k as this increases the per model training set size.

(a)

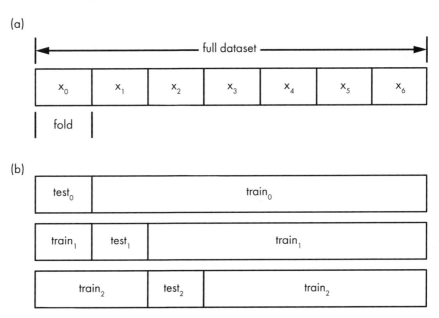

(b)

Figure 4-4: k-fold cross validation. Partitioning the dataset into non-overlapping regions, k=7(a). The first three train/test splits using first x_0 for test, then x_1 for test, and so on (b).

Once the k models are trained, you can evaluate them individually and average their metrics to get an idea of how a model trained on the full dataset would behave. See Chapter 11 to learn about ways to evaluate a model. If using k-fold cross validation to select among two or more models (say, between using k-NN or a Support Vector Machine[1]), repeat the full training and evaluation process for each type of model and compare their results.

---

1. These are examples of classical machine learning models. We'll learn more about them later in the book.

Once we have an idea of how well the model is performing on the averaged evaluation metrics, we can start over again and train the selected model type using *all* of the dataset for training. This is the advantage of *k*-fold cross validation: it lets you have your cake and eat it, too.

Look at Your Data

It's quite easy to assemble features and feature vectors, and then go ahead and put the training, validation, and test sets together without pausing to *look* at the data to see if it makes sense. This is especially true with deep learning models using huge collections of images or other multidimensional data. Here are a few problems you'll want to look out for:

Mislabeled data   Assume we're building a large dataset—one with hundreds of thousands of labeled samples. Further, assume that we're going to use the dataset to build a model that will be able to tell the difference between dogs and cats. Naturally, we need to feed the model many, many dog images and many, many cat images. No problem, you say; we'll just collect a lot of images using something like Google Images. Okay, that'll work. But if you simply set up a script to download image search results matching "dog" and "cat," you'll also get a lot of other images that are not of dogs or cats, or images that contain dogs and cats along with other things. The labels won't be perfect. While it is true that deep learning models can be resistant to such label noise, you want to avoid it whenever possible.

Missing or outlier data   Imagine you have a collection of feature vectors, and you have no idea how common it is that features are missing. If a large percentage of a particular feature is missing, that feature will become a hindrance to the model and you should eliminate it. Or, if there are extreme outliers in the data, you might want to remove those samples, especially if you're going to standardize, since outliers will strongly affect the mean subtracted from the feature values.

Searching for Problems in the Data

How can we look for these problems in the data? Well, for feature vectors, we can often load the dataset into a spreadsheet, if it isn't too large. Or we could write a Python script to summarize the data, feature by feature, or bring the data into a statistics program and examine it that way.

Typically, when summarizing values statistically, we look at the mean and standard deviation, both defined previously, as well as the largest value and the smallest value. We could also look at the median, which is the value we get when we sort the values from smallest to largest and pick the one in the middle. (If the number of values is even, we'd average the two middle values.) Let's look at one of the features from our earlier example. After sorting the values from smallest to largest, we can summarize the data in the following way.

x_2
0.0705
0.3408
0.9804
1.5362
1.7821
2.0085
2.1271
2.3190
2.3944
2.7561
2.7887
3.0150
3.9897
4.3465
4.8231

Mean ($\bar{x}$)	=	2.3519
Standard deviation (σ)	=	1.3128
Standard error (SE)	=	0.3390
Median	=	2.3190
Minimum	=	0.0705
Maximum	=	4.8231

We've already explored the concepts of mean, minimum, maximum, and standard deviation. The median is there, as well; I've highlighted it in the list of features on the left. Notice that after sorting, the median appears in the exact middle of the list. It's often known as the *50th percentile*, because the same amount of data is above it as below.

There is also a new value listed, the *standard error*, also called the *standard error of the mean*. This is the standard deviation divided by the square root of the number of values in the dataset:

$$SE = \frac{\sigma}{\sqrt{n}}$$

The standard error is a measure of the difference between our mean value, $\bar{x}$, and the mean value of the parent distribution. The basic idea is this: if we have more measurements, we'll have a better idea of the parent distribution that is generating the data, and so the mean value of the measurements will be closer to the mean value of the parent distribution.

Notice also that the mean and the median are relatively close to each other. The phrase *relatively close* has no rigorous mathematical meaning, of course, but we can use it as an ad hoc indicator that the data might be normally distributed, meaning we could reasonably replace the missing values by the mean (or median), as we saw previously.

The preceding values were computed easily using NumPy, as seen in Listing 4-3.

```
import numpy as np

❶ f = [0.3408,3.0150,4.3465,2.1271,2.7561,
       2.7887,4.8231,0.0705,3.9897,0.9804,
       2.3944,2.0085,1.7821,1.5362,2.3190]
  f = np.array(f)
```

```
print
print("mean  = %0.4f" % f.mean())
print("std   = %0.4f" % f.std())
❷ print("SE    = %0.4f" % (f.std()/np.sqrt(f.shape[0])))
print("median= %0.4f" % np.median(f))
print("min   = %0.4f" % f.min())
print("max   = %0.4f" % f.max())
```

Listing 4-3: Calculating basic statistics. See feature_stats.py.

After loading NumPy, we manually define the x_2 features (f) and turn them into a NumPy array ❶. Once the data is a NumPy array, calculating the desired values is straightforward, as all of them, except the standard error, are simple method or function calls. The standard error is calculated via the preceding formula ❷ where the first element of the tuple NumPy returns for the shape is the number of elements in a vector.

Numbers are nice, but pictures are often better. You can visualize the data with a *box plot* in Python. Let's generate one to view the standardized values of our dataset. Then we'll discuss what the plot is showing us. The code to create the plot is in Listing 4-4.

```
import numpy as np
import matplotlib.pyplot as plt

❶ d = [[ 0.6930, -1.1259, -1.5318,  0.9525,  1.1824],
       [ 0.5464, -0.0120,  0.5051, -0.0192, -0.1141],
       [ 0.8912,  1.3826,  1.5193, -1.1996, -1.1403],
       [ 1.1690,  0.4970, -0.1712, -0.5340,  0.3047],
       [-0.9221, -0.1071,  0.3079, -0.3885, -0.4753],
       [ 1.5699, -1.4767,  0.3327,  1.4714,  1.1807],
       [-0.3479,  0.4775,  1.8823, -1.4031, -0.7396],
       [ 0.0887, -0.4353, -1.7377, -1.2349,  1.7456],
       [ 1.0775,  0.9524,  1.2475,  0.7291, -1.1207],
       [-1.4657,  0.9250, -1.0446,  0.4262, -1.0279],
       [-1.3332,  1.4501,  0.0323,  1.1102, -0.8966],
       [ 0.3005, -1.4500, -0.2615,  1.7033, -0.2505],
       [-1.4377, -0.2472, -0.4340, -0.7032,  0.3362],
       [ 0.3016, -1.5527, -0.6213,  0.1780, -0.7517],
       [-1.1315,  0.7225, -0.0250, -1.0881,  1.7674]]
❷ d = np.array(d)
  plt.boxplot(d)
  plt.show()
```

Listing 4-4: A box plot of the standardized toy dataset. See box_plot.py.

The values themselves are in Table 4-6. We can store the data as a 2D array and make the box plot using Listing 4-4. We manually define the array ❶ and then plot it ❷. The plot is interactive, so experiment with the environment provided until you feel comfortable with it. The old-school floppy disk icon will store the plot to your disk.

The box plot generated by the program is shown in Figure 4-5.

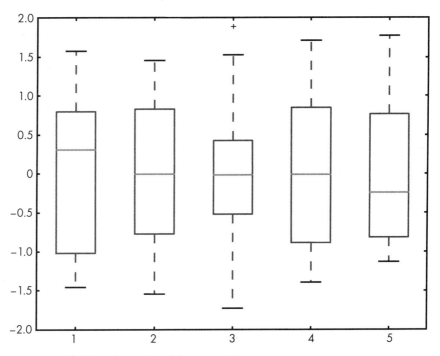

Figure 4-5: The box plot produced by Listing 4-4

How do we interpret the box plot? I'll show you by examining the box representing the standardized feature x_2, shown in Figure 4-6.

The lower box line, Q1, marks the end of the first quartile. This means that 25 percent of the data values for a feature are less than this value. The median, Q2, is the 50 percent mark, and therefore is the end of the second quartile. Half the data values are less than this value. The upper box line, Q3, is the 75 percent mark. The remaining 25 percent of the data values are above Q3.

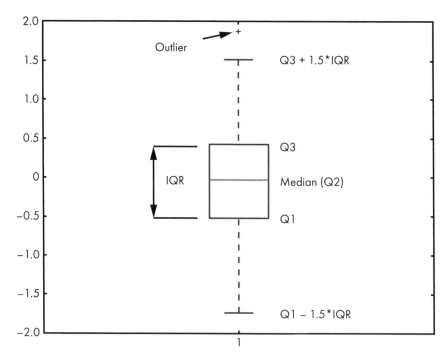

Figure 4-6: The standardized feature x_2 from our dataset

Two lines above and below the box are also shown. These are the *whiskers*. (Matplotlib calls them *fliers*, but this is an unconventional term.) The whiskers are the values at Q1 − 1.5 × IQR and Q3 + 1.5 × IQR. By convention, values outside this range are considered *outliers*.

Looking at outliers can be helpful, because you might realize they're mistakes in data entry and drop them from the dataset. Whatever you do with the outliers, however, be prepared to justify it should you ever plan on publishing or otherwise presenting results based on the dataset. Similarly, you might be able to drop samples with missing values, but make sure there's no systematic error causing the missing data, and check that you're not introducing bias into the data by dropping those samples. In the end, common sense should override slavish adherence to convention.

Cautionary Tales

So, at the risk of being repetitive, *look at your data*. The more you work with it, the more you will understand it, and the more effectively you will be able to make reasonable decisions about what goes in and what comes out, and *why*. Recall that the goal of the dataset is to faithfully and completely capture the parent distribution, or what the data will look like in the wild when the model is used.

Two quick anecdotes come to mind. They both illustrate ways models may well learn things we did not intend or even consider.

The first was told to me as an undergraduate student in the 1980s. In this story, an early form of neural network was tasked with detecting tank and non-tank images. The neural network seemed to work well in testing, but when used in the field, the detection rate dropped rapidly. The researchers realized that the tank images were taken on a cloudy day, and the non-tank were taken on a sunny day. The recognition system had not learned the difference between tanks and non-tanks at all; instead, it had learned the difference between cloudy and sunny days. The moral of this story is that the training set needs to include *all* of the conditions the model will see in the wild.

The second anecdote is more recent. I heard it in a talk at the Neural Information Processing Systems (NIPS) 2016 conference in Barcelona, Spain, and later found it repeated in the researchers' paper.[2] In this case, the authors, who were demonstrating their technique for getting a model to explain its decisions, trained a model that claimed to tell the difference between images of huskies and images of wolves. The model appeared to work rather well, and during the talk, the authors polled the audience composed of machine learning researchers about how believable the model was. Most thought it was a good model. Then, using their technique, the speaker revealed that the network had not learned much, if anything, about the difference between huskies and wolves. Instead, it had learned that the wolf pictures had snow in the background and the husky pictures did not.

Think about your data and be on the lookout for unintended consequences. Models are not human. We bring a lot of preconceived notions and unintended biases to the dataset.

Summary

In this chapter, we described the components of a dataset (classes, labels, features, feature vectors) and then characterized a good dataset, emphasizing the importance of ensuring that the dataset well represents the parent distribution. We then described basic data preparation techniques including how to scale data and one approach for dealing with missing features. After that, we learned how to separate the full dataset into training, validation, and test subsets and how to apply *k*-fold cross validation, which is especially useful with small datasets. We ended the chapter with tips on how to simply examine the data to make sure it makes sense.

In the next chapter, we'll take what we have learned in this chapter and apply it directly to construct the datasets we will use throughout the remainder of this book.

---

2. Ribeiro, Marco Tulio, Sameer Singh, and Carlos Guestrin. "Why Should I Trust You?: Explaining the Predictions of Any Classifier." *In Proceedings of the 22nd ACM SIGKDD International Conference on Knowledge Discovery and Data Mining*, pp. 1135–1144. ACM, 2016.

5

BUILDING DATASETS

The previous chapter had a lot of detailed advice. Now let's put it all into practice to build the datasets we'll use throughout the remainder of the book. Some of these datasets are well suited to traditional models, because they consist of feature vectors. Others are better suited to deep learning models that work with multidimensional inputs—in particular, images, or things that can be visualized as images.

We'll work through acquiring the raw data and preprocessing the data to make it suitable for our tools. We won't make actual training/validation/ test splits until we use these datasets for specific models. It is worth noting here that preprocessing the data to make it suitable for a model is often one of the most labor-intensive of machine learning tasks. All the same, if it is not done, or not done well, your model may end up being far less useful than you want it to be.

Irises

Perhaps the most classic of all machine learning datasets is the iris flower dataset, developed in 1936 by R. A. Fisher in his paper, "The Use of Multiple Measurements in Taxonomic Problems." It's a small dataset of three classes with 50 samples in each class. There are four features: sepal width, sepal length, petal width, and petal length, all in centimeters. The three classes are *I. setosa*, *I. versicolour*, and *I. virginica*. This dataset is built into sklearn, but we'll instead download it from the University of California, Irvine, Machine Learning Repository to practice working with externally sourced data and introduce a rich collection of datasets suitable for many traditional machine learning models. The main repository is located at *https://archive.ics .uci.edu/ml/index.php*, but you can download the irises dataset directly from *https://archive.ics.uci.edu/ml/datasets/iris/*.

At the time of this writing, this dataset has been downloaded nearly 1.8 million times. You can download it by selecting the **Data Folder** link near the top of the page, then right-clicking and saving the *iris.data* file, ideally to a new directory called *iris*. Let's take a look at the start of this file:

```
5.1,3.5,1.4,0.2,Iris-setosa
4.9,3.0,1.4,0.2,Iris-setosa
4.7,3.2,1.3,0.2,Iris-setosa
4.6,3.1,1.5,0.2,Iris-setosa
5.0,3.6,1.4,0.2,Iris-setosa
5.4,3.9,1.7,0.4,Iris-setosa
4.6,3.4,1.4,0.3,Iris-setosa
```

Because the class names at the end of each line are all the same, we should immediately suspect that the samples are sorted by class. Looking at the rest of the file confirms this. So, as emphasized in Chapter 4, we must be sure to randomize the data before training a model. Also, we need to replace the class names with integer labels. We can load the dataset into Python with the script in Listing 5-1.

```
import numpy as np

❶ with open("iris.data") as f:
      lines = [i[:-1] for i in f.readlines()]

❷ n = ["Iris-setosa","Iris-versicolor","Iris-virginica"]
  x = [n.index(i.split(",")[-1]) for i in lines if i != ""]
  x = np.array(x, dtype="uint8")

❸ y = [[float(j) for j in i.split(",")[:-1]] for i in lines if i != ""]
  y = np.array(y)

❹ i = np.argsort(np.random.random(x.shape[0]))
  x = x[i]
  y = y[i]
```

np.save("iris_features.npy", y)
  np.save("iris_labels.npy", x)

Listing 5-1: Loading the raw iris dataset and mapping to our standard format

First, we load the text file containing the data. The list comprehension removes the extraneous newline character ❶. Next, we create the vector of labels by converting the text label into an integer, 0–2. The last element in the list, created by splitting a line along commas, is the text label. We want NumPy arrays, so we turn the list into one. The uint8 is unnecessary, but since the labels are never negative and they're never larger than 2, we save a bit of space by making the data type an unsigned 8-bit integer ❷.

Creating the feature vectors as a 150-row by 4-column matrix comes next via a double list comprehension. The outer comprehension (i) moves over lines from the file, and the inner one (j) takes the list of measurements for each sample and turns them into floating-point numbers. We then convert the list of lists into a 2D NumPy array ❸. We finish by randomizing the dataset as we did previously ❹, and, finally, we write the NumPy arrays to disk so we can use them later ❺.

Figure 5-1 shows a box plot of the features. This is a well-behaved dataset, but the second feature does have some possible outliers. Because the features all have similar scales, we'll use the features as they are.

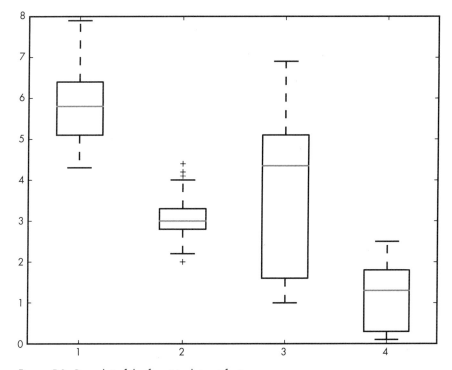

Figure 5-1: Box plot of the four iris dataset features

Breast Cancer

Our second dataset, the Wisconsin Diagnostic Breast Cancer dataset, is also in sklearn, and you can also download it from the UCI Machine Learning Repository. We'll follow the preceding procedure and download the dataset to see how to process it. This seems unnecessary, true, but just as it's crucial to build a good dataset to have any hope of training a good model, it's equally important to learn how to work with data sources that are not in the format we want. Should you one day decide to make machine learning and data science a career, you'll be faced with this issue on a near-daily basis.

Download the dataset by going to *https://archive.ics.uci.edu/ml/datasets/ Breast+Cancer+Wisconsin+(Diagnostic)/*. Then, click the **Data Folder** link, and save the *wdbc.data* file.

This dataset contains cell measurements taken from slides of fine-needle biopsies of breast masses. There are 30 continuous features and two classes: malignant (cancer, 212 samples) and benign (no cancer, 357 samples). This is also a popular dataset, with over 670,000 downloads. The first line of the file is shown here:

```
842302,M,17.99,10.38,122.8,1001,0.1184, ...
```

The first element in that line is a patient ID number that we don't need to worry about. The second element is the label—*M* for malignant, and *B* for benign. The rest of the numbers in the line are 30 measurements related to cell size. The features themselves are of different scales, so besides creating the raw dataset, we'll also create a standardized version. As this is the entirety of the dataset and we'll have to hold some of it back for testing, we don't need to record the per feature means and standard deviations in this case. If we were able to acquire more data generated in the same way, perhaps from an old file that was forgotten about, we would need to keep these values so that we could standardize the new inputs. The script to build this dataset, and to generate a summary box plot, is in Listing 5-2.

```
import numpy as np
import matplotlib.pyplot as plt

❶ with open("wdbc.data") as f:
      lines = [i[:-1] for i in f.readlines() if i != ""]

❷ n = ["B","M"]
  x = np.array([n.index(i.split(",")[1]) for i in lines],dtype="uint8")
  y = np.array([[float(j) for j in i.split(",")[2:]] for i in lines])
  i = np.argsort(np.random.random(x.shape[0]))
  x = x[i]
  y = y[i]
  z = (y - y.mean(axis=0)) / y.std(axis=0)

❸ np.save("bc_features.npy", y)
  np.save("bc_features_standard.npy", z)
```

```
np.save("bc_labels.npy", x)
plt.boxplot(z)
plt.show()
```

Listing 5-2: Loading the raw breast cancer dataset

The first thing we do is read in the raw text data ❶. We then extract each label and map it to 0 for benign and 1 for malignant. Note here that we used 1 for the natural target case, so that a model outputting a probability value is indicating likelihood of finding cancer ❷. We extract the 30 features per sample as floats using a nested list comprehension to first pull out the text of the features (i) and then map them to floats (j). This produces a nested list, which NumPy conveniently converts into a matrix of 569 rows and 30 columns.

Next, we randomize the dataset and calculate the standardized version by subtracting, per feature, the mean value of that feature and dividing by the standard deviation. We'll work with this version and examine it in the box plot of Figure 5-2 ❸, which shows all 30 features after standardization.

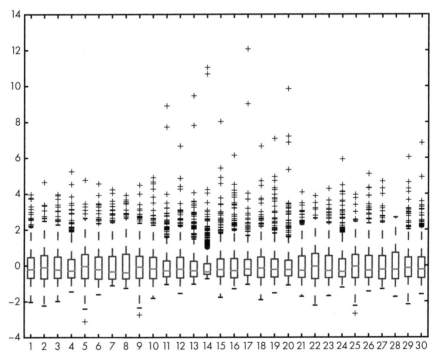

Figure 5-2: Box plot of the 30 breast cancer dataset features

We don't need to know in this case what the features represent. We'll work with the dataset under the assumption that the selected features are sufficient to the task of determining malignancy. Our models will indicate to us whether or not this is the case. The features are now all of the same scale as we can see by the location of the boxes on the y-axis: they're all covering basically the same range. One characteristic of the data is immediately evident—namely, that there are many apparent outliers, as called out by the interquartile range (see Figure 4-6). These aren't necessarily bad values, but they are an indicator that the data isn't normally distributed—it doesn't, per feature, follow a bell-curve-type distribution.

MNIST Digits

Our next dataset isn't typically composed of feature vectors, but is instead made up of thousands of small images of handwritten digits. This dataset is the workhorse of modern machine learning, and one of the first datasets deep learning researchers go to when looking to test new ideas. It's overused, but that's because it's so well understood and simple to work with.

The dataset has a long history, but the version we'll use, the most common version, is known simply as the *MNIST dataset*. The canonical source for the dataset, *http://yann.lecun.com/exdb/mnist/*, includes some background material. To save time, we'll use Keras to download and format the dataset.

Keras will return the dataset as 3D NumPy arrays. The first dimension is the number of images—60,000 for training and 10,000 for test. The second and third dimensions are the pixels of the images. The images are 28×28 pixels in size. Each pixel is an unsigned 8-bit integer, $[0, 255]$.

Because we want to work with models that expect vectors as inputs, and because we want to use this dataset to illustrate certain properties of models later in the book, we'll create additional datasets from this initial one. To do so, first we'll unravel the images to form feature vectors so that we can use this dataset with traditional models that expect vector inputs. Second, we'll use images, but we'll permute the order of the images in the dataset. We'll permute the order of the pixels of each image in the same way, so while the pixels will no longer be in the order that produces the digit image, the reordering will be deterministic, and applied consistently across all images. Third, we'll create an unraveled feature vector version of these permuted images. We'll use these additional datasets to explore differences between traditional neural networks and convolutional neural network models.

Use Listing 5-3 to build the dataset files.

```
import numpy as np
import keras
from keras.datasets import mnist
```

❶ (xtrn, ytrn), (xtst, ytst) = mnist.load_data()
```
idx = np.argsort(np.random.random(ytrn.shape[0]))
xtrn = xtrn[idx]
ytrn = ytrn[idx]
idx = np.argsort(np.random.random(ytst.shape[0]))
xtst = xtst[idx]
ytst = ytst[idx]

np.save("mnist_train_images.npy", xtrn)
np.save("mnist_train_labels.npy", ytrn)
```

```
np.save("mnist_test_images.npy", xtst)
np.save("mnist_test_labels.npy", ytst)
```

❷ ```
xtrnv = xtrn.reshape((60000,28*28))
xtstv = xtst.reshape((10000,28*28))
np.save("mnist_train_vectors.npy", xtrnv)
np.save("mnist_test_vectors.npy", xtstv)
```

❸ ```
idx = np.argsort(np.random.random(28*28))
for i in range(60000):
    xtrnv[i,:] = xtrnv[i,idx]
for i in range(10000):
    xtstv[i,:] = xtstv[i,idx]
np.save("mnist_train_scrambled_vectors.npy", xtrnv)
np.save("mnist_test_scrambled_vectors.npy", xtstv)
```

❹ ```
t = np.zeros((60000,28,28))
for i in range(60000):
    t[i,:,:] = xtrnv[i,:].reshape((28,28))
np.save("mnist_train_scrambled_images.npy", t)
t = np.zeros((10000,28,28))
for i in range(10000):
    t[i,:,:] = xtstv[i,:].reshape((28,28))
np.save("mnist_test_scrambled_images.npy", t)
```

*Listing 5-3: Loading and building the various MNIST datasets*

We start by telling Keras to load the MNIST dataset ❶. When run for the first time, Keras will show a message about downloading the dataset. After that, it won't show the message again.

The dataset itself is stored in four NumPy arrays. The first, xtrn, has a shape of (60000, 28, 28) for the 60,000 training images, each 28×28 pixels. The associated labels are in ytrn as integers, [0, 9]. The 10,000 test images are in xtst with labels in ytst. We also randomize the order of the samples and write the arrays to disk for future use.

Next, we unravel the training and test images and turn them into vectors of 784 elements ❷. Unraveling takes the first row of pixels followed by the second row and so on until all rows are laid end to end. We get 784 elements because $28 \times 28 = 784$.

Following this, we generate a permutation of the 784 elements in the unraveled vectors (idx) ❸.

We use the permuted vectors to form new, scrambled, digit images and store them on disk ❹. The scrambled images are made from the scrambled vectors by undoing the unravel operation. In NumPy, this is just a call to the reshape method of the vector arrays. Note that at no time do we alter the relative ordering of the images, so we need to store only one file each for the train and test labels.

Figure 5-3 shows representative digits from the MNIST dataset.
```

Figure 5-3: Representative MNIST digit images

We don't need to standardize the images, as we know they're all on the same scale already, since they're pixels. We'll sometimes scale them as we use them, but for now we can leave them on disk as byte grayscale images. The dataset is reasonably balanced; Table 5-1 shows the training distribution. Therefore, we don't need to worry about imbalanced data.

Table 5-1: Digit Frequencies for the MNIST Training Set

Digit	Count
0	5,923
1	6,742
2	5,958
3	6,131
4	5,842
5	5,421
6	5,918
7	6,265
8	5,851
9	5,949

CIFAR-10

CIFAR-10 is another standard deep learning dataset that's small enough for us to use without requiring a lot of training time or a GPU. As with MNIST, we can extract the dataset with Keras, which will download it the first time it's requested. The source page for CIFAR-10 is at *https://www.cs.toronto.edu/ %7Ekriz/cifar.html*.

It's worth perusing the page to learn more about where the dataset came from. It consists of 60,000 32×32 pixel RGB images from 10 classes, with 6,000 samples in each class. The training set contains 50,000 images, and the test set contains 10,000 images. The 10 classes are shown here in Table 5-2.

Table 5-2: CIFAR-10 Class Labels and Names

Label	Class
0	airplane
1	automobile
2	bird
3	cat
4	deer
5	dog
6	frog
7	horse
8	ship
9	truck

Figure 5-4 shows, row by row, a collection of representative images from each class. Let's extract the dataset, store it for future use, and create vector representations, much as we did for MNIST.

Figure 5-4: Representative CIFAR-10 images

The script to do all of this is in Listing 5-4.

```
import numpy as np
import keras
from keras.datasets import cifar10
```

❶ ```
(xtrn, ytrn), (xtst, ytst) = cifar10.load_data()
idx = np.argsort(np.random.random(ytrn.shape[0]))
xtrn = xtrn[idx]
ytrn = ytrn[idx]
idx = np.argsort(np.random.random(ytst.shape[0]))
xtst = xtst[idx]
ytst = ytst[idx]

np.save("cifar10_train_images.npy", xtrn)
np.save("cifar10_train_labels.npy", ytrn)
np.save("cifar10_test_images.npy", xtst)
np.save("cifar10_test_labels.npy", ytst)
```

❷ ```
xtrnv = xtrn.reshape((50000,32*32*3))
xtstv = xtst.reshape((10000,32*32*3))
np.save("cifar10_train_vectors.npy", xtrnv)
np.save("cifar10_test_vectors.npy", xtstv)
```

Listing 5-4: Loading and building the various CIFAR-10 datasets

We first load CIFAR-10 from Keras ❶. As with MNIST, the dataset will download automatically the first time that the code is run. And, as with MNIST, we randomize the train and test splits. The training data is in xtrn as a (50,000; 32; 32; 3) array. The last dimension is for the three color components for each pixel: red, green, and blue. The test data is similar, and is in xtst as a (10,000; 32; 32; 3) array. Finally, we write the randomized train and test images to disk. Next, we unravel the images to produce $32 \times 32 \times 3 = 3072$ element feature vectors representing the images ❷ and write them to disk.

Data Augmentation

As we saw in Chapter 4, the dataset is everything, so it needs to be as complete as possible. You'll normally achieve this by carefully selecting samples that fit within the range of inputs the model will encounter when you use it. Thinking back to our earlier analogy, we need the model to *interpolate* and not *extrapolate*. But sometimes, even though we have a wide range of possible samples, we don't have a lot of actual samples. This is where data augmentation can help.

Data augmentation uses the data in the existing dataset to generate new possible samples to add to the set. These samples are always based, in some way, on the existing data. Data augmentation is a powerful technique and is particularly helpful when our actual dataset is small. In a practical sense, data augmentation should probably be used whenever it's feasible.

Data augmentation takes the data we already have and modifies it to create new samples that could have plausibly come from the same parent distribution as our actual data. That means that if we were patient enough to keep collecting real data, we could measure those new samples. Sometimes data augmentation can go beyond what we would actually measure, yet still help the model learn to generalize to the actual data. For example, a model using images as input might benefit from unrealistic colors or backgrounds when the actual inputs to the model would never use those colors or backgrounds.

While data augmentation works in many situations and is a mainstay of deep learning, you won't always be able to use it because not all data can be realistically enhanced.

In this section, we'll take a look at why we'd want to consider using data augmentation and how we might go about doing it. We'll then augment two of the datasets we developed previously, so when we build models, we can see how augmentation affects the models' learning. As far as augmentation is concerned, here's a rule of thumb: in general, you should perform data augmentation whenever possible, especially if the dataset is small.

Why Should You Augment Training Data?

In Chapter 4, we encountered the curse of dimensionality. We saw that the solution to it, for many models, is to fill in the space of possible inputs with more and more training data. Data augmentation is one way we can fill in this space. We'll need to do this in the future; in Chapter 6, for example, we'll meet the k-Nearest Neighbor classifier, perhaps the simplest of all classifiers.

This classifier depends, critically, on having enough training data to adequately fill in the input feature space. If there are three features, then the space is three-dimensional and the training data will fit into some cube in that space. The more training data we have, the more samples we'll have in the cube, and the better the classifier will do. That's because the classifier measures the distance between points in the training data and that of a new, unknown feature vector and votes on what label to assign. The denser the space is with training points, the more often the voting process will succeed. Loosely speaking, data augmentation fills in this space. For most datasets, acquiring more data, more samples of the parent distribution, will not fill in every part of the feature space but will create a more and more complete picture of what the parent distribution looks like in the feature space.

When we work with modern deep learning models (Chapter 12), we'll see that data augmentation has additional benefits. During training, a neural network becomes conditioned to learn features of the training data. If the features the network learns to pay attention to are actually useful for distinguishing the classes, all is well. But, as we saw with the wolf and husky example of Chapter 4, sometimes the network learns the wrong thing, which can't be used to generalize to new inputs—like the fact that the wolf class images had snow in the background and the husky images did not.

Taking steps to avoid this tendency is known as *regularization*. Regularization helps the network learn important features of the training data, ones that generalize as we want them to. Data augmentation is—short of acquiring more actual data—perhaps the simplest way to regularize the network as it learns. It conditions the learning process to not pay attention to quirks of the particular samples selected for the training set but to instead focus on more general features of the data. At least, that is the hope.

An additional benefit of data augmentation is that it lessens the likelihood of overfitting when training. We'll discuss overfitting more in Chapter 9, but succinctly, it's what happens when the model learns the training data nearly perfectly without learning to generalize to new inputs. Using a small dataset can lead to overfitting if the model is able to basically memorize the training data. Data augmentation increases the dataset size, reducing the probability of overfitting and possibly allowing use of a model with a larger capacity. (Capacity is a nebulous concept. Think "bigger," in that the model can learn more of what is important in the training data, while still generalizing to new data.)

One extremely important point needs to be made about data augmentation as it relates to the training/validation/test split of the dataset: you *must* be sure that every augmented sample belongs to the same set. For example, if we augment sample X_{12345}, and this sample has been assigned to the training set, then we must ensure that *all* of the augmented samples based on X_{12345} are also members of the training set. This is so important that it's worth reiterating: *be sure to never mix an augmented sample based on an original sample between the training, validation, and test sets.*

If we don't follow this rule, our beliefs about the quality of the model will be unfounded, or at least partially unwarranted, because there will be samples in the validation and test sets that are, essentially, also in the training set, since they're based on the training data. This warning may seem unnecessary, but it's really easy to make this mistake, especially if working with others or with a database of some kind.

The correct way to augment data is *after* the training, validation, and test splits have been made. Then, augment at least the training data and label all the new samples as training data.

What about augmenting the validation and test splits? It isn't wrong to do so, and might make sense if you don't have a lot of either. I haven't run across any studies that tried to be rigorous about the effects of augmenting the validation and test data, but, conceptually, it shouldn't hurt, and might even help.

Ways to Augment Training Data

To augment a dataset, we need to generate new samples from it that are plausible, meaning they could really occur in the dataset. For images, this is straightforward; you can often rotate the image, or flip it horizontally or vertically. Other times, you can manipulate the pixels themselves to change the contrast or alter the colors. Some have even gone so far as to simply swap entire color bands—swapping the red channel with the blue channel, for example.

Of course, the manipulations must make sense. A subtle rotation might mimic a change in the camera's orientation, and a left-to-right flip might mimic the experience of looking in a mirror. But a top-to-bottom flip probably wouldn't be as realistic. True, a monkey might hang upside-down in a picture, but flipping the picture would flip the tree and the ground, as well. On the other hand, you might be able to do a top-to-bottom flip in an aerial image, which shows objects in any orientation.

Okay, so images are generally straightforward to augment, and it's easy to understand whether the augmentation makes sense. Augmentation of a feature vector is more subtle. It's not always clear how to do it, or if it's even possible. What can we do in that case?

Again, the guiding principle is that the augmentation makes sense. If we encoded color as a one-hot vector of, say, red, green, or blue, and an instance of a class can be red or green or blue, then one way to augment is to shift the color between red, green, and blue. If a sample can represent male or female, then we could also change those values to get a new sample of the same class but with a different gender.

These are unusual things to do, however. Typically, you try to augment continuous values, creating a new feature vector that still represents the original class. We'll examine one way to do this next by augmenting the iris dataset. After that, we'll augment the CIFAR-10 dataset to see how to work with images.

Augmenting the Iris Dataset

The iris dataset has 150 samples from three classes, each with four continuous features. We'll augment it by using *principal component analysis (PCA)*. This is an old technique, in use for over a century. It was common in machine learning before the advent of deep learning to combat the curse of dimensionality, because it can reduce the number of features in a dataset. It also has a variety of uses outside of machine learning.

Imagine that we have a dataset with only two features—for example, the first two features of the iris dataset. A scatter plot of these features will show us where the samples fall in 2D space. Figure 5-5 shows a plot of the first two features of the iris dataset for classes 1 and 2. The plot has shifted the origin to (0,0) by subtracting the mean value of each feature. This does not change the variance or scatter of the data, only its origin.

The plot in Figure 5-5 also shows two arrows. These are the two principal components of the data. Since the data is 2D, we have two components. If we had 100 features, then we would have up to 100 principal components. This is what PCA does: it tells you the directions of the variance of the data. These directions are the *principal components*.

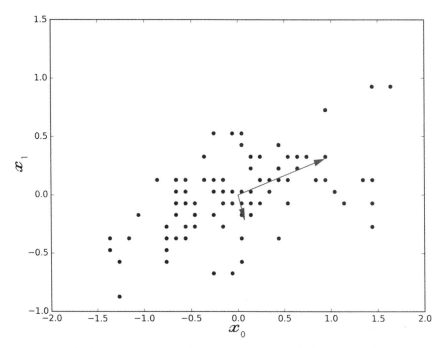

Figure 5-5: The first two iris features for classes 1 and 2, with their principal components

The principal components also tell you how much of the variance of the data is explained by each of these directions. In the plot, the length of the arrow corresponds to the fraction of the total variance explained by each component. As you can see, the largest component is along the diagonal that matches the greatest scatter of the points. Traditional machine learning uses PCA to reduce the number of features while still, hopefully, representing the dataset well. This is how PCA can help fight the curse of dimensionality: find the principal components and then throw the less influential ones away. However, for data augmentation, we want to keep all the components.

The code that produced Figure 5-5 is in Listing 5-5.

```
import numpy as np
import matplotlib.pylab as plt
from sklearn import decomposition

❶ x = np.load("../data/iris/iris_features.npy")[:,:2]
   y = np.load("../data/iris/iris_labels.npy")
   idx = np.where(y != 0)
   x = x[idx]
   x[:,0] -= x[:,0].mean()
   x[:,1] -= x[:,1].mean()

❷ pca = decomposition.PCA(n_components=2)
   pca.fit(x)
   v = pca.explained_variance_ratio_
```

```
❸ plt.scatter(x[:,0],x[:,1],marker='o',color='b')
  ax = plt.axes()
  x0 = v[0]*pca.components_[0,0]
  y0 = v[0]*pca.components_[0,1]
  ax.arrow(0, 0, x0, y0, head_width=0.05, head_length=0.1, fc='r', ec='r')
  x1 = v[1]*pca.components_[1,0]
  y1 = v[1]*pca.components_[1,1]
  ax.arrow(0, 0, x1, y1, head_width=0.05, head_length=0.1, fc='r', ec='r')
  plt.xlabel("$x_0$", fontsize=16)
  plt.ylabel("$x_1$", fontsize=16)
  plt.show()
```

Listing 5-5: Iris PCA plot

Much of the preceding code is to make the plot ❸. The imports are standard except for a new one from sklearn, the decomposition module. We load the iris dataset we previously saved, keeping only the first two features in x and the labels in y. We then keep only class 1 and class 2 features by excluding class 0. Next, we subtract the per feature means to center the data about the point (0,0) ❶.

Then we create the PCA object and fit the iris data to it ❷. There are two features, so the number of components in this case is also two. The PCA Python class mimics the standard approach of sklearn: it defines the model, then fits data to it. Once this is done, we have the principal components stored in pca and accessible via the components_ member variable. We set v to a vector representing the fraction of the variance in the data explained by each of the principal component directions. Since there are two components, this vector also has two components.

The components are always listed in decreasing order, so that the first component is the direction describing the majority of the variance, the second component is the next most important, and so on. In this case, the first component describes some 84 percent of the variance and the second describes the remaining 16 percent. We'll use this ordering when we generate new augmented samples. Here we use the fraction to scale the length of the arrows in the plot showing the principal component directions and relative importance.

How is Figure 5-5 useful for data augmentation? Once you know the principal components, you can use PCA to create derived variables, which means you rotate the data to align it with the principal components. The transform method of the PCA class does this by mapping an input—in our case, the original data—to a new representation where the variance is aligned with the principal components. This mapping is exact, and you can reverse it by using the inverse_transform method.

Doing this alone doesn't generate new samples for us. If we take the original data, x, transform it to the new representation, and then inverse transform it, we'll end up where we started, with x. But, if we transform x and then, before calling the inverse transform, *modify* some of the principal components, we'll return a new set of samples that are not x but are based on x. This is precisely what we want for data augmentation. Next, we'll see which components to modify, and how.

The components are ordered in pca by their importance. We want to keep the most important components as they are, because we want the inverse transform to produce data that looks much like the original data. We don't want to transform things too much, or the new samples won't be plausible instances of the class we claim they represent. We'll arbitrarily say that we want to keep the components that, cumulatively, represent some 90 percent to 95 percent of the variance in the data. These we won't modify at all. The remaining components will be modified by adding normally distributed noise. Recall that *normally distributed* means it follows the bell curve so that most of the time the value will be near the middle, which we'll set to 0, meaning no change to the component, and increasingly rarely to larger values. We'll add the noise to the existing component and call the inverse transform to produce new samples that are very similar but not identical to the originals.

The previous paragraph is pretty dense. The code will make things easier to understand. Our approach to generating augmented data is shown in Listing 5-6.

```
import numpy as np
from sklearn import decomposition

❶ def generateData(pca, x, start):
      original = pca.components_.copy()
      ncomp = pca.components_.shape[0]
      a = pca.transform(x)
      for i in range(start, ncomp):
          pca.components_[i,:] += np.random.normal(scale=0.1, size=ncomp)
      b = pca.inverse_transform(a)
      pca.components_ = original.copy()
      return b

  def main():
  ❷ x = np.load("../../../data/iris/iris_features.npy")
      y = np.load("../../../data/iris/iris_labels.npy")

      N = 120
      x_train = x[:N]
      y_train = y[:N]
      x_test = x[N:]
      y_test = y[N:]

      pca = decomposition.PCA(n_components=4)
      pca.fit(x)
      print(pca.explained_variance_ratio_)
      start = 2
  ❸ nsets = 10
```

```
    nsamp = x_train.shape[0]
    newx = np.zeros((nsets*nsamp, x_train.shape[1]))
    newy = np.zeros(nsets*nsamp, dtype="uint8")

❹ for i in range(nsets):
        if (i == 0):
            newx[0:nsamp,:] = x_train
            newy[0:nsamp] = y_train
        else:
            newx[(i*nsamp):(i*nsamp+nsamp),:] =
                            generateData(pca, x_train, start)
            newy[(i*nsamp):(i*nsamp+nsamp)] = y_train

❺ idx = np.argsort(np.random.random(nsets*nsamp))
    newx = newx[idx]
    newy = newy[idx]
    np.save("iris_train_features_augmented.npy", newx)
    np.save("iris_train_labels_augmented.npy", newy)
    np.save("iris_test_features_augmented.npy", x_test)
    np.save("iris_test_labels_augmented.npy", y_test)

main()
```

Listing 5-6: Augmenting the iris data with PCA. See iris_data_augmentation.py.

The main function ❷ loads the existing iris data, x, and the corresponding labels, y, and then calls PCA, this time using all four features of the dataset. This gives us the four principal components telling us how much of the
variance is explained by each component:

```
0.92461621 0.05301557 0.01718514 0.00518309
```

The first two principal components describe over 97 percent of the variance. Therefore, we'll leave the first two components alone, indices 0 and 1,
and start with index 2 when we want to generate new samples.

We next declare the number of sets we'll define ❸. A *set* here means a
new collection of samples. Since the samples are based on the original data,
x, with 150 samples, each new set will contain 150 samples as well. In fact,
they'll be in the same order as the original samples, so that the class label
that should go with each of these new samples is in the same order as the
class labels in y. We don't want to lose our original data, either, so nsets=10
puts the original data and nine new sets of samples based on that original
data—for a total of 1,500 samples—in the new dataset. We grab the number
of samples in x, 150, and define the arrays to hold our new features (newx)
and associated labels (newy).

Next, we loop to generate the new samples, one set of 150 at a time ❹.
The first pass simply copies the original data into the output arrays. The
remaining passes are similar, updating the source and destination indices
of the output arrays appropriately, but instead of assigning x, we assign the

output of generateData. When the loop is done, we scramble the order of the entire dataset and write it to disk ❺.

All of the magic is in generateData ❶. We pass in the PCA object (pca), the original data (x), and the starting principal component index (start). We set the last argument to 2 to leave the two most important components alone. We keep a copy of the actual components so we can reset the pca object before we return. Then we define ncomp, the number of principal components, for convenience and call the forward transformation mapping the original data along the principal components.

The loop updates the two least important components by adding a random value drawn from a normal curve with mean value 0 and a standard deviation of 0.1. Why 0.1? No special reason; if the standard deviation is small, then the new samples will be near the old samples, while if it's larger, they'll be farther away and possibly not representative of the class anymore. Next, we call the inverse transformation using the modified principal components and restore the actual components. Finally, we return the new set of samples.

Let's look at the new dataset, shown in Figure 5-6. The big gray dots are from our original dataset, and the smaller black dots are the augmented samples. As we can readily see, they all fall near an existing sample, which is what we would expect from modifying only the weakest of the principal components. Since we copied the original data into the augmented dataset, each big dot has a small dot at the center.

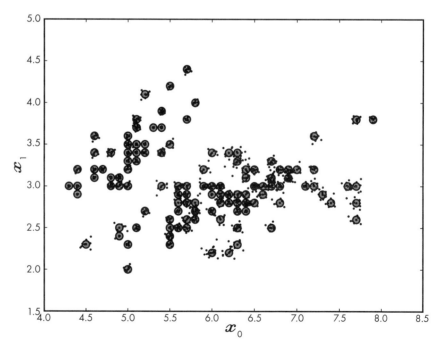

Figure 5-6: The first two features of the original iris dataset (large dots) and the augmented features generated by Listing 5-6 (small points)

This approach is appropriate for continuous features only, as was previously stated, and you should be careful to modify only the weakest of the principal components, and only by a small amount. Experimentation is important here. As an exercise, try applying the same technique to augment the breast cancer dataset, which also consists of continuous features.

Augmenting the CIFAR-10 Dataset

Augmenting the iris dataset involved a lot of discussion and some less than obvious math. Fortunately for us, augmenting images is generally a lot simpler, but still just as effective when training modern models. When we build convolutional neural network models (Chapter 12), we'll see how to do augmentation on the fly when training, a particularly helpful approach, but for now we'll do the augmentation first and build a new dataset with additional versions of the existing images.

Figure 5-4 shows representative images from each class in the CIFAR-10 dataset. These are color images stored as RGB data for the red, green, and blue channels. They were taken from ground level, so top and bottom flips do not make sense here, while left and right flips do. Translations—shifting the image in the x or y direction, or both—are one common technique. Small rotations are another common technique.

However, each of these raises an issue: what to do with pixels that have no data after the shift or rotate? If I shift an image 3 pixels to the left, I need to fill in the three columns on the right with something. Or, if I rotate to the right, there will be pixels at the upper right and lower left that need to be filled in. There are several ways to handle this. One is to simply leave the pixels black, or all 0 values, and let the model learn that there is no helpful information there. Another is to replace the pixels with the mean value of the image, which also provides no information and will, we hope, be ignored by the model. However, the most popular solution is to crop the image.

The image is 32×32 pixels. Pulling a random patch from the image of, say, 28×28 pixels is the equivalent of shifting the image by a random x or y position of up to 4 pixels without needing to worry about filling in anything. If we rotate the image first, which will require interpolation of the pixels, and then crop to remove the edge regions, we'll again have no empty pixels to worry about. Keras has tools for doing this via an image generator object used during training. When we're using Keras to build models, we'll make use of it, but for now, we'll do all of the work ourselves in order to understand the process.

We need to mention one point here. So far, we've talked about building a dataset for training a model. What should we do when we want to use the model? Do we hand the model random croppings of the test inputs as well? No. Instead, we hand the model a cropping centered on the image. So, for CIFAR-10, we would take each 32×32 test input and crop it to 28×28 by dropping the outer 6 pixels, then present that to the model. We do this because the center crop still represents the actual test image and not some augmented version of it.

Figure 5-7 illustrates what we mean by rotations, flips, random croppings for training, and center cropping for testing. In (a) we rotate the image and take a center crop. The output image is in the white square. In (b) we flip left to right and crop randomly. In (c), we take two random crops without flipping, and in (d) we take a center crop for testing, without any rotation or flip. Some people augment test images, but we won't do so here.

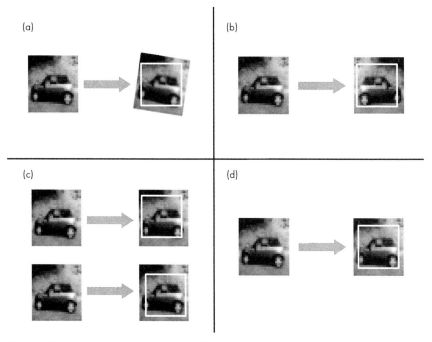

Figure 5-7: Rotate, then center crop (a). Flip left to right, then crop randomly (b). Two random crops during training (c). Center crop for testing, with no rotation or flip (d).

Listing 5-7 shows how to augment the CIFAR-10 training set with random crops, rotations, and flips.

```
import numpy as np
from PIL import Image

❶ def augment(im, dim):
    img = Image.fromarray(im)
    if (np.random.random() < 0.5):
        img = img.transpose(Image.FLIP_LEFT_RIGHT)
    if (np.random.random() < 0.3333):
        z = (32-dim)/2
        r = 10*np.random.random()-5
        img = img.rotate(r, resample=Image.BILINEAR)
        img = img.crop((z,z,32-z,32-z))
    else:
        x = int((32-dim-1)*np.random.random())
        y = int((32-dim-1)*np.random.random())
```

```
            img = img.crop((x,y,x+dim,y+dim))
        return np.array(img)

    def main():
❷    x = np.load("../data/cifar10/cifar10_train_images.npy")
     y = np.load("../data/cifar10/cifar10_train_labels.npy")
     factor = 10
     dim = 28
     z = (32-dim)/2
     newx = np.zeros((x.shape[0]*factor, dim,dim,3), dtype="uint8")
     newy = np.zeros(y.shape[0]*factor, dtype="uint8")
     k=0
❸    for i in range(x.shape[0]):
         im = Image.fromarray(x[i,:])
         im = im.crop((z,z,32-z,32-z))
         newx[k,...] = np.array(im)
         newy[k] = y[i]
         k += 1
         for j in range(factor-1):
             newx[k,...] = augment(x[i,:], dim)
             newy[k] = y[i]
             k += 1
     idx = np.argsort(np.random.random(newx.shape[0]))
     newx = newx[idx]
     newy = newy[idx]
     np.save("../data/cifar10/cifar10_aug_train_images.npy", newx)
     np.save("../data/cifar10/cifar10_aug_train_labels.npy", newy)

❹    x = np.load("../data/cifar10/cifar10_test_images.npy")
     newx = np.zeros((x.shape[0], dim,dim,3), dtype="uint8")
     for i in range(x.shape[0]):
         im = Image.fromarray(x[i,:])
         im = im.crop((z,z,32-z,32-z))
         newx[i,...] = np.array(im)
     np.save("../data/cifar10/cifar10_aug_test_images.npy", newx)
```

Listing 5-7: Augmenting the CIFAR-10 dataset. See cifar10_augment.py.

The main function loads the existing dataset and defines our augmentation factor, crop size, and a constant for defining a center crop ❷.

The new image will be put in newx, which has the following dimensions: $(500,000; 28; 28; 3)$; there are 50,000 training images, each with 32×32 pixels and three color bands. We set the augmentation factor to 10. Similarly, there will be 500,000 labels. The counter, k, will index into this new dataset. For every image in the old dataset, we'll create nine completely new versions and center crop the original ❶ ❸.

As the dataset consists of images, it's easiest to work with the data in image form, so we make the current sample an actual PIL image in order to easily crop it. This is the center crop of the original image. We store it in the new output array.

There are two Python idioms here that we'll see more than once. The first is to turn a NumPy array representing an image into a `PIL` image:

```
im = Image.fromarray(arr)
```

The second is to go the other way and turn a `PIL` image into a NumPy array:

```
arr = np.array(im)
```

We must be sure that the NumPy array is a valid image data type like unsigned byte (`uint8`). Use the `astype` NumPy array method to cast between types, remembering that you bear all responsibility for understanding what that casting entails.

Referring back to Listing 5-7, we are creating the nine versions of the current image. For each of these, we simply copy the label and assign the output array an augmented version. We'll describe the `augment` function shortly. Once the new dataset has been constructed, we scramble the order and write the augmented training dataset to disk ❸.

We're not quite done, however. We created an augmented training set that cropped the original 32×32 images to 28×28. We must, therefore, at least crop the original test set ❹. As we stated previously, we use a center crop and no augmentation of the test data. Therefore, we simply load the test dataset, define the new output test dataset, and run a loop that crops the 32×32 images to 28×28. When done, we write the cropped test data to disk. Note that we did not modify the *order* of the images in the test set; we simply cropped them, so we do not need to write a new file for the test labels.

The `augment` function ❶ is where all the action is. We immediately change the input NumPy array into an actual `PIL` image object. We next decide, with a 50-50 chance, whether or not we will flip the image left to right. Note that we do not crop the image just yet.

Next, we ask whether we should rotate the image or not. We select rotation with a probability of 33 percent (1 in 3 chance). Why 33 percent? No particular reason, but it seems that we might want to crop randomly more often than we rotate. We could even drop this probability down to 20 percent (1 in 5 chance). If we do rotate, we select the rotation angle, $[-5, 5]$ and then call the `rotate` method using bilinear interpolation to make the rotated image look a bit nicer than simply using the nearest neighbor, which is the `PIL` default. Next, we center crop the rotated image. This way, we will not get any black pixels on the edges where the rotation had no image information to work with.

If we do not rotate, we are free to select a random crop. We choose the upper-left corner of this random crop, ensuring that the cropped square will not exceed the dimensions of the original image. Finally, we convert the data back to a NumPy array and return.

Summary

In this chapter, we built four datasets that we'll use as examples through-out the rest of the book. The first two, irises and breast cancer histology, are based on feature vectors. The last two, MNIST and CIFAR-10, are repre-sented as images. We then learned about two data augmentation methods: augmenting a feature vector of continuous values using PCA and, more criti-cal for deep learning, augmenting images by basic transformations.

In the next chapter, we'll transition to our discussion of classical ma-chine learning models. In the chapter after that, we'll use these datasets with those models.

6

CLASSICAL MACHINE LEARNING

It's satisfying to be able to write "Classical Machine Learning" as it implies that there is something newer that makes older techniques "classical." Of course, we know by now that there is—deep learning—and we'll get to it in the chapters that follow. But first, we need to build our intuition by examining older techniques that will help cement concepts for us and, frankly, because the older techniques are still useful when the situation warrants.

It's tempting to include some sort of history here. To keep to the practical nature of this book, we won't, but a full history of machine learning is needed, and as of this writing, I have not found one. Historians reading this, please take note. I will say that machine learning is not new; the techniques of this chapter go back decades and have had considerable success on their own.

However, the successes were always limited in a way that deep learning has now largely overcome. Still, owning a hammer doesn't make everything a nail. You will encounter problems that are well suited to these older techniques. This might be because there's too little data available to train a deep model, because the problem is simple and easily solved by a classical technique, or because the operating environment is not conducive to a large, deep model (think microcontroller). Besides, many of these techniques are easier to understand, conceptually, than a deep model is, and all the comments of earlier chapters about building datasets, as well as the comments in Chapter 11 about evaluating models, still apply.

The following sections will introduce several popular classical models, not in great detail, but in essence. All of these models are supported by sklearn. In Chapter 7, we'll apply the models to some of the datasets we developed in Chapter 5. This will give us an idea of the relative performance of the models when compared to each other as well as giving us a baseline for comparing the performance of deep models in subsequent chapters.

We'll examine six classical models. The order in which we discuss them roughly tracks with the complexity of the type of model. The first three, Nearest Centroid, k-Nearest Neighbors, and Naïve Bayes, are quite simple to understand and implement. The last three, Decision Trees, Random Forests, and Support Vector Machines, are harder, but we'll do our best to explain what's going on.

Nearest Centroid

Assume we want to build a classifier and that we have a properly designed dataset of n classes (see Chapter 4). For simplicity, we'll assume that we have m samples of each of the n classes. This isn't necessary but saves us from adding many subscripts to things. Since our dataset is properly designed, we have training samples and test samples. We don't need validation samples in this case, so we can throw them into the training set. Our goal is to have a model that uses the training set to learn so we can apply the model to the test set to see how it will do with new, unknown samples. Here the sample is a feature vector of floating-point values.

The goal of selecting components for a feature vector is to end up with a feature vector that makes the different classes distinct in the feature space. Let's say that the feature vector has w features. This means we can think of the feature vector as the coordinates of a point in a w-dimensional space. If $w = 2$ or $w = 3$, we can graph the feature vectors. However, mathematically, there's no reason for us to restrict w to 2 or 3; all of what we describe here works in 100, 500, or 1000 dimensions. Note it won't work equally well: the dreaded curse of dimensionality will creep in and eventually require an exponentially large training dataset, but we'll ignore this elephant in the room for now.

If the features are well chosen, we might expect a plot of the points in the w-dimensional space to group the classes so that all of the samples from class 0 are near each other, and all of the samples from class 1 are near each other but distinct from class 0, and so forth. If this is our expectation, then how might we use this knowledge to assign a new, unknown sample to a particular class? Of course, this is the goal of classification, but in this case, given our assumption that the classes are well separated in the feature space, what is something simple we could do?

Figure 6-1 shows a hypothetical 2D feature space with four distinct classes. The different classes are clearly separated in this toy example. A new, unknown feature vector will fall into this space as a point. The goal is to assign a class label to the new point, either square, star, circle, or triangle.

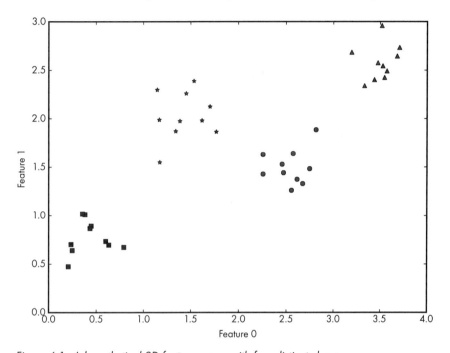

Figure 6-1: A hypothetical 2D feature space with four distinct classes

Since the points of Figure 6-1 are so well grouped, we might think that we could represent each group by an average position in the feature space. Instead of the 10 square points, we'd use a single point to represent the squares. This seems an entirely reasonable thing to do.

It turns out, the average point of a group of points has a name: the *centroid*, the center point. We know how to compute the average of a set of numbers: add them up and divide by how many we added. To find the centroid of a set of points in 2D space, we first find the average of all the x-axis coordinates and then the average of all the y-axis coordinates. If we have three dimensions, we'll do this for the x-, y-, and z-axes. If we have w dimensions, we'll do it for each of the dimensions. In the end, we'll have a single point that we can use to represent the entire group. If we do this for our toy example, we get Figure 6-2, where the centroid is shown as the large marker.

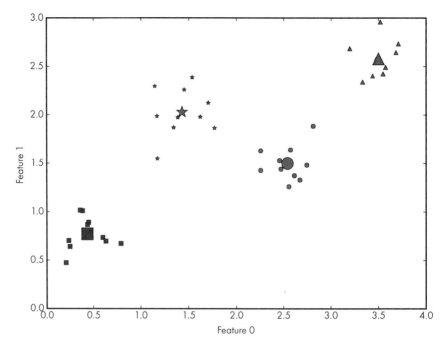

Figure 6-2: A hypothetical 2D feature space with four distinct classes and their centroids

How is the centroid helpful to us? Well, if a new, unknown sample is given to us, it will be a point in the feature space as mentioned previously. We can then measure the distance between this point and each of the centroids and assign the class label of the closest centroid. The idea of *distance* is somewhat ambiguous; there are many different ways to define distance. One obvious way is to draw straight line between the two points; this distance is known as the *Euclidean distance*, and it's easy enough to compute. If we have two points, (x_0, y_0) and (x_1, y_1) then the Euclidean distance between them is simply the following:

$$d = \sqrt{(x_0 - x_1)^2 + (y_0 - y_1)^2}$$

If we have three dimensions, the distance between two points becomes

$$d = \sqrt{(x_0 - x_1)^2 + (y_0 - y_1)^2 + (z_0 - z_1)^2}$$

which can be generalized to w dimensions for two points, x_0 and x_1, as

$$d = \sqrt{\sum_{i=0}^{w-1} (x_0^i - x_1^i)^2}$$

where x_0^i is the i-th component of the point x_0. This means, component by component, find the difference between the two points, square it, and add it to the squared difference of all the other components. Then, take the square root.

Figure 6-3 shows a sample point in the feature space as well as the distances to the centroids. The shortest distance is to the circle class, so we'd assign the new sample to that class.

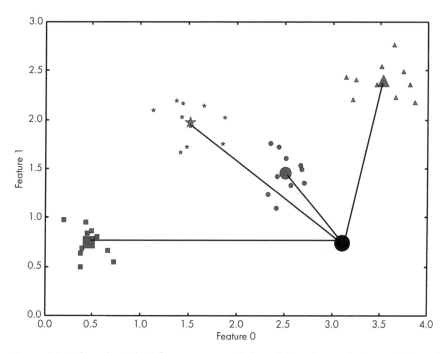

Figure 6-3: A hypothetical 2D feature space with four distinct classes, their centroids, and a new, unknown sample

The process we just implemented is known as a *Nearest Centroid* classifier. It's also sometimes called *template matching*. The centroids of the classes learned from the training data are used as a proxy for the class as a whole. Then, new samples use those centroids to decide on a label.

This seems so simple and perhaps even somewhat obvious, so why isn't this classifier used more? Well, there are several reasons. One has already been mentioned, the curse of dimensionality. As the number of features increases, the space gets larger and larger, and we need exponentially more training data to get a good idea of where the centroids should be. So, a large feature space implies that this might not be the right approach.

There's a more severe problem, however. Our toy example had very tight groups. What if the groups are more diffuse, even overlapping? Then the selection of the Nearest Centroid becomes problematic: how would we know whether the closest centroid represents class A or class B?

Still more severe is that a particular class might fall into *two* or more distinct groups. If we calculate the centroid of only the class as a whole, the centroid will be between the groups for the class and not represent either cluster well. We'd need to know that the class is split between groups and use multiple centroids for the class. If the feature space is small, we can plot it and see that the class is divided between groups. However, if the feature space is larger, there's no easy way for us to decide that the class is divided between multiple groups and that multiple centroids are required. Still, for elementary problems, this approach might be ideal. Not every application deals with difficult data. We might be building an automated system that needs to make simple, easy decisions on new inputs. In that case, this simple classifier might be a perfect fit.

k-Nearest Neighbors

As we saw earlier, one problem with a centroid approach is that the classes might be divided among multiple groups in the feature space. As the number of groups increases, so would the number of centroids necessary to specify the class. This implies another approach. Instead of computing per class centroids, what if we used the training data as is and selected the class label for a new input sample by finding the closest member of the training set and using its label?

This type of classifier is called a *Nearest Neighbor* classifier. If we look at only the closest sample in the training set, we are using one neighbor, so we call the classifier a *1-Nearest Neighbor* or *1-NN classifier*. But we don't need to look at only the nearest training point. We might want to look at several and then vote to assign a new sample the most common class label. In the event of a tie, we can select one of the class labels at random. If we use three nearest neighbors, we have a 3-NN classifier, and if we use k neighbors, we have a k-NN classifier.

Let's revisit the hypothetical dataset of Figure 6-1 but generate a new version where the tight clusters are more spread out. We still have two features and four classes with 10 examples each. Let's set $k = 3$, a typical value. To assign a label to a new sample, we plot the sample in the feature space and then find the three closest training data points to it. Figure 6-4 shows the three nearest neighbors for three unknown samples.

The three training data points closest to Sample A are square, square, and star. Therefore, by majority vote, we assign Sample A to the class square. Similarly, the three closest training data points for Sample B are circle, triangle, and triangle. Therefore, we declare Sample B to be of class triangle. Things are more interesting with Sample C. In this case, the three closest training samples are each from a different class: circle, star, and triangle. So, voting is a tie.

When this happens, the k-NN implementation has to make a choice. The simplest thing to do is select the class label at random since one might argue that any of the three are equally as likely. Alternatively, one might believe a little more strongly in the value of the distance between the unknown sample and the training data and select the one with the shortest distance. In this case, we'd label Sample C with class star, since that's the training sample closest to it.

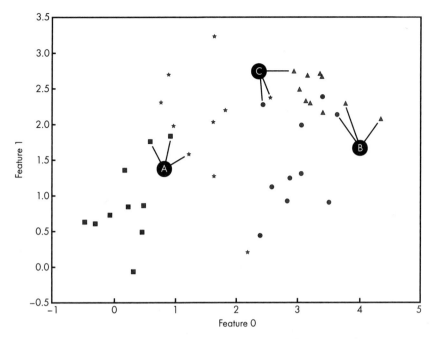

Figure 6-4: Applying k-NN for k=3 to three unknown samples A, B, and C

The beauty of a *k*-NN classifier is that the training data *is* the model—no training step is necessary. Of course, the training data must be carried around with the model and, depending upon the size of the training set, finding the *k* nearest neighbors for a new input sample might be computationally very expensive. People have worked for decades to try to speed up the neighbor search or store the training data more efficiently, but in the end, the curse of dimensionality is still there and still an issue.

However, some *k*-NN classifiers have performed very well: if the dimensionality of the feature space is small enough, *k*-NN might be attractive. There needs to be a balance between training data size, which leads to better performance but more storage and more laborious searching for neighbors, and the dimensionality of the feature space. The same sort of scenario that might make Nearest Centroid a good fit will also make *k*-NN a good fit. However, *k*-NN is perhaps more robust to diffuse and somewhat overlapping class groups than Nearest Centroid is. If the samples for a class are split between several groups, *k*-NN will be superior to Nearest Centroid.

Naïve Bayes

Widely used in natural language processing research, the *Naïve Bayes* classifier is simple to implement and straightforward to understand, though we'll have to include some math to do it. However, I promise, the description of what's happening will make the math understandable even if the notation isn't so familiar.

The technique uses Bayes' theorem (see Thomas Bayes' "An Essay Towards Solving a Problem in the Doctrine of Chances" published in 1763). The theorem relates probabilities, and its modern formulation is

$$P(A \mid B) = \frac{P(B \mid A)P(A)}{P(B)}$$

which uses some mathematical notation from probability theory that we need to describe to understand how we'll use this theorem to implement a classifier.

The expression $P(A \mid B)$ represents the probability that event A has occurred, given event B has already occurred. In this context, it's called the *posterior probability*. Similarly, $P(B \mid A)$ represents the probability that event B has occurred, given event A has occurred. We call $P(B \mid A)$ the *likelihood* of B, given A. Finally, $P(A)$ and $P(B)$ represent, respectively, the probability that event A has occurred, regardless of event B, and the probability that event B has occurred, regardless of event A. We call $P(A)$ the *prior probability* of A. $P(B)$ is the probability of B happening regardless of A.

Bayes' theorem gives us the probability of something happening (event A) given that we already know something else has happened (event B). So how does this help us classify? We want to know whether a feature vector belongs to a given class. We know the feature vector, but we don't know the class. So if we have a dataset of m feature vectors, where each feature vector has n features, $x = \{x_1, x_2, x_3, \ldots, x_n\}$, then we can replace the B in Bayes' theorem with each of the features in the feature vector. We can also replace A with y, the class label we want to assign to a new, unknown feature vector x. The theorem now looks like this:

$$P(y \mid x_1, x_2, x_3, \ldots, x_n) = \frac{P(x_1, x_2, x_3, \ldots, x_n \mid y)P(y)}{P(x_1, x_2, x_3, \ldots, x_n)}$$

Let's explain things a bit. Bayes' theorem states that if we know the likelihood of having x be our feature vector given that y is the class, and we know how often class y shows up (this is $P(y)$, the prior probability of y), then we can calculate the probability that the class of the feature vector x is y. If we are able to do this for all the possible classes, all the different y values, we can select the highest probability and label the input feature vector x as belonging to that class, y.

Recall that a training dataset is a set of pairs, (x^i, y^i), for a known feature vector, x^i, and a known class it belongs to, y^i. Here the i superscript is counting the feature vector and label pairs in the training dataset. Now, given a dataset like this, we can calculate $P(y)$ by making a histogram of how often each class label shows up in the training set. We believe that the training set fairly represents the parent distribution of possible feature vectors so that we can use the training data to calculate the values we need to make use of Bayes' theorem. (See Chapter 4 for techniques to ensure that the dataset is a good one.)

Once we have $P(y)$, we need to know the likelihood, $P(x_1, x_2, x_3, \ldots, x_n \mid y)$. Unfortunately, we can't calculate this directly. But all is not lost: we'll make an assumption that will let us move ahead. We'll assume that each of the features in x is *statistically independent*. This means that the fact that we measure a particular x_1 has nothing whatsoever to do with the values of any of the other $n - 1$ features. This isn't true always, or even most of the time, but in practice, it turns out that this assumption is often close enough to true that we can get by. This is why it's called *Naïve Bayes*, as it's naïve to assume the features are independent of each other. That assumption is most definitely not true, for example, when our input is an image. The pixels of an image are highly dependent upon each other. Pick one at random, and the pixels next to it are almost certainly within a few values of it.

When two events are independent, their *joint probability*, the probability that they both happen, is simply the product of their individual probabilities. The independence assumption lets us change the likelihood portion of Bayes' theorem like so:

$$P(x_1, x_2, x_3, \ldots, x_n | y) \approx \prod_{i=1}^{n} P(x_i | y)$$

The $\prod$ symbol means *multiplied together*, much like the $\sum$ symbol means *added together*. The right side of the equation is saying that if we know the probability of measuring a particular value of a feature, say feature x_i, given that the class label is y, we can get the likelihood of the entire feature vector x, given class label y, by multiplying each of the per feature probabilities together.

If our dataset consists of categorical values, or discrete values like integers (for example, age), then we can use the dataset to calculate the $P(x_i | y)$ values by building a histogram for each feature for each class. For example, if feature x_2 for class 1 has the following values

```
7, 4, 3, 1, 6, 5, 2, 8, 5, 4, 4, 2, 7, 1, 3, 1, 1, 3, 3, 3, 0, 3,
4, 4, 2, 3, 4, 5, 2, 4, 2, 3, 2, 4, 4, 1, 3, 3, 3, 2, 2, 4, 6, 5,
2, 6, 5, 2, 6, 6, 3, 5, 2, 4, 2, 4, 5, 4, 5, 5, 2, 5, 3, 4, 3, 1,
6, 6, 5, 3, 4, 3, 3, 4, 1, 1, 3, 5, 4, 4, 7, 0, 6, 2, 4, 7, 4, 3,
4, 3, 5, 4, 6, 2, 5, 4, 4, 5, 6, 5
```

then each value occurs with the following probability

```
0: 0.02
1: 0.08
2: 0.15
3: 0.20
4: 0.24
5: 0.16
6: 0.10
7: 0.04
8: 0.01
```

which comes from the number of times each value occurs divided by 100, the total number of values in the dataset.

This histogram is exactly what we need to find $P(x_2|y = 1)$, the probability for feature 2 when the class label is 1. For example, we can expect a new feature vector of class 1 to have $x_2 = 4$ about 24 percent of the time and to have $x_2 = 1$ about 8 percent of the time.

By building tables like this for each feature and each class label, we can complete our classifier for the categorical and discrete cases. For a new feature vector, we use the tables to find the probability that each feature would have that value. We multiply each of those probabilities together and then multiply by the prior probability of that class. This, repeated for each of the m classes in the dataset, will give us a set of m posterior probabilities. To classify the new feature vector, select the largest of these m values, and assign the corresponding class label.

How do we calculate $P(x_i|y)$ if the feature values are continuous? One way would be to bin the continuous values and then make tables as in the discrete case. Another is to make one more assumption. We need to make an assumption about the distribution of possible x_i feature values that we could measure. Most natural phenomena seem to follow a normal distribution. We discussed the normal distribution in Chapter 1. Let's assume, then, that the features all follow normal distributions. A normal distribution is defined by its mean value (μ, mu) and a standard deviation (σ, sigma). The mean value is just the average value we'd expect if we drew samples from the distribution repeatedly. The standard deviation is a measure of how wide the distribution is—how spread out it is around the mean value.

Mathematically, what we want to do is replace each $P(x_i|y)$ like so

$$P(x_i|y) \approx N(\mu_i, \sigma_i)$$

for each feature in our feature vector. Here $N(\mu_i, \sigma_i)$ is notation meaning a normal distribution centered around some mean value (μ) and defined by a spread (σ).

We don't really know the exact μ and σ values, but we can approximate them from the training data. For example, assume the training data consists of 25 samples, where the class label is 0. Further, assume that the following are the values of feature 3, that is, x_3, in those cases:

```
0.21457111,   4.3311102,    5.50481251,   0.80293956,   2.5051598,
2.37655204,   2.4296739,    2.84224169,  -0.11890662,   3.18819152,
1.6843311,    4.05982237,   4.14488722,   4.29148855,   3.22658406,
6.45507675,   0.40046778,   1.81796124,   0.2732696,    2.91498336,
1.42561983,   2.73483704,   1.68382843,   3.80387653,   1.53431146
```

Then we'd use $\mu_3 = 2.58$ and $\sigma_3 = 1.64$ when setting up the normal distribution for feature 3 for class 0 since the average of these values is 2.58, and the standard deviation, the spread around the mean value, is 1.64.

When a new unknown sample is given to the classifier, we would compute the probability of the given x_3 happening if the actual class was class 0 by using the following equation.

$$P(x_3 \mid y = 0) = \frac{1}{\sigma_3 \sqrt{2\pi}} e^{-\frac{1}{2}\left(\frac{x_3 - \mu_3}{\sigma_3}\right)^2}$$

This equation comes from the definition of a normal distribution with mean μ and standard deviation σ. It says that the likelihood of a particular feature value, given the class is y, is distributed around the mean value we measured from the training data according to the normal distribution. This is an assumption we are making on top of the independence assumption between features.

We use this equation for each of the features in the unknown feature vector. We'd then multiply the resulting probabilities together, and multiply that value by the prior probability of class 0 happening. We'd repeat this process for each of the classes. In the end, we'll have m numbers, the probabilities of the feature vector belonging to each of the m classes. To make a final decision, we'd do what we did before: select the largest of these probabilities and label the input as being of the corresponding class.

Some readers may complain that we ignored the denominator of Bayes' theorem. We did that because it's a constant across all the calculations, and since we always select the largest posterior probability, we really don't care whether we divide each value by a constant. We'll select the same class label, regardless.

Also, for the discrete case, it's possible that our training set does not have any instances of a value that rarely shows up. We ignored that, too, but it is a problem since if the value never shows up, the $P(x_i \mid y)$ we use would be 0, making the entire posterior probability 0. This often happens in natural language processing, where a particular word is rarely used. A technique called *Laplace smoothing* gets around this, but for our purposes, we claim that a "good" training set will represent *all* possible values for the features and simply press ahead. The sklearn `MultinomialNB` Naïve Bayes classifier for discrete data uses Laplace smoothing by default.

Decision Trees and Random Forests

The left side of Figure 6-5 shows an x-ray image of a puppy with a malformed right hip socket. Since the puppy is on its back in the x-ray, the right hip socket is on the left side of the image. The right side of Figure 6-5 shows the corresponding histogram of the pixel intensities (8-bit values, $[0, 255]$). There are two modes to this histogram, corresponding to the dark background and the lighter-intensity x-ray data. If we want to classify each pixel of the image into either background or x-ray, we can do so with the following rule: "If the pixel intensity is less than 11, call the pixel background."

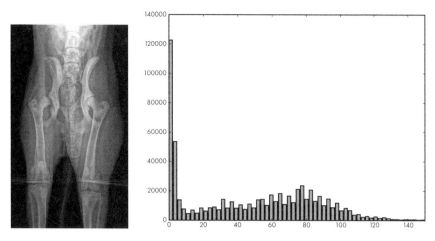

Figure 6-5: An x-ray image of a puppy (left). The corresponding histogram of 8-bit pixel values [0,255] (right).

This rule implements a decision made about the data based on one of the features, in this case, the pixel intensity value. Simple decisions like this are at the heart of *Decision Trees*, the classification algorithm we'll explore in this section. For completeness, if we apply the decision rule to each pixel in the image and output 0 or 255 (maximum pixel value) for background versus x-ray data, we get a mask showing us which pixels are part of the image. See Figure 6-6.

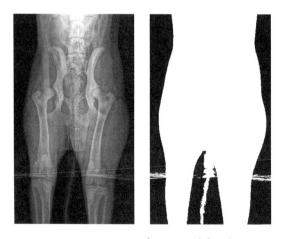

Figure 6-6: An x-ray image of a puppy (left). The corresponding pixel mask generated by the decision rule. White pixels are part of the x-ray image (right).

A Decision Tree is a set of nodes. The nodes either define a condition and branch based on the truth or falsehood of the condition, or select a particular class. Nodes that do not branch are called *leaf nodes*. Decision Trees are called *trees* because, especially for the binary case we'll consider here, they branch like trees. Figure 6-7 shows a Decision Tree learned by the sklearn `DecisionTreeClassifier` class for the full iris dataset using the first three features. See Chapter 5.

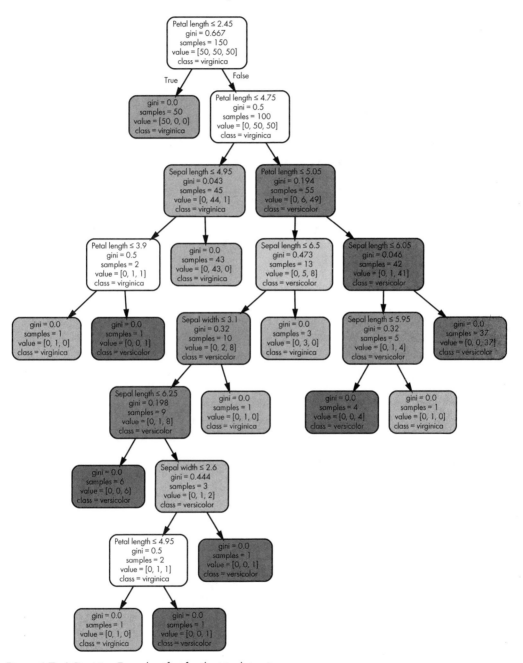

Figure 6-7: A Decision Tree classifier for the iris dataset

By convention, the first node in the tree, the *root*, is drawn at the top. For this tree, the root node asks the question, "Is the petal length $\leq$ 2.45?" If it is, the left branch is taken, and the tree immediately reaches a leaf node and assigns a label of "virginica" (class 0). We'll discuss the other information in the nodes shortly. If the petal length is not $\leq$ 2.45, the right branch is taken, leading to a new node that asks, "Is the petal length $\leq$ 4.75?" If so, we move to a node that asks a question about the sepal length. If not, we move to the right node and consider the petal length again. This process continues until a leaf is reached, which determines the class label.

The process just described is exactly how a Decision Tree is used after it's created. For any new feature vector, the series of questions is asked starting with the root node, and the tree is traversed until a leaf node is reached to decide the class label. This is a human-friendly way to move through the classification process, which is why Decision Trees are handy in situations where the "why" of the class assignment is as important to know as the class assignment itself. A Decision Tree can explain itself.

Using a Decision Tree is simple enough, but how is the tree created in the first place? Unlike the simple algorithms in the previous sections, the tree-building process is more involved, but not so involved that we can't follow through the main steps to build some intuition as to what goes into defining the tree.

Recursion Primer

Before we talk about the Decision Tree algorithm, however, we need to discuss the concept of *recursion*. If you're familiar with computer science, you probably already know that tree-like data structures and recursion go hand in hand. If not, don't worry; recursion is a straightforward but powerful concept. The essence of a recursive algorithm is that the algorithm repeats itself at different levels. When implemented as a function in a programming language, this generally means that the function calls itself on a smaller version of the problem. Naturally, if the function calls itself indefinitely, we'll have an infinite loop, so the recursion needs a stopping condition—something that says we no longer need to recurse.

Let's introduce the idea of recursion mathematically. The factorial of an integer, n, denoted $n!$, is defined to be

$$n! = n(n-1)(n-2)(n-3)\ldots(n-n+1)$$

which just means multiply together all the integers from 1 to n. By definition, $0! = 1$. Therefore, the factorial of 5 is 120 because

$$5! = 5 \times 4 \times 3 \times 2 \times 1 = 120$$

If we look at $5!$ we see that it is nothing more than $5 \times 4!$ or, in general, that, $n! = n \times (n-1)!$. Now, let's write a Python function to calculate factorials recursively using this insight. The code is simple, also a hallmark of many recursive functions, as Listing 6-1 shows.

```
def fact(n):
    if (n <= 1):
      return 1
    else:
      return n*fact(n-1)
```

Listing 6-1: Calculating the factorial

The code is a direct implementation of the rule that the factorial of *n* is *n* times the factorial of *n* − 1. To find the factorial of n, we first ask if n is 1. If it is, we know the factorial is 1 so we return 1—this is our stopping condition. If n is not 1, we know that the factorial of n is simply n times the factorial of n-1, which we find by calling fact with n-1 as the argument.

Building Decision Trees

The algorithm to build a Decision Tree is also recursive. Let's walk through what happens at a high level. The algorithm starts with the root node, determines the proper rule for that node, and then calls itself on the left and right branches. The call to the left branch will start again as if the left branch is the root node. This will continue until a stopping condition is met.

For a Decision Tree, the stopping condition is a leaf node (we'll discuss how a Decision Tree knows whether to create a leaf node next). Once a leaf node is created, the recursion terminates, and the algorithm returns to that leaf's parent node and calls itself on the right branch. The algorithm then starts again as if the right branch were the root node. Once both recursive calls terminate, and a node's left and right subtrees are created, the algorithm returns to that node's parent, and so on and so forth until the entire tree is constructed.

Now to get a little more specific. How is the training data used to build the tree? When the root node is defined, all the training data is present—say, all *n* samples. This is the set of samples used to pick the rule the root node implements. Once that rule has been selected and applied to the training samples, we have two new sets of samples: one for the left side (the true side) and one for the right side (the false side).

The recursion then works with these nodes, using their respective set of training samples, to define the rule for the left and right branches. Every time a branch node is created, the training set for that branch node gets split into samples that meet the rule and samples that don't meet the rule. A leaf node is declared when the set of training samples is either too small, of a sufficiently high proportion of one class, or the maximum tree depth has been reached.

By now you're probably wondering, "How do we select the rule for a branch node?" The rule relates a single input feature, like the petal length, to a particular value. The Decision Tree is a *greedy* algorithm; this means that at every node it selects the best rule for the current set of information available to it. In this case, this is the current set of training samples that are available to the node. The best rule is the one that best separates the classes into two groups. This implies that we need a way to select possible candidate rules and that we have a way to determine that a candidate rule is "best." The Decision Tree algorithm uses brute force to locate candidate rules. It runs through all possible combinations of features and values, making continuous values discrete by binning, and evaluates the purity of the left and right training sets after the rule is applied. The best-performing rule is the one kept at that node.

"Best performing" is determined by the *purity* of the split into left and right training sample subsets. One way to measure purity is to use the *Gini index*. This is the metric sklearn uses. The Gini index of each node in the iris example of Figure 6-7 is shown. It's calculated as

$$\text{Gini} = \sum_{i \neq j} P(y_i)P(y_j) = 1 - \sum_{i} P^2(y_i)$$

where $P(y_i)$ is the fraction of training examples in the subset for the current node that are of class i. A perfect split between classes, all of one class and none of the other, will result in a Gini index of 0. A 50-50 split has a Gini index of 0.5. The algorithm seeks to minimize the Gini index at each node by selecting the candidate rule that results in the smallest Gini index.

For example, in Figure 6-7 the right-hand node below the root has a Gini index of 0.5. This means that the rule for *the node above*, the root, will result in a subset of the training data that has petal length > 2.45, and that subset will be evenly divided between classes 1 and 2. This is the meaning of the "value" line in the node text. It shows the number of training samples in the subset that defined the node. The "class" line is the class that would be assigned if the tree were stopped at that node. It's simply the class label of the class that has the largest number of training samples in the node's subset. When the tree is used on new, unknown samples, it's run from root to a leaf, always.

Random Forests

Decision Trees are useful when the data is discrete or categorical or has missing values. Continuous data needs to be binned first (sklearn does this for you). Decision Trees have a bad habit, however, of *overfitting* the training data. This means that they are likely to learn meaningless statistical nuances of the training data that you happened to use, instead of learning meaningful general features of the data that are useful when applied to unknown data samples. Decision Trees also grow very large, as the number of features grows, unless managed by depth parameters.

Decision Tree overfitting can be mitigated by using *Random Forests*. In fact, unless your problem is simple, you probably want to look at using a Random Forest from the start. The following three concepts lead from a Decision Tree to a Random Forest:

- Ensembles of classifiers and voting between them
- Resampling of the training set by selecting samples *with replacement*
- Selection of random feature subsets

If we have a set of classifiers, each trained on different data or of a different type, like a k-NN and a Naïve Bayes, we can use their outputs to vote on the actual category to assign to any particular unknown sample. This is called an *ensemble* and, with diminishing returns as the number of classifiers increases, it will, in general, improve the performance over that of any individual classifier. We can employ a similar idea and imagine an ensemble, or *forest*, of Decision Trees, but unless we do something more with the training set, we'll have a forest of *exactly* the same tree because a particular set of training examples will always lead to the exact same Decision Tree. The algorithm to create a Decision Tree is deterministic—it always returns the same results.

A way to deal with the particular statistical nuances of the training set you have to work with is to select a new training set from the original training set but allow the same training set sample to be selected more than once. This is selection with replacement. Think of it as choosing colored marbles from a bag, but before you select the next marble, put the one you just selected back in the bag so you might pick it again. A new dataset selected in this way is known as a *bootstrap sample*. Building a collection of new datasets in this way is known as *bagging*, and it is models built from this collection of resampled datasets that build the Random Forest.

If we train multiple trees, each with a resampled training set with replacement, we'll get a forest of trees, each one slightly different from the others. This alone, along with ensemble voting, will probably improve things. However, there's one issue. If some of the features are highly predictive, they will dominate, and the resulting forest of trees will be very similar to one another and therefore suffer from very similar weaknesses. This is where the *random* of *Random Forest* comes into play.

Instead of just bagging, which changes the distribution of samples in the per tree training set but not the set of features examined, what if we also randomly selected, for each tree in the forest, a subset of the *features* themselves and trained on only those features? Doing this would break the correlation between the trees and increase the overall robustness of the forest. In practice, if there are n features per feature vector, each tree will randomly select $\sqrt{n}$ of them over which to build the tree. Random Forests are supported in sklearn as well.

Support Vector Machines

Our final classical machine learning model is the one that held neural networks at bay for most of the 1990s, the *Support Vector Machine (SVM)*. If the neural network is a highly data-driven, empirical approach to generating a model, the SVM is a highly elegant, mathematically founded, approach. We'll discuss the performance of an SVM at a conceptual level as the mathematics involved is beyond what we want to introduce here. If you're so inclined, the classic reference is "Support-Vector Networks" by Cortes and Vapnik (1995).

We can summarize what a Support Vector Machine is doing by gaining intuition about the concepts of margins, support vectors, optimization, and kernels. Let's look at each concept in turn.

Margins

Figure 6-8 shows a two-class dataset with two features. We've plotted each sample in the dataset with feature 1 along the x-axis and feature 2 along the y-axis. Class 0 is shown as circles, class 1 as diamonds. This is obviously a contrived dataset, one that's easily separated by plotting a line between the circles and the diamonds.

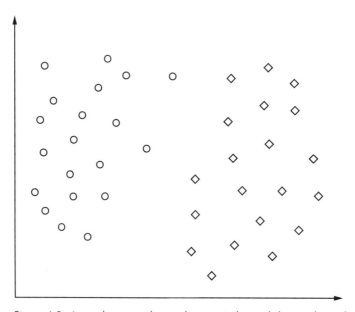

Figure 6-8: A toy dataset with two classes, circles and diamonds, and two features, x-axis and y-axis

A classifier can be thought of as locating one or more *planes* that split the space of the training data into homogeneous groups. In the case of Figure 6-8 the separating "plane" is a line. If we had three features, the separating plane would be a 2D plane. With four features, the separating plane would be three-dimensional, and for n dimensions the separating plane is $n - 1$ dimensional. Since the plane is multidimensional, we refer to it as a *hyperplane* and say that the goal of the classifier is to separate the training feature space into groups using hyperplanes.

If we look again at Figure 6-8, we can imagine an infinite set of lines that separate the training data into two groups, with all of class 0 on one side and all of class 1 on the other. Which one do we want to use? Well, let's think a bit about what the position of a line separating the two classes implies. If we draw a line more to the right side, just before any of the diamonds, we'll have separated the training data, but only barely so. Recall, we're using the training data as a surrogate for the true distribution of samples of each class. The more training data we have, the more faithfully we'll know that true distribution. However, we don't really know it.

A new, unknown sample, which must be of class 0 or class 1, will fall somewhere on the graph. It's reasonable to believe that there are class 1 (diamond) samples in the wild that will fall even closer to the circles than any of the samples in the training set. If the separating line is too close to the diamonds, we run the risk of calling valid class 1 samples *class 0* because the separating line is too far to the right. We can make a similar claim if we place the separating line very close to the class 0 points (circles). Then we run the risk of mislabeling class 0 samples as *class 1* (diamonds).

Therefore, in the absence of more training data, it seems most reasonable to choose the separating line that is as far from both classes as possible. This is the line that is farthest from the rightmost circles while still being as far to the left of the diamonds as possible. This line is the maximal margin location, where the *margin* is defined as the distance from the closest sample points. Figure 6-9 shows the maximal margin location as the heavy line with the maximum margin indicated by the two dotted lines. The goal of an SVM is to locate the maximum margin position, as this is the location where we can be most certain to not misclassify new samples, given the knowledge gained from the training set.

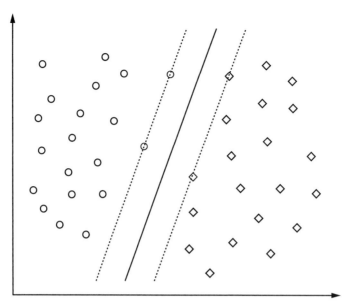

Figure 6-9: The toy dataset of Figure 6-8 with the maximal margin separating line (heavy) and the maximum margins (dotted)

Support Vectors

Look again at Figure 6-9. Notice the four training data points on the margin? These are the training samples that define the margin, or, in other words, support the margin; hence they are *support vectors*. This is the origin of the name *Support Vector Machine*. The support vectors define the margin, but how can we use them to locate the margin position? Here is where we'll simplify things a bit to avoid a large amount of complex vector mathematics that will only muddy the waters for us. For a more mathematical treatment, see "A Tutorial on Support Vector Machines for Pattern Recognition" by Christopher Burges (1998).

Optimization

Mathematically, we can find the maximum margin hyperplane by solving an optimization problem. Recall that in an optimization problem, we have a quantity that depends on certain parameters, and we want to find the set of parameter values that makes the quantity as small or as large as possible.

In the SVM case, the orientation of the hyperplane can be specified by a vector, $\vec{w}$. There is also an offset, b, which we must find. Finally, before we can do the optimization, we need to change the way we specify the class labels. Instead of using 0 or 1 for y_i, the label of the i-th training sample, x_i, we'll use -1 or $+1$. This will let us define the condition of the optimization problem more simply.

So, mathematically, what we want is to find $\vec{w}$ and b so that the quantity $\frac{1}{2}||\vec{w}||^2$ is as small as possible, given that $y_i(\vec{w} \cdot \vec{x} - b) \geq 1$ for all y_i labels and x_i training vectors in the dataset. This sort of optimization problem is readily solved via a technique called *quadratic programming*. (We're ignoring another important mathematical step here: the actual optimization problem solved uses a Lagrangian to solve the dual form, but again, we'll try to avoid muddying the waters too much.)

The preceding formulation is for a case where the dataset, assumed to have only two classes, can be separated by a hyperplane. This is the linearly separable case. In reality, as we well appreciate by now, not every dataset can be separated this way. So, the full form of the optimization problem includes a fudge factor, C, which affects the size of the margin found. This factor shows up in the sklearn SVM class and needs to be specified to some level. From a practical point of view, C is a *hyperparameter* of the SVM, a value that we need to set to get the SVM to train properly. The right value of C is problem dependent. In general, any parameter of a model that is not learned by the model but must be set to use the model, like C for an SVM or k for k-NN, is a hyperparameter.

Kernels

There's one more mathematical concept we need to introduce, with suitable hand waving. The preceding description is for a linear SVM and uses the training data directly (the $\vec{x}$'s). The nonlinear case maps the training data to another space by passing it through a function, typically called $\phi(\vec{x})$, that produces a new version of the training data vector, $\vec{x}$. The SVM algorithm uses inner products, $\vec{x}^T \vec{z}$, which means that the mapped version will use $\phi(\vec{x})^T \phi(\vec{z})$. In this notation, vectors are thought of as a column of numbers so that T, the transpose, produces a row vector. Then normal matrix multiplication of a $1 \times n$ row vector and an $n \times 1$ column vector will result in a 1×1 output, which is a scalar. The inner product is typically written as

$$K(\vec{x}, \vec{z}) = \phi(\vec{x})^T \phi(\vec{z})$$

and the function $K(\vec{x}, \vec{z})$ is called a *kernel*. The linear kernel is simply $\vec{x}^T \vec{z}$, but other kernels are possible. The *Gaussian kernel* is a popular one, also known as a *radial basis function (RBF)* kernel. In practical use, this kernel introduces a new parameter, apart from C, which is γ. This parameter relates to how spread out the Gaussian kernel is around a particular training point, with smaller values extending the range of influence of the training sample. Typically, one uses a grid search over C and, if using the RBF kernel, γ, to locate the best performing model.

To summarize, then, a Support Vector Machine uses the training data, mapped through a kernel function, to optimize the orientation and location of a hyperplane that produces the maximum margin between the hyperplane and the support vectors of the training data. The user needs to select the kernel function and associated parameters like C and γ so that the model best fits the training data.

Support Vector Machines dominated machine learning in the 1990s and early 2000s, before the advent of deep learning. This is because they're trained efficiently and don't need extensive computational resources to be successful. Since the arrival of deep learning, however, SVMs have fallen somewhat by the wayside because powerful computers have enabled neural networks to do what previously was not possible with more limited computing resources. Still, SVMs have a place at the table. One popular approach uses a large neural network trained on a particular dataset as a preprocessor for a different dataset with an SVM trained on the output of the neural network (minus the top layers).

Summary

In this chapter, we introduced six of the most common classic machine learning models: Nearest Centroid, k-NN, Näive Bayes, Decision Tree, Random Forest, and SVMs. These models are classic because they have been used for decades. They are also still relevant if the conditions they support best are present. At times, the classic model is still the correct choice. An experienced machine learning practitioner will know when to fall back to the classics.

In the next chapter, we'll use each of these models, via sklearn, to perform a number of experiments that will build our intuition of how the models work and when to use them.

7

EXPERIMENTS WITH CLASSICAL MODELS

In Chapter 6, we introduced several classical machine learning models. Let's now take the datasets we built in Chapter 5 and use them with these models to see how well they perform. We'll use sklearn to create the models and then we'll compare them by looking at how well they do on the held-out test sets.

This will give us a good overview of how to work with sklearn and help us build intuition about how the different models perform relative to one another. We'll use three datasets: the iris dataset, both original and augmented; the breast cancer dataset; and the vector form of the MNIST handwritten digits dataset.

Experiments with the Iris Dataset

We'll start with the iris dataset. This data set has four continuous features—the measurements of the sepal length, sepal width, petal length, and petal width—and three classes—different iris species. There are 150 samples, 50 each from the three classes. In Chapter 5, we applied PCA augmentation to the dataset, so we actually have two versions we can work with: the original 150 samples and the 1200 augmented training samples. Both can use the same test set.

We'll use sklearn to implement versions of the Nearest Centroid, *k*-NN, Naïve Bayes, Decision Tree, Random Forest, and SVM models we outlined in Chapter 6. We'll quickly see how powerful and elegant the sklearn toolkit is since our tests are virtually all identical across the models. The only thing that changes is the particular class we instantiate.

Testing the Classical Models

The code for our initial tests is in Listing 7-1.

```
import numpy as np
from sklearn.neighbors import NearestCentroid
from sklearn.neighbors import KNeighborsClassifier
from sklearn.naive_bayes import GaussianNB, MultinomialNB
from sklearn.tree import DecisionTreeClassifier
from sklearn.ensemble import RandomForestClassifier
from sklearn.svm import SVC

❶ def run(x_train, y_train, x_test, y_test, clf):
      clf.fit(x_train, y_train)
      print("    predictions  :", clf.predict(x_test))
      print("    actual labels:", y_test)
      print("    score = %0.4f" % clf.score(x_test, y_test))
      print()

def main():
❷   x = np.load("../data/iris/iris_features.npy")
    y = np.load("../data/iris/iris_labels.npy")
    N = 120
    x_train = x[:N]; x_test = x[N:]
    y_train = y[:N]; y_test = y[N:]
❸   xa_train=np.load("../data/iris/iris_train_features_augmented.npy")
    ya_train=np.load("../data/iris/iris_train_labels_augmented.npy")
    xa_test =np.load("../data/iris/iris_test_features_augmented.npy")
    ya_test =np.load("../data/iris/iris_test_labels_augmented.npy")

    print("Nearest Centroid:")
❹   run(x_train, y_train, x_test, y_test, NearestCentroid())
    print("k-NN classifier (k=3):")
    run(x_train, y_train, x_test, y_test,
        KNeighborsClassifier(n_neighbors=3))
    print("Naive Bayes classifier (Gaussian):")
❺   run(x_train, y_train, x_test, y_test, GaussianNB())
    print("Naive Bayes classifier (Multinomial):")
    run(x_train, y_train, x_test, y_test, MultinomialNB())
```

```
❻ print("Decision Tree classifier:")
   run(x_train, y_train, x_test, y_test, DecisionTreeClassifier())
   print("Random Forest classifier (estimators=5):")
   run(xa_train, ya_train, xa_test, ya_test,
       RandomForestClassifier(n_estimators=5))

❼ print("SVM (linear, C=1.0):")
   run(xa_train, ya_train, xa_test, ya_test, SVC(kernel="linear", C=1.0))
   print("SVM (RBF, C=1.0, gamma=0.25):")
   run(xa_train, ya_train, xa_test, ya_test,
       SVC(kernel="rbf", C=1.0, gamma=0.25))
   print("SVM (RBF, C=1.0, gamma=0.001, augmented)")
   run(xa_train, ya_train, xa_test, ya_test,
       SVC(kernel="rbf", C=1.0, gamma=0.001))
❽ print("SVM (RBF, C=1.0, gamma=0.001, original)")
   run(x_train, y_train, x_test, y_test,
       SVC(kernel="rbf", C=1.0, gamma=0.001))
```

Listing 7-1: Classic models using the iris dataset. See iris_experiments.py.

First, we import the necessary classes and modules. Notice that each of the classes represents a single type of model (classifier). For the Naïve Bayes classifier, we're using two versions: the Gaussian version, GaussianNB, because the features are continuous values, and MultinomialNB for the discrete case to illustrate the effect of choosing a model that's inappropriate for the dataset we're working with. Because sklearn has a uniform interface for its classifiers, we can simplify things by using the same function to train and test any particular classifier. That function is run ❶. We pass in the training features (x_train) and labels (y_train) along with the test features and labels (x_test, y_test). We also pass in the particular classifier object (clf).

The first thing we do inside run is fit the model to the data by calling fit with the training data samples and labels. This is the training step. After the model is trained, we can test how well it does by calling the predict method with the held-out test data. This method returns the predicted class label for each sample in the test data. We held back 30 samples from the original 150 so predict will return a vector of 30 class label assignments, which we print. Next, we print the actual test labels so we can compare them visually with the predictions. Finally, we use the score method to apply the classifier to the test data (x_test) using the known test labels (y_test) to calculate the overall accuracy.

The accuracy is returned as a fraction between 0 and 1. If every test sample were given the wrong label, the accuracy would be 0. Even random guessing will do better than that, so a return value of 0 is a sign that something is amiss. Since there are three classes in the iris dataset, we'd expect a classifier that guesses the class at random to be right about one-third of the time and return a value close to 0.3333. The actual score is calculated as

$$\text{score} = N_c/(N_c + N_w)$$

where N_c is the number of test samples for which the predicted class is correct; that is, it matches the class label in y_test. N_w is the number of test samples where the predicted class does not match the actual class label.

Now that we have a way to train and test each classifier, all we need to do is load the datasets and run a series of experiments by creating different classifier objects and passing them to run. Back inside of main, we begin by loading the original iris dataset and separating it into train and test cases ❷. We also load the augmented iris dataset that we created in Chapter 5 ❸. By design, the two test sets are identical, so regardless of which training set we use, the test set will be the same. This simplifies our comparisons.

We then define and execute the Nearest Centroid classifier ❹. The output is shown here:

```
Nearest Centroid:
 predictions  :[011202120211112202201101102211]
 actual labels:[011202120211112202201101102211]
 score = 1.0000
```

We've removed spaces to make a visual comparison between the predicted and actual class labels easier. If there's an error, the corresponding value, 0–2, will not match between the two lines. The score is also shown. In this case, it's 1.0, which tells us that the classifier was perfect in its predictions on the held-out test set. This isn't surprising; the iris dataset is a simple one. Because the iris dataset was randomized when created in Chapter 5, you might get a different overall score. However, unless your randomization was particularly unfortunate, you should have a high test score.

Based on what we learned in Chapter 6, we should expect that if the Nearest Centroid classifier is perfect on the test data, then all the other more sophisticated models will likewise be perfect. This is generally the case here, but as we'll see, careless selection of model type or model hyperparameter values will result in inferior performance even from a more sophisticated model.

Look again at Listing 7-1, where we train a Gaussian Naïve Bayes classifier by passing an instance of GaussianNB to run ❺. This classifier is also perfect and returns a score of 1.0. This is the correct way to use continuous values with a Naïve Bayes classifier. What happens if we instead use the discrete case even though we have continuous features? This is the MultinomialNB classifier, which assumes the features are selected from a discrete set of possible values. For the iris dataset, we can get away with defining such a classifier because the feature values are non-negative. However, because the features are not discrete, this model is not perfect and returns the following:

```
Naive Bayes classifier (Multinomial):
 predictions  :[011202220211122202202101102221]
 actual labels:[011202120211112202201101102211]
 score = 0.8667
```

Here we see that the classifier is only 86.7 percent accurate on our test samples. If we need discrete counts for the probabilities, why did this approach work at all in this case? The answer is evident in the sklearn source code for the `MultinomialNB` classifier. The method that counts feature frequencies per class uses `np.dot` so that even if the feature values are continuous, the output will be a valid number, though not an integer. Still, mistakes were made, so we shouldn't be happy. We should instead be careful to select the proper classifier type for the actual data we're working with.

The next model we train in Listing 7-1 is a Decision Tree ❻. This classifier is perfect on this dataset, as is the Random Forest trained next. Note, the Random Forest is using five estimators, meaning five random trees are created and trained; voting between the individual outputs determines the final class label. Note also that the Random Forest is trained on the augmented iris dataset, xa_train, because of the limited number of training samples in the unaugmented dataset.

We then train several SVM classifiers ❼, also on the augmented dataset. Recall that SVMs have two parameters we control: the margin constant, `C`, and `gamma` used by the Gaussian kernel.

The first is a linear SVM, meaning we need a value for the margin constant (`C`). We define `C` to be 1.0, the default value for sklearn. This classifier is perfect on the test data, as is the following classifier using the Gaussian kernel, for which we also set γ to 0.25. The `SVC` class defaults to auto for `gamma`, which sets γ to $1/n$, where n is the number of features. For the iris dataset, $n = 4$ so $\gamma = 0.25$.

Next, we train a model with very small γ. The classifier is still perfect on the test data. Lastly, we train the same type of SVM, but instead of the augmented training data, we use the original training data ❽. This classifier is not perfect:

```
SVM (RBF, C=1.0, gamma=0.001, original)
 predictions   :[0222020202222222202202202202220]
 actual labels:[0112021202111122022011011022211]
 score = 0.5667
```

In fact, it's rather dismal. It never predicts class 1 and is right only 56.7 percent of the time. This shows that data augmentation is valuable as it turned a lousy classifier into a good one—at least, good as far as we can know from the small test set we are using!

Implementing a Nearest Centroid Classifier

What if we were stranded on a deserted island and didn't have access to sklearn? Could we still quickly build a suitable classifier for the iris dataset? The answer is "yes," as Listing 7-2 shows. This code implements a quick-and-dirty Nearest Centroid classifier for the iris dataset.

```
import numpy as np

❶ def centroids(x,y):
      c0 = x[np.where(y==0)].mean(axis=0)
      c1 = x[np.where(y==1)].mean(axis=0)
      c2 = x[np.where(y==2)].mean(axis=0)
      return [c0,c1,c2]

❷ def predict(c0,c1,c2,x):
      p = np.zeros(x.shape[0], dtype="uint8")
      for i in range(x.shape[0]):
          d = [((c0-x[i])**2).sum(),
               ((c1-x[i])**2).sum(),
               ((c2-x[i])**2).sum()]
          p[i] = np.argmin(d)
      return p

  def main():
❸     x = np.load("../data/iris/iris_features.npy")
      y = np.load("../data/iris/iris_labels.npy")
      N = 120
      x_train = x[:N]; x_test = x[N:]
      y_train = y[:N]; y_test = y[N:]
      c0, c1, c2 = centroids(x_train, y_train)
      p = predict(c0,c1,c2, x_test)
      nc = len(np.where(p == y_test)[0])
      nw = len(np.where(p != y_test)[0])
      acc = float(nc) / (float(nc)+float(nw))
      print("predicted:", p)
      print("actual    :", y_test)
      print("test accuracy = %0.4f" % acc)
```

Listing 7-2: A quick-and-dirty Nearest Centroid classifier for the iris dataset. See iris_centroids.py.

We load the iris data and separate it into train and test sets as before ❸. The centroids function returns the centroids of the three classes ❶. We can easily calculate these by finding the per feature means of each training sample of the desired class. This is all it takes to train this model. If we compare the returned centroids with those in the preceding trained NearestCentroid classifier (see the centroids_ member variable), we get precisely the same values.

Using the classifier is straightforward, as predict shows ❷. First, we define the vector of predictions, one per test sample (x). The loop defines d, a vector of Euclidean distances from the current test sample, x[i], to the three class centroids. The index of the smallest distance in d is the predicted class label (p[i]).

Let's unpack d a bit more. We set d to a list of three values, the distances from the centroids to the current test sample. The expression

```
((c0-x[i])**2).sum()
```

is a bit dense. The phrase c0-x[i] returns a vector of four numbers—four because we have four features. These are the differences between the centroid of class 0 and the test sample feature value. This quantity is squared, which squares each of the four values. This squared vector is summed, element by element, to return the distance measure.

Strictly speaking, we're missing a final step. The actual distance between c0 and x[i] is the square root of this value. Since we're simply looking for the smallest distance to each of the centroids, we don't need to calculate the square root. The smallest value will still be the smallest value, whether we take the square root of all the values or not. Running this code produces the same output as we saw previously for the Nearest Centroid classifier, which is encouraging.

The iris dataset is extremely simple, so we shouldn't be surprised by the excellent performance of our models even though we saw that careless selection of model type and hyperparameters will cause us trouble. Let's now look at a larger dataset with more features, one that was not meant as a toy.

Experiments with the Breast Cancer Dataset

The two-class breast cancer dataset we developed in Chapter 5 has 569 samples, each with 30 features, all measurements from a histology slide. There are 212 malignant cases (class 1) and 357 benign cases (class 0). Let's train our classic models on this dataset and see what sort of results we get. As all the features are continuous, let's use the normalized version of the dataset. Recall that a normalized dataset is one where, per feature in the feature vector, each value has the mean for that feature subtracted and then is divided by the standard deviation:

$$x' = \frac{x - \bar{x}}{\sigma}$$

Normalization of the dataset maps all the features into the same overall range so that the value of one feature is similar to the value of another. This helps many model types and is a typical data preprocessing step, as we discussed in Chapter 4.

Two Initial Test Runs

First, we'll do a quick run with a single test split, as we did in the previous section. The code is in Listing 7-3 and mimics the code we described previously, where we pass in the model instance, train it, and then score it using the testing data.

```
import numpy as np
from sklearn.neighbors import NearestCentroid
from sklearn.neighbors import KNeighborsClassifier
from sklearn.naive_bayes import GaussianNB, MultinomialNB
from sklearn.tree import DecisionTreeClassifier
from sklearn.ensemble import RandomForestClassifier
from sklearn.svm import SVC

def run(x_train, y_train, x_test, y_test, clf):
    clf.fit(x_train, y_train)
    print("    score = %0.4f" % clf.score(x_test, y_test))
    print()

def main():
    x = np.load("../data/breast/bc_features_standard.npy")
    y = np.load("../data/breast/bc_labels.npy")
  ❶ N = 455
    x_train = x[:N];   x_test = x[N:]
    y_train = y[:N];   y_test = y[N:]

    print("Nearest Centroid:")
    run(x_train, y_train, x_test, y_test, NearestCentroid())
    print("k-NN classifier (k=3):")
    run(x_train, y_train, x_test, y_test,
        KNeighborsClassifier(n_neighbors=3))
    print("k-NN classifier (k=7):")
    run(x_train, y_train, x_test, y_test,
        KNeighborsClassifier(n_neighbors=7))
    print("Naive Bayes classifier (Gaussian):")
    run(x_train, y_train, x_test, y_test, GaussianNB())
    print("Decision Tree classifier:")
    run(x_train, y_train, x_test, y_test, DecisionTreeClassifier())
    print("Random Forest classifier (estimators=5):")
    run(x_train, y_train, x_test, y_test,
        RandomForestClassifier(n_estimators=5))
    print("Random Forest classifier (estimators=50):")
    run(x_train, y_train, x_test, y_test,
        RandomForestClassifier(n_estimators=50))
    print("SVM (linear, C=1.0):")
    run(x_train, y_train, x_test, y_test, SVC(kernel="linear", C=1.0))
    print("SVM (RBF, C=1.0, gamma=0.03333):")
    run(x_train, y_train, x_test, y_test,
        SVC(kernel="rbf", C=1.0, gamma=0.03333))
```

Listing 7-3: Initial models using the breast cancer dataset. See bc_experiments.py.

As before, we load the dataset and split it into training and testing data. We keep 455 of the 569 samples for training (80 percent), and the remaining 114 samples are the test set (74 benign, 40 malignant). The dataset is already randomized, so we skip that step here. We then train nine models: Nearest Centroid (1), k-NN (2), Naïve Bayes (1), Decision Tree (1), Random Forest (2), linear SVM (1), and an RBF SVM (1). For the Support Vector Machines, we use the default C value, and for γ, we use $1/30 = 0.033333$ since we have 30 features. Running this code gives us the scores in Table 7-1.

Table 7-1: Breast Cancer Model Scores

Model type	Score
Nearest Centroid	0.9649
3-NN classifier	0.9912
7-NN classifier	0.9737
Naïve Bayes (Gaussian)	0.9825
Decision Tree	0.9474
Random Forest (5)	0.9298
Random Forest (50)	0.9737
Linear SVM ($C = 1$)	0.9737
RBF SVM ($C = 1$, $\gamma = 0.03333$)	0.9825

Note the number in parentheses for the Random Forest classifiers is the number of estimators (number of trees in the forest).

A few things jump out at us. First, perhaps surprisingly, the simple Nearest Centroid classifier is right nearly 97 percent of the time. We also see that all the other classifiers are doing better than the Nearest Centroid, except for the Decision Tree and the Random Forest with five trees. Somewhat surprisingly, the Naïve Bayes classifier does very well, matching the RBF SVM. The $k = 3$ Nearest Neighbor classifier does best of all, 99 percent accurate, even though we have 30 features, meaning our 569 samples are points scattered in a 30-dimensional space. Recall, a weakness of k-NN is the curse of dimensionality: it requires more and more training samples as the number of features increases. The results with all the classifiers are good, so this is a hint to us that the separation between malignant and benign is, for this dataset, distinct. There isn't much overlap between the two classes using these features.

So, are we done with this dataset? Hardly! In fact, we've just begun. What happens if we run the code a second time? Do we get the same scores? Would we expect not to? A second run gives us Table 7-2.

Table 7-2: Breast Cancer Scores, Second Run

Model type	Score
Nearest Centroid	0.9649
3-NN classifier	0.9912
7-NN classifier	0.9737
Naïve Bayes (Gaussian)	0.9825
Decision Tree	**0.9386**
Random Forest (5)	**0.9474**
Random Forest (50)	**0.9649**
Linear SVM (C = 1)	0.9737
RBF SVM (C = 1, γ = 0.03333)	0.9825

We've highlighted the scores that changed. Why would anything change? A bit of reflection leads to an *aha!* moment: the Random Forest is just that, random, so naturally we'd expect different results run to run. What about the Decision Tree? In sklearn, the Decision Tree classifier will randomly select a feature and find the best split, so different runs will also lead to different trees. This is a variation on the basic decision tree algorithm we discussed in Chapter 6.

All the other algorithms are fixed: for a given training dataset, they can lead to only one model. As an aside, the SVM implementation in sklearn does use a random number generator, so at times different runs will give slightly different results, but, conceptually, we'd expect the same model for the same input data. The tree-based classifiers, however, do change between training runs. We'll explore this variation more next. For now, we need to add some rigor to our quick analysis.

The Effect of Random Splits

Let's change the split between training and testing data and see what happens to our results. We don't need to list all the code again since the only change is to how x_train and x_test are defined. Before splitting, we randomize the order of the full dataset but do so by first fixing the pseudorandom number seed so that each run gives the same ordering to the dataset.

Looking again at Listing 7-3, insert the following code before ❶ so that we generate a fixed permutation of the dataset (idx).

```
np.random.seed(12345)
idx = np.argsort(np.random.random(y.shape[0]))
x = x[idx]
y = y[idx]
```

It's fixed because we fixed the pseudorandom number generator seed value. We then reorder the samples (x) and labels (y) accordingly before splitting into train and test subsets as before. Running this code gives us the results in Table 7-3.

Table 7-3: Breast Cancer Scores After Randomizing the Dataset

Model type	Score
Nearest Centroid	0.9474
3-NN classifier	0.9912
7-NN classifier	0.9912
Naïve Bayes (Gaussian)	0.9474
Decision Tree	0.9474
Random Forest (5)	0.9912
Random Forest (50)	1.0000
Linear SVM ($C = 1$)	0.9649
RBF SVM ($C = 1$, $\gamma = 0.03333$)	0.9737

Notice these are entirely different from our earlier results. The *k*-NN classifiers are both equally good, the SVM classifiers are worse, and the 50-tree Random Forest achieves perfection on the test set. So, what is happening? Why are we getting all these different results run to run?

We're seeing the effect of the random sampling that builds the train and test splits. The first split just happened to use an ordering of samples that gave good results for one model type and less good results for other model types. The new split favors different model types. Which is correct? Both. Recall what the dataset represents: a sampling from some unknown parent distribution that generates the data that we actually have. If we think in those terms, we see that the dataset we have is an incomplete picture of the true parent distribution. It has biases, though we don't know what they are necessarily, and is deficient in that there are parts of the parent distribution that the dataset does not represent well.

Further, when we split the data after randomizing the order, we might end up with a "bad" mix in the train or test portion—a mix of the data that does a poor job of representing the true distribution. If so, we might train a model to recognize a slightly different distribution that does not match the true distribution well, or the test set might be a bad mix and not be a fair representation of what the model has learned. This effect is even more pronounced when the proportion of the classes is such that one or more are rare and possibly not present in the train or test split. This is precisely the issue that caused us to introduce the idea of *k*-fold cross-validation in Chapter 4. With *k*-fold validation, we'll be sure to use every sample as both train and test at some point and buy ourselves some protection against a bad split by averaging across all the folds.

However, before we apply *k*-fold validation to the breast cancer dataset, we should notice one essential thing. We modified the code of Listing 7-3 to fix the pseudorandom number seed so that we could reorder the dataset in exactly the same way each time we run. We then ran the code and saw the results. If we rerun the code, we'll get *exactly* the same output, even for the tree-based classifiers. This is not what we saw earlier. The tree classifiers are *stochastic*—they will generate a unique tree or forest each time—so we should expect the results to vary somewhat from run to run. But now they don't vary; we get the same output each time. By setting the NumPy pseudorandom number seed explicitly, we fixed not only the ordering of the dataset, but also the ordering of the *pseudorandom sequence* sklearn will use to generate the tree models. This is because sklearn is also using the NumPy pseudorandom number generator. This is a subtle effect with potentially serious consequences and in a larger project might be very difficult to pick up as a bug. The solution is to set the seed to a random value after we're done reordering the dataset. We can do this by adding one line after y = y[idx]

```
np.random.seed()
```

so that the pseudorandom number generator is reset by using the system state, typically read from */dev/urandom*. Now when we run again, we'll get different results for the tree models, as before.

Adding k-fold Validation

To implement *k*-fold validation, we first need to pick a value for *k*. Our dataset has 569 samples. We want to split it so that there are a decent number of samples per fold because we want to make the test set a reasonable representation of the data. This argues toward making *k* small. However, we also want to average out the effect of a bad split, so we might want *k* to be larger. As with most things in life, a balance must be sought. If we set *k* = 5, we'll get 113 samples per split (ignoring the final four samples, which should have no meaningful impact). This leaves 80 percent for training and 20 percent for test for each combination of folds, a reasonable thing to do. So, we'll use *k* = 5, but we'll write our code so that we can vary *k* if we want.

We already have an approach for training multiple models on a train/test split. All we need to add is code to generate each of the *k* folds and then train the models on them. The code is in Listing 7-4 and Listing 7-5, which show the helper functions and main function, respectively. Let's start with Listing 7-4.

```
import numpy as np
from sklearn.neighbors import NearestCentroid
from sklearn.neighbors import KNeighborsClassifier
from sklearn.naive_bayes import GaussianNB, MultinomialNB
from sklearn.tree import DecisionTreeClassifier
from sklearn.ensemble import RandomForestClassifier
from sklearn.svm import SVC
import sys

def run(x_train, y_train, x_test, y_test, clf):
    clf.fit(x_train, y_train)
    return clf.score(x_test, y_test)

def split(x,y,k,m):
```

```
❶ ns = int(y.shape[0]/m)
   s = []
   for i in range(m):
    ❷ s.append([x[(ns*i):(ns*i+ns)],
                 y[(ns*i):(ns*i+ns)]])
   x_test, y_test = s[k]
   x_train = []
   y_train = []
   for i in range(m):
       if (i==k):
           continue
       else:
           a,b = s[i]
           x_train.append(a)
           y_train.append(b)
❸ x_train = np.array(x_train).reshape(((m-1)*ns,30))
   y_train = np.array(y_train).reshape((m-1)*ns)
   return [x_train, y_train, x_test, y_test]

def pp(z,k,s):
    m = z.shape[1]
    print("%-19s: %0.4f +/- %0.4f | " % (s, z[k].mean(),
        z[k].std()/np.sqrt(m)), end='')
    for i in range(m):
        print("%0.4f " % z[k,i], end='')
    print()
```

Listing 7-4: Using k-fold validation to evaluate the breast cancer dataset. Helper functions. See bc_kfold.py.

Listing 7-4 begins by including all the modules we used before and then defines three functions: run, split, and pp. The run function looks familiar. It takes a train set, test set, and model instance, trains the model, and then scores the model against the test set. The pp function is a pretty-print function to show the per split scores along with the average score across all the splits. The average is shown as the mean ± the standard error of the mean. Recall that an sklearn score is the overall accuracy of the model on the test set, or the fraction of times that the model predicted the actual class of the test sample. Perfection is a score of 1.0, and complete failure is 0.0. Complete failure is rare because even random guessing will get it right some fraction of the time.

The only interesting function in Listing 7-4 is split. Its arguments are the full dataset, x, the corresponding labels, y, the current fold number, k, and the total number of folds, m. We'll divide the full dataset into m distinct sets, the folds, and use the k-th fold as test while merging the remaining $m - 1$ folds into a new training set. First, we set the number of samples per fold ❶. The loop then creates a list of folds, s. Each element of this list contains the feature vectors and labels of the fold ❷.

The test set is simple, it's the *k*-th fold, so we set those values next (x_test, y_test). The loop then takes the remaining $m - 1$ folds and merges them into a new training set, x_train, with labels, y_train.

The two lines after the loop are a bit mysterious ❸. When the loop ends, x_train is a *list*, each element of which is a list representing the feature vectors of the fold we want in the training set. So we first make a NumPy array of this list and then reshape it so that x_train has 30 columns, the number of features per vector, and $n_s(m - 1)$ rows, where n_s is the number of samples per fold. Thus x_train becomes x minus the samples we put into the test fold, those of the *k*-th fold. We also build y_train so that the correct label goes with each the feature vector in x_train.

Listing 7-5 shows us how to use the helper functions.

```
def main():
    x = np.load("../data/breast/bc_features_standard.npy")
    y = np.load("../data/breast/bc_labels.npy")
    idx = np.argsort(np.random.random(y.shape[0]))
    x = x[idx]
    y = y[idx]
❶   m = int(sys.argv[1])
    z = np.zeros((8,m))

    for k in range(m):
        x_train, y_train, x_test, y_test = split(x,y,k,m)
        z[0,k] = run(x_train, y_train, x_test, y_test,
                    NearestCentroid())
        z[1,k] = run(x_train, y_train, x_test, y_test,
                    KNeighborsClassifier(n_neighbors=3))
        z[2,k] = run(x_train, y_train, x_test, y_test,
                    KNeighborsClassifier(n_neighbors=7))
        z[3,k] = run(x_train, y_train, x_test, y_test,
                    GaussianNB())
        z[4,k] = run(x_train, y_train, x_test, y_test,
                    DecisionTreeClassifier())
        z[5,k] = run(x_train, y_train, x_test, y_test,
                    RandomForestClassifier(n_estimators=5))
        z[6,k] = run(x_train, y_train, x_test, y_test,
                    RandomForestClassifier(n_estimators=50))
        z[7,k] = run(x_train, y_train, x_test, y_test,
                    SVC(kernel="linear", C=1.0))

    pp(z,0,"Nearest"); pp(z,1,"3-NN")
    pp(z,2,"7-NN");     pp(z,3,"Naive Bayes")
    pp(z,4,"Decision Tree");     pp(z,5,"Random Forest (5)")
    pp(z,6,"Random Forest (50)");     pp(z,7,"SVM (linear)")
```

Listing 7-5: Using k*-fold validation to evaluate the breast cancer dataset. Main code. See* bc_kfold.py.

The first thing we do in `main` is load the full dataset and randomize the ordering. The number of folds, `m`, is read from the command line ❶ and used to create the output array, `z`. This array holds the per fold scores for each of the eight models we'll train, so it has shape $8 \times m$. Recall, when running a Python script from the command line, any arguments passed after the script name are available in `sys.argv`, a list of strings. This is why the argument is passed to `int` to convert it to an integer ❶.

Next, we loop over the m folds, where k is the fold that we'll be using for test data. We create the split and then use the split to train the eight model types we trained previously. Each call to `run` trains a model of the type passed in and returns the score found by running that model against the k-th fold as test data. We store these results in `z`. Finally, we use `pp` to display the per model type and per fold scores along with the average score over all the folds.

A sample run of this code, for $k = 5$ and showing only the mean score across folds, gives the results in Table 7-4.

Table 7-4: Breast Cancer Scores as Mean Over Five Folds

Model	Mean $\pm$ SE
Nearest Centroid	0.9310 ± 0.0116
3-NN	0.9735 ± 0.0035
7-NN	0.9717 ± 0.0039
Naïve Bayes	0.9363 ± 0.0140
Decision Tree	0.9027 ± 0.0079
Random Forest (5)	0.9540 ± 0.0107
Random Forest (50)	0.9540 ± 0.0077
SVM (linear)	0.9699 ± 0.0096

Here we're showing the average performance of each model over all folds. One way to understand the results is that this is the sort of performance we should expect, per model type, if we were to train the model using *all* of the data in the dataset and test it against new samples from the same parent distribution. Indeed, in practice, we would do just this, as we can assume that the reason behind making the model in the first place is to use it for some purpose going forward.

Run the code a second time with $k = 5$. A new set of outputs appears. This is because we're randomizing the order of the dataset on every run (Listing 7-5). This makes a new set of splits and implies that each model will be trained on a different subset mix of the full dataset on each run. So, we should expect different results. Let's run the code 1,000 times with $k = 5$. Note, training this many models takes about 20 minutes on a very standard desktop computer. For each run we'll get an average score over the five folds. We then compute the mean of these averages, which is known as the *grand mean*. Table 7-5 shows the results.

Table 7-5: Breast Cancer Scores as Grand Mean Over 1,000 Runs with Five Folds

Model	Grand mean $\pm$ SE
Nearest Centroid	0.929905 $\pm$ 0.000056
3-NN	0.966334 $\pm$ 0.000113
7-NN	0.965496 $\pm$ 0.000110
Naïve Bayes	0.932973 $\pm$ 0.000095
Decision Tree	0.925706 $\pm$ 0.000276
Random Forest (5)	0.948378 $\pm$ 0.000213
Random Forest (50)	0.958845 $\pm$ 0.000135
SVM (linear)	0.971871 $\pm$ 0.000136

We can take these grand means as an indication of how well we'd expect each model to do against a new set of unknown feature vectors. The small standard errors of the mean are an indication of how well the mean value is known, not how well a model of that type trained on a dataset will necessarily perform. We use the grand mean to help us order the models so we can select one over another.

Ranking the models from highest score to lowest gives the following:

1. SVM (linear)
2. k-NN ($k = 3$)
3. k-NN ($k = 7$)
4. Random Forest (50)
5. Random Forest (5)
6. Naïve Bayes (Gaussian)
7. Nearest Centroid
8. Decision Tree

This is interesting given that we might expect the SVM to be best, but would likely assume the Random Forests to do better than k-NN. The Decision Tree was not as good as we thought, and was less accurate than the Nearest Centroid classifier.

Some comments are in order here. First, note that these results are derived from the training of 8,000 different models on 1,000 different orderings of the dataset. When we study neural networks, we'll see much longer training times. Experimenting with classical machine learning models is generally easy to do since each change to a parameter doesn't require a lengthy training session.

Second, we didn't try to optimize any of the model hyperparameters. Some of these hyperparameters are indirect, like assuming that the features are normally distributed so that the Gaussian Naïve Bayes classifier is a reasonable choice, while others are numerical, like the number of neighbors in k-NN or the number of trees in a Random Forest. If we want to thoroughly develop a good classifier for this dataset using a classic model, we'll have to explore some of these hyperparameters. Ideally, we'd repeat the experiments many, many times for each new hyperparameter setting to arrive at a tight mean value for the score, as we have previously with the grand means over 1,000 runs. We'll play a bit more with hyperparameters in the next section, where we see how we can search for good ones that work well with our dataset.

Searching for Hyperparameters

Let's explore the effect of some of the hyperparameters on various model types. Specifically, let's see if we can optimize our choice of k for k-NN, forest size for Random Forest, and the C margin size of the linear SVM.

Fine-Tuning Our k-NN Classifier

Because the number of neighbors in a k-NN classifier is an integer, typically odd, it's straightforward to repeat our five-fold cross validation experiment while varying k for $k \in \{1, 3, 5, 7, 9, 11, 13, 15\}$. To do this, we need only change the main loop in Listing 7-5 so that each call to run uses KNeighborsClassifier with a different number of neighbors, as follows.

```
for k in range(m):
    x_train, y_train, x_test, y_test = split(x,y,k,m)
    z[0,k] = run(x_train, y_train, x_test, y_test,
                KNeighborsClassifier(n_neighbors=1))
    z[1,k] = run(x_train, y_train, x_test, y_test,
                KNeighborsClassifier(n_neighbors=3))
    z[2,k] = run(x_train, y_train, x_test, y_test,
                KNeighborsClassifier(n_neighbors=5))
    z[3,k] = run(x_train, y_train, x_test, y_test,
                KNeighborsClassifier(n_neighbors=7))
    z[4,k] = run(x_train, y_train, x_test, y_test,
                KNeighborsClassifier(n_neighbors=9))
    z[5,k] = run(x_train, y_train, x_test, y_test,
                KNeighborsClassifier(n_neighbors=11))
    z[6,k] = run(x_train, y_train, x_test, y_test,
                KNeighborsClassifier(n_neighbors=13))
    z[7,k] = run(x_train, y_train, x_test, y_test,
                KNeighborsClassifier(n_neighbors=15))
```

The grand mean of the scores for 1,000 repetitions of the five-fold cross-validation code using a different random ordering of the full dataset each time gives the results in Table 7-6.

Table 7-6: Breast Cancer Scores as Grand Mean for Different k Values and Five-Fold Validation

k	Grand mean $\pm$ SE
1	0.951301 ± 0.000153
3	0.966282 ± 0.000112
5	0.965998 ± 0.000097
7	0.96520 ± 0.000108
9	**0.967011 ± 0.000100**
11	0.965069 ± 0.000107
13	0.962400 ± 0.000106
15	0.959976 ± 0.000101

We've highlighted the $k = 9$ because it returned the highest score. This indicates that we might want to use $k = 9$ for this dataset.

Fine-Tuning Our Random Forest

Let's look at the Random Forest model. The sklearn `RandomForestClassifier` class has quite a few hyperparameters that we could manipulate. To avoid being excessively pedantic, we'll seek only an optimal number of trees in the forest. This is the n_estimators parameter. As we did for k in k-NN, we'll search over a range of forest sizes and select the one that gives the best grand mean score for 1,000 runs at five folds each per run.

This is a one-dimensional grid-like search. We varied k by one, but for the number of trees in the forest, we need to cover a larger scale. We don't expect there to be a meaningful difference between 10 trees in the forest or 11, especially considering that each Random Forest training session will lead to a different set of trees even if the number of trees is fixed. We saw this effect several times in the previous section. Instead, let's vary the number of trees by selecting from $n_t \in \{5, 20, 50, 100, 200, 500, 1000, 5000\}$ where n_t is the number of trees in the forest (number of estimators). Running this search gives us the grand means in Table 7-7.

Table 7-7: Breast Cancer Scores as Grand Mean for Different Random Forest Sizes and Five-Fold Validation

n_t	Grand mean $\pm$ SE
5	0.948327 ± 0.000206
20	0.956808 ± 0.000166
50	0.959048 ± 0.000139
100	0.959740 ± 0.000130
200	0.959913 ± 0.000122
500	0.960049 ± 0.000117
750	0.960147 ± 0.000118
1000	0.960181 ± 0.000116

The first thing to notice is that the differences are very small, though if you run the Mann–Whitney U test, you'll see that the difference between $n_t = 5$ (worst) and $n_t = 1000$ (best) is statistically significant. However, the difference between $n_t = 200$ and $n_t = 1000$ is not significant. Here we need to make a judgment call. Setting $n_t = 1000$ did give the best result but it's indistinguishable, for practical purposes, from $n_t = 500$ or even $n_t = 100$. Since runtime for a Random Forest scales linearly in the number of trees, using $n_t = 100$ results in a classifier that is on average $10\times$ faster than using $n_t = 1000$. So, depending upon the task, we might select $n_t = 100$ over $n_t = 1000$ for that reason.

Fine-Tuning Our SVMs

Let's turn our attention to the linear SVM. For the linear kernel, we'll adjust C. Note, sklearn has other parameters, as it did for the Random Forest, but we'll leave them at their default settings.

What range of C should we search over? The answer is problem dependent but the sklearn default value of $C = 1$ is a good starting point. We'll select C values around 1 but over several orders of magnitude. Specifically, we'll select from $C \in \{0.001, 0.01, 0.1, 1.0, 2.0, 10.0, 50.0, 100.0\}$. Running one thousand five-fold validations, each for a different random ordering of the full dataset, gives grand means as shown in Table 7-8.

Table 7-8: Breast Cancer Scores as Grand Mean for Different SVM C Values and Five-Fold Validation

C	Grand mean $\pm$ SE
0.001	0.938500 $\pm$ 0.000066
0.01	0.967151 $\pm$ 0.000089
0.1	0.975943 $\pm$ 0.000101
1.0	0.971890 $\pm$ 0.000141
2.0	0.969994 $\pm$ 0.000144
10.0	0.966239 $\pm$ 0.000154
50.0	0.959637 $\pm$ 0.000186
100.0	0.957006 $\pm$ 0.000189

$C = 0.1$ gives the best accuracy. While, statistically, the difference between $C = 0.1$ and $C = 1$ is meaningful, in practice the difference is only about 0.4 percent, so the default value of $C = 1$ would likewise be a reasonable choice. Further refinement of C is possible because we see that $C = 0.01$ and $C = 2$ give the same accuracy, while $C = 0.1$ is higher than either, implying that if the C curve is smooth, there's a maximum accuracy for some C in $[0.01, 2.0]$.

Finding the right C for our dataset is a crucial part of successfully using a linear SVM. Our preceding rough run used a one-dimensional grid search. We do expect, since C is continuous, that a plot of the accuracy as a function of C will also be smooth. If that's the case, one can imagine searching for the right C, not with a grid search but with an optimization algorithm.

In practice, however, the randomness of the ordering of the dataset and its effect on the output of *k*-fold cross-validation results will probably make any *C* found by an optimization algorithm too specific to the problem at hand. Grid search over a larger scale, with possibly one level of refinement, is sufficient in most cases. The take-home message is: do spend some time looking for the proper *C* value to maximize the effectiveness of the linear SVM.

Observant readers will have noticed that the preceding analysis has ignored the RBF kernel SVM. Let's revisit it now and see how to do a simple two-dimensional grid search over *C* and γ, where γ is the parameter associated with the RBF (Gaussian) kernel. sklearn has the GridSearchCV class to perform sophisticated grid searching. We're not using it here to be pedagogical and show how to do simple grid searches directly. It's especially important for this kernel to select good values for both of these parameters.

For the search, we'll use the same range of *C* values as we used for the linear case. For γ we'll use powers of two, 2^p, times the sklearn default value, $1/30 = 0.03333$ for $p \in [-4, 3]$. The search will, for the current *C* value, do five-fold validation over the dataset for each γ value before moving to the next *C* value so that all pairs of (C, γ) are considered. The pair that results in the largest score (accuracy) will be output. The code is in Listing 7-6.

```
import numpy as np
from sklearn.svm import SVC

def run(x_train, y_train, x_test, y_test, clf):
    clf.fit(x_train, y_train)
    return clf.score(x_test, y_test)

def split(x,y,k,m):
    ns = int(y.shape[0]/m)
    s = []
    for i in range(m):
        s.append([x[(ns*i):(ns*i+ns)], y[(ns*i):(ns*i+ns)]])
    x_test, y_test = s[k]
    x_train = []
    y_train = []
    for i in range(m):
        if (i==k):
            continue
        else:
            a,b = s[i]
            x_train.append(a)
            y_train.append(b)
    x_train = np.array(x_train).reshape(((m-1)*ns,30))
    y_train = np.array(y_train).reshape((m-1)*ns)
    return [x_train, y_train, x_test, y_test]

def main():
    m = 5
```

```
x = np.load("../data/breast/bc_features_standard.npy")
y = np.load("../data/breast/bc_labels.npy")
idx = np.argsort(np.random.random(y.shape[0]))
x = x[idx]
y = y[idx]

❶ Cs = np.array([0.01,0.1,1.0,2.0,10.0,50.0,100.0])
  gs = (1./30)*2.0**np.array([-4,-3,-2,-1,0,1,2,3])
  zmax = 0.0
❷ for C in Cs:
      for g in gs:
          z = np.zeros(m)
          for k in range(m):
              x_train, y_train, x_test, y_test = split(x,y,k,m)
              z[k] = run(x_train, y_train, x_test, y_test,
                  SVC(C=C,gamma=g,kernel="rbf"))
      ❸ if (z.mean() > zmax):
              zmax = z.mean()
              bestC = C
              bestg = g
  print("best C    = %0.5f" % bestC)
  print("    gamma = %0.5f" % bestg)
  print("    accuracy= %0.5f" % zmax)
```

Listing 7-6: A two-dimensional grid search for C and γ for an RBF kernel SVM. Breast cancer dataset. See bc_rbf_svm_search.py.

The two helper functions, run and split, are exactly the same as we used before (see Listing 7-4); all the action is in main. We fix the number of folds at five and then load and randomize the full dataset.

We then define the specific C and γ values to search over ❶. Note how gs is defined. The first part is $1/30$, the reciprocal of the number of features. This is the default value for γ used by sklearn. We then multiply this factor by an array, $(2^{-4}, 2^{-3}, 2^{-1}, 2^0, 2^1, 2^2, 2^3)$, to get the final γ values we'll search over. Notice that one of the γ values is exactly the default sklearn uses since $2^0 = 1$.

The double loop ❷ iterates over all possible pairs of C and γ. For each one, we do five-fold validation to get a set of five scores in z. We then ask if the mean of this set is greater than the current maximum (z_{max}) and if so, update the maximum and keep the C and γ values as our current bests ❸. When the loops over C and γ exit, we have our best values in bestC and bestg.

If we run this code repeatedly, we'll get different outputs each time. This is because we're randomizing the order of the full dataset, which will alter the subsets in the folds, leading to a different mean score over the folds. For example, 10 runs produced the output in Table 7-9.

Table 7-9: Breast Cancer Scores for an RBF SVM
with Different C and γ Values Averaged Over 10 Runs

C	γ	accuracy
1	0.03333	0.97345
2	0.03333	0.98053
10	0.00417	0.97876
10	0.00417	0.97699
10	0.00417	0.98053
10	0.01667	0.98053
10	0.01667	0.97876
10	0.01667	0.98053
1	0.03333	0.97522
10	0.00417	0.97876

These results hint that $(C, \gamma) = (10, 0.00417)$ is a good combination. If we use these values to generate a grand mean over 1,000 runs of five-fold validation as before, we get an overall accuracy of 0.976991, or 97.70 percent, which is the highest grand mean accuracy of any model type we trained on the breast cancer histology dataset.

The breast cancer dataset is not a large dataset. We were able to use k-fold validation to find a good model that worked well with it. Now, let's move from a pure vector-only dataset to one that is actually image-based and much larger, the MNIST dataset.

Experiments with the MNIST Dataset

The last dataset we'll work with in this chapter is the vector version of the MNIST handwritten digit dataset (see Chapter 5). Recall, this dataset consists of 28×28 pixel grayscale images of handwritten digits, [0, 9], one digit centered per image. This dataset is by far the most common workhorse dataset in machine learning, especially in deep learning, and we'll use it throughout the remainder of the book.

Testing the Classical Models

MNIST contains 60,000 training images, roughly evenly split among the digits, and 10,000 test images. Since we have a lot of training data, at least for classic models like those we're concerned with here, we won't make use of k-fold validation, though we certainly could. We'll train on the training data and test on the testing data and trust that the two come from a common parent distribution (they do).

Since our classic models expect vector inputs, we'll use the vector form of the MNIST dataset we created in Chapter 5. The images are unraveled so that the first 28 elements of the vector are row 0, the next 28 are row 1, and so on for an input vector of $28 \times 28 = 784$ elements. The images are stored as 8-bit grayscale, so the data values run from 0 to 255. We'll consider three versions of the dataset. The first is the raw byte version. The second is a version where we scale the data to [0, 1) by dividing by 256, the number of possible grayscale values. The third is a normalized version where, per "feature" (really, pixel), we subtract the mean of that feature across the dataset and then divide by the standard deviation. This will let us explore how the range of the feature values affects things, if at all.

Figure 7-1 shows examples of the original images and the resulting normalized vectors raveled back into images and scaled [0, 255]. Normalizing affects the appearance but does not destroy spatial relationships among the parts of the digit images. Just scaling the data to [0, 1) will result in images that look the same as those on the top of Figure 7-1.

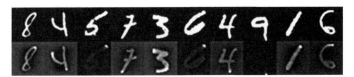

Figure 7-1: Original MNIST digits (top) and normalized versions used by the models (bottom)

The code we'll use is very similar to what we used previously, but for reasons that will be explained next, we will replace the SVC class with a new SVM class, LinearSVC. First, take a look at the helper functions in Listing 7-7.

```python
import time
import numpy as np
from sklearn.neighbors import NearestCentroid
from sklearn.neighbors import KNeighborsClassifier
from sklearn.naive_bayes import GaussianNB, MultinomialNB
from sklearn.tree import DecisionTreeClassifier
from sklearn.ensemble import RandomForestClassifier
from sklearn.svm import LinearSVC
from sklearn import decomposition

def run(x_train, y_train, x_test, y_test, clf):
    s = time.time()
    clf.fit(x_train, y_train)
    e_train = time.time() - s
    s = time.time()
    score = clf.score(x_test, y_test)
    e_test = time.time() - s
    print("score = %0.4f (time, train=%8.3f, test=%8.3f)"
        % (score, e_train, e_test))

def train(x_train, y_train, x_test, y_test):
    print("    Nearest Centroid        : ", end='')
    run(x_train, y_train, x_test, y_test, NearestCentroid())
    print("    k-NN classifier (k=3)    : ", end='')
```

```
run(x_train, y_train, x_test, y_test,
    KNeighborsClassifier(n_neighbors=3))
print("    k-NN classifier (k=7)    : ", end='')
run(x_train, y_train, x_test, y_test,
    KNeighborsClassifier(n_neighbors=7))
print("    Naive Bayes (Gaussian)   : ", end='')
run(x_train, y_train, x_test, y_test, GaussianNB())
print("    Decision Tree            : ", end='')
run(x_train, y_train, x_test, y_test, DecisionTreeClassifier())
print("    Random Forest (trees=  5) : ", end='')
run(x_train, y_train, x_test, y_test,
    RandomForestClassifier(n_estimators=5))
print("    Random Forest (trees= 50) : ", end='')
run(x_train, y_train, x_test, y_test,
    RandomForestClassifier(n_estimators=50))
print("    Random Forest (trees=500) : ", end='')
run(x_train, y_train, x_test, y_test,
    RandomForestClassifier(n_estimators=500))
print("    Random Forest (trees=1000): ", end='')
run(x_train, y_train, x_test, y_test,
    RandomForestClassifier(n_estimators=1000))
print("    LinearSVM (C=0.01)       : ", end='')
run(x_train, y_train, x_test, y_test, LinearSVC(C=0.01))
print("    LinearSVM (C=0.1)        : ", end='')
run(x_train, y_train, x_test, y_test, LinearSVC(C=0.1))
print("    LinearSVM (C=1.0)        : ", end='')
run(x_train, y_train, x_test, y_test, LinearSVC(C=1.0))
print("    LinearSVM (C=10.0)       : ", end='')
run(x_train, y_train, x_test, y_test, LinearSVC(C=10.0))
```

Listing 7-7: Training differently scaled versions of the MNIST dataset using classic models. Helper functions. See mnist_experiments.py.

The run function of Listing 7-7 is also similar to those used previously, except we've added code to time how long training and testing takes. These times are reported along with the score. We added this code for MNIST because, unlike the tiny iris and breast cancer datasets, MNIST has a larger number of training samples so that runtime differences among the model types will start to show themselves. The train function is new, but all it does is wrap calls to run for the different model types.

Now take a look at Listing 7-8, which contains the main function.

```
def main():
    x_train = np.load("mnist_train_vectors.npy").astype("float64")
    y_train = np.load("mnist_train_labels.npy")
    x_test = np.load("mnist_test_vectors.npy").astype("float64")
    y_test = np.load("mnist_test_labels.npy")

    print("Models trained on raw [0,255] images:")
```

```
    train(x_train, y_train, x_test, y_test)
    print("Models trained on raw [0,1) images:")
    train(x_train/256.0, y_train, x_test/256.0, y_test)

❶  m = x_train.mean(axis=0)
    s = x_train.std(axis=0) + 1e-8
    x_ntrain = (x_train - m) / s
    x_ntest  = (x_test - m) / s

    print("Models trained on normalized images:")
    train(x_ntrain, y_train, x_ntest, y_test)

❷  pca = decomposition.PCA(n_components=15)
    pca.fit(x_ntrain)
    x_ptrain = pca.transform(x_ntrain)
    x_ptest = pca.transform(x_ntest)

    print("Models trained on first 15 PCA components of normalized images:")
    train(x_ptrain, y_train, x_ptest, y_test)
```

Listing 7-8: Training differently scaled versions of the MNIST dataset using classic models. Main function. See mnist_experiments.py.

The main function of Listing 7-8 loads the data and then trains the models using the raw byte values. It then repeats the training using a scaled [0, 1) version of the data and a scaled version of the testing data. These are the first two versions of the dataset we'll use.

Normalizing the data requires knowledge of the per feature means and standard deviations ❶. Note, we add a small value to the standard deviations to make up for pixels that have a standard deviation of zero. We can't divide by zero, after all. We need to normalize the test data, but which means and which standard deviations should we use? Generally, we have more training data than testing data, so using the means and standard deviations from the training data makes sense; they are a better representation of the true means and standard deviations of the parent distribution that generated the data in the first place. However, at times, there may be slight differences between the training and testing data distributions, in which case it might make sense to consider the testing means and standard deviations. In this case, because the MNIST training and test datasets were created together, there's no difference, so the training values are what we'll use. Note that the same per feature means and standard deviations will need to be used for all new, unknown samples, too.

Next, we apply PCA to the dataset just as we did for the iris data in Chapter 5 ❷. Here we're keeping the first 15 components. These account for just over 33 percent of the variance in the data and reduce the feature vector from 784 features (the pixels) to 15 features (the principal components). Then we train the models using these features.

Running this code produces a wealth of output that we can learn from. Let's first consider the scores per model type and data source. These are in

Table 7-10; values in parentheses are the number of trees in the Random Forest.

Table 7-10: MNIST Model Scores for Different Preprocessing Steps

Model	Raw [0,255]	Scaled [0,1]	Normalized	PCA
Nearest Centroid	0.8203	0.8203	0.8092	0.7523
k-NN (k = 3)	0.9705	0.9705	0.9452	0.9355
k-NN (k = 7)	0.9694	0.9694	0.9433	0.9370
Naïve Bayes	0.5558	0.5558	0.5239	0.7996
Decision Tree	0.8773	0.8784	0.8787	0.8403
Random Forest (5)	0.9244	0.9244	0.9220	0.8845
Random Forest (50)	0.9660	0.9661	0.9676	0.9215
Random Forest (500)	0.9708	0.9709	0.9725	0.9262
Random Forest (1000)	0.9715	0.9716	0.9719	0.9264
LinearSVM (C = 0.01)	0.8494	0.9171	0.9158	0.8291
LinearSVM (C = 0.1)	0.8592	0.9181	0.9163	0.8306
LinearSVM (C = 1.0)	0.8639	0.9182	0.9079	0.8322
LinearSVM (C = 10.0)	0.8798	0.9019	0.8787	0.7603

Look at the Nearest Centroid scores. These make sense as we move from left to right across the different versions of the dataset. For the raw data, the center location of each of the 10 classes leads to a simple classifier with an accuracy of 82 percent—not too bad considering random guessing would have an accuracy closer to 10 percent (1/10 for 10 classes). Scaling the data by a constant won't change the relative relationship between the per class centroids so we'd expect the same performance in column 2 of Table 7-10 as in column 1.

Normalizing, however, does more than divide the data by a constant. We saw the effect clearly in Figure 7-1. This alteration, at least for the MNIST dataset, changes the centroids' relationships to each other and results in a decrease in accuracy to 80.9 percent.

Finally, using PCA to reduce the number of features from 784 to 15 has a severe negative impact, resulting in an accuracy of only 75.2 percent. Note the word *only*. In the past, before the advent of deep learning, an accuracy of 75 percent on a problem with 10 classes would generally have been considered to be pretty good. Of course, it really isn't. Who would get in a self-driving car that has an accident one time out of every four trips? We want to do better.

Let's consider the k-NN classifiers next. We see similar performance for both k = 3 and k = 7 and the same sort of trend as we saw with the Nearest Centroid classifier. This is to be expected given how similar the two types of models actually are. The difference in accuracy between the two (centroid and k-NN) is dramatic, however. An accuracy of 97 percent is generally regarded as good. But still, who would opt for elective surgery with a 3 percent failure rate?

Things get interesting when we look at the Naïve Bayes classifier. Here all the versions of the dataset perform poorly, though still five times better than guessing. We see a large jump in accuracy with the PCA processed dataset, from 56 percent to 80 percent. This is the only model type to improve after using PCA. Why might this be? Remember, we're using Gaussian Naïve Bayes, which means our independence assumption is coupled with an assumption that the continuous feature values are, per feature, really drawn from a normal distribution whose parameters, the mean and standard deviation, we can estimate from the feature values themselves.

Now recall what PCA does, geometrically. It's the equivalent of rotating the feature vectors onto a new set of coordinates aligned with the largest orthogonal directions derivable from the dataset. The word *orthogonal* implies that no part of a direction overlaps with any other part of any other direction. Think of the x-, y-, and z-axes of a three-dimensional plot. No part of the x is along the y or z, and so forth. This is what PCA does. Therefore, PCA makes the first assumption of Naïve Bayes more likely to be true, that the new features are indeed independent of each other. Add in the Gaussian assumption as to the distribution of the per pixel values, and we have an explanation for what we see in Table 7-10.

The tree-based classifiers, Decision Tree and Random Forest, perform much the same until we get to the PCA version of the dataset. Indeed, there is no difference between the raw data and the data scaled by 256. Again, this is to be expected as all scaling by a constant does is scale the decision thresholds for each of the nodes in the body of the tree or trees. As before, working with reduced dimensionality vectors via PCA results in a loss of accuracy because potentially important information has been discarded.

For any data source, we see scores that make sense relative to each other. As before, the single Decision Tree performs worst, which it should except for simple cases since it's competing against a collection of trees via the Random Forests. For the Random Forests, we see that the score improves as the number of trees in the forest increases—again expected. However, the improvement comes with diminishing returns. There's a significant improvement when going from 5 trees to 50 trees, but a minimal improvement in going from 500 trees to 1,000 trees.

Before we look at the SVM results, let's understand why we made the switch from the SVC class to LinearSVC. As the name suggests, LinearSVC implements only a linear kernel. The SVC class is more generic and can implement other kernels, so why switch?

The reason has to do with runtime. In computer science, there are specific definitions of complexity and an entire branch devoted to the analysis of algorithms and how they perform as their inputs scale larger and larger. All we'll concern ourselves with here is *big-O* notation. This is a way of characterizing how the runtime of an algorithm changes as the input (or the number of inputs) gets larger and larger.

For example, a classic bubble sort algorithm works just fine on a few dozen numbers to be sorted. But, as the input gets larger (more numbers to be sorted), the runtime increases not linearly but quadratically, meaning the time to sort the numbers, t, is proportional to the *square* of the number of numbers to be sorted, $t \propto n^2$, which is written as $\mathcal{O}(n^2)$. So, the bubble sort is an order n^2 algorithm. In general, we want algorithms that are better than n^2, more like n, written as $\mathcal{O}(n)$, or even independent of n, written as $\mathcal{O}(1)$. It turns out that the kernel algorithm for training an SVM is *worse* than $\mathcal{O}(n^2)$ so that when the number of training samples increases, the runtime explodes. This is one reason for the switch from the SVC class to LinearSVC, which doesn't use kernels.

The second reason for the switch has to do with the fact that Support Vector Machines are designed for binary classification—only two classes. The MNIST dataset has 10 classes, so something different has to be done. There are multiple approaches. According to the sklearn documentation, the SVC class uses a *one-versus-one* approach that trains pairs of classifiers, one class versus another: class 0 versus class 1, class 1 versus class 2, class 0 versus class 2, and so on. This means it ends up training not one but $m(m-1)/2$ classifiers for $m = 10$ classes, or $10(10-1)/2 = 45$ separate classifiers. This isn't efficient in this case. The LinearSVC classifier uses a *one-versus-rest* approach. This means it trains an SVM to classify "0" versus "1–9", then "1" versus "0, 2–9", and so on, for a total of only 10 classifiers, one for each digit.

It's with the SVM classifiers that we see a definite benefit to scaling the data versus the raw byte inputs. We also see that the optimal C value is likely between $C = 0.1$ and $C = 1.0$. Note that simple $[0, 1)$ scaling leads to SVM models that outperform (for this one dataset!) the models trained on the normalized data. The effect is small but consistent for different C values. And, as we saw before, dropping the dimensionality from 784 features to only 15 features via PCA leads to a rather large loss of accuracy. PCA seems not to have helped in this case. We'll come back to it in a bit and see if we can understand why.

Analyzing Runtimes

Let's now look at the runtime performance of the algorithms. Table 7-11 shows the train and test times, in seconds, for each model type and dataset version.

Look at the test times. This is how long each model takes to classify all 10,000 digit images in the test set. The first thing that jumps out at us is that k-NN is slow. Classifying the test set takes over 10 minutes when full feature vectors are used! It's only when we drop down to the first 15 PCA components that we see reasonable k-NN runtimes. This is a good example of the price we pay for a seemingly simple idea. Recall, the k-NN classifier finds the k closest training samples to the unknown sample we wish to classify. Here *closest* means in a Euclidean sense, like the distance between two points on a graph, except in this case we don't have two or three dimensions but 784.

Table 7-11: Training and Testing Times (Seconds) for Each Model Type

Model	Raw [0,255]		Scaled [0,1]		Normalized		PCA	
	train	test	train	test	train	test	train	test
Nearest Centroid	0.23	0.03	0.24	0.03	0.24	0.03	0.01	0.00
K-NN (K = 3)	33.24	747.34	33.63	747.22	33.66	699.58	0.09	3.64
K-NN (K = 7)	33.45	746.00	33.69	746.65	33.68	709.62	0.09	4.65
Naïve Bayes	0.80	0.88	0.85	0.90	0.83	0.94	0.02	0.01
Decision Tree	25.42	0.03	25.41	0.02	25.42	0.02	2.10	0.00
Random Forest (5)	2.65	0.06	2.70	0.06	2.61	0.06	1.20	0.03
Random Forest (50)	25.56	0.46	25.14	0.46	25.27	0.46	12.06	0.25
Random Forest (500)	252.65	4.41	249.69	4.47	249.19	4.45	121.10	2.51
Random Forest (1000)	507.52	8.86	499.23	8.71	499.10	8.91	242.44	5.00
LinearSVM (C = 0.01)	169.45	0.02	5.93	0.02	232.93	0.02	16.91	0.00
LinearSVM (C = 0.1)	170.58	0.02	36.00	0.02	320.17	0.02	37.46	0.00
LinearSVM (C = 1.0)	170.74	0.02	96.34	0.02	488.06	0.02	66.49	0.00
LinearSVM (C = 10.0)	170.46	0.02	154.34	0.02	541.69	0.02	86.87	0.00

Therefore, for each of the test samples, we need to find the $k = 3$ or $k = 7$ closest points in the training data. The naïve way to do this is to calculate the distance between the unknown sample and each of the 60,000 training samples, sort them, look at the k smallest distances, and vote to decide the output class label. This is a lot of work because we have 60,000 training samples and 10,000 test samples for a total of 600,000,000 distance calculations. It isn't as bad as all that because sklearn automatically selects the algorithm used to find the nearest neighbors, and decades of research has uncovered "better than brute force" approaches. Curious readers will want to investigate the terms *K-D-tree* and *Ball tree* (sometimes called *Metric tree*). See "An Empirical Comparison of Exact Nearest Neighbor Algorithms" by Kibriya and Frank (2007). Still, because of the extreme difference in runtimes between the other model types and k-NN, it's necessary to remember just how slow k-NN can be if the dataset is large.

The next slowest test times are for the Random Forest classifiers. We understand why the forest with 500 trees takes 10 times longer to run than the forest with 50 trees; we have 10 times as many trees to evaluate. Training times also scale linearly. Reducing the size of the feature vectors with PCA improves things but not by a factor of 50 (784 features divided by 15 PCA features ≈ 50), so the performance difference is not primarily influenced by the size of the feature vector.

The linear SVMs are the next slowest to train after the Random Forests, but their execution time is extremely low. Long training times and short classification (inference) times are a hallmark of many model types. The simplest models are quick to train and quick to use, like Nearest Centroid or Naïve Bayes, but in general, "slow to train, quick to use" is a safe assumption. It's especially true of neural networks.

Using PCA hurt the performance of the models except for the Naïve Bayes classifier. Let's do an experiment to see the effect of PCA as the number of PCA components changes.

Experimenting with PCA Components

For Tables 7-10 and 7-11, we selected 15 PCA components that represented about 33 percent of the variance in the dataset. This value was selected at random. You could imagine training models using some other number of principal components.

Let's examine the effect of the number of PCA components used on the accuracy of the resulting model. We'll vary the number of components from 10 to 780, which is basically all the features in the image. For each number of components, we'll train a Naïve Bayes classifier, a Random Forest of 50 trees, and a linear SVM with $C = 1.0$. The code to do this is in Listing 7-9.

```
def main():
    x_train = np.load("../data/mnist/mnist_train_vectors.npy")
                     .astype("float64")
    y_train = np.load("../data/mnist/mnist_train_labels.npy")
    x_test = np.load("../data/mnist/mnist_test_vectors.npy").astype("float64")
    y_test = np.load("../data/mnist/mnist_test_labels.npy")
    m = x_train.mean(axis=0)
    s = x_train.std(axis=0) + 1e-8
    x_ntrain = (x_train - m) / s
    x_ntest  = (x_test - m) / s

    n = 78
    pcomp = np.linspace(10,780,n, dtype="int16")
    nb=np.zeros((n,4))
    rf=np.zeros((n,4))
    sv=np.zeros((n,4))
    tv=np.zeros((n,2))

    for i,p in enumerate(pcomp):
     ❶ pca = decomposition.PCA(n_components=p)
        pca.fit(x_ntrain)
```

```
        xtrain = pca.transform(x_ntrain)
        xtest = pca.transform(x_ntest)
        tv[i,:] = [p, pca.explained_variance_ratio_.sum()]
 ❷  sc,etrn,etst =run(xtrain, y_train, xtest, y_test, GaussianNB())
        nb[i,:] = [p,sc,etrn,etst]
        sc,etrn,etst =run(xtrain, y_train, xtest, y_test,
                        RandomForestClassifier(n_estimators=50))
        rf[i,:] = [p,sc,etrn,etst]
        sc,etrn,etst =run(xtrain, y_train, xtest, y_test, LinearSVC(C=1.0))
        sv[i,:] = [p,sc,etrn,etst]

    np.save("mnist_pca_tv.npy", tv)
    np.save("mnist_pca_nb.npy", nb)
    np.save("mnist_pca_rf.npy", rf)
    np.save("mnist_pca_sv.npy", sv)
```

Listing 7-9: Model accuracy as a function of the number of PCA components used. See mnist_pca.py.

First, we load the MNIST dataset and compute the normalized version. This is the version that we'll use with PCA. Next, we set up storage for the results. The variable pcomp stores the specific number of PCA components that will be used from 10 to 780 in steps of 10. Then we start a loop over the number PCA components. We find the requested number of components (p) and map the dataset to the actual dataset trained and tested (xtrain, xtest) ❶.

We also store the actual amount of variance in the dataset explained by the current number of principal components (tv). We'll plot this value later to see how quickly the number of components covers the majority of the variance in the dataset.

Next, we train and test a Gaussian Naïve Bayes classifier using the current number of features ❷. The run function called here is virtually identical to that used in Listing 7-7 except that it returns the score, the training time, and the testing time. These are captured and put into the appropriate output array (nb). Then we do the same for the Random Forest and linear SVM.

When the loop completes, we have all the data we need and we store the NumPy arrays on disk for plotting. Running this code takes some time, but the output, when plotted, leads to Figure 7-2.

The solid curve shows the fraction of the total variance in the dataset explained by the current number of PCA components (x-axis). This curve will reach a maximum of 1.0 when all the features in the dataset are used. It's helpful in this case because it shows how quickly adding new components explains major orientations of the data. For MNIST, we see that about 90 percent of the variance is explained by using less than half the possible number of PCA components.

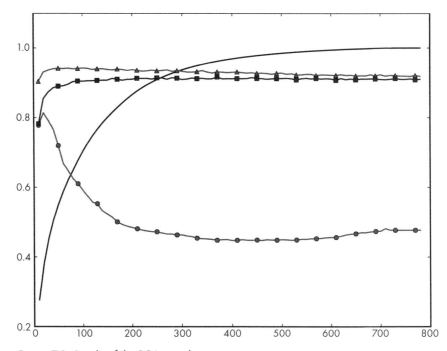

Figure 7-2: Results of the PCA search

The remaining three curves plot the accuracy of the resulting models on the test data. The best-performing model, in this case, is the Random Forest with 50 trees (triangles). This is followed by the linear SVM (squares) and then Naïve Bayes (circles). These curves show how the number of PCA components tracks with accuracy, and while the Random Forest and SVM change only slowly as PCA changes, we see that the Naïve Bayes classifier rapidly loses accuracy as the number of PCA components increases. Even the Random Forest and SVM decrease as the number of PCA components increases, which we might expect because the curse of dimensionality will eventually creep in. It seems likely that the dramatically different behavior of the Naïve Bayes classifier is due to violations of the independence assumption as the number of components used increases.

The maximum accuracy and the number of PCA components where it occurs are shown in Table 7-12.

Table 7-12: Maximum Accuracy on MNIST by Model and Number of Components

Model	Accuracy	Components	Variance
Naïve Bayes	0.81390	20	0.3806
Random Forest (50)	0.94270	100	0.7033
Linear SVM (C = 1.0)	0.91670	370	0.9618

Table 7-12 tracks with the plot in Figure 7-2. Interestingly, the SVM does not reach a maximum until nearly all the features in the original dataset are used. Also, the best accuracy found for the Random Forest and SVM is not as good as seen previously for other versions of the dataset that did not use PCA. So, for these models, PCA is not a benefit; it is, however, for the Naïve Bayes classifier.

Scrambling Our Dataset

Before we leave this section, let's look at one more experiment that we'll come back to in Chapter 9 and again in Chapter 12. In Chapter 5, we made a version of the MNIST dataset that scrambled the order of the pixels in the digit images. The scrambling wasn't random: the same pixel in each input image was moved to the same position in the output image, resulting in images that, at least to us, no longer look like the original digit, as Figure 7-3 shows. How might this scrambling affect the accuracy of the models we've been using in this chapter?

Figure 7-3: Original MNIST digits (top) and scrambled versions of the same digit (bottom).

Let's repeat the experiment code of Listing 7-8, this time running only the scaled [0, 1) version of the scrambled MNIST images. Since the only difference to the original code is the source filenames and the fact that we call run only once, we'll forgo a new listing.

Placing the accuracy results side by side gives us Table 7-13.

Table 7-13: MNIST Scores by Model Type for Unscrambled and Scrambled Digits

Model	Unscrambled [0,1)	Scrambled [0,1)
Nearest Centroid	0.8203	0.8203
k-NN (k = 3)	0.9705	0.9705
k-NN (k = 7)	0.9694	0.9694
Naïve Bayes	0.5558	0.5558
Decision Tree	0.8784	0.8772
Random Forest (5)	0.9244	0.9214
Random Forest (50)	0.9661	0.9651
Random Forest (500)	0.9709	0.9721
Random Forest (1000)	0.9716	0.9711
LinearSVM (C = 0.01)	0.9171	0.9171
LinearSVM (C = 0.1)	0.9181	0.9181
LinearSVM (C = 1.0)	0.9182	0.9185
LinearSVM (C = 10.0)	0.9019	0.8885

Here we see virtually no difference between the scrambled and unscrambled results. In fact, for several models, the results are identical. For stochastic models, like the Random Forests, the results are still very similar. Is this surprising? Perhaps at first, but if we think about it for a bit, we realize that it really shouldn't be.

All of the classic models are holistic: they operate on the entire feature vector as a single entity. While we can't see the digits anymore because our vision does not operate holistically, the *information* present in the image is still there, so the models are just as happy with the scrambled as unscrambled inputs. When we get to Chapter 12, we'll encounter a different result of this experiment.

Classical Model Summary

What follows is a summary of the pros and cons related to each of the classical model types we have explored in this chapter. This can be used as a quick list for future reference. It will also take some of the observations we made via our experiments and make them more concrete.

Nearest Centroid

This is the simplest of all the models and can serve as a baseline. It's seldom adequate unless the task at hand is particularly easy. The single centroid for each class is needlessly restrictive. You could use a more generalized approach that first finds an appropriate number of centroids for each class and then groups them together to build the classifier. In the extreme, this approaches k-NN but is still simpler in that the number of centroids is likely far less than the number of training samples. We'll leave the implementation of this variation as an exercise for the motivated reader.

Pros

As we saw in this chapter, the implementation of a Nearest Centroid classifier takes only a handful of code. Additionally, Nearest Centroid is not restricted to binary models and readily supports multiclass models, like the irises. Training is very fast and since only one centroid is stored per class, the memory overhead is likewise very small. When used to label an unknown sample, run time is also very small because the distance from the sample to each class centroid is all that needs to be computed.

Cons

Nearest Centroid makes a simplistic assumption about the distribution of the classes in the feature space—one that's seldom met in practice. As a consequence of this assumption, the Nearest Centroid classifier is only highly accurate when the classes form a single tight group in the feature space and the groups are distant from each other like isolated islands.

k-Nearest Neighbors

This is the simplest model to train since there's no training: we store the training set and use it to classify new instances by finding the k nearest training set vectors and voting.

Pros

As just mentioned, no training required makes k-NN particularly attractive. It also can perform quite well, especially if the number of training samples is large relative to the dimensionality of the feature space (that is, the number of features in the feature vector). Multiclass support is implicit and doesn't require a special approach.

Cons

The simplicity of "training" comes at a cost: classification is slow because of the need to look at every training example to find the nearest neighbors to the unknown feature vector. Decades of research, still underway, have sped up the search to improve the naïve implementation of looking at every training sample every time, but, as we saw in this chapter, classification is still slow, especially when compared to the speed of other model types (for example, SVM).

Naïve Bayes

This model is conceptually simple and efficient, and surprisingly valid even when the core assumption of feature independence isn't met.

Pros

Naïve Bayes is fast to train and fast to classify with, both positives. It also supports multiclass models instead of just binary, and other than continuous features. As long as the probability of a particular feature value can be computed, we can apply Naïve Bayes.

Cons

The feature independence assumption central to Naïve Bayes is seldom true in practice. The more correlated the features (the more a change in, say, feature x_2 implies that x_3 will change), the poorer the performance of the model (in all likelihood).

While Naïve Bayes works directly with discrete valued features, using continuous features often involves a second level of assumption, as when we assumed that the continuous breast cancer dataset features were well represented as samples from a Gaussian distribution. This second assumption, which is also likely seldom true in practice, means that we need to estimate the parameters of the distribution from the dataset instead of using histograms to stand in for the actual feature probabilities.

Decision Trees

This model is useful when it's important to be able to understand, in human terms, why a particular class was selected.

Pros

Decision Trees are reasonably fast to train. They're also fast to use for classifying. Multiclass models are not a problem and are not restricted to using just continuous features. A Decision Tree can justify its answer by showing the particular steps used to reach a decision: the series of questions asked from the root to the leaf.

Cons

Decision Trees are prone to overfitting—to learning elements of the training data that are not generally true of the parent distribution. Also, interpretability degrades as the tree increases in size. Tree depth needs to be balanced with the quality of the decisions (labels) as the leaves of the tree. This directly affects the error rate.

Random Forests

This is a more powerful form of Decision Tree that uses randomness to reduce the overfitting problem. Random Forests are one of the best performing of the classic model types and apply to a wide range of problem domains.

Pros

Like Decision Trees, Random Forests support multiclass models and other than continuous features. They are reasonably fast to train and to use for inference. Random Forests are also robust to differences in scale between features in the feature vector. In general, the accuracy improves, with diminishing returns, as the size of the forest grows.

Cons

The easy interpretability of a Decision Tree disappears with a Random Forest. While each tree in the forest can justify its decision, the combined effect of the forest as a whole can be difficult to understand.

The inference runtime of a forest scales linearly with the number of trees. However, this can be mitigated by parallelization since each tree in the forest is making a calculation that does not depend on any other tree until combining the output of all trees to make an overall decision.

As stochastic models, the overall performance of a forest varies from training session to training session for the same dataset. In general, this isn't an issue, but a pathological forest could exist—if possible, train the forest several times to get a sense of the actual performance.

Support Vector Machines

Before the "rebirth" of neural networks, Support Vector Machines were generally considered to provide the pinnacle of model performance when they were applicable and well-tuned.

Pros

SVMs can give show excellent performance when properly tuned. Inference is very fast once trained.

Cons

Multiclass models are not directly supported. Extensions for multiclass problems require training multiple models whether using one-versus-one or one-versus-rest approaches. Additionally, SVMs expect only continuous features and feature scaling matters; normalization or other scaling is often necessary to get good performance.

Large datasets are difficult to train when using other than linear kernels, and SVMs often require careful tuning of margin and kernel parameters (C, γ), though this can be mitigated somewhat by search algorithms that seek the best hyperparameter values.

When to Use Classical Models

The classical models may be *classic*, but they are still appropriate under the right conditions. In this section, we'll discuss when you should consider a classical model instead of a more modern approach.

Handling Small Datasets

One of the best reasons for working with a classic model is when the dataset is small. If you have only a few tens or hundreds of examples, then a classic model might be a good fit, whereas a deep learning model might not have enough training data to condition itself to the problem. Of course, there are exceptions. A deep neural network can, via transfer learning, sometimes learn from relatively few examples. Other approaches, like zero-shot or few-shot learning, may also allow a deep network to learn from a small dataset. However, these techniques are far beyond the scope of what we want to address in this book. For us, the rule of thumb is: when the dataset is small, consider using a classic model.

Dealing with Reduced Computational Requirements

Another reason to consider a classic model is when computational requirements must be kept to a minimum. Deep neural networks are notoriously demanding of computational resources. The thousands, millions, and even billions of connections in a deep network all require extensive calculation.

Implementing such a model on a small handheld device, or on an embedded microcontroller, will not work, or at least not work in any reasonable timeframe.

In such cases, you might consider a classic model that doesn't require a lot of overhead. Simple models like Nearest Centroid or Naïve Bayes are good candidates. So are Decision Trees and Support Vector Machines, once trained. From the previous experiments, k-NN is probably not a good candidate unless the feature space or training set is small. This leads to our next rule of thumb: when computation must be kept to a minimum, consider using a classic model.

Having Explainable Models

Some classic models can explain themselves by revealing exactly *how* they arrived at their answer for a given unknown input. This includes Decision Trees, by design, but also k-NN (by showing the labels of the k voters), Nearest Centroid (by virtue of the selected centroid), and even Naïve Bayes (by the selected posterior probability). By way of contrast, deep neural networks are black boxes—they do not explain themselves—and it's an active area of research to learn how to get a deep network to give some reason for its decision. This research has not been entirely unsuccessful, to be sure, but it's still far from looking like the decision path in a tree classifier. Therefore, we can give another rule of thumb: when it's essential to know how the classifier makes its decision, consider using a classic model.

Working with Vector Inputs

Our final rule of thumb, acknowledging, of course, that there are indeed others we could give, has to do with the form of the inputs to the model. Modern deep learning systems often work with inputs that are not an amalgamation of separate features put into a single vector but instead are multidimensional inputs, such as images, where the "features" (pixels) are not different from each other but of the same kind and often highly correlated (the red pixel of the apple likely has a red pixel next to it, for example). A color image is a three-dimensional beast: there are three color images, one for the red channel, one for the blue channel, and one for the green channel. If the inputs are images from other sources, like satellites, there might be four to eight or more channels per image. A convolutional neural network is designed precisely for inputs such as these and will look for spatial patterns characteristic of the classes the network is trying to learn about. See Chapter 12 for more details.

But if the input to the model is a vector, especially a vector where the particular features are not related to each other (the key assumption of the Naïve Bayes classifier), then a classic model might be appropriate, since there's no need to look for structure among the features beyond the global interpretation that the classic models perform by considering the input as a single monolithic entity. Therefore, we might give the rule as: when the input is a feature vector without spatial structure (unlike an image), especially if the features are not related to each other, consider using a classic model.

It's important to remember that these are rule-of-thumb suggestions, and that they aren't always applicable to a particular problem. Also, it's possible to use deep networks even if these rules seem to apply; it's just that they may not give the best performance, or might be overkill, like using a shotgun to kill a fly. The main point of this book is to build intuition so that when a situation arises, we'll know how to use the techniques we are exploring to maximum advantage. Pasteur said, "In the fields of observation, chance favors only the prepared mind" (lecture at the University of Lille, December 1854), and we wholeheartedly agree.

Summary

In this chapter, we worked with six common classical machine learning models: Nearest Centroid, k-Nearest Neighbors, Naïve Bayes, Decision Trees, Random Forests, and Support Vector Machines. We applied them to three datasets that were developed in Chapter 5: irises, breast cancer, and MNIST digits. We used the results of the experiments with these datasets to gain insight into the strengths and weaknesses of each model type along with the effect of different data preprocessing steps. We ended the chapter with a discussion of the classic models and when it might be appropriate to use them.

In the next chapter, we'll move on from the classic models and begin our exploration of neural networks, the backbone of modern deep learning.

8

INTRODUCTION TO NEURAL NETWORKS

Neural networks are the heart of deep learning. In Chapter 9, we'll take a deep dive into what we'll call *traditional neural networks*. However, before we do that, we'll introduce the anatomy of a neural network, followed by a quick example.

Specifically, we'll present the components of a *fully connected feedforward neural network*. Visually, you can imagine the network as shown in Figure 8-1. We'll refer to this figure often in this chapter and the next. Your mission, should you choose to accept it, is to commit this figure to memory to save wear and tear on the book by flipping back to it repeatedly.

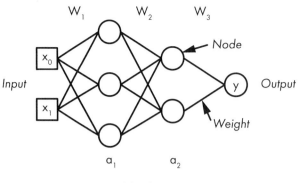

Figure 8-1: A sample neural network

After discussing the structure and parts of a neural network, we'll explore training our example network to classify irises. From this initial experiment, Chapter 9 will lead us to gradient descent and the backpropagation algorithm—the standard way that neural networks, including advanced deep neural networks, are trained. This chapter is intended as a warm-up. The heavy lifting starts in Chapter 9.

Anatomy of a Neural Network

A *neural network* is a graph. In computer science, a *graph* is a series of *nodes*, universally drawn as circles, connected by *edges* (short line segments). This abstraction is useful for representing many different kinds of relationships: roads between cities, who knows whom on social media, the structure of the internet, or a series of basic computational units that can be used to approximate any mathematical function.

The last example is, of course, deliberate. Neural networks are universal function approximators. They use a graph structure to represent a series of computational steps mapping an input feature vector to an output value, typically interpreted as a probability. Neural networks are built in layers. Conceptually, they act from left to right, mapping an input feature vector to the output(s) by passing values along the edges to the nodes. Note, the nodes of a neural network are often referred to as *neurons*. We'll see why shortly. The nodes calculate new values based on their inputs. The new values are then passed to the next layer of nodes and so on until the output nodes are reached. In Figure 8-1, there's an input layer on the left, a hidden layer to its right, another hidden layer right of that, and a single node in the output layer.

The previous section included the phrase *fully connected feedforward neural network* without much explanation. Let's break it down. The *fully connected* part means every node of a layer has its output sent to every node of the next layer. The *feedforward* part means that information passes from left to right through the network without being sent back to a previous layer; there is no *feedback*, no looping, in the network structure. This leaves only the *neural network* part.

The Neuron

Personally, I have a love/hate relationship with the phrase *neural network*. The phrase itself comes from the fact that in a very crude approximation, the basic unit of the network resembles a neuron in a brain. Consider Figure 8-2, which we'll describe in detail shortly.

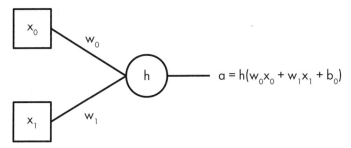

$$a = h(w_0 x_0 + w_1 x_1 + b_0)$$

Figure 8-2: A single neural network node

Recalling that our visualization of a network always moves from left to right, we see that the node (the circle) accepts input from the left, and has a single output on the right. Here there are two inputs, but it might be hundreds.

Many inputs mapped to a single output echo how a neuron in the brain works: structures called dendrites accept input from many other neurons, and the single axon is the output. I love this analogy because it leads to a cool way of talking and thinking about the networks. But I hate the analogy because these artificial neurons are, operationally, quite different from real ones, and the analogy quickly falls apart. There is an anatomical similarity to actual neurons, but they're not the same, and it leads to confusion on the part of those who are not familiar with machine learning, causing some to believe that computer scientists are truly building artificial brains or that the networks think. The meaning of the word *think* is hard to pin down, but to me it doesn't apply to what a neural network does.

Returning now to Figure 8-2, we see two squares on the left, a bunch of lines, a circle, a line on the right, and a bunch of labels with subscripts. Let's sort this out. If we understand Figure 8-2, we'll be well on our way to understanding neural networks. Later, we'll see an implementation of our visual model in code and be surprised to learn how simple it can be.

Everything in Figure 8-2 focuses on the circle. This is the actual node. In reality, it implements a mathematical function called the *activation function*, which calculates the output of the node, a single number. The two squares are the inputs to the node. This node accepts features from an input feature vector; we use squares to differentiate from circles, but the input might just as well have come from another group of circular nodes in a previous network layer.

Each input is a number, a single scalar value, which we're calling x_0 and x_1. These inputs move to the node along the two line segments labeled w_0 and w_1. These line segments represent *weights*, the strength of the connection. Computationally, the inputs (x_0, x_1) are multiplied by the weights (w_0, w_1), summed, and given to the activation function of the node. Here we're calling the activation function h, a fairly common thing to call it.

The value of the activation function is the output of the node. Here we're calling this output a. The inputs, multiplied by the weights, are added together and given to the activation function to produce an output value. We have yet to mention the b_0 value, which is also added in and passed to the activation function. This is the *bias* term. It's an offset used to adjust the input range to make it suitable for the activation function. In Figure 8-2, we added a zero subscript. There is a bias value for each node in each layer, so the subscript here implies that this node is the first node in the layer. (Remember computer people always count from zero, not one.)

This is all that a neural network node does: a neural network node accepts multiple inputs, $x_0, x_1, \ldots$, multiplies each by a weight value, $w_0, w_1, \ldots$, sums these products along with the bias term, b, and passes this sum to the activation function, h, to produce a single scalar output value, a:

$$a = h(w_0 x_0 + w_1 x_1 + \cdots + b)$$

That's it. Get a bunch of nodes together, link them appropriately, figure out how to train them to set the weights and biases, and you have a useful neural network. As you'll see in the next chapter, training a neural network is no easy feat. But once trained, they're simple to use: feed it a feature vector, and out comes a classification.

As an aside, we've been calling these graphs *neural networks*, and will continue to do so, sometimes using the abbreviation *NN*. If you read other books or papers, you might see them called *artificial neural networks (ANNs)* or even *multi-layer perceptrons (MLPs)*, as in the sklearn `MLPClassifier` class name. I recommend sticking with *neural network*, but that's just me.

Activation Functions

Let's talk about activation functions. The activation function for a node takes a single scalar input, the sum of the inputs times the weights plus the bias, and does something to it. In particular, we need the activation function to be nonlinear so that the model can learn complex functions. Mathematically, it's easiest to see what a nonlinear function is by stating what a linear function is and then saying that any mapping that is not linear is . . . nonlinear.

A *linear function*, g, has output that is directly proportional to the input, $g(x) \propto x$, where $\propto$ means *proportional to*. Alternatively, the graph of a linear function is a straight line. Therefore, any function whose graph is not a straight line is a nonlinear function.

For example, the function

$$g(x) = 3x + 2$$

is a linear function because its graph is a straight line. A constant function like $g(x) = 1$ is also linear. However, the function

$$g(x) = x^2 + 2$$

is a nonlinear function because the exponent of x is 2. Transcendental functions are also nonlinear. *Transcendental functions* are functions like $g(x) = \log x$, or $g(x) = e^x$, where $e = 2.718...$ is the base of the natural logarithm. *Trigonometric functions* like sine and cosine, their inverses, and functions like tangent that are built from sine and cosine are also transcendental functions. These functions are transcendental because you cannot form them as finite combinations of elementary algebra operations. They are nonlinear because their graphs are not straight lines.

The network needs nonlinear activation functions; otherwise, it will be able to learn only linear mappings, and linear mappings are not sufficient to make the networks generally useful. Consider a trivial network of two nodes, each with one input. This means there's one weight and one bias value per node, and the output of the first node is the input of the second. If we set $h(x) = 5x - 3$, a linear function, then for input x the network computes output a_1 to be

$$a_1 = h(w_1 a_0 + b_1)$$

$$= h(w_1 h(w_0 x + b_0) + b_1)$$

$$= h(w_1(5(w_0 x + b_0) - 3) + b_1)$$

$$= h(w_1(5w_0 x + 5b_0 - 3) + b_1)$$

$$= h(5w_1 w_0 x + 5w_1 b_0 - 3w_1 + b_1)$$

$$= 5(5w_1 w_0 x + 5w_1 b_0 - 3w_1 + b_1) - 3$$

$$= (25w_1 w_0)x + (25w_1 b_0 - 15w_1 + 5b_1 - 3)$$

$$= Wx + B$$

for $W = 25w_1 w_0$ and $B = 25w_1 b_0 - 15w_1 + 5b_1 - 3$, which is also a linear function, another line with slope W and intercept B since neither W nor B depend on x. Therefore, a neural network with linear activation functions would learn only a linear model since the composition of linear functions is also linear. It's precisely this limitation of linear activation functions that caused the first neural network "winter" in the 1970s: research into neural networks was effectively abandoned because they were thought to be too simple to learn complex functions.

Okay, so we want nonlinear activation functions. Which ones? There are an infinite number of possibilities. In practice, a few have risen to the top because of their proven usefulness or nice properties or both. Traditional neural networks used either sigmoid activation functions or hyperbolic tangents. A *sigmoid* is

$$\sigma(x) = \frac{1}{1 + e^{-x}}$$

and the *hyperbolic tangent* is

$$\tanh(x) = \frac{e^x - e^{-x}}{e^x + e^{-x}} = \frac{e^{2x} - 1}{e^{2x} + 1}$$

Plots of both of these functions are in Figure 8-3, with the sigmoid on the top and the hyperbolic tangent on the bottom.

The first thing to notice is that both of these functions have roughly the same "S" shape. The sigmoid runs from 0 as you go further left along the x-axis to 1 as you go to the right. At 0, the function value is 0.5. The hyperbolic tangent does the same but goes from −1 to +1 and is 0 at $x = 0$.

More recently, the sigmoid and hyperbolic tangent have been replaced by the *rectified linear unit*, or *ReLU* for short. The ReLU is simple, and has convenient properties for neural networks. Even though the word *linear* is in the name, the ReLU is a nonlinear function—its graph is not a straight line. When we discuss backpropagation training of neural networks in Chapter 9, we'll learn why this change has happened.

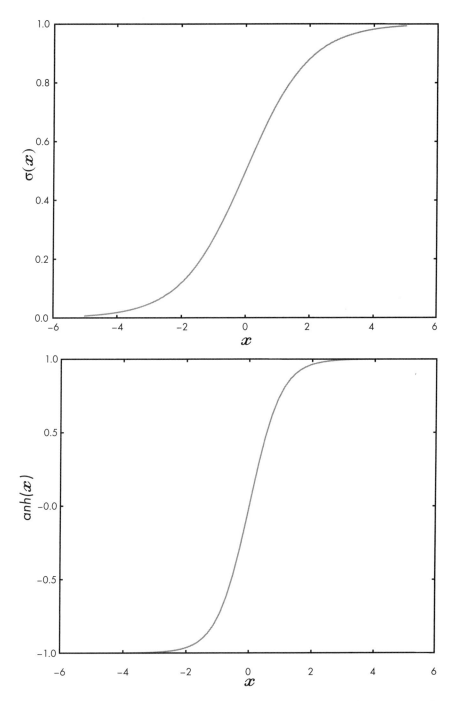

Figure 8-3: A sigmoid function (top) and a hyperbolic tangent function (bottom). Note that the y-axis scales are not the same.

The ReLU is as follows and is shown in Figure 8-4.

$$\text{ReLU}(x) = \max(0, x) = \begin{cases} 0, & \text{if } x < 0 \\ x, & \text{otherwise} \end{cases}$$

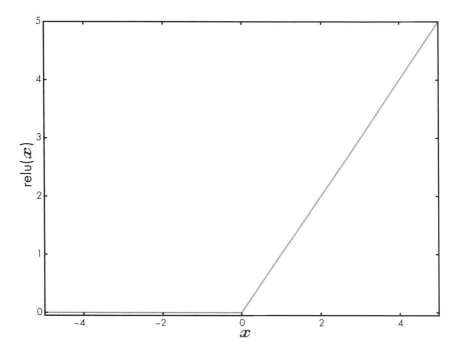

Figure 8-4: The rectified linear activation function, ReLU(x) = max(0,x)

ReLU is called *rectified* because it removes the negative values and replaces them with 0. In truth, the machine learning community uses several different versions of this function, but all are essentially replacing negative values with a constant or some other value. The piecewise nature of the ReLU is what makes it nonlinear and, therefore, suitable for use as a neural network activation function. It's also computationally simple, far faster to calculate than either the sigmoid or the hyperbolic tangent. This is because the latter functions use e^x, which, in computer terms, means a call to the exp function. This function is typically implemented as a sum of terms of a series expansion, translating into dozens of floating-point operations in place of the single `if` statement necessary to implement a ReLU. Small savings like this add up in an extensive network with potentially thousands of nodes.

Architecture of a Network

We've discussed nodes and how they work, and hinted that nodes are connected to form networks. Let's look more closely at how nodes are connected, the *architecture* of the network.

Standard neural networks like the ones we are working with in this chapter are built in layers, as you saw in Figure 8-1. We don't need to do this, but as we'll see, this buys us some computational simplicity and greatly simplifies training. A feedforward network has an input layer, one or more hidden layers, and an output layer. The input layer is simply the feature vector, and the output layer is the prediction (probability). If the network is for a multiclass problem, the output layer might have more than one node, with each node representing the model's prediction for each of the possible classes of inputs.

The hidden layers are made of nodes, and the nodes of layer i accept as input the output of the nodes of layer $i - 1$ and pass their outputs to the inputs of the nodes of layer $i + 1$. The connections between the layers are typically fully connected, meaning every output of every node of layer $i - 1$ is used as an input to every node of layer i, hence *fully connected*. Again, we don't need to do this, but it simplifies the implementation.

The number of hidden layers and the number of nodes in each hidden layer define the architecture of the network. It has been proven that a single hidden layer with enough nodes can learn any function mapping. This is good because it means neural networks are applicable to machine learning problems since, in the end, the model acts as a complex function mapping inputs to output labels and probabilities. However, like many theoretical results, this does not mean that it's practical for a single layer network to be used in all situations. As the number of nodes (and layers) in a network grows, so, too, does the number of parameters to learn (weights and biases), and therefore the amount of training data needed goes up as well. It's the curse of dimensionality again.

Issues like these stymied neural networks for a second time in the 1980s. Computers were too slow to train large networks, and, regardless, there was usually too little data available to train the network anyway. Practitioners knew that if both of these situations changed, then it would become possible to train large networks that would be far more capable than the small networks of the time. Fortunately for the world, the situation changed in the early 2000s.

Selecting the proper neural network architecture has a huge impact on whether or not your model will learn anything. This is where experience and intuition come in. Selecting the right architecture is the dark art of using neural networks. Let's try to be more helpful by giving some (crude) rules of thumb:

- If your input has definite spatial relationships, like the parts of an image, you might want to use a convolutional neural network instead (Chapter 12).

- Use no more than three hidden layers. Recall, in theory, one sufficiently large hidden layer is all that is needed, so use as few hidden layers as necessary. If the model learns with one hidden layer, then add a second to see if that improves things.

- The number of nodes in the first hidden layer should match or (ideally) exceed the number of input vector features.

- Except for the first hidden layer (see previous rule), the number of nodes per hidden layer should be the same as or some value between the number of nodes in the previous layer and the following layer. If layer $i - 1$ has N nodes and layer $i + 1$ has M nodes, then layer i might be good with $N \leq x \leq M$ nodes.

The first rule says that a traditional neural network best applies to situations where your input does not have spatial relationships—that is, you have a feature vector, not an image. Also, when your input dimension is small, or when you do not have a lot of data, which makes it hard to train a larger convolutional network, you should give a traditional network a try. If you do think you are in a situation where a traditional neural network is called for, start small, and grow it as long as performance improves.

Output Layers

The last layer of a neural network is the output layer. If the network is modeling a continuous value, known as *regression*, a use case we're ignoring in this book, then the output layer is a node that doesn't use an activation function; it simply reports the argument to h in Figure 8-2. Note that this is the same as saying that the activation function is the identity function, $h(x) = x$.

Our neural networks are for classification; we want them to output a decision value. If we have two classes labeled 0 and 1, we make the activation function of the final node a sigmoid. This will output a value between 0 and 1 that we can interpret as a likelihood or probability that the input belongs to class 1. We make our classification decision based on the output value with a simple rule: if the activation value is less than 0.5, call the input class 0; otherwise, call it class 1. We'll see in Chapter 11 how changing this threshold of 0.5 can be used to tune a model's performance for the task at hand.

If we have more than two classes, we need to take a different approach. Instead of a single node in the output layer, we'll have N output nodes, one for each class, each one using the identity function for h. Then, we apply a *softmax* operation to these N outputs and select the output with the largest softmax value.

Let's illustrate what we mean by softmax. Suppose we have a dataset with four classes in it. What they represent doesn't really matter; the network doesn't know what they represent, either. The classes are labeled 0, 1, 2, and 3. So, $N = 4$ means our network will have four output nodes, each one using the identity function for h. This looks like Figure 8-5, where we have also shown the softmax operation and the resulting output vector.

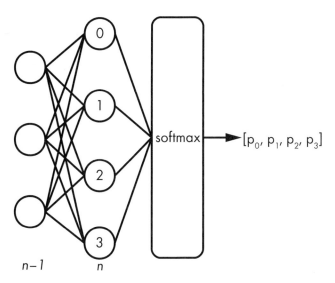

Figure 8-5: The last hidden layer n-1 and output layer (n, nodes numbered) for a neural network with four classes. The softmax operation is applied, producing a four-element output vector, $[p_0, p_1, p_2, p_3]$.

We select the index of the largest value in this output vector as the class label for the given input feature vector. The softmax operation ensures that the elements of this vector sum to 1, so we can again be a bit sloppy and call these values the probability of belonging to each of the four classes. That is why we take only the largest value to decide the output class label.

The softmax operation is straightforward: the probability for each of the outputs is simply

$$p_i = \frac{e^{a_i}}{\sum_j e^{a_j}}$$

where a_i is the i-th output, and the denominator is the sum over all the outputs. For the example, $i = 0, 1, 2, 3$, and the index of the largest value will be the class label assigned to the input.

As an example, assume the output of the four last layer nodes is

$$a_0 = 0.2$$

$$a_1 = 1.3$$

$$a_2 = 0.8$$

$$a_3 = 2.1$$

Then calculate the softmax as follows:

$$p_0 = e^{0.2} / (e^{0.2} + e^{1.3} + e^{0.8} + e^{2.1}) = 0.080$$

$$p_1 = e^{1.3} / (e^{0.2} + e^{1.3} + e^{0.8} + e^{2.1}) = 0.240$$

$$p_2 = e^{0.8} / (e^{0.2} + e^{1.3} + e^{0.8} + e^{2.1}) = 0.146$$

$$p_3 = e^{2.1} / (e^{0.2} + e^{1.3} + e^{0.8} + e^{2.1}) = 0.534$$

Select class 3 because p_3 is the largest. Note that the sum of the p_i values is 1.0, as we would expect.

Two points should be mentioned here. In the preceding equations, we used the sigmoid to calculate the output of the network. If we set the number of classes to 2 and calculate the softmax, we'll get two output values: one will be some p, and the other will be $1 - p$. This is identical to the sigmoid alone, selecting the probability of the input being of class 1.

The second point has to do with implementing the softmax. If the network outputs, the a values, are large, then e^a might be very large, which is something the computer will not like. Precision will be lost, at least, or the value might overflow and make the output meaningless. Numerically, if we subtract the largest a value from all the others before calculating the softmax, we'll take the exponential over smaller values that are less likely to overflow. Doing this for the preceding example gives new a values

$$a_0' = 0.2 - 2.1 = -1.9$$

$$a_1' = 1.3 - 2.1 = -0.8$$

$$a_2' = 0.8 - 2.1 = -1.3$$

$$a_3' = 2.1 - 2.1 = 0.0$$

where we subtract 2.1 because that is the largest a value. This leads to precisely the same p values we found before, but this time protected against overflow in the case that any of the a values are too large.

Representing Weights and Biases

Before we move on to an example neural network, let's revisit the weights and biases and see that we can greatly simplify the implementation of a neural network by viewing it in terms of matrices and vectors.

Consider the mapping from an input feature vector of two elements to the first hidden layer with three nodes (a_1 in Figure 8-1). Let's label the edges between the two layers (the weights) as w_{ij} with $i = 0, 1$ for the inputs x_0 and x_1 and $j = 0, 1, 2$ for the three hidden layer nodes numbered from top to bottom of the figure. Additionally, we need three bias values that are not shown in the figure, one for each hidden node. We'll call these b_0, b_1, and b_2, again, top to bottom.

In order to calculate the outputs of the activation functions, h, for the three hidden nodes, we need to find the following.

$$a_0 = h(w_{00}x_0 + w_{10}x_1 + b_0)$$

$$a_1 = h(w_{01}x_0 + w_{11}x_1 + b_1)$$

$$a_2 = h(w_{02}x_0 + w_{12}x_1 + b_2)$$

But, remembering how matrix multiplication and vector addition work, we see that this is exactly

$$\vec{a} = h\left(\begin{bmatrix} w_{00} & w_{10} \\ w_{01} & w_{11} \\ w_{02} & w_{12} \end{bmatrix} \begin{bmatrix} x_0 \\ x_1 \end{bmatrix} + \begin{bmatrix} b_0 \\ b_1 \\ b_2 \end{bmatrix}\right) = h(W\vec{x} + \vec{b})$$

where $\vec{a} = (a_0, a_1, a_2)$, $\vec{x} = (x_0, x_1)$, $\vec{b} = (b_0, b_1, b_2)$, and W is a 3×2 matrix of weight values. In this case, the activation function, h, is given a vector of input values and produces a vector of output values. This is simply applying h to every element of $W\vec{x} + \vec{b}$. For example, applying h to a vector $\vec{x}$ with three elements is

$$h(\vec{x}) = h((x_0, x_1, x_2)) = (h(x_0), h(x_1), h(x_2))$$

with h applied separately to each element of $\vec{x}$.

Since the NumPy Python module is designed to work with arrays, and matrices and vectors are arrays, we arrive at the pleasant conclusion that the weights and biases of a neural network can be stored in NumPy arrays and we need only simple matrix operations (calls to np.dot) and addition to work with a fully connected neural network. Note this is why we want to use fully connected networks: their implementation is straightforward.

To store the network of Figure 8-1, we need a weight matrix and bias vector between each layer, giving us three matrices and three vectors: a matrix and vector each for the input to the first hidden layer, the first hidden layer to the second, and the second hidden layer to the output. The weight matrices are of dimensions 3×2, 2×3, and 1×2, respectively. The bias vectors are of length 3, 2, and 1.

Implementing a Simple Neural Network

In this section, we'll implement the sample neural network of Figure 8-1 and train it on two features from the iris dataset. We'll implement the network from scratch but use sklearn to train it. The goal of this section is to see how straightforward it is to implement a simple neural network. Hopefully, this will clear some of the fog that might be hanging around from the discussion of the previous sections.

The network of Figure 8-1 accepts an input feature vector with two features. It has two hidden layers, one with three nodes and the other with two nodes. It has one sigmoid output. The activation functions of the hidden nodes are also sigmoids.

Building the Dataset

Before we look at the neural network code, let's build the dataset we'll train against and see what it looks like. We know the iris dataset already, but for this example, we'll use only two classes and only two of the four features. The code to build the train and test datasets is in Listing 8-1.

```
import numpy as np
❶ d = np.load("iris_train_features_augmented.npy")
  l = np.load("iris_train_labels_augmented.npy")
  d1 = d[np.where(l==1)]
  d2 = d[np.where(l==2)]
❷ a=len(d1)
  b=len(d2)
  x = np.zeros((a+b,2))
  x[:a,:] = d1[:,2:]
  x[a:,:] = d2[:,2:]
❸ y = np.array([0]*a+[1]*b)
  i = np.argsort(np.random.random(a+b))
  x = x[i]
  y = y[i]
❹ np.save("iris2_train.npy", x)
  np.save("iris2_train_labels.npy", y)
❺ d = np.load("iris_test_features_augmented.npy")
  l = np.load("iris_test_labels_augmented.npy")
  d1 = d[np.where(l==1)]
  d2 = d[np.where(l==2)]
  a=len(d1)
  b=len(d2)
  x = np.zeros((a+b,2))
  x[:a,:] = d1[:,2:]
  x[a:,:] = d2[:,2:]
  y = np.array([0]*a+[1]*b)
  i = np.argsort(np.random.random(a+b))
  x = x[i]
```

```
y = y[i]
np.save("iris2_test.npy", x)
np.save("iris2_test_labels.npy", y)
```

Listing 8-1: Building the simple example dataset. See nn_iris_dataset.py.

This code is straightforward data munging. We start with the augmented dataset and load the samples and labels ❶. We want only class 1 and class 2, so we find the indices of those samples and pull them out. We're keeping only features 2 and 3 and put them in x ❷. Next, we build the labels (y) ❸. Note, we recode the class labels to 0 and 1. Finally, we scramble the order of the samples and write the new dataset to disk ❹. Last of all, we repeat this process to build the test samples ❺.

Figure 8-6 shows the training set. We can plot it in this case because we have only two features.

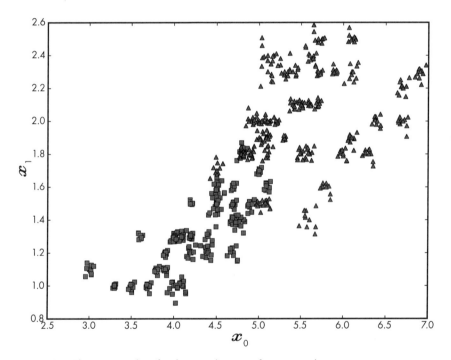

Figure 8-6: The training data for the two-class, two-feature iris dataset

We immediately see that this dataset is not trivially separable. There is no simple line we can draw that will correctly split the training set into two groups, one all class 0 and the other all class 1. This makes things a little more interesting.

Implementing the Neural Network

Let's see how to implement the network of Figure 8-1 in Python using NumPy. We'll assume that it's already trained, meaning we already know all the weights and biases. The code is in Listing 8-2.

```
import numpy as np
import pickle
import sys

def sigmoid(x):
    return 1.0 / (1.0 + np.exp(-x))

def evaluate(x, y, w):
❶   w12,b1,w23,b2,w34,b3 = w
    nc = nw = 0
    prob = np.zeros(len(y))
    for i in range(len(y)):
        a1 = sigmoid(np.dot(x[i], w12) + b1)
        a2 = sigmoid(np.dot(a1, w23) + b2)
        prob[i] = sigmoid(np.dot(a2, w34) + b3)
        z  = 0 if prob[i] < 0.5 else 1
❷   if (z == y[i]):
            nc += 1
        else:
            nw += 1
    return [float(nc) / float(nc + nw), prob]

❸ xtest = np.load("iris2_test.npy")
  ytest = np.load("iris2_test_labels.npy")
❹ weights = pickle.load(open("iris2_weights.pkl","rb"))
  score, prob = evaluate(xtest, ytest, weights)
  print()
  for i in range(len(prob)):
      print("%3d:  actual: %d  predict: %d  prob: %0.7f" %
      (i, ytest[i], 0 if (prob[i] < 0.5) else 1, prob[i]))
  print("Score = %0.4f" % score)
```

Listing 8-2: Using the trained weights and biases to classify held-out test samples. See nn_iris_evaluate.py.

Perhaps the first thing we should notice is how short the code is. The evaluate function implements the network. We also need to define sigmoid as NumPy does not have it natively. The main code loads the test samples (xtest) and associated labels (ytest) ❸. These are the files generated by the preceding code, so we know that xtest is of shape 23×2 because we have 23 test samples, and each has two features. Similarly, ytest is a vector of 23 labels.

When we train this network, we'll store the weights and biases as a list of NumPy arrays. The Python way to store a list on disk is via the pickle module, so we use pickle to load the list from disk ❹. The list weights has six elements representing the three weight matrices and three bias vectors that define the network. These are the "magic" numbers that our training has conditioned to the dataset. Finally, we call evaluate to run each of the test samples through the network. This function returns the score (accuracy) and the output probabilities for each sample (prob). The remainder of the code displays the sample number, actual label, predicted label, and associated output probability of being class 1. Finally, the score (accuracy) is shown.

The network is implemented in evaluate; let's see how. First, pull the individual weight matrices and bias vectors from the supplied weight list ❶. These are NumPy arrays: w12 is a 2×3 matrix mapping the two-element input to the first hidden layer with three nodes, w23 is a 3×2 matrix mapping the first hidden layer to the second hidden layer, and w34 is a 2×1 matrix mapping the second hidden layer to the output. The bias vectors are b1, three elements; b2, two elements; and b3, a single element (a scalar).

Notice the weight matrices are not of the same shape as we previously indicated they would be. They are transposes. This is because we're multiplying vectors, which are treated as 1×2 matrices, by the weight matrices. Because scalar multiplication is commutative, meaning $ab = ba$, we see that we're still calculating the same argument value for the activation function.

Next, evaluate sets the number correct (nc) and number wrong (nw) counters to 0. These are for calculating the overall score across the entire test set. Similarly, we define prob, a vector to hold the output probability value for each of the test samples.

The loop applies the entire network to each test sample. First, we map the input vectors to the first hidden layer and calculate a_1, a vector of three numbers, the activation for each of the three hidden nodes. We then take these first hidden layer activations and calculate the second hidden layer activations, a_2. This is a two-element vector as there are two nodes in the second hidden layer. Next, we calculate the output value for the current input vector and store it in the prob array. The class label, z, is assigned by checking if the output value of the network is < 0.5 or not. Finally, we increment the correct (nc) or incorrect (nw) counters based on the actual label for this sample (y[i]) ❷. When all samples have been passed through the network, the overall accuracy is returned as the number of correctly classified samples divided by the total number of samples.

This is all well and good; we can implement a network and pass input vectors through it to see how well it does. If the network had a third hidden layer, we would pass the output of the second hidden layer (a2) through it before calculating the final output value.

Training and Testing the Neural Network

The code in Listing 8-2 applies the trained model to the test data. To train the model in the first place, we'll use sklearn. The code to train the model is in Listing 8-3.

```
import numpy as np
import pickle
from sklearn.neural_network import MLPClassifier
```

```
    xtrain= np.load("iris2_train.npy")
    ytrain= np.load("iris2_train_labels.npy")
    xtest = np.load("iris2_test.npy")
    ytest = np.load("iris2_test_labels.npy")

❶ clf = MLPClassifier(
    ❷ hidden_layer_sizes=(3,2),
    ❸ activation="logistic",
        solver="adam", tol=1e-9,
        max_iter=5000,
        verbose=True)
    clf.fit(xtrain, ytrain)
    prob = clf.predict_proba(xtest)
    score = clf.score(xtest, ytest)

❹ w12 = clf.coefs_[0]
    w23 = clf.coefs_[1]
    w34 = clf.coefs_[2]
    b1 = clf.intercepts_[0]
    b2 = clf.intercepts_[1]
    b3 = clf.intercepts_[2]
    weights = [w12,b1,w23,b2,w34,b3]
    pickle.dump(weights, open("iris2_weights.pkl","wb"))

    print()
    print("Test results:")
    print("  Overall score: %0.7f" % score)
    print()
    for i in range(len(ytest)):
        p = 0 if (prob[i,1] < 0.5) else 1
        print("%03d: %d - %d, %0.7f" % (i, ytest[i], p, prob[i,1]))
    print()
```

Listing 8-3: Using sklearn to train the iris neural network. See nn_iris_mlpclassifier.py.

First, we load the training and testing data from disk. These are the same files we created previously. Then we set up the neural network object, an instance of MLPClassifier ❶. The network has two hidden layers, the first with three nodes and the second with two nodes ❷. This matches the architecture in Figure 8-1. The network is also using *logistic* layers ❸. This is another name for a sigmoid layer. We train the model by calling fit just as we did for other sklearn model types. Since we set verbose to True, we'll get output showing us the loss for each iteration.

Calling predict_proba gives us the output probabilities on the test data. This method is also supported by most other sklearn models. This is the model's certainty as to the assigned output label. We then call score to calculate the score over the test set as we have done before.

We want to store the learned weights and biases so we can use them with our test code. We can pull them directly from the trained model ❹. These are packed into a list (weights) and dumped to a Python pickle file.

The remaining code prints the results of running the sklearn trained model against the held-out test data. For example, a particular run of this code gives

```
Test results:
  Overall score: 1.0000000

000: 0 - 0, 0.0705069
001: 1 - 1, 0.8066224
002: 0 - 0, 0.0308244
003: 0 - 0, 0.0205917
004: 1 - 1, 0.9502825
005: 0 - 0, 0.0527558
006: 1 - 1, 0.9455174
007: 0 - 0, 0.0365360
008: 1 - 1, 0.9471218
009: 0 - 0, 0.0304762
010: 0 - 0, 0.0304762
011: 0 - 0, 0.0165365
012: 1 - 1, 0.9453844
013: 0 - 0, 0.0527558
014: 1 - 1, 0.9495079
015: 1 - 1, 0.9129983
016: 1 - 1, 0.8931552
017: 0 - 0, 0.1197567
018: 0 - 0, 0.0406094
019: 0 - 0, 0.0282220
020: 1 - 1, 0.9526721
021: 0 - 0, 0.1436263
022: 1 - 1, 0.9446458
```

indicating that the model was perfect against the small test dataset. The output shows the sample number, the actual class label, the assigned class label, and the output probability of being class 1. If we run the pickle file holding the sklearn network's weights and biases through our evaluation code, we see that the output probabilities are precisely the same as the preceding code, indicating that our hand-generated neural network implementation is working correctly.

Summary

In this chapter, we discussed the anatomy of a neural network. We described the architecture, the arrangement of nodes, and the connections between them. We discussed the output layer nodes and the functions they compute. We then saw that all the weights and biases could be conveniently represented by matrices and vectors. Finally, we presented a simple network for classifying a subset of the iris data and showed how it could be trained and evaluated.

Now that we have our feet wet, let's move on and dive into the theory behind neural networks.

9

TRAINING A NEURAL NETWORK

In this chapter, we'll discuss how to train a neural network. We'll look at the standard approaches and tricks being used in the field today. There will be some math, some hand-waving, and a whole host of new terms and concepts. But you don't need to follow the math at a deep level: we'll gloss over things as needed to get the main point across.

This chapter is perhaps the most challenging in the book, at least conceptually. It certainly is mathematically. While it's crucially important to building intuition and understanding, sometimes we get impatient and like to dive into things first to test the waters. Thanks to preexisting libraries, we can do that here. If you want to play around with neural networks before learning how they work, jump to Chapter 10 before coming back here to fill in the theory. But do come back.

It's possible to learn to use powerful toolkits like sklearn and Keras without understanding how they work. That approach should not satisfy anyone, though the temptation is real. Understanding how these algorithms work is well worth your time.

A High-Level Overview

Let's begin this chapter with an overview of the concepts we'll discuss. Read it, but don't fret if the concepts are unclear. Instead, try to get a feel for the overall process.

The first step in training a neural network is selecting intelligent initial values for the weights and biases. We then use *gradient descent* to modify these weights and biases so that we reduce the error over the training set. We'll use the average value of the loss function to measure the error, which tells us how wrong the network currently is. We know if the network is right or wrong because we have the expected output for each input sample in the training set (the class label).

Gradient descent is an algorithm that requires gradients. For now, think of gradients as measures of steepness. The larger the gradient, the steeper the function is at that point. To use gradient descent to search for the smallest value of the loss function, we need to be able to find gradients. For that, we'll use *backpropagation*. This is the fundamental algorithm of neural networks, the one that allows them to learn successfully. It gives us the gradients we need by starting at the output of the network and moving back through the network toward the input. Along the way, it calculates the gradient value for each weight and bias.

With the gradient values, we can use the gradient descent algorithm to update the weights and biases so that the next time we pass the training samples through the network, the average of the loss function will be less than it was before. In other words, our network will be less wrong. This is the goal of training, and we hope it results in a network that has learned general features of the data.

Learning general features of the dataset requires *regularization*. There are many approaches to regularization, and we'll discuss the main ones. Without regularization, the training process is in danger of overfitting, and we could end up with a network that doesn't generalize. But with regularization, we can be successful and get a useful model.

So, the following sections introduce gradient descent, backpropagation, loss functions, weight initialization, and, finally, regularization. These are the main components of successful neural network training. We don't need to understand these in all their gory mathematical details; instead, we need to understand them conceptually so we can build an intuitive approach to what it means to train a neural network. With this intuition, we'll be able to make meaningful use of the parameters that sklearn and Keras give us for training.

Gradient Descent

The standard way to train a neural network is to use gradient descent.

Let's parse the phrase *gradient descent*. We already know what the word *descent* means. It means to go down from somewhere higher up. What about *gradient*? The short answer is that a gradient indicates how quickly something changes with respect to how fast something else changes. Measuring how much one thing changes as another changes is something we're all familiar with. We all know about speed, which is how position changes as time changes. We even say it in words: *miles per hour* or *kilometers per hour*.

You're probably already familiar with the gradient in another context. Consider the equation of a line

$$y = mx + b$$

where m is the slope and b is the y-axis intercept. The slope is how quickly the line's y position changes with each change in the x position. If we know two points that are on the line, (x_0, y_0) and (x_1, y_1), then we can calculate the slope as

$$m = \frac{y_0 - y_1}{x_0 - x_1}$$

which, in words, we might say as "y's per x." It's a measure of how steep or shallow the line is: its gradient. In mathematics, we often talk about a change in a variable, and the notation for that is to put a Δ (delta) in front. So, we might write the slope of a line as

$$m = \frac{\Delta y}{\Delta x}$$

to drive home the point that the slope is the change in y for each change in x. Fortunately for us, it turns out that not only do lines have a slope at each point, but also most functions have a slope at each point. However, except for straight lines, this slope changes from point to point. A picture will help here. Consider Figure 9-1.

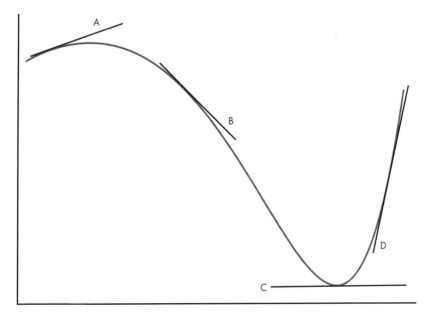

Figure 9-1: A function with several tangent lines indicated

The graph in Figure 9-1 is of a polynomial. Notice the lines drawn on the figure that are just touching the function. These are *tangent* lines. And as lines, they have a slope we can see in the plot. Now imagine moving one of the lines over the function so that it continues to touch the function at only one point; imagine how the slope of the line changes as it moves.

It turns out that how the slope changes over the function is itself a function, and it's called the *derivative*. Given a function and x value, the derivative tells us the slope of the function at that point, x. The fact that functions have derivatives is a fundamental insight of calculus, and of fundamental importance to us.

The notion of a derivative is essential because for single variable functions, the derivative at the point x is the gradient at x; it's the direction in which the function is changing. If we want to find the minimum of the function, the x that gives us the smallest y, we want to move in the direction *opposite* to the gradient as that will move us in the direction of the minimum.

The derivative is written in many different ways, but the way that echoes the idea of the slope, how y changes for a change in x, is

$$\frac{dy}{dx}$$

We'll return to this form next when discussing the backpropagation algorithm. That's it for the gradient; now let's take a closer look at descent.

Finding Minimums

Since we want a model that makes few mistakes, we need to find the set of parameters that lead to a small value for the loss function. In other words, we need to find a *minimum* of the loss function.

Look again at Figure 9-1. The minimum is on the right, where tangent line C is. We can see it's the minimum, and notice that the gradient is 0 there. This tells us we're at a minimum (or maximum). If we start at B, we see that the slope of the tangent line is negative (down and to the right). Therefore, we need to move to an x value in the positive direction because this is opposite to the sign of the gradient. Doing this will take us closer to the minimum at C. Similarly, if we start at D, the slope of the tangent line is positive (up and to the right) meaning we need to move in the negative x direction, again toward C, to move closer to the minimum. All of this hints at an algorithm for finding the minimum of a function: pick a starting point (an x value) and use the gradient to move to a lower point.

For simple functions of just x, like those of Figure 9-1, this approach will work nicely, assuming we start in a good place like B or D. When we move to more than one dimension, it turns out that this approach will still work nicely provided we start in a good place with our initial guess.

Working still with Figure 9-1 and assuming we're starting at B, we see that the gradient tells us to move to the right, toward C. But how do we select the next x value to consider, to move us closer to C? This is the step size, and it tells us how big a jump we make from one x position to the next. Step size is a parameter we have to choose, and in practice this value, called the *learning rate*, is often fluid and gets smaller and smaller as we move, under the assumption that as we move, we get closer and closer to the minimum value and therefore need smaller and smaller steps.

This is all well and good, even intuitive, but we have a small problem. What if instead of starting at B or D, we start at A? The gradient at A is pointing us to the left, not the right. In this case, our simple algorithm will fail—it will move us to the left, and we'll never reach C. The figure shows only one minimum, at C, but we can easily imagine a second minimum, say to the left of A, that doesn't go as low (doesn't have as small a y value) as C. If we start at A, we'll move toward this minimum, and not the one at C. Our algorithm will fall into a *local minimum*. Once in, our algorithm can't get us out, and we won't be able to find the global minimum at C. We'll see that this is a genuine issue for neural networks, but one that for modern deep networks is, almost magically, not much of an issue after all.

So how does all of this help us train a neural network? The gradient tells us how a small change in x changes y. If x is one of the parameters of our network and y is the error given by the loss function, then the gradient tells us how much a change in that parameter affects the overall error of the network. Once we know that, we're in a position to modify the parameter by an amount based on the gradient, and we know that this will move us toward a minimum error. When the error over the training set is at a minimum, we can claim that the network has been trained.

Let's talk a bit more about the gradients and parameters. All of our discussion to this point, based on Figure 9-1, has been rather one-dimensional; our functions are functions of x only. We talked about changing one thing, the position along the x-axis, to see how it affects the y position. In reality, we're not working with just one dimension. Every weight and bias in our network is a parameter, and the loss function value depends upon all of them. For the simple network in Figure 8-1 alone, there are 20 parameters, meaning that the loss function is a 20-dimensional function. Regardless, our approach remains much the same: if we know the gradient for each parameter, we can still apply our algorithm in an attempt to locate a set of parameters minimizing the loss.

Updating the Weights

We'll talk about how to get gradient values in a bit, but for the time being let's assume we have them already. We'll say that we have a set of numbers that tells us how, given the current configuration of the network, a change in any weight or bias value changes the loss. With that knowledge, we can apply gradient descent: we adjust the weight or bias by some fraction of that gradient value to move us, collectively, toward a minimum of the entire loss function.

Mathematically, we update each weight and bias using a simple rule:

$$w \leftarrow w - \eta \Delta w$$

Here w is one of the weights (or biases), η (eta) is the learning rate (the step size), and Δw is the gradient value.

Listing 9-1 gives an algorithm for training a neural network using gradient descent.

---

1. Pick some intelligent starting values for the weights and biases.
2. Run the training set through the network using its current weights and biases and calculate the average loss.
3. Use this loss to get the gradient for each weight and bias.
4. Update the weight or bias value by the step size times the gradient value.
5. Repeat from step 2 until the loss is low enough.

Listing 9-1: Gradient descent in five (deceptively) simple steps

The algorithm appears simple, but as they say, the devil is in the details. We have to make choices at every step, and every choice we make will prompt further questions. For example, step 1 says to "Pick some intelligent starting values." What should they be? It turns out that successfully training a neural network depends critically on choosing good initial values. We already saw how this might be so in our preceding example using Figure 9-1 where if we start at A, we won't find the minimum at C. Much research has been conducted over the years related to step 1.

Step 2 is straightforward; it's the forward-pass through the network. We haven't talked in detail about the loss function itself; for now, just think of it as a function measuring the effectiveness of the network on the training set.

Step 3 is a black box for the time being. We'll explore how to do it shortly. For now, assume we can find the gradient values for each parameter.

Step 4 follows the form of the previous equation that moves the parameter from its current value to one that will reduce the overall loss. In practice, the simple form of this equation is not sufficient; there are other terms, like momentum, that preserve some fraction of the previous weight change for the next iteration (next pass of the training data through the network) so that parameters do not change too wildly. We'll revisit momentum later. For now, let's look at a variation of gradient descent, the one that is actually used to train deep networks.

Stochastic Gradient Descent

The previous steps describe gradient descent training of a neural network. As we might expect, in practice there are many different flavors of this basic idea. One that's in widespread use and works well empirically is called *stochastic gradient descent (SGD)*. The word *stochastic* refers to a random process. We'll see next why the word *stochastic* goes before *gradient descent* in this case.

Batches and Minibatches

Step 2 of Listing 9-1 says to run the complete training set through the network using the current values of the weights and biases. This approach is called *batch training*, so named because we use all of the training data to estimate the gradients. Intuitively, this is a reasonable thing to do: we've carefully constructed the training set to be a fair representation of the unknown parent process that generates the data, and it's this parent process we want the network to successfully model for us.

If our dataset is small, like the original iris dataset of Chapter 5, then batch training makes sense. But what if our training dataset isn't small? What if it's hundreds of thousands or even millions of samples? We'll be facing longer and longer training times.

We've run into a problem. We want a large training set as that will (hopefully) better represent the unknown parent process that we want to model. But the larger the training set, the longer it takes to pass each sample through the network, get an average value for the loss, and update the weights and biases. We call passing the entire training set through the network an *epoch*, and we'll need many dozens to hundreds of epochs to train the network. Doing a better job of representing the thing we want to model means longer and longer computation times because of all the samples that must be passed through the network.

This is where SGD comes into play. Instead of using all the training data on each pass, let's alternatively select a small subset of the training data and use the average loss calculated from it to update the parameters. We'll calculate an "incorrect" gradient value because we're estimating the loss over the full training set using only a small sample, but we'll save a lot of time.

Let's see how this sampling plays out with a simple example. We'll define a vector of 100 random bytes using NumPy:

```
>>> d = np.random.normal(128,20,size=100).astype("uint8")
>>> d
130, 141,  99, 106, 135, 119,  98, 147, 152, 163, 118, 149, 122,
133, 115, 128, 176, 132, 173, 145, 152,  79, 124, 133, 158, 111,
139, 140, 126, 117, 175, 123, 154, 115, 130, 108, 139, 129, 113,
129, 123, 135, 112, 146, 125, 134, 141, 136, 155, 152, 101, 149,
137, 119, 143, 136, 118, 161, 138, 112, 124,  86, 135, 161, 112,
117, 145, 140, 123, 110, 163, 122, 105, 135, 132, 145, 121,  92,
118, 125, 154, 148,  92, 142, 118, 128, 128, 129, 125, 121, 139,
152, 122, 128, 126, 126, 157, 124, 120, 152
```

Here the byte values are normally distributed around a mean of 128. The actual mean of the 100 values is 130.9. Selecting subsets of these values, 10 at a time, gives us an estimate of the actual mean value

```
>>> i = np.argsort(np.random.random(100))
>>> d[i[:10]].mean()
138.9
```

with repeated subsets leading to estimated means of 135.7, 131.7, 134.2, 128.1, and so forth.

None of the estimated means are the actual mean, but they are all close to it. If we can estimate the mean from a random subset of the full dataset, we can see by analogy that we should be able to estimate the gradients of the loss function with a subset of the full training set. Since the sample is randomly selected, the resulting gradient values are randomly varying estimates. This is why we add the word *stochastic* in front of *gradient descent*.

Because passing the full training set through the network on each weight and bias update step is known as *batch training*, passing a subset through is known as *minibatch training*. You will hear people use the term *minibatch* quite frequently. A minibatch is the subset of the training data used for each stochastic gradient descent step. Training is usually some number of epochs, where the relationship between epochs and minibatches is as follows:

$$1 \text{ epoch} = \left(\frac{\textit{number of training set samples}}{\textit{minibatch size}} \right) \text{ minibatches}$$

In practice, we don't really want to select the minibatches at random from the full training set. If we do that, we run the risk of not using all the samples: some might never be selected, and others might be selected too often. Typically, we randomize the order of the training samples and select fixed-size blocks of samples sequentially whenever a minibatch is required. When all available training samples are used, we can shuffle the full training set order and repeat the process. Some deep learning toolkits don't even do this; they instead cycle through the same set of minibatches again.

Convex vs. Nonconvex Functions

SGD sounds like a concession to practicality. In theory, it seems that we'd never want to use it, and we might expect that our training results will suffer because of it. However, the opposite is generally true. In some sense, gradient descent training of a neural network shouldn't work at all because we're applying an algorithm meant for convex functions to one that is nonconvex. Figure 9-2 illustrates the difference between a convex function and a nonconvex function.

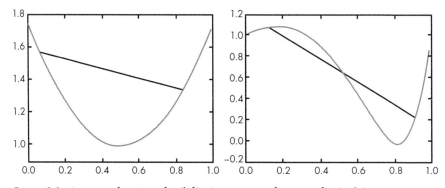

Figure 9-2: A convex function of x (left). A nonconvex function of x (right).

A convex function is such that a line segment between any two points on the function does not cross the function at any other point. The black line on the left of Figure 9-2 is one example, and any such segment will not cross the function at any other point, indicating that this is a convex function. However, the same can't be said of the curve on the right of Figure 9-2. This is the curve from Figure 9-1. Here the black line does cross the function.

Gradient descent is designed to find the minimum when the function is convex, and because it relies only on the gradient, the first derivative, it's sometimes known as a *first-order* optimization method. Gradient descent should not work, in general, with nonconvex functions because it runs the risk of getting trapped in a local minimum instead of finding the global minimum. Again, we saw this with the example in Figure 9-1.

Here's where stochastic gradient descent helps. In multiple dimensions, the gradient will point in a direction that isn't necessarily toward the nearest minimum of the loss function. This means that our step will be in a slightly wrong direction, but that somewhat wrong direction might help us avoid getting trapped somewhere we don't want to be.

The situation is more complicated, of course, and more mysterious. The machine learning community has been struggling with the contradiction between the obvious success of using first-order optimization on the nonconvex loss function and the fact that it shouldn't work at all.

Two ideas are emerging. The first is what we just stated, that stochastic gradient descent helps by actually moving us in a slightly wrong direction. The second idea, which seems to be pretty much proven now, is that, for the loss functions used in deep learning, it turns out that there are many, many local minimums and that these are all basically the same, so that landing in almost any one of them will result in a network that performs well.

Some researchers argue that most gradient descent learning winds up on a *saddle point*; this is a place that looks like a minimum but isn't. Imagine a saddle for a horse and place a marble in the middle. The marble will sit in place, but you could push the marble in a certain direction and have it roll off the saddle. The argument, not without some justification, is that most training ends on a saddle point, and better results are possible with a better algorithm. Again, however, even the saddle point, if it is one, is still for practical purposes a good place to be, so the model is successful regardless.

In practice, then, we should use stochastic gradient descent because it leads to better overall learning and reduces the training time by not requiring full batches. It does introduce a new hyperparameter, the minibatch size, that we must select at some point before training.

Ending Training

We haven't yet discussed a critical question: when should we stop training? Remember that in Chapter 5, we went through some effort to create training sets, validation sets, and test sets. This is where we'll use the validation sets. While training, we can use the accuracy, or some other metric, on the validation set to decide when to stop. If using SGD, we typically run the validation set through the network for each minibatch or set of minibatches to compute the accuracy. By tracking the accuracy on the validation set, we can decide when to stop training.

If we train for a long time, eventually two things usually happen. The first is that the error on the training set goes toward zero; we get better and better on the training set. The second is that the error on the validation set goes down and then, eventually, starts to go back up.

These effects are due to overfitting. The training error goes down and down as the model learns more and more to represent the parent distribution that generated the dataset. But, eventually, it will stop learning general things about the training set. At this point, we're overfitting, and we want to stop training because the model is no longer learning general features and is instead learning minutiae about the particular training set we're using. We can watch for this by using the validation set while training. Since we don't use the samples in the validation set to update the weights and biases of the network, it should give us a fair test of the current state of the network. When overfitting starts, the error on the validation set will begin to go up from a minimum value. What we can do then is to keep the weights and biases that produced the minimum value on the validation set and claim that those represent the best model.

We don't want to use any data that has influenced training to measure the final effectiveness of our network. We use the validation set to decide when to stop training, so characteristics of the samples in the validation set have also influenced the final model; this means we can't strongly rely on the validation set to give us an idea of how the model will behave on new data. It's only the held-out test set, unused until we declare victory over training, that gives us some idea of how we might expect the model to perform on data in the wild. So, just as it is anathema to report training set accuracy as a measure of how good the model is, it's also anathema to report the validation set accuracy.

Updating the Learning Rate

In our generic update equation for changing the weights and biases based on the gradient, we introduced a hyperparameter, η (eta), the learning rate or step size. It's a scale factor indicating how much we should update the weight or bias based on the gradient value.

We previously stated that the learning rate doesn't need to be fixed and that it could, and even should, get smaller and smaller as we train under the assumption that we need smaller and smaller steps to get to the actual minimum value of the loss function. We didn't state how we should actually update the learning rate.

There's more than one way to update the step size, but some are more helpful than others. The `MLPClassifier` class of sklearn, which uses SGD solvers, has three options. The first is to never change the learning rate—just leave η at its initial value, η_0. The second is to scale η so that it decreases with epochs (minibatches) according to

$$\eta = \frac{\eta_0}{t^p}$$

where η_0 is set by the user, t is the iteration (epoch, minibatch), and p is an exponent on t, also picked by the user. The sklearn default p is 0.5—that is, scale by $\sqrt{t}$, which seems a reasonable default.

The third option is to adapt the learning rate by watching the loss function value. As long as the loss is decreasing, leave the learning rate where it is. When the loss stops decreasing for a set number of minibatches, divide the learning rate by some value like 5, the sklearn default. If we never change the learning rate, and it's too large, we might end up moving around the minimum without ever being able to reach it because we're consistently stepping over it. It's a good idea then to decrease the learning rate when using SGD. Later in the book, we'll encounter other optimization approaches that automatically adjust the learning rate for us.

Momentum

There's one last wrinkle in SGD we have to cover. As we saw previously, the weight update equation for both gradient descent and SGD is

$$w \leftarrow w - \eta \Delta w$$

We update the weight by the learning rate (η) times the gradient, which we are representing here as Δw.

A common and powerful trick is to introduce a *momentum* term that adds back some fraction of the previous Δw, the update of the prior minibatch. The momentum term prevents the w parameter from changing too quickly in response to a particular minibatch. Adding in this term gives us

$$w_{i+1} \leftarrow w_i - \eta \Delta w_i + \mu \Delta w_{i-1}$$

We've added subscripts to indicate the next pass through the network ($i + 1$), the current pass (i), and the previous pass ($i - 1$). The previous pass Δw is the one we need to use. A typical value for μ (mu), the momentum, is around 0.9. Virtually all toolkits implement momentum in some form, including sklearn.

Backpropagation

We've been operating under the assumption that we know the gradient value for each parameter. Let's discuss how the backpropagation algorithm gives us these magic numbers. The backpropagation algorithm is perhaps the single most important development in the history of neural networks as it enables the training of large networks with hundreds, thousands, millions, and even billions of parameters. This is especially true of the convolutional networks we'll work with in Chapter 12.

The backpropagation algorithm itself was published by Rumelhart, Hinton, and Williams in 1986 in their paper "Learning Representations by Backpropagating Errors." It's a careful application of the chain rule for derivatives. The algorithm is called *backpropagation* because it works backward from the output layer of the network toward the input layer, propagating the error from the loss function down to each parameter of the network. Colloquially, the algorithm is known as *backprop*; we'll use that term here, so we sound more like native machine learning experts.

Adding backprop into the training algorithm for gradient descent, and tailoring it to SGD, gives us the algorithm in Listing 9-2.

---

1. Pick some intelligent starting values for the weights and biases.
2. Run a minibatch through the network using its current weights and biases and calculate the average loss.
3. Use this loss and backprop to get the gradient for each weight and bias.
4. Update the weight or bias value by the step size times the gradient value.
5. Repeat from step 2 until the loss is low enough.

Listing 9-2: Stochastic gradient descent with backprop

Step 2 of Listing 9-2 is referred to as the *forward pass*; step 3 is the *backward pass*. The forward pass is also how we'll use the network after it's finally trained. The backward pass is backprop calculating the gradients for us so that we can update the parameters in step 4.

We'll describe backprop twice. First, we'll do so with a simple example and work with the actual derivatives. Second, we'll work with a more abstract notation to see how backprop applies to actual neural networks in a general sense. There is no way to sugarcoat this: this section involves derivatives, but we already have a good intuitive sense of what those are from our discussion of gradient descent, so we should be in good shape to proceed.

Backprop, Take 1

Suppose we have two functions, $z = f(y)$ and $y = g(x)$, meaning $z = f(g(x))$. We know that the derivative of the function g gives us dy/dx, which tells us how y changes when x changes. Similarly, we know that the derivative of the function f will give us dz/dy. The value of z depends upon the composition of f and g, meaning the output of g is the input to f, so if we want to find an expression for dz/dx, how z changes with x, we need a way to link through the composed functions. This is what the chain rule for derivatives gives us:

$$\frac{dz}{dx} = \frac{dz}{dy}\frac{dy}{dx}$$

This notation is especially nice because we can imagine the dy "term" canceling just as it would if these were actual fractions.

How does this help us? In a neural network, the output of one layer is the input to the next, which is composition, so we can see intuitively that the chain rule might apply. Remember that we want the values that tell us how the loss function changes with respect to the weights and biases. Let's call the loss function L and any given weight or bias w. We want to calculate $\partial L/\partial w$ for all the weights and biases.

Alarm bells should be going off in your head. The previous paragraph slipped in new notation. So far, we've been writing derivatives as dy/dx, but the derivative for the loss with respect to a weight was written as $\partial L/\partial w$. What is this fancy ∂?

When we had a function of one variable, just x, there was only one slope at a point to talk about. As soon as we have a function with more than one variable, the idea of the slope at a point becomes ambiguous. There are an infinite number of lines tangent to the function at any point. So we need the idea of the *partial derivative*, which is the slope of the line in the direction of the variable we're considering when all other variables are treated as fixed. This tells us how the output will change as we change only the one variable. To note that we are using a partial derivative, we shift from d to ∂, which is just a script d.

Let's set up a straightforward network so that we can see how the chain rule leads directly to the expressions we want. We're looking at the network in Figure 9-3, which consists of an input, two hidden layers of a single node each, and an output layer.

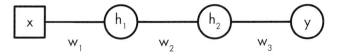

Figure 9-3: A simple network to illustrate the chain rule

For simplicity, we'll ignore any bias values. Additionally, let's define the activation function to be the identity function, $h(x) = x$. This simplification removes the derivative of the activation function to make things more transparent.

For this network, the forward pass computes

$$h_1 = w_1 x$$

$$h_2 = w_2 h_1$$

$$y = w_3 h_2$$

which follows the form we've used previously, chaining things together by making the output of one layer the input to the next. This gives us the output of the network, y, for input x. If we're looking to train the network, we'll have a training set, a set of pairs, $(x_i, \hat{y}_i)$, $i = 0, 1, \ldots$, that are examples of what the output should be for a given input. Note that the forward pass moved from the input, x, to the output, y. We'll next see why the backward pass moves from the output to the input.

Now let's define the loss function, $\mathcal{L}$, to be the squared error between y, the network output for a given input x, and $\hat{y}$, the output we should get. Functionally, the loss looks like the following.

$$\mathcal{L} = \frac{1}{2}(y - \hat{y})^2$$

For simplicity, we're ignoring the fact that the loss is a mean over the training set or some minibatch drawn from it. The factor of $\frac{1}{2}$ is not strictly necessary but it's commonly used to make the derivative a bit nicer. Since we're looking to minimize the loss for a particular set of weights, it doesn't matter that we're always multiplying the loss by a constant factor of $\frac{1}{2}$—the smallest loss will still be the smallest loss regardless of its actual numeric value.

To use gradient descent, we need to find how the loss changes with the weights. In this simple network, that means we need to find three gradient values, one each for w_1, w_2, and w_3. This is where the chain rule comes into play. We'll write the equations first and then talk about them:

$$\frac{\partial \mathcal{L}}{\partial w_3} = \frac{\partial \mathcal{L}}{\partial y} \frac{\partial y}{\partial w_3}$$

$$\frac{\partial \mathcal{L}}{\partial w_2} = \frac{\partial \mathcal{L}}{\partial y} \frac{\partial y}{\partial h_2} \frac{\partial h_2}{\partial w_2}$$

$$\frac{\partial \mathcal{L}}{\partial w_1} = \frac{\partial \mathcal{L}}{\partial y} \frac{\partial y}{\partial h_2} \frac{\partial h_2}{\partial h_1} \frac{\partial h_1}{\partial w_1}$$

The order of these equations shows why this algorithm is called *backprop-agation*. To get the partial derivative for the output layer parameter, we need only the output and the loss, y and $\mathcal{L}$. To get the partial derivative for the middle layer weight, we need the following two partial derivatives from the output layer:

$$\frac{\partial \mathcal{L}}{\partial y}$$

$$\frac{\partial y}{\partial h_2}$$

Finally, to get the partial derivative for the input layer weight, we need partial derivatives from the output and middle layer. In effect, we have moved backward through the network propagating values from later layers.

For each of these equations, the right-hand side matches the left-hand side if we imagine the "terms" canceling like fractions. Since we selected a particularly simple form for the network, we can calculate the actual gradients by hand. We need the following gradients, from the right-hand side of the preceding equations.

$$\frac{\partial \mathcal{L}}{\partial y} = (y - \hat{y})$$

$$\frac{\partial y}{\partial w_3} = h_2 = w_2 h_1 = w_2 w_1 x$$

$$\frac{\partial y}{\partial h_2} = w_3$$

$$\frac{\partial h_2}{\partial w_2} = h_1 = w_1 x$$

$$\frac{\partial h_2}{\partial h_1} = w_2$$

$$\frac{\partial h_1}{\partial w_1} = x$$

The $\partial \mathcal{L} / \partial y$ comes from the form we selected for the loss and the rules of differentiation from calculus.

Putting these back into the equations for the gradients of the weights gives us

$$\frac{\partial \mathcal{L}}{\partial w_3} = (y - \hat{y})w_2 w_1 x$$

$$\frac{\partial \mathcal{L}}{\partial w_2} = (y - \hat{y})w_3 w_1 x$$

$$\frac{\partial \mathcal{L}}{\partial w_1} = (y - \hat{y})w_3 w_2 x$$

After a forward pass, we have numeric values for all the quantities on the right-hand side of these equations. Therefore, we know the numeric value of the gradients. The update rule from gradient descent then tells us to change the weights like the following.

$$w_3 \leftarrow w_3 - \eta \frac{\partial \mathcal{L}}{\partial w_3} = w_3 - \eta(y - \hat{y})w_2 w_1 x$$

$$w_2 \leftarrow w_2 - \eta \frac{\partial \mathcal{L}}{\partial w_2} = w_2 - \eta(y - \hat{y})w_3 w_1 x$$

$$w_1 \leftarrow w_1 - \eta \frac{\partial \mathcal{L}}{\partial w_1} = w_1 - \eta(y - \hat{y})w_3 w_2 x$$

where η is the learning rate parameter defining how large a step to take when updating.

To recap, we need to use the chain rule, the heart of the backprop algorithm, to find the gradients we need to update the weights during training. For our simple network, we were able to work out the value of these gradients explicitly by moving backward through the network from the output toward the input. Of course, this is just a toy network. Let's now take a second look at how to use backprop in a more general sense to calculate the necessary gradients for any network.

Backprop, Take 2

Let's begin by revisiting the loss function and introducing some new notation. The loss function is a function of all the parameters in the network, meaning that every weight and bias value contributes to it. For example, the loss for the network of Figure 8-1, which has 20 weights and biases, could be written as

$$\text{loss} = \mathcal{L}(w_{00}^{(1)}, w_{01}^{(1)}, w_{02}^{(1)}, w_{10}^{(1)}, w_{11}^{(1)}, w_{12}^{(1)}, b_0^{(1)}, b_1^{(1)}, b_2^{(1)},$$

$$w_{00}^{(2)}, w_{01}^{(2)}, w_{10}^{(2)}, w_{11}^{(2)}, w_{20}^{(2)}, w_{21}^{(2)}, b_0^{(2)}, b_1^{(2)},$$

$$w_{00}^{(3)}, w_{10}^{(3)}, b_0^{(3)})$$

Note we've introduced a new notation for the parameters:

$$w_{jk}^{(i)}$$

This represents the weight that links the j-th input, an output of the $i - 1$ layer, to the k-th node of layer i. We also have

$$b_k^{(i)}$$

to represent the bias value for the k-th node of the i-th layer. Here layer 0 is the input layer itself. The parentheses on the exponent are a label, the layer number; they should not be interpreted as actual exponents. Therefore,

$$w_{20}^{(2)}$$

is the weight from the third output of the first layer to the first node of the second layer. This is the highlighted weight in Figure 9-4. Remember that we always number nodes top to bottom, starting with 0.

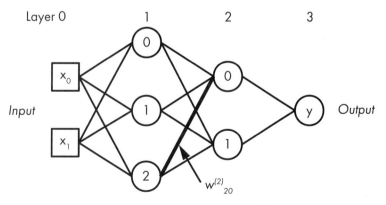

Figure 9-4: The network of Figure 8-1 with weight $w^{(2)}{}_{20}$ marked with a bold line

This notation is a bit daunting, but it will let us reference any weight or bias of the network precisely. The number we need to use backprop is the partial derivative of the loss with respect to each weight or bias. Therefore, what we want to find ultimately is written, in all its glorious mathematical notation, as

$$\frac{\partial \mathcal{L}}{\partial w_{jk}^{(i)}}$$

This gives us the slope: the amount the loss will change for a change in the weight linking the k-th node of the i-th layer to the j-th output of the $i - 1$ layer. A similar equation gives us the partial derivatives of the biases.

We can simplify this cumbersome notation by dealing only with the layer number understanding that buried in the notation is a vector (biases, activations) or matrix (weights) so that we want to find

$$\frac{\partial \mathcal{L}}{\partial w^{(i)}} \text{ and } \frac{\partial \mathcal{L}}{\partial b^{(i)}}$$

These correspond to a matrix for all the weights linking layer $i - 1$ to i, and a vector for all the biases of layer i, respectively.

We'll protect our notational sanity by looking at things in terms of vectors and matrices. Let's start with the output layer and see what that buys us. We know that the activations of the output layer, layer L, are found via

$$a^{(L)} = h(W^{(L)}a^{(L-1)} + b^{(L)})$$

with a being the activations from layer $L - 1$, b the bias vector for layer L, and W the weight matrix between layers $L - 1$ and L. The activation function is h.

Additionally, we'll define the argument to h to be $z^{(L)}$

$$z^{(L)} \equiv W^{(L)}a^{(L-1)} + b^{(L)}$$

and call $\partial \mathcal{L}/\partial z^{(l)}$ the *error*, the contribution to the loss from the inputs to layer l. Next, we define

$$\delta^{(l)} \equiv \frac{\partial \mathcal{L}}{\partial z^{(l)}}$$

so that we can work with δ (delta) from now on.

For the output layer, we can write δ as

$$\delta^{(L)} = \frac{\partial \mathcal{L}}{\partial z^{(L)}} = \frac{\partial \mathcal{L}}{\partial a^{(L)}} \cdot h'(z^{(L)})$$

The notation $h'(z^{(L)})$ is another way to write the derivative of h (with respect to z) evaluated at $z^{(L)}$. The $\cdot$ represents elementwise multiplication. This is the way NumPy works when multiplying two arrays of the same size so that if $C = A \cdot B$, then $C_{ij} = A_{ij}B_{ij}$. Technically, this product is called the *Hadamard product*, named for the French mathematician Jacques Hadamard.

The preceding means that to use backpropagation, we need a loss function that can be differentiated—a loss function for which a derivative exists at every point. This isn't too much of a burden; the loss functions we'll examine in the next section meet this criterion. We also need an activation function that can be differentiated so we can find $h'(z)$. Again, the activation functions we have considered so far are essentially all differentiable.

NOTE *I say "essentially" because the derivative of the ReLU is undefined at x = 0. The derivative from the left is 0 while the derivative from the right is 1. In practice, implementations choose a particular value to return should the argument to the derivative of the ReLU be exactly 0. For example, TensorFlow simply asks if the argument is less than or equal to 0 and, if it is, returns 0 as the derivative. Otherwise, it returns 1. This works because, numerically, there is so much rounding off happening to floating-point values during calculations that it's unlikely the value passed to the derivative of the ReLU function was actually meant to be identically 0.*

The equation for δ tells us the error due to the inputs to a particular layer. We'll see next how to use this to get the error from each weight of a layer.

With $\delta^{(L)}$ in hand, we can propagate the error down to the next layer via

$$\delta^{(l)} = ((W^{(l+1)})^T \delta^{l+1}) \cdot h'(z^{(l)})$$

where, for the next-to-last layer, $l + 1 = L$. The T represents matrix transpose. This is a standard matrix operation that involves a reflection across the diagonal so that if

$$A = \begin{bmatrix} 1 & 2 & 3 \\ 4 & 5 & 6 \\ 7 & 8 & 9 \end{bmatrix}$$

then

$$A^T = \begin{bmatrix} 1 & 4 & 7 \\ 2 & 5 & 8 \\ 3 & 6 & 9 \end{bmatrix}$$

We need the transpose of the weight matrix because we are going in the opposite direction from the forward pass. If there are three nodes in layer l and two in layer $l + 1$, then the weight matrix between them, W, is a 2×3 matrix, so Wx is a two-element vector. In backprop, we are going from layer $l + 1$ to layer l, so we transpose the weight matrix to map the two-element vector, here δ, to a three-element vector for layer l.

The $\delta^{(l)}$ equation is used for every layer moving backward through the network. The output layer values are given by $\delta^{(L)}$, which starts the process.

Once we have the errors per layer, we can finally find the gradient values we need. For the biases, the values are the elements of δ for that layer

$$\frac{\partial \mathcal{L}}{\partial b_j^{(l)}} = \delta_j^{(l)}$$

for the j-th element of the bias for the l-th layer. For the weights, we need

$$\frac{\partial \mathcal{L}}{\partial w_{kj}^{(l)}} = a_k^{(l-1)} \delta_j^{(l)}$$

linking the k-th output of the previous layer to the j-th error for the current layer, l.

Using the preceding equations for each layer of the network gives us the set of weight and bias gradient values needed to continue applying gradient descent.

As I hope you can see from this rather dense section, we can use a convenient mathematical definition of the error to set up an iterative process that moves the error from the output of the network back through the layers of the network to the input layer. We cannot calculate the errors for a layer without already knowing the errors for the layer after it, so we end up propagating the error backward through the network, hence the name *backpropagation*.

Loss Functions

The *loss function* is used during training to measure how poorly the network is doing. The goal of training is to make this value as small as possible, while still generalizing to the true characteristics of the data. In theory, we can create any loss function we want if we feel it's relevant to the problem at hand. If you read the deep learning literature, you'll see papers do this all the time. Still, most research falls back on a few standard loss functions that, empirically, do a good job most of the time. We'll discuss three of those here: absolute loss (sometimes called L_1 loss), mean squared error (sometimes called L_2 loss), and cross-entropy loss.

Absolute and Mean Squared Error Loss

Let's start with the absolute and mean squared error loss functions. We'll discuss them together because they're very similar mathematically.

We've seen mean squared error already in our discussion of backprop. Absolute loss is new. Mathematically, the two equations are

$$\mathcal{L}_{\text{abs}} = |y - \hat{y}|$$

$$\mathcal{L}_{\text{MSE}} = \frac{1}{2}(y - \hat{y})^2$$

where we've labeled them *abs* for *absolute value* and *MSE* for *mean squared error*, respectively. Note that we'll always use y for the network output, the output from the forward pass with input x. We'll always use $\hat{y}$ for the known training class label, which is always an integer label starting with 0.

Even though we're writing the loss functions in a simple form, we need to remember that when used, the value is really the mean of the loss over the training set or minibatch. This is also the origin of *mean* in *mean squared error*. Therefore, we really should be writing this:

$$\mathcal{L}_{\text{MSE}} = \frac{1}{N} \sum_{i=1}^{N} \frac{1}{2}(y_i - \hat{y}_i)^2 = \frac{1}{2N} \sum_{i=1}^{N} (y_i - \hat{y}_i)^2$$

Here we're finding the average of the squared error loss over the N values in the training set (or minibatch).

Both of these loss functions are reasonable if we consider what they are measuring. We want the network to output a value that matches the expected value, the sample label. The difference between these two is an indication of how wrong the network output is. For the absolute loss, we find the difference and drop the sign, which is what the absolute value does. For the MSE loss, we find the difference and then square it. This also makes the difference positive because multiplying a negative number by itself always results in a positive number. As mentioned in the "Backpropagation" section on page 200, the $\frac{1}{2}$ factor on the MSE loss simplifies the derivative of the loss function but does not change how it works.

The absolute loss and MSE are different, however. The MSE is more sensitive to outliers. This is because we're squaring the difference, and a plot of $y = x^2$ grows quickly as x, the difference, gets larger. For the absolute loss, this effect is minimized because there is no squaring; the difference is merely the difference.

In truth, neither of these loss functions are commonly used for neural networks when the goal of the network is *classification*, which is our implicit assumption in this book. It's more common to use the cross-entropy loss, presented next. We want the network output to lead to the correct class label for the input. However, it's entirely possible to train a network to output a continuous real value instead. This is called *regression*, and both of these loss functions are quite useful in that context.

Cross-Entropy Loss

Even though we can use the absolute and MSE loss functions in training a neural network for classification, the most commonly used loss is the *cross-entropy loss* (closely related to the log-loss). This loss function assumes the output of the network is a softmax (vector) for the multiclass case or a sigmoid (logistic, scalar) for the binary case. Mathematically, it looks like this for M classes in the multiclass case:

$$\mathcal{L}_{\text{ent}} = -\sum_{i}^{M} \hat{y}_j \log y_j \text{ (multiclass case)}$$

$$\mathcal{L}_{\text{ent}} = -\hat{y} \log(y) + (1 - \hat{y}) \log(1 - y) \text{ (binary case)}$$

What is the cross-entropy doing that often makes it a better choice for training a neural network for classification? Let's think about the multiclass case with softmax outputs. The definition of *softmax* means that the network outputs can be thought of as probability estimates of the likelihood that the input represents each of the possible classes. If we have three classes, we might get a softmax output that looks like this:

$$y = (0.03, 0.87, 0.10)$$

This output roughly means that the network thinks there is a 3 percent chance the input is of class 0, an 87 percent chance it is of class 1, and a 10 percent chance it is of class 2. This is the output vector, y. We compute the loss by supplying the actual label via a vector where 0 means *not this class* and 1 means *this class*. So, the $\hat{y}$ vector associated with the input that led to this y would be

$$\hat{y} = (0, 1, 0)$$

for an overall loss value of

$$\mathcal{L}_{\text{ent}} = -(0(\log 0.03) + 1(\log 0.87) + 0(\log 0.10)) = 0.139262$$

The three predictions of the network can be thought of together as a probability distribution, just like the one we get when we sum together the likelihoods of different outcomes for throwing two dice. We also have a known probability distribution from the class label. For the preceding example, the actual class is class 1, so we made a probability distribution that assigns no chance to classes 0 and 2, and 100 percent probability to class 1, the actual class. As the network trains, we expect the output distribution to be closer and closer to $(0, 1, 0)$, the distribution for the label.

Minimizing the cross-entropy drives the network toward better and better predictions of the probability distribution for the different classes we want the network to learn about. Ideally, these output distributions will look like the training labels: 0 for all classes except the actual class, which has an output of 1.

For classification tasks, we usually use the cross-entropy loss. The sklearn `MLPClassifier` class uses cross-entropy. Keras supports cross-entropy loss as well, but provides many others, including absolute and mean squared error.

Weight Initialization

Before we can train a neural network, we need to initialize the weights and biases. Step 1 of Listing 9-1 on gradient descent says to "Pick some intelligent starting values for the weights and biases."

The initialization techniques examined here all depend upon selecting random numbers in some range. More than that, the random numbers need to be either uniform over that range or normally distributed. *Uniformly distributed* means that all the values in the range are equally likely to be selected. This is what you get for each number, 1 through 6, if you roll a fair die many times over. Normally distributed values were introduced in Chapter 4. These are values with a particular mean, the most likely value returned, and a range around the mean over which the likelihood of a value being selected falls off gradually toward 0 according to a parameter known as the *standard deviation*. This is the classic bell curve shape. Either distribution can be used. The main point is that the initial weights are not all the same value (like 0) because if they are, all gradients will be the same during backprop, and each weight will change in the same way. The initial weights need to be different to break this symmetry and allow individual weights to adapt themselves to the training data.

In the early days of neural networks, people initialized the weights and biases by choosing values in $[0, 1)$ uniformly ($U(0, 1)$) or by drawing them from the standard normal distribution, $N(0, 1)$, with a mean of 0 and a standard deviation of 1. These values were often multiplied by some small constant, like 0.01. In many cases, this approach works, at least for simple networks. However, as networks became more complex, this simple approach fell apart. Networks initialized in this way had trouble learning, and many failed to learn at all.

Let's fast-forward several decades and a great deal of research later. Researchers realized that precisely how the weights of a particular layer should be initialized depended primarily on a few things: the type of activation function used and the number of weights coming into the layer (f_{in}) and, possibly, going out (f_{out}). These realizations led to the main initialization approaches in use today.

The sklearn `MLPClassifier` class uses *Glorot initialization*. This is also sometimes called *Xavier initialization*, though some toolkits mean something different when they use that term.[1] (Note *Xavier* and *Glorot* actually refer to the same person.) Let's see how sklearn uses Glorot initialization. The key method in `MLPClassifier` for initializing the weights is `_init_coef`. This method uses a uniform distribution and sets the range for it so that the weights are in

$$\left[-\sqrt{\frac{A}{f_{in} + f_{out}}}, \ \sqrt{\frac{A}{f_{in} + f_{out}}} \right]$$

where the bracket notation indicates the smallest possible value selected (left) to the largest possible value (right). As the distribution is uniform, every value in that range is equally likely to be selected.

We did not yet specify what A is. This value depends upon the activation function used. According to the literature, if the activation function is a sigmoid (logistic), then $A = 2$ is suggested. Otherwise, $A = 6$ is recommended.

Now to confuse things. Some toolkits, like Caffe, use an alternate form of Xavier initialization by which they mean a multiplier on samples from a standard normal distribution. In that case, we initialize the weights with draws from

$$N(0, 1)\sqrt{\frac{1}{f_{in}}} \ \text{(alternate Xavier initialization)}$$

To add even more confusion, the introduction of the rectified linear unit (ReLU) resulted in a further recommended change. This is known now as *He initialization* and it replaces the 1 in Xavier initialization with a 2:

$$N(0, 1)\sqrt{\frac{2}{f_{in}}} \ \text{(He initialization, ReLU only)}$$

For more on this, see "Delving Deep into Rectifiers: Surpassing Human-Level Performance on ImageNet Classification" by Kaiming He et al.

The key point with these initialization schemes is that the old-school "small random value" is replaced by a more principled set of values that take the network architecture into account via f_{in} and f_{out}.

The preceding discussion ignored bias values. This was intentional. While it might be okay to initialize the bias values instead of leaving them all 0, prevailing wisdom, which is fickle and fluid, currently says it's best to initialize them all to 0. That said, sklearn `MLPClassifier` initializes the bias values in the same way as the weights.

---

1. For more on these, see Glorot, Xavier, and Yoshua Bengio. "Understanding the Difficulty of Training Deep Feedforward Neural Networks."

Overfitting and Regularization

The goal of training a model is for it to learn essential, general features of the parent distribution the dataset is sampled from. That way, when the model encounters new inputs, it's prepared to interpret them correctly. As we've seen in this chapter, the primary method for training a neural network involves optimization—looking for the "best" set of parameters so that the network makes as few errors as possible on the training set.

However, it's not enough to simply look for the best set of values that minimizes the training error. If we make no mistakes when classifying the training data, it's often the case that we've overfitted and haven't actually learned general features of the data. This is more likely the situation with traditional models, neural network or classical, and less so with deep models like the convolutional networks of Chapter 12.

Understanding Overfitting

We've mentioned overfitting from time to time before now but have not gained any good intuition as to what it is. One way to think of overfitting is to consider a separate problem, the problem of fitting a function to a set of points. This is known as *curve fitting*, and one approach to it is to optimize some measure of error over the points by finding parameters to the function that minimize the error. This should sound familiar. It's exactly what we do when training a neural network.

As an example of curve fitting, consider the following points:

x	y
0.00	50.0
0.61	–17.8
1.22	74.1
1.83	29.9
2.44	114.8
3.06	55.3
3.67	66.0
4.28	89.1
4.89	128.3
5.51	180.8
6.12	229.7
6.73	229.3
7.34	227.7
7.95	354.9
8.57	477.1
9.18	435.4
9.79	470.1

We want to find a function, $y = f(x)$, that describes these points—a function that might have been the parent function these points were measured from, albeit noisily.

Typically, when curve fitting, we already know the form of the function; it's the parameters we're looking for. But what if we didn't know the exact form of the function, only that it was some kind of polynomial? In general, a polynomial looks like this for some maximum exponent, n:

$$y = a_0 + a_1x + a_2x^2 + a_3x^3 + \cdots + a_nx^n$$

The goal of fitting a polynomial to a dataset is to find the parameters, $a_0, a_1, a_2, \ldots, a_n$. The method for doing this usually minimizes the squared difference between y, a given output for a given x position, and $f(x)$, the function output at the same x for the current set of parameters. This should sound very familiar, as we discussed using precisely this type of loss function for training a neural network.

How does this relate to overfitting? Let's plot the previous dataset, along with the result of fitting two different functions to it. The first function is

$$y = a_0 + a_1x + a_2x^2$$

which is a quadratic function, the type of function you may have learned to hate as a beginning algebra student. The second function is

$$y = a_0 + a_1x + a_2x^2 + a_3x^3 + \cdots + a_{14}x^{14} + a_{15}x^{15}$$

which is a 15th-degree polynomial. The results are shown in Figure 9-5.

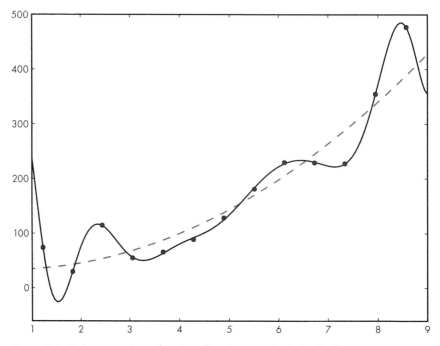

Figure 9-5: A dataset and two functions fit to it: a quadratic (dashed) and a 15th-degree polynomial (solid)

Which function does a better job of capturing the general trend of the dataset? The quadratic clearly follows the general trend of the data, while the 15th-degree polynomial is all over the place. Look again at Figure 9-5. If all we use to decide that we have fit the data well is the distance between the data points and the corresponding function value, we'd say that the 15th-degree polynomial is the better fit; it passes through nearly all the data points, after all. This is analogous to training a neural network and achieving perfection on the training set. The cost of that perfection might well be a poor ability to generalize to new inputs. The quadratic fit of Figure 9-5 did not hit the data points, but it did capture the general trend of the data, making it more useful should we want to make predictions about the y values we'd expect to get for a new x value.

When a human wants to fit a curve to something like our sample dataset, they usually look at the data and, noticing the general trend, select the function to fit. It might also be the case that the expected functional form is already known from theory. If we want to be analogous to neural networks, however, we'll find ourselves in a situation where we don't know the proper function to fit, and need to find a "best" one from the space of functions of x along with its parameters.

Hopefully, this example drives home the idea that training a neural network is not an optimization problem like other optimization problems—we need something to push the function the network is learning in a direction that captures the essence of the data without falling into the trap of paying too much attention to specific features of the training data. That something is regularization, and you need it, especially for large networks that have a huge capacity.

Understanding Regularization

Regularization is anything that pushes the network to learn the relevant features of the parent distribution and not the details of the training set. The best form of regularization is increasing the size and representative nature of the training set. The larger the dataset and the better it represents all the types of samples the network will encounter in the wild, the better it will learn. Of course, we're typically forced to work with a finite training set. The machine learning community has spent, and is spending, untold time and energy learning how to get more from smaller datasets.

In Chapter 5, we encountered perhaps the second-best way to regularize a model, data augmentation. This is a proxy for having a larger dataset, where we use the data we do have to generate new training samples that are plausibly from the parent distribution. For example, we considered increasing a limited set of training images by simple rotations, flips, and shifts of the images already in the training set. Data augmentation is powerful, and you should use it when possible. It's particularly easy to apply when working with images as inputs, though in Chapter 5 we also saw a way to augment a dataset consisting of continuously valued vectors.

We now have two tricks in our regularization toolbox: more data and data augmentation. These are the best tricks to know, but there others that you should use when available. Let's look at two more: L2 regularization and dropout. The former is now standard and widely supported by the toolkits, including sklearn and Keras. The latter is powerful and was a game changer when it appeared in 2012.

L2 Regularization

A model with a few weights that have large values is somehow less simple than a model that has smaller weights. Therefore, keeping the weights small will hopefully allow the network to implement a simpler function better suited to the task we want it to learn.

We can encourage the weights to be small by using L2 regularization. *L2 regularization* adds a term to the loss function so that the loss becomes

$$\mathcal{L} = \mathcal{L}(x, y, w, b) + \frac{\lambda}{2} \sum_i w_i^2$$

where the first term is whatever loss we're already using, and the second term is the new L2 regularization term. Notice that the loss is a function of the input (x), the label (y), the weights (w), and the biases (b), where we mean all the weights and all the biases of the network. The regularization term is a sum over all the weights in the network and only the weights. The "L2" label is what causes us to square the weights.

Here *L2* refers to the type of norm or distance. You might be familiar with the equation for the distance between two points on the plane: $d^2 = (x_2 - x_1)^2 + (y_2 - y_1)^2$. This is the *Euclidean distance*, also known as the *L2 distance*, because the values are squared. This is why the regularization term is called *L2* and the weight values are squared. It's also possible to use an L1 loss term, where instead of squaring the weights, one uses the absolute value. In practice, L2 regularization is more common and, at least empirically, seems to work better for neural network classifiers.

The λ (lambda) multiplier sets the importance of this term; the larger it is, the more it dominates the overall loss used to train the network. Typical values of λ are around 0.0005. We'll see in a little bit why the multiplier is $\lambda/2$ and not just λ.

What is the L2 term doing? Recall that the loss is the thing we want to minimize while training. The new L2 term sums the squares of the weights of the network. If weights are large, the loss is large, and that's something we don't want while training. Smaller weights make the L2 term smaller, so gradient descent will favor small weights, whether they are positive or negative, since we square the weight value. If all the weights of the network are relatively small, and none strongly dominate, then the network will use all of the weights to represent the data, and this is a good thing when it comes to preventing overfitting.

L2 regularization is also known as *weight decay* because of what the L2 term does during backprop. Backprop gives us the partial derivative of the loss function with respect to w_i. Adding L2 regularization means that the partial derivative of the total loss now adds in the partial derivative of the

L2 term itself with respect to any particular weight, w_i. The derivative of $\frac{\lambda}{2}w^2$ is λw; the $\frac{1}{2}$ cancels the factor of 2 that would otherwise be there. Also, since we want the partial derivative with respect to a specific weight, w_i, all the other parts of the L2 term go to 0. The net effect is that the update for weight w_i during gradient descent becomes

$$w_i \leftarrow w_i - \eta \frac{\partial \mathcal{L}}{\partial w_i} - \eta \lambda w_i$$

where η (eta) is the learning rate, and we are ignoring any additional momentum term. The $\eta \lambda w_i$ term is new. It is due to L2 regularization, and we can see that it's pushing the weights toward 0 as training progresses because both η and λ are < 1, so on each minibatch, we're subtracting some small fraction of the weight value. The weight can still increase, but to do so, the gradient of the original loss must be large.

We previously stated that the form of the loss function is up to us, the developer of the network. A regularization term isn't the only kind of term we can add to the loss function. As we did with the L2 term, we can create and add terms to change the behavior of the network during training and help it learn what we want it to learn. This is a powerful technique that can be used to customize various aspects of what a neural network learns.

Dropout

Dropout took the machine learning community by storm when it appeared in 2012, see "Imagenet Classification with Deep Convolutional Neural Networks" by Alex Krizhevsky et al. As of Fall 2020, this paper has been cited over 70,000 times, and as one well-known machine learning researcher told me privately at the time, "If we had had dropout in the 1980s, this would be a different world now." So, what is dropout, and why was everyone so excited by it?

To answer that question, we need to review the concept of ensembles of models. We talked about them a bit in Chapter 6. An ensemble is a group of models, all slightly different and all trained on the same dataset or a slightly different version of the dataset. The idea is straightforward: since training most models involves randomness, training multiple similar models should result in a set that is mutually reinforcing—one where the set of outputs can be combined to produce a result that is better than any one model alone. Ensembles are useful, and we use them often, but they come at a price in terms of runtime. If it takes x milliseconds to run a sample through a neural network, and we have an ensemble of 20 networks, then our evaluation time (inference time) has jumped to $20x$ milliseconds, ignoring the possibility of parallel execution. In some situations, that is unacceptable (to say nothing of the storage and power requirements for 20 big networks versus 1). Since the net result of an ensemble of models is better overall performance, we can say that an ensemble is a kind of regularizer as well since it embodies the "wisdom of the crowd."

Dropout takes the ensemble idea to an extreme but does so only during training and without creating a second network so that in the end, we still have one model to deal with. Like many good ideas in statistics, this one requires randomness. Right now, when we train the network, we do a forward pass using the current weights and biases. What if, during that forward pass, we randomly assign a 0 or a 1 to each node of the network so that nodes with a 1 are used in the next layer while nodes with a 0 are dropped out? We'd effectively be running the training samples through a different neural network configuration each time. For example, see Figure 9-6.

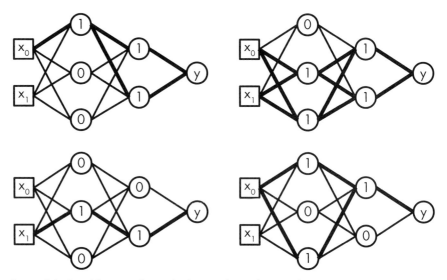

Figure 9-6: Possible networks used when applying dropout during training

Here we show the network of Figure 8-1 but with a 0 or 1 for each of the hidden nodes. This 0 or 1 determines whether the output is used or not. The heavy lines in the network show the connections that are still valid. In other words, the heavy lines show the network that was actually used to create the output accumulated for backprop. If we do this for each training sample, we can readily see that we'll be training a vast number of neural networks, each trained on a single sample. Moreover, since the weights and biases persist between forward passes, all the networks will share those weights in the hope that the process will reinforce good weight values that represent the essence of the dataset. As we've mentioned several times in this chapter, learning the essence of the data is the goal of training; we want to generalize well to new data from the same virtual parent distribution that generated the training set in the first place. Dropout is serious regularization.

I previously said that we "randomly assign a 0 or a 1" to the nodes. Do we assign them equally? The probability with which we drop nodes in a layer is something we get to specify. Let's call it p. Typically, p = 0.5, meaning about 50 percent of the nodes in a layer will be dropped for each training sample. Setting p = 0.8 would drop 80 percent of the nodes, while p = 0.1 would drop only 10 percent. Sometimes a different probability is used for different layers of the network, especially the first input layer, which should use a smaller probability than the hidden nodes. If we drop too many of the inputs, we'll lose the source of the signal we're trying to get the network to recognize. Dropout applied to the input layer can be thought of as a form of data augmentation.

Conceptually, dropout is training a large set of networks that share weights. The output of each of these networks can be combined with the others via a geometric mean, assuming we use a softmax output. The geometric mean of two numbers is the square root of their product. The geometric mean of n numbers is the nth root of their product. In the case of dropout, it turns out that this can be approximated by using the entire network with all the weights multiplied by the probability that they would be included. Given we said p is the probability that a node is dropped, the weights need to be multiplied by $1 - p$, as that is the probability the node would not be dropped. So, if we fix $p = 0.5$ and use it for all the nodes, then the final network is the one where all the weights are divided by 2.

As of this writing, sklearn's `MLPClassifier` class does not support dropout, but Keras most certainly does, so we'll see dropout again in Chapter 12.

Summary

Because this is an important chapter, let's review what we've learned in a little more depth. In this chapter, we described how to train a neural network using gradient descent and backpropagation. The overall sequence of steps is as follows:

1. Select the architecture of the model. This means the number of layers, their sizes, and the type of activation function.
2. Initialize the weights and biases of the network using intelligently selected initial values.
3. Run a minibatch of training samples through the network and compute the mean loss over the minibatch. We discussed common loss functions.
4. Using backpropagation, calculate the contribution of each weight and bias to the overall loss for the minibatch.
5. Using gradient descent, update the weight and bias values of the model based on the contributions found via backpropagation. We discussed stochastic gradient descent and its relationship to the concept of minibatches.
6. Repeat from step 3 until the desired number of epochs or minibatches have been processed, or the loss has dropped below some threshold, or stopped changing much, or when the score on a validation set of samples has reached its minimum value.
7. If the network isn't learning well, apply regularization and train again. We looked at L2 regularization and dropout in this chapter. Data augmentation, or increasing the size or representativeness of the training set, can also be thought of as regularization.

The goal of training a neural network is to learn the parameters of a model that generalizes well to unseen inputs. This is the goal of all supervised machine learning. For a neural network, we know it's able to approximate any function, with enough capacity and enough training data. Naïvely, we may think that we are doing nothing more than ordinary optimization, but, in an important sense, we are not. Perfection on the training set is often not a good thing; it's often a sign of overfitting. Instead, we want the model to learn a function that captures the essential nature of the function implied by the training set. We use the test data to give us confidence that we've learned a useful function.

In the next chapter, we'll get real and explore traditional neural networks through a series of experiments using sklearn.

10

EXPERIMENTS WITH NEURAL NETWORKS

In Chapter 9, we discussed the theory behind neural networks. In this chapter, we'll trade equations for code and run a number of experiments designed to increase our intuition regarding the essential parameters of neural networks: architecture and activation functions, batch size, base learning rate, training set size, L2 regularization, momentum, weight initialization, feature ordering, and the precision of the weights and biases.

To save space and eliminate tedious repetition, we won't show the specific code for each experiment. In most cases, the code is only trivially different from the previous example; we're usually changing only the particular argument to the MLPClassifier constructor we're interested in. The code for each experiment is included in the set of files associated with this book, and we'll list the network parameters and the name of the file. When necessary, we'll provide code to clarify a particular approach. We'll show the code for the first experiment in its entirety.

Our Dataset

We'll be working with the MNIST dataset's vector form, which we assembled in Chapter 5. Recall that this dataset consists of 28×28 pixel 8-bit grayscale images of handwritten digits, $[0, 9]$. In vector form, each 28×28 image is unraveled into a vector of $28 \times 28 = 784$ elements, all bytes ($[0, 255]$). The unraveling lays each row end to end. Therefore, each sample has 784 elements and an associated label. The training set has 60,000 samples, while the test set has 10,000. For our experiments, we won't use all of the data in the training set. This is to help illustrate the effect of network parameters and to keep our training times reasonable. Refer back to Figure 5-3 for representative MNIST digits.

The MLPClassifier Class

The MLPClassifier class follows the same format as the other sklearn classifiers. There is a constructor and the expected methods: fit for training, score for applying the classifier to test data, and predict to make a prediction on unknown inputs. We'll also use predict_proba to return the actual predicted per class probabilities. The constructor has many options:

```
MLPClassifier(hidden_layer_sizes=(100, ), activation='relu',
    solver='adam', alpha=0.0001, batch_size='auto',
    learning_rate='constant', learning_rate_init=0.001,
    power_t=0.5, max_iter=200, shuffle=True,
    random_state=None, tol=0.0001, verbose=False,
    warm_start=False, momentum=0.9, nesterovs_momentum=True,
    early_stopping=False, validation_fraction=0.1, beta_1=0.9,
    beta_2=0.999, epsilon=1e-08)
```

Here we've provided the default values for each parameter. See the sklearn documentation page at *http://scikit-learn.org/* for a complete description of each parameter. We'll set some of these to specific values, and others will be changed for the experiments while still others are relevant in only specific situations. The key parameters we'll work with are in Table 10-1.

The following set of experiments explores the effect of various MLPClassifier parameters. As mentioned, we'll show all the code used for the first experiment, understanding that only small changes are needed to perform the other experiments. At times, we'll show little code snippets to make the change concrete.

Table 10-1: Important `MLPClassifier` Constructor Keywords and Our Default Values for Them

Keyword	Description
hidden_layer_sizes	Tuple giving the hidden layer sizes
activation	Activation function type; for example, ReLU
alpha	L2 parameter—we called it λ (lambda)
batch_size	Minibatch size
learning_rate_init	The learning rate, η (eta)
max_iter	Number of training epochs
warm_start	Continue training or start again
momentum	Momentum
solver	Solver algorithm ("sgd")
nesterovs_momentum	Use Nesterov momentum (False)
early_stopping	Use early stopping (False)
learning_rate	Learning rate schedule ("constant")
tol	Stop early if loss change < tol (1e-8)
verbose	Output to console while training (False)

Architecture and Activation Functions

When designing a neural network, we immediately face two fundamental questions: what architecture and what activation function? These are arguably the most important deciding factors for a model's success. Let's explore what happens when we train a model using different architectures and activation functions while holding the training dataset fixed.

The Code

As promised, for this first experiment we'll show the code in its entirety, starting with the helper functions in Listing 10-1.

```
import numpy as np
import time
from sklearn.neural_network import MLPClassifier

def run(x_train, y_train, x_test, y_test, clf):
    s = time.time()
```

```
        clf.fit(x_train, y_train)
        e = time.time()-s
        loss = clf.loss_
        weights = clf.coefs_
        biases = clf.intercepts_
        params = 0
        for w in weights:
            params += w.shape[0]*w.shape[1]
        for b in biases:
            params += b.shape[0]
        return [clf.score(x_test, y_test), loss, params, e]

def nn(layers, act):
    return MLPClassifier(solver="sgd", verbose=False, tol=1e-8,
            nesterovs_momentum=False, early_stopping=False,
            learning_rate_init=0.001, momentum=0.9, max_iter=200,
            hidden_layer_sizes=layers, activation=act)
```

Listing 10-1: Helper functions for experimenting with the architecture and activation function. See mnist_nn_experiments.py.

Listing 10-1 imports the usual modules and then defines two helper functions, run and nn. Starting with nn, we see that all it does is return an instance of MLPClassifier using the hidden layer sizes and the given activation function type.

The hidden layer sizes are given as a tuple, where each element is the number of nodes in the corresponding layer. Recall that sklearn works with only fully connected layers, so a single number is all we need to specify the size. The input samples given for training determine the size of the input layer. Here the input samples are vectors representing the digit images, so there are $28 \times 28 = 784$ nodes in the input layer.

What about the output layer? It's not specified explicitly because it depends on the number of classes in the training labels. The MNIST dataset has 10 classes, so there will be 10 nodes in the output layer. When the predict_proba method is called to get an output probability, sklearn applies a softmax over the 10 outputs. If the model is binary, meaning the only class labels are 0 and 1, then there is only one output node, a logistic (sigmoid), representing the probability of belonging to class 1.

Now let's look at the parameters we passed in to MLPClassifier. First, we explicitly state that we want to use the SGD solver. The solver is the approach used to modify the weights and biases during training. All the solvers use backprop to calculate the gradients; how we use those gradients varies. Plain vanilla SGD is good enough for us right now.

Next, we set a low tolerance so that we'll train the requested number of epochs (max_iter). We also turn off Nesterov momentum (a variant of standard momentum) and early stopping (generally useful but not desired here).

The initial learning rate is set to the default value of 0.001, as is the value of standard momentum, 0.9. The number of epochs is arbitrarily set to 200 (the default), but we'll explore this more in the experiments that follow.

Please indulge your curiosity at all times and see what changing these values does to things. For consistency's sake, we'll use these values as defaults throughout unless they are the parameters we want to experiment with.

The other helper function in Listing 10-1 is run. This function will train and test the classifier object it's passed using the standard sklearn fit and score methods. It also does some other things that we have not seen before.

In particular, after timing how long training takes, we extract the final training loss value, the network weights, and the network biases from the MLPClassifier object so that we can return them. The MLPClassifier class minimizes the log-loss, which we described in Chapter 9. We store the log-loss in the loss_ member variable. The size of this value, and how it changes during training, gives us a clue as to how well the network is learning. In general, the smaller the log-loss, the better the network is doing. As you explore neural networks more and more, you'll begin to develop intuition for what a good loss value is and whether the training process is learning quickly or not by how rapidly the loss changes.

The weights and biases are stored in the coefs_ and intercepts_ member variables. These are lists of NumPy matrices (weights) and vectors (biases), respectively. Here we use them to calculate the number of parameters in the network by summing the number of elements in each matrix and vector. This is what the two small loops in the run function do. Finally, we return all this information, including the score against the test set, to the main function. The main function is shown in Listing 10-2.

```
def main():
    x_train = np.load("mnist_train_vectors.npy").astype("float64")/256.0
    y_train = np.load("mnist_train_labels.npy")
    x_test = np.load("mnist_test_vectors.npy").astype("float64")/256.0
    y_test = np.load("mnist_test_labels.npy")

    N = 1000
    x_train = x_train[:N]
    y_train = y_train[:N]
    x_test  = x_test[:N]
    y_test  = y_test[:N]

    layers = [
        (1,), (500,), (800,), (1000,), (2000,), (3000,),
        (1000,500), (3000,1500),
        (2,2,2), (1000,500,250), (2000,1000,500),
    ]

    for act in ["relu", "logistic", "tanh"]:
        print("%s:" % act)
        for layer in layers:
            scores = []
            loss = []
            tm = []
```

```
for i in range(10):
    s,l,params,e = run(x_train, y_train, x_test, y_test,
                       nn(layer,act))
    scores.append(s)
    loss.append(l)
    tm.append(e)
s = np.array(scores)
l = np.array(loss)
t = np.array(tm)
n = np.sqrt(s.shape[0])
print("    layers: %14s, score= %0.4f +/- %0.4f,
        loss = %0.4f +/- %0.4f (params = %6d, time = %0.2f s)" % \
        (str(layer), s.mean(), s.std()/n, l.mean(),
         l.std()/n, params, t.mean()))
```

Listing 10-2: The main *function for experimenting with the architecture and activation function. See* mnist_nn_experiments.py.

We first load the MNIST train and test data stored in x_train (samples) and y_train (labels), and x_test and y_test. Notice that we divide the samples by 256.0 to make them floats in the range [0, 1). This normalization is the only preprocessing we'll do in this chapter.

As the full training set has 60,000 samples and we want to run many training sessions, we'll use only the first 1,000 samples for training. We'll likewise keep the first 1,000 test samples. Our goal in this chapter is to see relative differences as we change parameters, not to build the best model possible, so we'll sacrifice the quality of the model to get results in a reasonable timeframe. With 1,000 training samples, we'll have only 100 instances of each digit type, on average. We'll vary the number of training samples for specific experiments.

The layers list holds the different architectures we'll explore. Ultimately, we'll pass these values to the hidden_layer_sizes argument of the MLPClassifier constructor. Notice that we'll examine architectures ranging from a single hidden layer with a single node to three hidden layers with up to 2,000 nodes per layer.

The main loop runs over three activation function types: rectified linear unit, logistic (sigmoid) unit, and the hyperbolic tangent. We'll train a model for each combination of activation function type and architecture (layers). Moreover, since we know neural network training is stochastic, we'll train 10 models for each combination and report the mean and standard error of the mean, so we're not thrown off by a particularly bad model that isn't representative.

NOTE *When you run the code in the experiments that follow, you'll likely generate warning messages from sklearn like this one:*

```
ConvergenceWarning: Stochastic Optimizer: Maximum iterations (200) reached
and the optimization hasn't converged yet.
```

The messages are sklearn's way of telling you that the number of training iterations completed before sklearn felt that the network had converged to a good set of weights. The warnings are safe to ignore and can be disabled completely by adding -W ignore *to the command line when you run the code; for example:*

```
$ python3 -W ignore mnist_nn_experiments.py
```

The Results

Running this code takes several hours to complete, and produces output with lines that look something like this:

```
layers:(3000,1500), score=0.8822+/-0.0007, loss=0.2107+/-0.0006
(params=6871510, time=253.42s)
```

This tells us that using a ReLU activation function, and an architecture with two hidden layers of 3,000 and 1,500 nodes each, the models had an average score of 88.2 percent and an average final training loss of 0.21 (remember that lower is better). It also tells us that the neural network had a total of nearly 6.9 million parameters and took, on average, a little more than four minutes to train.

Table 10-2 summarizes the scores for the various network architectures and activation function types.

Table 10-2: Mean Score (mean ± SE) on the MNIST Test Set as a Function of the Architecture and Activation Function Type

Architecture	ReLU	Tanh	Logistic (sigmoid)
1	0.2066 ± 0.0046	0.2192 ± 0.0047	0.1718 ± 0.0118
500	0.8616 ± 0.0014	0.8576 ± 0.0011	0.6645 ± 0.0029
800	0.8669 ± 0.0014	0.8612 ± 0.0011	0.6841 ± 0.0030
1000	0.8670 ± 0.001	0.8592 ± 0.0014	0.6874 ± 0.0028
2000	0.8682 ± 0.0008	0.8630 ± 0.0012	0.7092 ± 0.0029
3000	0.8691 ± 0.0005	0.8652 ± 0.0011	0.7088 ± 0.0024
1000; 500	0.8779 ± 0.0011	0.8720 ± 0.0011	0.1184 ± 0.0033
3000; 1500	0.8822 ± 0.0007	0.8758 ± 0.0009	0.1221 ± 0.0001
1000; 500; 250	0.8829 ± 0.0011	0.8746 ± 0.0012	0.1220 ± 0.0000
2000; 1000; 500	0.8850 ± 0.0007	0.8771 ± 0.0010	0.1220 ± 0.0000

In each case, we show the mean score on the reduced test set averaged over the 10 models trained (plus or minus the standard error of the mean). There is quite a bit of information in this table, so let's look at it carefully.

If we look at the activation type, we immediately see something is off. The results for the logistic activation function show improved scores as the single hidden layer gets larger, something we might expect to see, but when we move to more than one hidden layer, the network fails to train. We know that it was unable to train because the scores on the test set are abysmal. If you check the output, you'll see that the loss values do not go down. If the loss value does not decrease while training proceeds, something is wrong.

It's not immediately evident why training failed for the logistic activation function case. One possibility is a bug in sklearn, but this is rather unlikely given how widely used the toolkit is. The most likely culprit has to do with network initialization. The sklearn toolkit uses the standard, commonly used initialization schemes we discussed in Chapter 8. But these are tailored for ReLU and tanh activation functions and may not be performing well for the logistic case.

For our purposes, we can view this failure as a glaring sign that the logistic activation function is not a good one to use for the hidden layers. Sadly, this is precisely the activation function that was widely used throughout much of the early history of neural networks, so we were shooting ourselves in the foot from the beginning. No wonder it took so long for neural networks to finally find their proper place! From here on out, we'll ignore the logistic activation function results.

Consider again the scores for the single hidden layer networks (see Table 10-2, rows 1–6). For the ReLU and tanh activation functions, we see a steady improvement in the performance of the networks. Also, note that in each case, the ReLU activation function slightly outperforms tanh for the same number of nodes in the hidden layer, though these differences are likely not statistically significant with only 10 models per architecture. Still, it follows a general observation prevalent in the community: ReLU is preferred to tanh.

If we look at the remaining rows of Table 10-2, we see that adding a second and even third hidden layer continues to improve the test scores but with diminishing returns. This is also a widely experienced phenomenon that we should look at a little more closely. In particular, we should consider the number of parameters in the models of Table 10-2. This makes the comparison a bit unfair. If, instead, we train models that have closely matched numbers of parameters, then we can more fairly compare the performance of the models. Any differences in performance we see can be plausibly attributed to the number of layers used since the overall number of parameters will be virtually the same.

By modifying the layers array in Listing 10-2, we can train multiple versions of the architectures shown in Table 10-3. The number of nodes per layer was selected to parallel the overall number of parameters in the models.

Table 10-3: Model Architectures Tested to Produce Figure 10-1

Architecture	Number of parameters
1000	795,010
2000	1,590,010
4000	3,180,010
8000	6,360,010
700; 350	798,360
1150; 575	1,570,335
1850; 925	3,173,685
2850; 1425	6,314,185
660; 330; 165	792,505
1080; 540; 270	1,580,320
1714; 857; 429	3,187,627
2620; 1310; 655	6,355,475

Where did the magic numbers in Table 10-3 come from? We first picked the single-layer sizes we wanted to test. We then determined the number of parameters in models with those architectures. Next, we crafted two-layer architectures using the rules of thumb from Chapter 8 so that the number of parameters in those models will be close to the corresponding number of parameters in the single-layer models. Finally, we repeated the process for three-layer models. Doing things this way lets us compare the performance of the models for very similar numbers of parameters. In essence, we're fixing the number of parameters in the model and altering only the way they interact with each other.

Training models as we did in Listing 10-2, but this time averaging 25 models instead of just 10, gives us Figure 10-1.

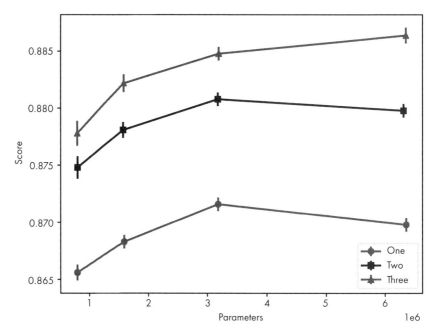

Figure 10-1: Scores (mean ± E) on the MNIST test set for the architectures of Table 10-3 as a function of the number of parameters in the network

Let's parse Figure 10-1. First, note that the x-axis, the number of parameters in the model, is given in millions. Second, we can compare the three lines going vertically as those models all have similar numbers of parameters. The legend tells us which plot represents models with one, two, or three hidden layers.

Looking at the leftmost points, representing the smallest models in each case, we see that changing from a single layer to two layers gives us a jump in model performance. Also, moving from two layers to three results in another, smaller rise. This repeats for all the layer sizes moving left to right. We'll address the dip in performance between the two largest models for single- and double-layer architectures in a bit. Fixing the number of parameters but increasing the depth of the network (number of layers) results in better performance. We might be tempted here to say, "Go deep, not wide," but there will be cases where this doesn't work. Still, it's worth remembering: more layers can help, not just a wider layer with more nodes.

What about the dip for the largest models in the one- and two-layer cases? These are the rightmost points of Figure 10-1. Recall, the models used to make the plot were trained with only 1,000 samples each. For the largest models, there likely wasn't enough data to adequately train such a wide model. If we were to increase the number of training samples, which we can do because we have 60,000 to choose from for MNIST, we might see the dip go away. I'll leave this as an exercise for the reader.

Batch Size

Let's now turn our attention to how batch size affects training. Recall that here *batch size* means minibatch size, a subset of the full training set used in the forward pass to calculate the average loss over the minibatch. From this loss, we use backprop to update the weights and biases. Processing a single minibatch, then, results in a single gradient-descent step—a single update to the parameters of the network.

We'll train a fixed-size subset of MNIST for a set number of epochs with different minibatch sizes to see how that affects the final test scores. Before we do that, however, we need to understand, for epochs and minibatches, the process sklearn uses to train a neural network.

Let's look briefly at the actual sklearn source code for the MLPClassifier class, in the _fit_stochastic method, found at *https://github.com/scikit-learn/ scikit-learn/blob/7389dba/sklearn/neural_network/multilayer_perceptron.py*. Understanding that this method is an internal one and might change from version to version, we see code that looks like this:

```
for it in range(self.max_iter):
  X, y = shuffle(X, y, random_state=self._random_state)
  accumulated_loss = 0.0
  for batch_slice in gen_batches(n_samples, batch_size):
    activations[0] = X[batch_slice]
    batch_loss, coef_grads, intercept_grads = self._backprop(
      X[batch_slice], y[batch_slice], activations, deltas,
      coef_grads, intercept_grads)
    accumulated_loss += batch_loss * (batch_slice.stop -
                                      batch_slice.start)
    grads = coef_grads + intercept_grads
    self._optimizer.update_params(grads)
  self.n_iter_ += 1
```

There are two for loops, the first over the number of epochs (`max_iter`), and the second over the number of minibatches present in the training data. The `gen_batches` function returns minibatches from the training set. In reality, it returns slice indices with `X[batch_slice]` returning the actual training samples, but the effect is the same. The calls to `_backprop` and `update_params` complete the gradient descent step for the current minibatch.

An *epoch* is a full pass through the minibatches present in the training set. The minibatches themselves are groupings of the training data so that looping over the minibatches uses all the samples in the training set once. If the number of training samples is not an integer multiple of the minibatch size, the final minibatch will be smaller than expected, but that will not affect training in the long run.

We can view this graphically as in Figure 10-2, where we see how an epoch is built from the minibatches in the training set. In Figure 10-2, the entire training set is represented as the epoch with n samples. A minibatch has m samples, as indicated. The last minibatch is smaller than the rest to indicate that the n/m might not be an integer.

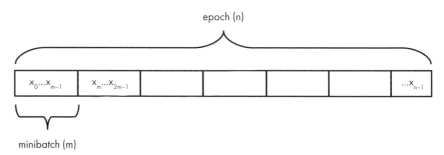

Figure 10-2: The relationship between epochs (n), minibatches (m), and samples $\{x_0, x_1, \ldots, x_{n-1}\}$

Figure 10-2 also implies that the order of the samples in the training set is essential, which is why we shuffled the datasets when we made them. The sklearn toolkit will also rearrange the samples after every epoch during training if desired. As long as a minibatch is, statistically, a random sample from the training set as a whole, things should be okay. If the minibatch is not, then it might give a biased view of the gradient direction during backprop.

Our minibatch experiment will fix the number of MNIST training samples at 16,384 while we vary the minibatch size. We'll also fix the number of epochs at 100. The scores we report are the mean and standard error for five different runs of the same model, each with a different random initialization. The MLPClassifier object is therefore instantiated via

```
MLPClassifier(solver="sgd", verbose=False, tol=1e-8,
    nesterovs_momentum=False, early_stopping=False,
    learning_rate_init=0.001, momentum=0.9, max_iter=100,
    hidden_layer_sizes=(1000,500), activation="relu",
    batch_size=bz)
```

This code indicates that all of the models have two hidden layers of 1,000 and 500 nodes, respectively, making the architecture of the entire network 784-1000-500-10 when adding in the nodes of the input and output layers. The only parameter that varies when defining a network is the batch_size. We'll use the batch sizes in Table 10-4 along with the number of gradient descent steps taken for each epoch (see Figure 10-2).

Table 10-4: Minibatch Sizes and the Corresponding Number of Gradient Descent Steps per Epoch

Minibatch size	SGD steps per epoch
2	8,192
4	4,096
8	2,048
16	1,024
32	512
64	256
128	128
256	64
512	32
1,024	16
2,048	8
4,096	4
8,192	2
16,384	1

When the minibatch size is 2, over 8,000 gradient descent steps will be taken per epoch, but when the minibatch size is 8,192, only 2 gradient descent steps are taken. Fixing the number of epochs should favor a smaller minibatch size since there will be correspondingly more gradient descent steps, implying more opportunity to move toward the optimal set of network parameters.

Figure 10-3 plots the mean score as a function of the minibatch size. The code that generated the data for the plot is in the *mnist_nn_experiments _batch_size.py* file. The plotting code itself is in *mnist_nn_experiments_batch _size_plot.py*. The curve that concerns us for the moment is the one using circles. We'll explain the square symbol curve shortly.

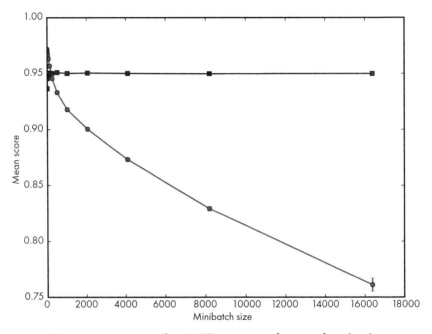

Figure 10-3: Average score on the MNIST test set as a function of minibatch size (mean ± SE) for a fixed number of epochs (100) regardless of the minibatch size (circles) or a fixed number of minibatches (squares)

Here we've fixed the number of epochs at 100, so by varying the minibatch size, we vary the number of gradient steps: the larger the minibatch, the *fewer* gradient steps we take. Because the minibatch is larger, the steps themselves are based on a more faithful representation of the actual gradient direction; however, the number of steps is reduced because there are fewer minibatches per epoch, leading to poorer convergence: we are not reaching a good minimum of the loss function.

A more "fair" test might be to see what happens when we adjust the number of epochs so that the number of *minibatches* examined is constant regardless of the minibatch size. One way to do that is to note that the number of minibatches per epoch is n/m, where n is the number of training samples, and m is the number of minibatches. If we call the overall number of minibatches we want to run M, then, to hold it fixed, we need to set the number of *epochs* to

$$E = \frac{Mm}{n}$$

so that regardless of m, we perform a total of M gradient descent steps during training.

Let's keep the same set of minibatches but alter the number of epochs according to the preceding equation. We need to select M, the overall number of minibatches (gradient descent steps). Let's set it to $M = 8,192$ so that the number of epochs is an integer in each case. When the minibatch size is 2, we use one epoch to get 8,192 minibatches. And when the minibatch size is 16,384 (n is still also 16,384 samples), we get 8,192 epochs. If we do this, we get a completely different set of results, the square symbol curve in Figure 10-3, where we see that the mean score is pretty much a constant representing the constant number of gradient descent updates performed during training. When the minibatch size is small, corresponding to points near 0 in Figure 10-3, we do see a degradation in performance, but after a certain minibatch size, the performance levels off, reflecting the constant number of gradient descent updates combined with a reasonable estimate of the true gradient from using a large enough minibatch.

For the set of base neural network parameters, specifically for a fixed learning rate, fixing the number of epochs results in reduced performance because of the design of sklearn. Fixing the number of minibatches examined results in mainly constant performance.

Base Learning Rate

In Chapter 9, we introduced the basic equation for updating the weights of a neural network during training:

$$w \leftarrow w - \eta \Delta w$$

Here η (eta) is the learning rate, the parameter that controls the step size based on the gradient value, Δw. In sklearn, η is specified via the `learning _rate_init` parameter. During training, the learning rate is often reduced, so that the step sizes get smaller the closer we get to the training minimum (hopefully!). For our experiments here, however, we're using a constant learning rate, so whatever value we set `learning_rate_init` to persists throughout the entire training session. Let's see how this value affects learning.

For this experiment, we fix the minibatch size at 64 samples and the architecture to $(1000, 500)$, meaning two hidden layers with 1,000 and 500 nodes, respectively. We then look at two main effects. The first is what we get when we fix the number of epochs regardless of the base learning rate. In this case, we'll always take a set number of gradient descent steps during training. The second case fixes the *product* of the base learning rate and the number of epochs. This case is interesting because it looks at the effect on the test score of fewer large steps versus many small steps. The code for these experiments is in *mnist_experiments_base_lr.py*. The training set is the first 20,000 MNIST samples.

The first experiment fixes the epochs at 50 and loops over different base learning rates:

```
[0.2, 0.1, 0.05, 0.01, 0.005, 0.001, 0.0005, 0.0001]
```

The second uses the same base learning rates but varies the number of epochs so that in each case the product of the base learning rate and epochs is 1.5. This leads to the following number of epochs matched to the preceding base learning rates:

```
[8, 15, 30, 150, 300, 1500, 3000, 15000]
```

Running the two experiments takes some time. When they're complete, we can plot the test score as a function of the base learning rate size. Doing this gives us Figure 10-4.

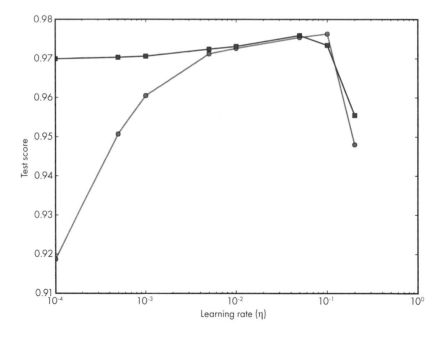

Figure 10-4: MNIST test scores as a function of the base learning rate. The circles represent the fixed epochs case. The squares are the fixed product of the base learning rate and the epochs case.

Figure 10-4 shows two plots. In the first plot, using circles, the number of epochs was fixed at 50. Fixing the number of epochs fixes the number of gradient descent steps taken during training. We then vary the learning rate. The larger the learning rate, the bigger the steps we'll take.

Imagine walking over a football field, attempting to get to the very center from one of the corners in a limited number of steps. If we take large steps, we might move over a lot of ground quickly, but we won't be able to zero in on the center because we'll keep stepping past it. If we take tiny steps, we'll cover only a short distance from the corner toward the center. We might be on track, but since we're allowed only a certain number steps, we can't reach the center. Intuitively, we can perhaps convince ourselves that there is a sweet spot where the step size and the number of steps we get to take combine to get us to the center.

We see this effect in the circle plot of Figure 10-4. The leftmost point represents the case of tiny steps. We do relatively poorly because we haven't traversed enough of the error space to find the minimum. Similarly, the rightmost point represents taking very large steps. We do poorly because we keep stepping past the minimum. The best score happens when the number of steps we get to make and the size of those steps work together to move us to the minimum. In the figure, this happens when the base learning rate is 0.1.

Now let's look at the square symbol plot in Figure 10-4. This plot comes from the scores found when the product of the base learning rate and the number of epochs is constant, meaning small learning rates will run for a large number of epochs. For the most part, the test scores are the same for all base learning rates except the very largest. In our walking over the football field thought experiment, the square symbol plot corresponds to taking a few large steps or very many small steps. We can imagine both approaches getting us close to the center of the field, at least until our step size is too large to let us land at the center.

Some readers might be objecting at this point. If we compare the first three points of both the circle and square plots in Figure 10-4, we see a large gap. For the circles, the performance improves as the base learning rate increases. For the squares, however, the performance remains high and constant regardless of the base learning rate. For the circles, we trained for 50 epochs, always. This is a more significant number of epochs than were used for the squares plot for the corresponding base learning rates. This means that in the circles' case, we stomped around quite a bit after we got near the center of the field. For the case of the squares, however, we limited the number of epochs, so we stopped walking when we were near the center of the field, hence the improved performance. This implies that we need to adjust the number of epochs (gradient descent steps taken) to match the learning rate so that we get near to the minimum of the loss function quickly, without a lot of stomping around, but not so quickly that we are taking large steps that won't let us converge on the minimum.

Thus far we've been holding the learning rate constant throughout training. Because of space considerations, we can't fully explore the effect of changing the learning rate during training. Still, we can at least use our football field thought experiment to help us visualize why changing the learning rate during training makes sense. Recall, the network is initialized intelligently but randomly. This means we start somewhere on the field at random. The odds are low that this arbitrary position is near the center, the minimum of the error surface, so we do need to apply gradient descent to move us closer to the center. At first, we might as well take significant steps to move quickly through the field. Since we are following the gradient, this moves us toward the center. If we keep taking large steps, however, we might overshoot the center. After taking a few large steps, we might think it wise to start taking smaller steps, believing that we are now closer to our goal of reaching the center. The more we walk, the smaller our steps so we can get as close to the center as possible. This is why the learning rate is typically reduced during training.

Training Set Size

We've mentioned that the number of samples in the training set affects performance significantly. Let's use the MNIST data to quantify this assertion. For this experiment, we'll vary the number of training set samples while adjusting the number of epochs so that in each case, we take (approximately) 1,000 gradient descent steps during training. The code for this experiment is in *mnist_nn_experiments_samples.py*. In all cases, the minibatch size is 100, and the architecture of the network has two hidden layers of 1,000 and 500 nodes, respectively. Figure 10-5 shows the results of this experiment.

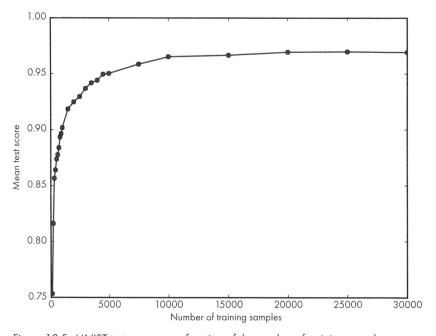

Figure 10-5: MNIST test scores as a function of the number of training samples

Figure 10-5 is particularly satisfying because it shows exactly what we'd expect to see. If we have too little training data, we cannot learn to generalize well because we're training the model with a very sparse sample from the parent distribution. As we add more and more training data, we'd expect a potentially rapid rise in the performance of the network since the training set is a better and better sample of the parent distribution we're asking the model to learn.

Figure 10-5 shows that increasing the training set size results in diminishing returns. Moving from 1,000 to 5,000 training set samples results in a substantial improvement in performance, but moving from 5,000 to even 10,000 samples gives us only a small performance boost, and further increases in the training set size level off at some ceiling performance. We can think of this level region as having reached some capacity—that the model has pretty much learned all it will learn from the dataset. At this point, we might think of enlarging the network architecture to see if we get a jump in test set scores provided we have enough training samples available.

L2 Regularization

In Chapter 9, we discussed regularization techniques that improve network generalization, including L2 regularization. We saw that L2 regularization, which adds a new term to the loss function during training, is functionally equivalent to weight decay and penalizes the network during training if the weights get large.

In sklearn, the parameter controlling the strength of L2 regularization is `alpha`. If this parameter is 0, there is no L2 regularization, while the regularization increases in intensity as `alpha` increases. Let's explore the effect of L2 regularization on our MNIST networks.

For this experiment, we'll fix the minibatch size at 64. We'll also set the momentum to 0 so that the effect we see is due to L2 regularization alone. Finally, we'll use a smaller network with two hidden layers of 100 and 50 nodes each and a small training set of the first 3,000 MNIST samples. The code is in *mnist_nn_experiments_L2.py*.

Unlike the previous experiments, in this case, we'd like to evaluate the test data after each training epoch so that we can watch the network learn over the training process. If it is learning, the error on the test set will go down as the number of training epochs increases. We know that sklearn will loop over all the minibatches in the dataset for one epoch, so we can set the number of training epochs to 1. However, if we set `max_iter` to 1 and then call the `fit` method, the next time we call `fit`, we'll start over with a newly initialized network. This won't help us at all; we need to preserve the weights and biases between calls to `fit`.

Fortunately for us, the creators of sklearn thought ahead and added the `warm_start` parameter. If this parameter is set to `True`, a call to `fit` will *not* re-initialize the network but will use the existing weights and biases. If we set `max_iter` to 1 and `warm_start` to `True`, we'll be able to watch the network learn by calling `score` after each epoch of training. Calling `score` gives us the accuracy on the test data. If we want the error, the value we need to track is 1 − `score`. This is the value we plot as a function of epoch. The `alpha` values we'll plot are

```
[0.0, 0.1, 0.2, 0.3, 0.4]
```

We've made these rather large compared to the default so we can see the effect.

Focusing on the test error only, the code for evaluating a single epoch is:

```
def epoch(x_train, y_train, x_test, y_test, clf):
    clf.fit(x_train, y_train)
    val_err = 1.0 - clf.score(x_test, y_test)
    clf.warm_start = True
    return val_err
```

Here, `fit` is called to perform one epoch of training. Then we calculate the error on the test set and store it in `val_err`. Setting `warm_start` to `True` after calling `fit` ensures that the first call to `epoch` will properly initialize the network, but subsequent calls will keep the weights and biases from the previous call.

Training then happens in a simple loop:

```
def run(x_train, y_train, x_test, y_test, clf, epochs):
    val_err = []
    clf.max_iter = 1
    for i in range(epochs):
        verr = epoch(x_train, y_train, x_test, y_test, clf)
        val_err.append(verr)
    return val_err
```

This loop collects the per epoch results and returns them to the `main` function, which itself loops over the α values we're interested in.

Let's run this code and plot `val_err`, the test error, as a function of the number of epochs for each `alpha`. Figure 10-6 is the result.

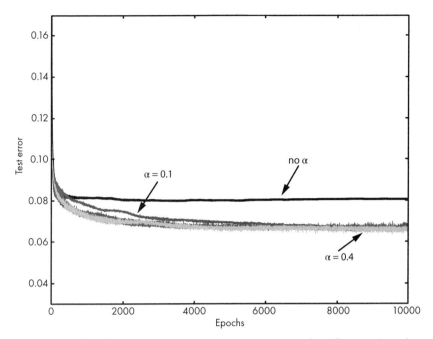

Figure 10-6: MNIST test error as a function of training epoch for different values of α

The first thing we notice in Figure 10-6 is that any nonzero value for α produces a lower test error compared to not using L2 regularization at all. We can conclude that L2 regularization is helpful. The different α values all result in approximately the same test error, but larger values are slightly more effective and reach a lower test error sooner. Compare α = 0.1 to α = 0.4, for example.

Notice that larger α values seem noisier: the plot is thicker as the error jumps around more, relative to the smaller α values. To understand this, think about the total loss minimized during training. When α is large, we're placing more importance on the L2 term relative to the network's error over the minibatch. This means that when we ask the network to adjust the weights and biases during backprop, it'll be more strongly affected by the magnitude of the parameters of the network than the training data itself. Because the network is focusing less on reducing the loss due to the training data, we might expect the per epoch test error to vary more.

Momentum

Momentum alters the weight update during training by adding in a fraction of the gradient value used to update the weight in the previous minibatch. The fraction is specified as a multiplier on the previous gradient value, [0, 1]. We covered momentum in Chapter 9.

Let's see how changing this parameter affects training. In this case, the setup for the experiment is simple. It's identical to the approach used previously for L2 regularization, but instead of fixing the momentum parameter (μ) and varying the L2 weight (α), we'll fix $\alpha = 0.0001$ and vary μ. All the other parts remain the same: training by single epochs, the network configuration, and so forth. See the file *mnist_nn_experiments_momentum.py*.

We'll explore these momentum values:

```
[0.0, 0.3, 0.5, 0.7, 0.9, 0.99]
```

They range from no momentum term ($\mu = 0$) to a large momentum term ($\mu = 0.99$). Running the experiment produces Figure 10-7.

In Figure 10-7, we see three distinct regions. The first, represented by no momentum or relatively small momentum values ($\mu = 0.3$, $\mu = 0.5$), shows the highest test set error. The second shows improvement with moderate momentum values ($\mu = 0.7$, $\mu = 0.9$), including the "standard" (sklearn default) value of 0.9. In this case, however, a large momentum of 0.99 lowers the test set error from about 7.5 percent to about 6 percent. Momentum helps and should be used, especially with values near the standard of 0.9. In practice, people seldom seem to alter the momentum much, but as this example shows, sometimes it makes a big difference to the results.

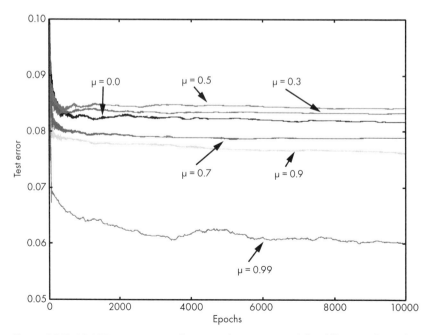

Figure 10-7: MNIST test error as a function of training epoch for different values of μ

Note that we severely limited the training set to a mere 3,000 samples, about 300 per digit, which likely made momentum matter more because the training set was a small and less complete of a sample of the parent distribution we want the model to learn. Increasing the training set size to 30,000 results in a different, and more typical, ordering of the plot, where a momentum of 0.9 is the best option.

Weight Initialization

Once treated rather cavalierly, the initial set of values used for the weights and biases of a network is now known to be extremely important. The simple experiment of this section shows this plainly.

The sklearn toolkit initializes the weights and biases of a neural network by calling the _init_coef method of the MLPClassifier class. This method selects weights and biases randomly according to the Glorot algorithm we discussed in Chapter 9. This algorithm sets the weights and biases to values sampled uniformly from the range

$$\left[-\sqrt{\frac{A}{f_{in} + f_{out}}}, \ \sqrt{\frac{A}{f_{in} + f_{out}}} \ \right]$$

where f_{in} is the number of inputs and f_{out} is the number of outputs for the current layer being initialized. If the activation function is a sigmoid, $A = 2$; otherwise, $A = 6$.

If we play a little trick, we can change the way that sklearn initializes the network and thereby experiment with alternative initialization schemes. The trick uses Python's object-oriented programming abilities. If we make a subclass of MLPClassifier, let's call it simply Classifier, we can override the _init_coef method with our own. Python also allows us to add new member variables to a class instance arbitrarily, which gives us all we need.

The remainder of the experiment follows the format of the previous sections. We'll ultimately plot the test error by epoch of the MNIST digits trained on a subset of the full data for different initialization approaches. The model itself will use the first 6,000 training samples, a minibatch size of 64, a constant learning rate of 0.01, a momentum of 0.9, an L2 regularization parameter of 0.2, and an architecture with two hidden layers of 100 and 50 nodes each. See *mnist_nn_experiments_init.py* for this experiment's code.

We'll test four new weight initialization schemes along with the standard Glorot approach of sklearn. The schemes are shown in Table 10-5.

Table 10-5: Weight Initialization Schemes

Name	Equation	Description
Glorot	$\left[-\sqrt{\frac{6}{f_{in}+f_{out}}},\ \sqrt{\frac{6}{f_{in}+f_{out}}} \right]$	sklearn default
He	$N(0,1)\sqrt{\frac{2}{f_{in}}}$	He initialization for ReLU
Xavier	$N(0,1)\sqrt{\frac{1}{f_{in}}}$	Alternate Xavier
Uniform	$0.01(U(0,1)\text{-}0.5)$	Classic small uniform
Gaussian	$0.005N(0,1)$	Classic small Gaussian

Recall that $N(0,1)$ refers to a sample from a bell curve with a mean of 0 and a standard deviation of 1 while $U(0,1)$ refers to a sample drawn uniformly from $[0,1)$, meaning all values in that range are equally likely except 1.0. Each of the new initialization methods sets the bias values to 0, always. However, sklearn's Glorot implementation sets the bias values in the same way it sets the weights.

NOTE *As mentioned in Chapter 9, both* Xavier *and* Glorot *refer to the same person, Xavier Glorot. We're differentiating here because the form we're calling* Xavier *is referred to as such in other machine learning toolkits like Caffe, and the equation used is different from the equation used in the original paper.*

This all sounds nice and neat, but how to implement it in code? First, we define a new Python class, `Classifier`, which is a subclass of `MLPClassifier`. As a subclass, the new class immediately inherits all the functionality of the superclass (`MLPClassifier`) while allowing us the freedom to override any of the superclass methods with our own implementation. We simply need to define our own version of `_init_coef` with the same arguments and return values. In code, it looks like this:

```
class Classifier(MLPClassifier):
    def _init_coef(self, fan_in, fan_out):
        if (self.init_scheme == 0):
            return super(Classifier, self)._init_coef(fan_in, fan_out)
        elif (self.init_scheme == 1):
            weights = 0.01*(np.random.random((fan_in, fan_out))-0.5)
            biases = np.zeros(fan_out)
        elif (self.init_scheme == 2):
            weights = 0.005*(np.random.normal(size=(fan_in, fan_out)))
            biases = np.zeros(fan_out)
        elif (self.init_scheme == 3):
            weights = np.random.normal(size=(fan_in, fan_out))* \
                            np.sqrt(2.0/fan_in)
            biases = np.zeros(fan_out)
        elif (self.init_scheme == 4):
            weights = np.random.normal(size=(fan_in, fan_out))* \
```

```
                    np.sqrt(1.0/fan_in)
          biases = np.zeros(fan_out)
```

The initialization we perform depends on the value of `init_scheme`. This is a new member variable that we use to select the initialization method (see Table 10-6).

Table 10-6: Initialization Scheme and `init_scheme` Value

Value	Initialization method
0	sklearn default
1	Classic small uniform
2	Classic small Gaussian
3	He initialization
4	Alternate Xavier

We set the variable immediately after creating the `Classifier` object.

We know that training a network more than once results in slightly different performance because of the way the network is initialized. Therefore, training a single network for each initialization type will likely lead to a wrong view of how well the initialization performs because we might hit a bad set of initial weights and biases. To mitigate this, we need to train multiple versions of the network and report the average performance. Since we want to plot the test error as a function of the training epoch, we need to track the test error at each epoch for each training of each initialization scheme. This suggests a three-dimensional array:

```
test_err = np.zeros((trainings, init_types, epochs))
```

We have trainings trainings of each initialization type (init_types) for a maximum of epochs epochs.

With all of this in place, the generation and storage of the actual experiment output is straightforward, if rather slow, taking the better part of a day to run:

```
for i in range(trainings):
    for k in range(init_types):
        nn = Classifier(solver="sgd", verbose=False, tol=0,
                nesterovs_momentum=False, early_stopping=False,
                learning_rate_init=0.01, momentum=0.9,
                hidden_layer_sizes=(100,50), activation="relu", alpha=0.2,
                learning_rate="constant", batch_size=64, max_iter=1)
        nn.init_scheme = k
        test_err[i,k,:] = run(x_train, y_train, x_test, y_test, nn, epochs)
np.save("mnist_nn_experiments_init_results.npy", test_err)
```

Here nn is the classifier instance to train, `init_scheme` sets the initialization scheme to use, and `run` is the function we defined earlier to train and test the network incrementally.

If we set the number of training sessions to 10, the number of epochs to 4,000, and plot the mean test error per epoch, we get Figure 10-8.

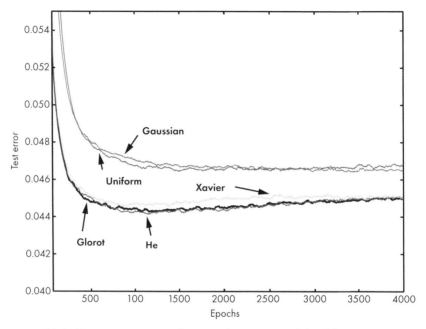

Figure 10-8: MNIST test error as a function of training epoch for different weight initialization methods (mean over 10 training runs)

Let's understand what the figure is showing us. The five initialization approaches are marked, each pointing to one of the five curves in the figure. The curves themselves are familiar to us by now; they show the test set error as a function of the training epoch. In this case, the value plotted for each curve is the average over 10 training runs of the same network architecture initialized with the same approach but different random values.

We immediately see two distinct groups of results. On the top, we have the test error for the classic initialization approaches using small uniform or normally distributed values (Gaussian). On the bottom, we have the results for the more principled initialization in current use. Even this basic experiment shows the effectiveness of modern initialization approaches quite clearly. Recall, the classic approaches were part of the reason neural networks had a bad name a few decades ago. Networks were finicky and difficult to train in large part because of improper initialization.

Looking at the bottom set of results, we see that for this experiment, there is little difference between the sklearn default initialization, which we are calling *Glorot*, and the initialization approach of He. The two plots are virtually identical. The plot labeled *Xavier* is slightly worse at first , but toward the end of our training runs matches the other two. Sklearn is using a good initialization strategy.

The plot also shows us something else. For the classic initialization approaches, we see the test set error level off and remain more or less constant. For the modern initialization approaches, we observe the test error increase slightly with the training epoch. This is particularly true for the Glorot and He methods. This increase is a telltale sign of overfitting: as we keep training, the model stops learning general features of the parent distribution and starts to focus on specific features of the training set. We didn't plot the training set error, but it would be going down even as the test set error starts to rise. The lowest test set error is at about 1,200 epochs. Ideally, this would be where we stop training because we have the most reliable evidence that the model is in a good place to correctly predict new, unseen inputs. Further training tends to degrade model generalization.

Why did the increase in the test error happen? The likely cause of this effect is too small of a training set, only 6,000 samples. Also, the model architecture is not very large, with only 100 and 50 nodes in the hidden layers.

This section dramatically demonstrates the benefit of using current, state-of-the-art network initialization. When we explore convolutional neural networks in Chapter 12, we'll use these approaches exclusively.

Feature Ordering

We'll end our MNIST experiments with a bit of fun that we'll return to again when we're exploring convolutional neural networks. All of the experiments so far use the MNIST digits as a vector made by laying the rows of the digit images end to end. When we do this, we know that the elements of the vector are related to each other in a way that will reconstruct the digit should we take the vector and reshape it into a 28×28 element array. This means, except for the end of one row and the beginning of the next, that the pixels in the row are still part of the digit—the spatial relationship of the components of the image is preserved.

However, if we scramble the pixels of the image, but always scramble the pixels in the same way, we'll destroy the local spatial relationship between the pixels. This local relationship is what we use when we look at the image to decide what digit it represents. We look for the top part of a 5 to be a straight line segment and the bottom portion to curve on the right side, and so forth.

Look at Figure 7-3. The figure shows MNIST digit images on the top row and what the same digit images look like after scrambling (bottom). In Chapter 7, we showed that this scrambling does not affect the accuracy of classic machine learning models; the models consider the inputs holistically, not by local spatial relationships as we do. Is this true for neural networks as well? Also, if true, will the network learn as quickly with the scrambled inputs as it does with the original images? Let's find out.

The code for this experiment is found in *mnist_nn_experiments_scrambled* *.py*, where we simply define our now expected neural network model

```
MLPClassifier(solver="sgd", verbose=False, tol=0,
  nesterovs_momentum=False, early_stopping=False,
  learning_rate_init=0.01, momentum=0.9,
  hidden_layer_sizes=(100,50), activation="relu",
  alpha=0.2, learning_rate="constant", batch_size=64, max_iter=1)
```

and train it on the first 6,000 MNIST digit samples—first as usual, and then using the scrambled versions. We compute the test set error as a function of the epoch and average the results over 10 runs before plotting. The result is Figure 10-9.

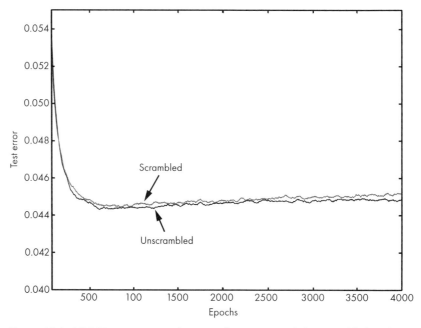

Figure 10-9: MNIST test error as a function of training epoch for scrambled and unscrambled digits

In the figure, we see the answer to our earlier questions. First, yes, traditional neural networks do interpret their input vectors holistically, like the classic models. Second, yes, the network learns just as rapidly with the scrambled digits as it does with the unscrambled ones. The difference between the scrambled and unscrambled curves in Figure 10-9 is not statistically significant.

These results indicate that (traditional) neural networks "understand" their inputs in their entirety and do not look for local spatial relationships. We'll see a different outcome to this experiment when we work with convolutional neural networks (Chapter 12). It's precisely this lack of spatial awareness (assuming images as inputs) that limited neural networks for so long and led to the development of convolutional neural networks, which are spatially aware.

Summary

In this chapter, we explored the concepts developed in Chapters 8 and 9 via experiments with the MNIST dataset. By varying key parameters associated with the network architecture and gradient descent learning process, we increased our intuition as to how the parameters influence the overall performance of the network. Space considerations prevented us from thoroughly exploring all the MLPClassifier options, so I encourage you to experiment more on your own. In particular, experiment with using the different solvers, Nesterov momentum, early stopping, and, particularly crucial for training convolutional neural networks, nonconstant learning rates.

The next chapter explores techniques and metrics for evaluating the performance of machine learning models. This interlude before we jump to convolutional neural networks will supply us with tools we can use to help understand the performance of more advanced model types.

11

EVALUATING MODELS

So far, we've evaluated models by looking at their accuracy on a held-out test set. This is natural and intuitive, but as we'll learn in this chapter, it's not all that we can, or should, do to evaluate a model.

We'll begin this chapter by defining metrics and delineating some basic assumptions. Then we'll look at why we need more than just accuracy. We'll introduce the concept of a confusion matrix and spend time discussing the metrics we can derive from it. From there, we'll jump to performance curves, which are the best way to compare different models together. Finally, we'll extend the idea of a confusion matrix to the multiclass case. We won't say all there is to say about performance metrics, as this area is still somewhat evolving. However, by the end of this chapter, you'll be familiar with the sorts of numbers that people involved in machine learning will throw around and have a good understanding of what they mean.

Definitions and Assumptions

There are many other metrics besides accuracy that we can use to help us evaluate how well a model is performing. These allow us to reasonably compare models. Let's start by defining the word *metric*. For us, a metric is a number or set of numbers that represents something about how well the model is doing.

The value of the metric increases or decreases as the performance of the model increases or decreases, or possibly vice versa. At times, we'll be a bit sloppy and refer to graphs as metrics as well since we use them to judge the performance of a model.

We're concerned with evaluating a model for which we have a single held-out test set. We'll assume that we followed the advice of Chapter 4 and built three datasets: a training set to teach the model, a validation set to decide when the model was done training, and a held-out test set to evaluate the trained model. We've now trained our model, thereby utilizing the training and validation sets, and want to know how well we've done.

We have another, implicit assumption in this chapter. It's a crucial one: we assume that the held-out test set is a good representation of the parent distribution that generated the data. Put another way, the held-out test set must represent the sort of data the model will encounter in the wild in as many ways as possible. For example, the frequency with which particular classes appear in the test set should match, as far as is practical, the expected rates that will be encountered when the model is used.

This is necessary because the training set is conditioning the model to expect a particular distribution, a particular set of characteristics, and if the data given to the model when it's used has different characteristics, the model won't perform well. A difference in distribution between the training set and the set of data presented to the model when it's used is one of the most common reasons deployed machine learning models fail in actual use.

Why Accuracy Is Not Enough

A binary classifier outputs a single decision for a particular input: class 0 or class 1. Let's define the following,

N_c, the number of test examples the model correctly classified
N_w, the number of test examples the model got wrong

Then, the overall accuracy of this model, a number between 0 and 1, is

$$\mathrm{ACC} = \frac{N_c}{N_c + N_w}$$

This is the accuracy as we have been using it throughout the book. Note, in this chapter, we will use *ACC* when we mean the overall accuracy.

This seems like a pretty reasonable metric, but there are a couple of good reasons not to trust this number too much. For example, N_c and N_w tell us nothing about the relative frequency of each class. What if one class is rare? Let's see how that might affect things.

If the model is 95 percent accurate (ACC = 0.95), we might be happy. However, let's say the frequency (read *prior probability*) of class 1 is only 5 percent, meaning that on average, if we draw 100 samples from the test set, about 5 of them will be of class 1 and the other 95 will be of class 0. We see that a model that predicts all inputs are of class 0 will be right 95 percent of the time. But consider this: our model might be returning only class 0 for all inputs. If we stick with the overall accuracy, we might think we have a good model when, in fact, we have a terrible model that we could implement in two lines of Python as

```python
def predict(x):
    return 0
```

In this code, we say that the class is 0 regardless of the input feature vector, x. No one would be satisfied with such a model.

The prior probabilities of the classes affect how we should think about the overall accuracy. However, if we know the following

N_0, the number of class 0 instances in our test set
N_1, the number of class 1 instances in our test set
C_0, the number of class 0 instances our model found
C_1, the number of class 1 instances our model found

we can easily compute the accuracy per class:

$$ACC_0 = \frac{C_0}{N_0}$$

$$ACC_1 = \frac{C_1}{N_1}$$

$$ACC = \frac{C_0 + C_1}{N_0 + N_1}$$

The final expression is just another way to compute the overall accuracy because it tallies all of the correct classifications divided by the number of samples tested.

The per class accuracy is better than the overall accuracy because it accounts for any imbalance in the frequency of the respective classes in the test set. For our previous hypothetical test set with the frequency of class 1 at 5 percent, if the classifier were predicting class 0 for all inputs, we would detect it because our per class accuracies would be $ACC_0 = 1.0$ and $ACC_1 = 0.0$. This makes sense. We'd get every class 0 sample correct and every class 1 sample wrong (we'd call them class 0 anyway). Per class accuracies will show up again when we consider evaluating multiclass models.

A more subtle reason to not just use the overall accuracy is that being wrong might bring a much higher cost than being right. This introduces something outside just the test set: it introduces the meaning we assign to class 0 and class 1. For example, if our model is testing for breast cancer, perhaps using the dataset we created in Chapter 5, reporting class 1 (malignant) when, in fact, the sample does not represent a malignant case might cause anxiety for the woman waiting for her test results. With further testing, however, she'll be shown to not have breast cancer after all. But consider the other case. A benign result that is actually malignant might mean that she will not receive treatment, or receive it too late, which could very well be fatal. The relative cost of one class versus another isn't the same and might literally mean the difference between life and death. The same could be said of a self-driving car that thinks the child playing in the middle of the road is an empty soda can, or any number of other real-world examples.

We use models in the real world, so their outputs are connected to the real world, and sometimes the cost associated with an output is significant. Using just the overall accuracy of a model can be misleading because it does not take the cost of an error into account.

The 2 x 2 Confusion Matrix

The models we've worked with so far have all ultimately assigned each input a class label. For example, a neural network with a logistic output is interpreted as a probability of membership of class 1. Using a typical threshold of 0.5 lets us assign a class label: if the output is < 0.5, call the input class 0; otherwise, call it class 1. For other model types, the decision rule is different (for example, voting in k-NN), but the effect is the same: we get a class assignment for the input.

If we run our entire test set through our model and apply the decision rule, we get the assigned class label along with the true class label for each sample. Again, thinking only of the binary classifier case, we have four possible outcomes for each input sample in regards to the assigned class and the true class (see Table 11-1).

Table 11-1: Possible Relationships Between the True Class Label and the Assigned Class Label for a Binary Classifier

Assigned class	True class	Case
0	0	True negative (TN)
0	1	False negative (FN)
1	0	False positive (FP)
1	1	True positive (TP)

The *Case* label defines how we'll talk about these situations. If the actual class of the input is class 0 and the model assigns class 0, we have a correctly identified negative case, so we have a *true negative*, or *TN*. If the actual class is class 1 and the model assigns class 1, we have a correctly identified positive case, so we have a *true positive*, or *TP*. However, if the actual class is class 1 and the model assigns class 0, we have a positive case wrongly called a negative case, so we have a *false negative*, or *FN*. Finally, if the actual class is 0 and the model assigns class 1, we have a negative case wrongly called a positive case, so we have a *false positive*, or *FP*.

We can place each of the inputs in our test set into one, and only one, of these cases. Doing this lets us tally the number of times each case appears in the test set, which we can present nicely as a table (see Table 11-2).

Table 11-2: Definition of the Class Labels in the 2 × 2 Table

	Actual class 1	Actual class 0
Model assigns class 1	TP	FP
Model assigns class 0	FN	TN

I have placed the case labels (TP, FP, and so forth) in the location where the actual tally counts would go for each case.

This table is called a 2 × 2 *confusion matrix* (or 2 × 2 *contingency table*). It is 2 × 2 because there are two rows and two columns. It is a confusion matrix because it shows us at a glance how the classifier is performing and, especially, where it is confused. The classifier is confused when it assigns an instance of one class to the other class. In the 2 × 2 table, this confusion shows up as counts that are not along the main diagonal of the table (upper left to lower right). These are the FP and FN entries. A model that performs flawlessly on the test set will have FP = 0 and FN = 0; it will make no mistakes in assigning class labels.

In Chapter 7, we experimented with the breast cancer dataset built in Chapter 5. We reported the performance of classic models against this dataset by looking at their overall accuracy. This is what the sklearn score method returns. Let's now instead look at some 2 × 2 tables generated from the test set for these models.

The code we are looking at is in the file *bc_experiments.py*. This code trains multiple classic model types. Instead of using the overall accuracy, however, let's introduce a new function that computes the entries in the 2 × 2 table (Listing 11-1):

```
def tally_predictions(clf, x, y):
    p = clf.predict(x)
    score = clf.score(x,y)
    tp = tn = fp = fn = 0
    for i in range(len(y)):
        if (p[i] == 0) and (y[i] == 0):
            tn += 1
        elif (p[i] == 0) and (y[i] == 1):
            fn += 1
```

```
        elif (p[i] == 1) and (y[i] == 0):
            fp += 1
        else:
            tp += 1
    return [tp, tn, fp, fn, score]
```

Listing 11-1: Generating tally counts

This function accepts a trained sklearn model object (clf), the test samples (x), and the corresponding actual test labels (y). The first thing this function does is use the sklearn model to predict a class label for each of the test samples; the result is stored in p. It then calculates the overall score, and loops over each of the test samples and compares the predicted class label (p) to the actual known class label (y) to see if that sample is a true positive, true negative, false positive, or false negative. When done, all of these values are returned.

Applying tally_predictions to the output of *bc_experiments.py* gives us Table 11-3. Here, the sklearn model type is given.

Table 11-3: 2 × 2 Tables for the Breast Cancer Test Set

Nearest Centroid	Actual 1	Actual 0
Model assigns 1	43	4
Model assigns 0	2	65

3-NN	Actual 1	Actual 0
Model assigns 1	45	1
Model assigns 0	0	68

Decision Tree	Actual 1	Actual 0
Model assigns 1	44	6
Model assigns 0	1	63

SVM (linear)	Actual 1	Actual 0
Model assigns 1	45	4
Model assigns 0	0	65

In Table 11-3, we see four 2 × 2 tables corresponding to the test set applied to the respective models: Nearest Centroid, 3-NN, Decision Tree, and linear SVM. From the tables alone, we see that the best-performing model was the 3-NN as it had only one false positive and no false negatives. This means that the model never called a true malignant case benign and only once called a benign case malignant. Given our discussion in the previous section, we see that this is an encouraging result.

Look now at the results for the Nearest Centroid and the Decision Tree. The overall accuracies for these models are 94.7 percent and 93.9 percent, respectively. From the accuracy alone, we might be tempted to say that the Nearest Centroid model is better. However, if we look at the 2 × 2 tables, we see that even though the Decision Tree had more false positives (6), it had only one false negative, while the Nearest Centroid had two false negatives. Again, in this case, a false negative means a missed cancer detection with potentially serious consequences. So, for this dataset, we want to minimize false negatives even if that means we need to tolerate a small increase in false positives. Therefore, we'll select the Decision Tree over the Nearest Centroid model.

Metrics Derived from the 2 x 2 Confusion Matrix

Looking at the raw 2×2 table is helpful, but even more helpful are the metrics derived from it. Let's look at several of these in this section to see how they can help us interpret the information in the 2×2 table. Before we start, however, we should keep in mind that the metrics we'll discuss are sometimes a bit controversial. There is still healthy academic debate as to which are best to use when. Our intention here is to introduce them via examples, and to describe what it is that they are measuring. As a machine learning practitioner, you'll encounter virtually all of these from time to time, so it's wise to at least be familiar with them.

Deriving Metrics from the 2 x 2 Table

The first metrics are derived directly from the values in the 2×2 table: TP, TN, FP, FN. Think of these as the bread-and-butter metrics. They're easy to compute and easy to understand. Recall the general form of the 2×2 table from Table 11-2. We'll now define two other quantities:

$$\text{True positive rate (TPR)} = \frac{TP}{TP + FN}$$

$$\text{True negative rate (TNR)} = \frac{TN}{TN + FP}$$

The *true positive rate (TPR)* is the probability that an actual instance of class 1 will be correctly identified by the model. The TPR is frequently known by other names: *sensitivity*, *recall*, and *hit rate*. You will likely see it referred to as *sensitivity* in medical literature.

The *true negative rate (TNR)* is the probability that an actual instance of class 0 will be correctly identified by the model. The TNR is also known as the *specificity*, again, particularly so in medical literature. Both of these quantities, as probabilities, have a value between 0 and 1; higher is better. A perfect classifier will have TPR = TNR = 1.0; this happens when it makes no mistakes so that FP = FN = 0, always.

The TPR and TNR need to be understood together to assess a model. For example, we previously mentioned that if class 1 is rare and the model always predicts class 0, it will have high accuracy. If we look at TPR and TNR in that case, we'll see that the TNR is 1 because the model never assigns an instance of class 0 to class 1 (FP = 0). However, the TPR is 0 for the very same reason, all actual instances of class 1 will be misidentified as false negatives; they get assigned to class 0. Therefore, the two metrics together immediately indicate that the model is not a good one.

What about the breast cancer case where a false negative might be fatal? How do we want the TPR and TNR to look in this case? Ideally, of course, we want them to both be as high as possible, but we might be willing to use the model anyway if the TPR is very high while the TNR might be lower. In that situation, we know that actual breast cancers, when presented, are detected almost always. Why? Because the false negative count (FN) is virtually 0, so the denominator of the TPR is about TP, which implies a TPR of about 1.0. If, on the other hand, we tolerate false positives (actual negative instances called malignant by the model), we see that the TNR might be well below 1.0 because the denominator of the TNR includes the FP counts.

The TPR and TNR tell us something about the likelihood that the model will pick up actual class 1 and class 0 instances. What it does not tell us, however, is how much faith we should put into the output of the model. For example, if the model says "class 1," should we believe it? To make that assessment, we need two other metrics derived directly from the 2×2 table:

$$\text{Positive predictive value (PPV)} = \frac{\text{TP}}{\text{TP} + \text{FP}}$$

$$\text{Negative predictive value (NPV)} = \frac{\text{TN}}{\text{TN} + \text{FN}}$$

The *positive predictive value (PPV)* is most often known as the *precision*. It's the probability that when the model says the instance is of class 1, it is of class 1. Similarly, the *negative predictive value (NPV)* is the probability that the model is correct when it claims an instance is of class 0. Both of these values are also numbers between 0 and 1, where higher is better.

The only difference between the TPR and the PPV is whether we consider false negatives or false positives in the denominator. By including the false positives, the instances the model says are of class 1 when they are really of class 0; we get the probability that the model output is correct.

For the case of a model that always predicts class 0, the PPV is undefined because both the TP and FP are zero. All of the class 1 instances are pushed into the FN count, and the TN count includes all the actual class 0 instances. For the case where TPR is high, but TNR is not, we have a nonzero FP count so that the PPV goes down. Let's make up an example to see why this is so and how we might understand it.

Let's say that our breast cancer model has produced the following 2×2 table (Table 11-4).

Table 11-4: A Hypothetical 2×2 Table for a Breast Cancer Dataset

	Actual 1	Actual 0
Model assigns 1	312	133
Model assigns 0	6	645

In this example, the metrics we have covered so far are

$$TPR = 0.9811$$
$$TNR = 0.8398$$
$$PPV = 0.7011$$
$$NPV = 0.9908$$

This means a truly malignant case will be called malignant by the model 98 percent of the time, but a benign case will be called benign only 84 percent of the time. The PPV of 70 percent implies that when the model says "malignant," there is only a 70 percent chance that the case is malignant; however, because of the high TPR, we know that buried in the "malignant" outputs are virtually all of the actual breast cancer cases. Notice also that this implies a high NPV, so when the model says "benign," we have very high confidence that the instance is not breast cancer. This is what makes the model useful even if the PPV is less than 100 percent. In a clinical setting, this model will warrant further testing when it says "malignant" but in general, no further testing will likely be needed if it says "benign." Of course, what acceptable levels of these metrics are depends upon the use case for the model. Some might call an NPV of only 99.1 percent too low given the potentially very high cost of missing a cancer detection. Thoughts like these likely also motivate the recommended frequency of screening.

There are two additional basic metrics we can easily derive from the 2×2 table:

$$\text{False positive rate (FPR)} = \frac{FP}{FP + TN}$$

$$\text{False negative rate (FNR)} = \frac{FN}{FN + TP}$$

These metrics tell us the likelihood that a sample will be a false positive if the actual class is class 0 or a false negative if the actual class is class 1, respectively. The FPR will show up again later when we talk about using curves to assess models. Notice that FPR = 1 – TNR and FNR = 1 – TPR.

Calculating these basic metrics is straightforward, especially if we use the output of the `tally_predictions` function defined previously as the input (Listing 11-2):

```
def basic_metrics(tally):
    tp, tn, fp, fn, _ = tally
    return {
        "TPR": tp / (tp + fn),
        "TNR": tn / (tn + fp),
        "PPV": tp / (tp + fp),
        "NPV": tn / (tn + fn),
```

```
        "FPR": fp / (fp + tn),
        "FNR": fn / (fn + tp)
    }
```

Listing 11-2: Calculating basic metrics

We break up the list returned by `tally_predictions`, disregarding the accuracy, and then build and return a dictionary containing each of the six basic metrics we described. Of course, robust code would check for pathological cases where the denominators are zero, but we've ignored that code here to preserve clarity in the presentation.

Using Our Metrics to Interpret Models

Let's use `tally_predictions` and `basic_metrics` to interpret some models. We'll work with the vector form of the MNIST data but keep only digits 3 and 5 so that we have a binary classifier. The code is similar to that found in *mnist_experiments.py*, which we used in Chapter 7.

Keeping only digits 3 and 5 leaves us with 11,552 training samples (6,131 3s; 5,421 5s) and 1,902 test samples of which 1,010 are 3s and 892 are 5s. The actual code is in *mnist_2x2_tables.py* with selected output in Table 11-5.

Table 11-5: Selected Output from MNIST 3 vs. 5 Models and Corresponding Basic Metrics

Model	TP	TN	FP	FN
Nearest Centroid	760	909	101	132
3-NN	878	994	16	14
Naïve Bayes	612	976	34	280
RF 500	884	1,003	7	8
LinearSVM	853	986	24	39

Model	TPR	TNR	PPV	NPV	FPR	FNR
Nearest Centroid	0.8520	0.9000	0.8827	0.8732	0.1000	0.1480
3-NN	0.9843	0.9842	0.9821	0.9861	0.0158	0.0157
Naïve Bayes	0.6851	0.9663	0.9474	0.7771	0.0337	0.3139
RF 500	0.9910	0.9931	0.9921	0.9921	0.0069	0.0090
LinearSVM	0.9563	0.9762	0.9726	0.9620	0.0238	0.0437

In Table 11-5, we see the raw counts at the top and the metrics defined in this section at the bottom. Lots of numbers! Let's parse things a bit to see what's going on. We'll concentrate on the metrics at the bottom of the table. The first two columns show the true positive rate (sensitivity, recall) and the true negative rate (specificity). These values should be examined together.

If we look at the Nearest Centroid results, we see TPR = 0.8520 and TNR = 0.9000. Here class 1 is a five, and class 0 is a three. So, the Nearest Centroid classifier will call 85 percent of the fives it sees "five." Similarly, it will call 90 percent of the threes it sees "three." While not too shabby, we should not be impressed. Looking down the columns, we see that two models performed very well for these metrics: 3-NN and the Random Forest with 500 trees. In both cases, the TPR and TNR were nearly identical and quite close to 1.0. This is a sign of the model performing well. Absolute perfection would be TPR = TNR = PPV = NPV = 1.0 and FPR = FNR = 0.0. The closer we get to perfection, the better. If attempting to pick the best model for this classifier, we would likely choose the Random Forest because it was the closest to perfection on the test set.

Let's look briefly at the Naïve Bayes results. The TNR (specificity) is reasonably high, about 97 percent. However, the TPR (sensitivity) of 68.5 percent is pathetic. Roughly speaking, only two out of every three 5's presented to this model will be correctly classified. If we examine the next two columns, the positive and negative predictive values, we see a PPV of 94.7 percent, meaning when the model does happen to say the input is a five, we can be somewhat confident that it is a five. However, the negative predictive value isn't so good at 77.7 percent. Looking at the top portion of Table 11-5 shows us what is happening in this case. The FP count is only 34 out of 1010 threes in the test set, but the FN count is high: 280 of the fives were labeled "three." This is the source of the low NPV for this model.

Here is a good rule of thumb for these metrics: a well-performing model has TPR, TNR, PPV, and NPV very close to 1.0, and FPR and FNR very close to 0.0.

Look again at Table 11-5, particularly the lower metrics for the Random Forest. As their names suggest, the FPR and FNR values are rates. We can use them to estimate how often FP and FN will occur when using the model. For example, if we present the model with $N = 1,000$ cases that are threes (class 0), we can use the FPR to estimate how many of them the model will call fives (class 1):

$$\text{estimated number of FP} = \text{FPR} \times N = 0.0069(1000) \approx 7$$

A similar calculation gives us the estimated number of FN for $N = 1000$: instances that are really 5's:

$$\text{estimated number of FN} = \text{FNR} \times N = 0.0090(1000) = 9$$

The same holds for the TPR and TNR, which also have "rate" in their names ($N = 1000$ each for actual threes and fives):

$$\text{estimated number of TP} = \text{TPR} \times N = 0.9910(1000) = 991$$
$$\text{estimated number of FN} = \text{FNR} \times N = 0.9931(1000) = 993$$

These calculations show how well this model performs on the test data.

More Advanced Metrics

Let's look in this section at what I'm arbitrarily calling *more advanced metrics*. I say they are more advanced because instead of using the 2×2 table entries directly, they are built from values calculated from the table itself. In particular, we'll examine five advanced metrics: informedness, markedness, F1 score, Cohen's kappa, and the Matthews correlation coefficient (MCC).

Informedness and Markedness

Informedness and *markedness* go together. They are somewhat less well known than other metrics in this section, but they will hopefully be better known in the future. I said earlier that TPR (sensitivity) and TNR (specificity) should be interpreted together. The informedness (also called Youden's J statistic) does just that:

$$\text{Informedness} = \text{TPR} + \text{TNR} - 1$$

Informedness is a number in $[-1, +1]$ that combines both the TPR and TNR. The higher the informedness is, the better. An informedness of 0 implies random guessing, while an informedness of 1 implies perfection (on the test set). An informedness of less than 0 might suggest a model that is worse than random guessing. An informedness of -1 implies that all true positive instances were called negatives, and vice versa. In that case, we could swap the label the model wants to assign to each input and get a quite good model. Only pathological models lead to negative informedness values.

The markedness combines the positive and negative predictive values in the same way that informedness combines TPR and TNR:

$$\text{Markedness} = \text{PPV} + \text{NPV} - 1$$

We see that it has the same range as informedness. The informedness says something about how well the model is doing at correctly labeling inputs from each class. The markedness says something about how well the model is doing at being correct when it does claim a particular label for a particular input, be it class 0 or class 1. Random guessing will give a markedness near 0 and perfection a markedness near 1.

I like that the informedness and markedness each capture essential aspects of the model's performance in a single number. Some claim that these metrics are unbiased by the prior probabilities of the particular classes. This means if class 1 is significantly less common than class 0, the informedness and markedness are not affected. For in-depth details, see "Evaluation: From Precision, Recall and F-measure to ROC, Informedness, Markedness, and Correlation" by David Martin Powers.

F1 Score

The *F1 score*, rightly or wrongly, is widely used, and we should be familiar with it. The F1 score combines two basic metrics into one. Its definition is straightforward in terms of precision (PPV) and recall (TPR):

$$F1 = \frac{2 \cdot \text{precision} \cdot \text{recall}}{\text{precision} + \text{recall}} = \frac{2 \cdot \text{PPV} \cdot \text{TPR}}{\text{PPV} + \text{TPR}}$$

The F1 score is a number in [0, 1], where higher is better. Where does this formula come from? It's not obvious in this form, but the the F1 score is the harmonic mean of the precision and recall. A *harmonic mean* is the reciprocal of the arithmetic mean of the reciprocals. Like this,

$$F1 = \left(\frac{1}{2} \left(\frac{1}{\text{precision}} + \frac{1}{\text{recall}} \right) \right)^{-1}$$

$$= \left(\frac{\text{precision} + \text{recall}}{2 \cdot \text{precision} \cdot \text{recall}} \right)^{-1}$$

$$= \frac{2 \cdot \text{precision} \cdot \text{recall}}{\text{precision} + \text{recall}}$$

One criticism of the F1 score is that it does not take the true negatives into account as informedness does (via the TNR). If we look at the definition of PPV and TPR, we see that both of these quantities depend entirely on the TP, FP, and FN counts from the 2×2 table, but not the TN count. Additionally, the F1 score places equal weight on the precision and the recall. Precision is affected by false positives, while recall is affected by false negatives. From the previous breast cancer model, we saw that the human cost of a false negative is substantially higher than a false positive. Some argue that this must be taken into account when evaluating model performance, and indeed it should. However, if the relative costs of a false positive and a false negative are the same, the F1 score will have more meaning.

Cohen's Kappa

Cohen's kappa is another statistic commonly found in machine learning. It attempts to account for the possibility that the model might put the input into the correct class by accident. Mathematically, the metric is defined as

$$\kappa = \frac{p_o - p_e}{1 - p_e}$$

where p_o is the observed accuracy and p_e is the accuracy expected by chance. For a 2×2 table, these values are defined to be

$$p_o = (TP + TN)/N$$

$$p_e = \frac{(TP + FN)(TP + FP)}{N^2} + \frac{(TN + FP)(TN + FN)}{N^2}$$

with N being the total number of samples in the test set.

Cohen's kappa is generally between 0 and 1. 0 means a complete disagreement between the assigned class labels and the given class labels. A negative value indicates worse than chance agreement. A value near 1 indicates strong agreement.

Matthews Correlation Coefficient

Our final metric is *Matthews correlation coefficient (MCC)*. It is the geometric mean of the informedness and markedness. In that sense, it is, like the F1 score, a combination of two metrics into one.

The MCC is defined as

$$MCC = \frac{TP \cdot TN - FP \cdot FN}{\sqrt{(TP + FP)(TP + FN)(TN + FP)(TN + FN)}}$$

which, mathematically, works out to the geometric mean of the informedness and markedness:

$$MCC = \sqrt{Informedness \cdot Markedness}$$

The MCC is favored by many because it takes the full 2×2 table into account, including the relative frequency of the two classes (the class prior probabilities). This is something that the F1 score does not do because it ignores the true negatives.

The MCC is a number between 0 and 1, with higher being better. If considering only one value as a metric for evaluating a binary model, make it the MCC. Note, there are four sums in the denominator of the MCC. If one of these sums is 0, the entire denominator will be 0, which is a problem since we cannot divide by 0. Fortunately, in that case, the denominator can be replaced with 1 to give a still meaningful result. A well-performing model has MCC close to 1.0.

Implementing Our Metrics

Let's write a function to construct these metrics from a given 2×2 table. The code is shown in Listing 11-3:

```
from math import sqrt
def advanced_metrics(tally, m):
```

```
tp, tn, fp, fn, _ = tally
n = tp+tn+fp+fn
po = (tp+tn)/n
pe = (tp+fn)*(tp+fp)/n**2 + (tn+fp)*(tn+fn)/n**2

return {
    "F1": 2.0*m["PPV"]*m["TPR"] / (m["PPV"] + m["TPR"]),
    "MCC": (tp*tn - fp*fn) / sqrt((tp+fp)*(tp+fn)*(tn+fp)*(tn+fn)),
    "kappa": (po - pe) / (1.0 - pe),
    "informedness": m["TPR"] + m["TNR"] - 1.0,
    "markedness": m["PPV"] + m["NPV"] - 1.0
}
```

Listing 11-3: Calculating advanced metrics

For the sake of simplicity, we're not checking if the MCC denominator is 0 as a full implementation would.

This code takes the tallies and basic metrics as arguments and returns a new dictionary with the more advanced metrics. Let's see how our MNIST example from Table 11-5 looks when we calculate the advanced metrics.

Table 11-6 shows the metrics of this section for the MNIST 3 versus 5 models. A few things are worth noticing. First, the F1 score is always higher than the MCC or Cohen's kappa. In a way, the F1 score is overly optimistic. As previously noted, the F1 score does not take the true negatives into account, while both the MCC and Cohen's kappa do.

Table 11-6: Selected Output from MNIST 3 vs. 5 Models and Corresponding Advanced Metrics

Model	F1	MCC	Cohen's κ	Informedness	Markedness
Nearest Centroid	0.8671	0.7540	0.7535	0.7520	0.7559
3-NN	0.9832	0.9683	0.9683	0.9685	0.9682
Naïve Bayes	0.7958	0.6875	0.6631	0.6524	0.7244
RF 500	0.9916	0.9842	0.9842	0.9841	0.9842
LinearSVM	0.9644	0.9335	0.9334	0.9325	0.9346

Another thing to note is that well-performing models, like 3-NN and the Random Forest, score highly in all of these metrics. When the model performs well, the difference between the F1 score and MCC is smaller than when the model is doing poorly (Naïve Bayes, for example). Notice also that the MCC is always between the informedness and markedness, as a geometric mean will be. Finally, from the values in Table 11-5 and Table 11-6, we see that the best-performing model is the Random Forest, based on the MCC of 0.9842.

In this section, and the two before it, we looked at quite a few metrics and saw how they could be calculated and interpreted. A well-performing model will score highly on all of these metrics. This is the hallmark of a good model. It's when the models we're evaluating are less than sterling that the relative differences between the metrics, and the meaning of the metrics, really comes into play. That's when we need to consider specific metric values and the cost associated with the mistakes the models are making (FP and FN). In those cases, we have to use our judgment and problem-specific factors to decide which model is ultimately selected.

Now, let's shift gears and take a look at a graphical way of evaluating model performance.

The Receiver Operating Characteristics Curve

They say that a picture is worth a thousand words. In this section, we'll learn that a picture—more accurately, a curve—can be worth upward of a dozen numbers. That is, we'll learn how to turn the output of a model into a curve that captures more of the performance than the metrics of the previous sections can. Specifically, we'll learn about the widely used *receiver operating characteristics (ROC) curve*: what it is, how to plot it, and how to use sklearn to plot it for us.

Gathering Our Models

To make the curve, we need a model that outputs a probability of belonging to class 1. In the previous sections, we used models that output a class label so that we could tally the TP, TN, FP, and FN counts. For our ROC curves, we still need these counts, but instead of the class label as model output, we need the probability of class 1 membership. We'll apply different thresholds to these probabilities to decide what label to give the input.

Fortunately for us, traditional neural networks (and the deep networks we will see in Chapter 12) output the necessary probability. If we're using sklearn, other classical models can also be made to output a probability estimate, but we'll ignore that fact here to keep things simple.

Our test case is a series of neural networks trained to decide between even MNIST digits (class 0) and odd MNIST digits (class 1). Our inputs are the vector form of the digits that we've been using up to this point in the book. We can use the training and test data we created in Chapter 5—we only need to recode the labels so that digits 0, 2, 4, 6, and 8 are class 0, while digits 1, 3, 5, 7, and 9 are class 1. That is easily accomplished with a few lines of code:

```
old = np.load("mnist_train_labels.npy")
new = np.zeros(len(old), dtype="uint8")
new[np.where((old % 2) == 0)] = 0
new[np.where((old % 2) == 1)] = 1
np.save("mnist_train_even_odd_labels.npy", new)

old = np.load("mnist_test_labels.npy")
new = np.zeros(len(old), dtype="uint8")
new[np.where((old % 2) == 0)] = 0
```

```
new[np.where((old % 2) == 1)] = 1
np.save("mnist_test_even_odd_labels.npy", new)
```

The directory paths point to the same place the other MNIST data is
stored. We use the fact that the remainder when an even number is divided
by 2 is always 0 or 1 depending on whether the number is even or odd.

What models will we test? To emphasize the difference between the respective models, we'll intentionally train models that we know are far from
ideal. In particular, we'll use the following code to generate the models and
produce the probability estimates:

```
import numpy as np
from sklearn.neural_network import MLPClassifier

def run(x_train, y_train, x_test, y_test, clf):
    clf.fit(x_train, y_train)
    return clf.predict_proba(x_test)

def nn(layers):
    return MLPClassifier(solver="sgd", verbose=False, tol=1e-8,
            nesterovs_momentum=False, early_stopping=False, batch_size=64,
            learning_rate_init=0.001, momentum=0.9, max_iter=200,
            hidden_layer_sizes=layers, activation="relu")

def main():
    x_train = np.load("mnist_train_vectors.npy").astype("float64")/256.0
    y_train = np.load("mnist_train_even_odd_labels.npy")
    x_test = np.load("mnist_test_vectors.npy").astype("float64")/256.0
    y_test = np.load("mnist_test_even_odd_labels.npy")
    x_train = x_train[:1000]
    y_train = y_train[:1000]
    layers = [(2,), (100,), (100,50), (500,250)]
    mlayers = ["2", "100", "100x50", "500x250"]
    for i,layer in enumerate(layers):
        prob = run(x_train, y_train, x_test, y_test, nn(layer))
        np.save("mnist_even_odd_probs_%s.npy" % mlayers[i], prob)
```

The code can be found in the file *mnist_even_odd.py*. The run and nn
functions should be familiar. We used virtually identical versions in Chapter 10, where nn returns a configured MLPClassifier object and run trains the
classifier and returns the prediction probabilities on the test set. The main
function loads the train and test sets, limits the training set to the first 1,000
samples (about 500 even and 500 odd), then loops over the hidden layer
sizes we will train. The first two are single hidden layer networks with 2 and
100 nodes, respectively. The last two are two hidden layer networks with
100×50 and 500×250 nodes per layer.

Plotting Our Metrics

The output of `clf.predict_proba` is a matrix with as many rows as there are test samples (ten thousand in this case). The matrix has as many columns as there are classes; since we're dealing with a binary classifier, there are two columns per sample. The first is the probability that the sample is even (class 0), and the second is the probability of the sample being odd (class 1). For example, the first 10 outputs for one of the models are shown in Table 11-7.

Table 11-7: Example Model Output Showing the Assigned per Class Probabilities Along with the Actual Original Class Label

Class 0	Class 1	Actual label
0.009678	0.990322	3
0.000318	0.999682	3
0.001531	0.998469	7
0.007464	0.992536	3
0.011103	0.988897	1
0.186362	0.813638	7
0.037229	0.962771	7
0.999412	0.000588	2
0.883890	0.116110	6
0.999981	0.000019	6

The first column is the probability of being even, and the second is the probability of being odd. The third column is the actual class label for the sample showing that the predictions are spot on. The odd digits have high class 1 probabilities and low class 0 probabilities, while the opposite is true for the even samples.

When we build a 2×2 table from the performance of a model on a held-out test set, we get a collection of TP, TN, FP, and FN numbers from which we can calculate all the metrics of the previous sections. This includes the true positive rate (TPR, sensitivity) and the false positive rate (FPR, equal to 1 − specificity). Implicit in the table is the threshold we used to decide when the model output should be considered class 1 or class 0. In the previous sections, this threshold was 0.5. If the output is $\geq$ 0.5, we assign the sample to class 1; otherwise, we assign it to class 0. Sometimes you'll see this threshold added as a subscript like $TPR_{0.5}$ or $FPR_{0.5}$.

Mathematically, we can consider the TPR and FPR calculated from a 2×2 table to be a point on the FPR (x-axis) versus TPR (y-axis) plane, specifically, the point (FPR, TPR). Since both FPR and TPR range from 0 to 1, the point (FPR, TPR) will lie somewhere within a square of length 1 with the lower-left corner of the square at the point (0,0) and the upper-right corner at the point (1,1). Every time we change our decision threshold, we get a new 2×2 table leading to a new point on the FPR versus TPR plane. For example, if we change our decision threshold from 0.5 to 0.3 so that each output class 1 probability of 0.3 or higher is called class 1, we'll get a new 2×2 table and a new point, $(\text{FPR}_{0.3}, \text{TPR}_{0.3})$, on the plane. As we systematically change the decision threshold from high to low, we generate a sequence of points that we can connect to form a curve.

Curves generated by changing a parameter in this way are called *parametric curves*. The points are functions of the threshold. Let's call the threshold value θ (theta) and vary it from near 1 to near 0. Doing so lets us calculate a set of points, $(\text{FPR}_{\theta}, \text{TPR}_{\theta})$, which, when plotted, lead to a curve in the FPR versus TPR plane. As noted earlier, this curve has a name: the receiver operating characteristics (ROC) curve. Let's look at an ROC curve and explore what such a curve can tell us.

Exploring the ROC Curve

Figure 11-1 shows the ROC curve for the MNIST even-versus-odd model with a single hidden layer of 100 nodes.

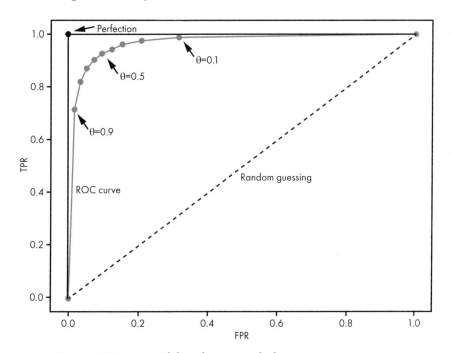

Figure 11-1: An ROC curve with key elements marked

The labeled points represent the FPR and TPR for the given threshold values. The dashed line is the diagonal from (0,0) to (1,1). This dashed line represents a classifier that guesses its output randomly. The closer our curve is to this dashed line, the less powerful the model is. If your curve lies on top of the line, you might as well flip a coin and assign the label that way. Any curve below the dashed line is performing *worse* than random guessing. If the model were entirely wrong, meaning it calls all class 1 instances class 0, and *vice versa*, a curious thing happens: we can turn the entirely wrong model into a perfectly correct model by changing all class 1 output to class 0 and all class 0, output to class 1. It's unlikely that you will run across a model this bad.

The ROC curve in Figure 11-1 has a single point labeled *perfection* in the upper-left corner of the graph. This is the ideal we are striving for. We want our ROC curve to move up and to the left toward this point. The closer we get the curve to this point, the better the model is performing against our test set. A perfect model will have an ROC curve that jumps up vertically to this point and then horizontally to the point (1,1). The ROC curve in Figure 11-1 is going in the right direction and represents a reasonably well-performing model.

Notice the labeled θ values. We can select a level of performance from the model by adjusting θ. In this case, the typical default value of 0.5 gives us the best performance because that threshold value returns a TPR and FPR with the best balance, the point closest to the upper left of the graph. However, there are reasons we might want to use a different θ value. If we make θ small, say 0.1, we move along the curve toward the right. Two things happen. First, the TPR goes up to about 0.99, meaning we correctly assign about 99 percent of the real class 1 instances handed to the model to class 1. Second, the FPR also goes up, to about 0.32, meaning we will simultaneously call about 32 percent of the true negatives (class 0) class 1 as well. If our problem is such that we can tolerate calling some negative instances "positive," knowing that we now have a meager chance of doing the opposite, calling a positive case "negative," we might choose to change the threshold to 0.1. Think of the previous breast cancer example: we never want to call a positive case "negative," so we tolerate more false positives to know we are not mislabeling any actual positives.

What does it mean to move the threshold (θ) to 0.9? In this case, we've moved along the curve to the left, to a point with a very low false-positive rate. We might do this if we want to know with a high degree of confidence that when the model says "class 1," it is an instance of class 1. This means we want a high positive predictive value (PPV, precision). Recall the definition of the PPV:

$$PPV = \frac{TP}{TP + FP}$$

The PPV is high if FP is low. Setting θ to 0.9 makes the FP low for any given test set. For the ROC curve of Figure 11-1, moving to θ = 0.9 implies an FPR of about 0.02 and a TPR of about 0.71 for a PPV of about 0.97. At θ = 0.9, when the model outputs "class 1," there is a 97 percent chance that the model is correct. In contrast, at θ = 0.1, the PPV is about 76 percent. A high threshold can be used in a situation where we are interested in definitely locating an example of class 1 without caring that we might not detect all class 1 instances.

Changing the threshold θ moves us along the ROC curve. As we do so, we should expect the metrics of the previous section to also change as a function of θ. Figure 11-2 shows us how the MCC and PPV change with θ.

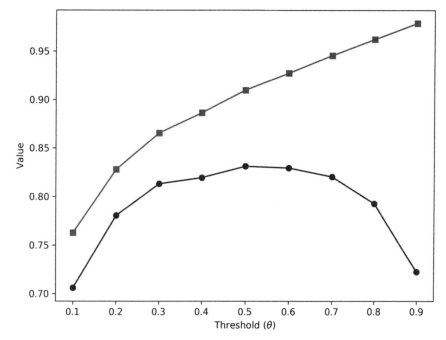

Figure 11-2: How MCC (circles) and PPV (squares) change as the decision threshold (θ) changes for the MNIST even/odd model of Figure 11-1

In the figure, we see that as the threshold goes up, so does the PPV. The model becomes more confident when it declares an input a member of class 1. However, this is tempered by the change in MCC, which, as we previously saw, is an excellent single metric measure of overall model performance. In this case, the highest MCC is at θ = 0.5, with MCC falling off as the threshold increases or decreases.

Comparing Models with ROC Analysis

The ROC curve gives us a significant amount of information. It's also handy for comparing models, even if those models are radically different from each other in architecture or approach. However, care must be taken when making the comparison so that the test sets used to generate the curves are ideally the same or very nearly the same.

Let's use ROC analysis to compare the different MNIST even/odd digit models that we trained previously. We'll see if this helps us to choose between them.

Figure 11-3 shows the ROC curves for these models with an inset expanding the upper-left corner of the graph to make it easier to distinguish one model from the other. The number of nodes in each hidden layer is indicated to identify the models.

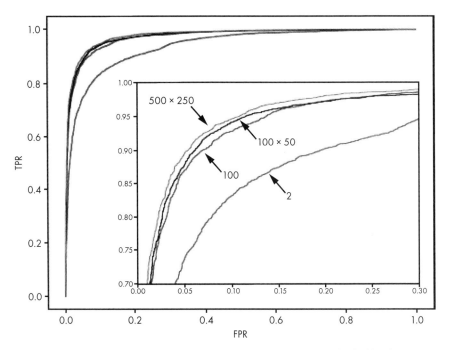

Figure 11-3: ROC curves for the MNIST even/odd models. The model hidden layer sizes are indicated.

We immediately see that one ROC curve is significantly different from the other three. This is the ROC curve for the model with a single hidden layer with two nodes. All the other ROC curves are above this one. As a general rule, if one ROC curve is entirely above another, then the model that generated the curve can be considered superior. All of the larger MNIST even/odd models are superior to the model with only two nodes in its hidden layer.

The other three models are quite close to each other, so how do we choose one? The decision isn't always clear-cut. Following our rule of thumb about ROC curves, we should select the two-layer model with 500 and 250 nodes, respectively, as its ROC curve is above the others. However, we might hesitate depending upon our use case. This model has over 500,000 parameters. Running it requires use of all of those parameters. The 100×50 model contains slightly more than 80,000 parameters. That's less than one-fifth the number of the larger model. We might decide that processing speed considerations eclipse the small improvement in the overall performance of the larger model and select the smaller model. The ROC analysis showed us that doing so involves only a minor performance penalty.

Another factor to consider when comparing ROC curves visually is the slope of the curve when the FPR is small. A perfect model has a vertical slope since it jumps immediately from the point (0,0) to (0,1). Therefore, the better model will have an ROC curve that has a steeper slope in the low FPR region.

A commonly used metric derived from the ROC curve is the area under it. This area is usually abbreviated as *AUC* or, in medical circles, *Az*. A perfect ROC curve has an AUC of 1.0 since the curve jumps from (0,0) to (0,1) and then over to (1,1), forming a square of side 1 with an area of 1. A model that guesses randomly (the diagonal line in the ROC plot) has an AUC of 0.5, the area of the triangle formed by the dashed diagonal line. To calculate the area under an arbitrary ROC curve, one needs to perform numerical integration. Fortunately for us, sklearn knows how to do this, so we don't need to. We'll see this shortly.

People often report the AUC, but as time goes by, I'm less and less in favor of it. The main reason is that AUC replaces the highly informative graph with a single number, but different ROC curves can lead to the same AUC. If the AUC of two curves is the same, but one leans far to the right while the other has a steep slope in the low FPR region, we might be tempted to think the models are roughly equivalent in terms of performance, when, in reality, the model with the steeper slope is likely the one we want because it will reach a reasonable TPR without too many false positives.

Another caution when using the AUC is that the AUC changes only a small amount for even fairly significant changes in other parameters. This makes it difficult for humans to judge well based on AUC values that are only slightly different from each other. For example, the AUC of the MNIST even/odd model with two nodes in its hidden layer is 0.9373, while the AUC of the model with 100 nodes is 0.9722. Both are well above 0.9 out of a possible 1.0, so, are they both about the same? We know that they are not, since the ROC curves clearly show the two-node model to be well below the other.

Generating an ROC Curve

We are now ready to learn how to create an ROC curve. The easy way to get the ROC curve, and AUC, is to use sklearn:

```
import os
import sys
import numpy as np
import matplotlib.pylab as plt
from sklearn.metrics import roc_auc_score, roc_curve

def main():
    labels = np.load(sys.argv[1])
    probs = np.load(sys.argv[2])
    pname = sys.argv[3]

    auc = roc_auc_score(labels, probs[:,1])
    roc = roc_curve(labels, probs[:,1])
    print("AUC = %0.6f" % auc)

    plt.plot(roc[0], roc[1], color='r')
    plt.plot([0,1],[0,1], color='k', linestyle=':')
```

```
plt.xlabel("FPR")
plt.ylabel("TPR")
plt.tight_layout(pad=0, w_pad=0, h_pad=0)
plt.savefig(pname, dpi=300)
plt.show()
```

This routine reads a set of labels and the associated per class probabilities, such as the output generated by the code in the previous section. It then calls the sklearn functions roc_auc_score and roc_curve to return the AUC and the ROC points, respectively. The ROC curve is plotted, saved to disk, and displayed.

We need not use sklearn as a black box. We can generate the ROC curve points ourselves quickly enough. We load the same inputs, the labels, and the per class probabilities, but instead of calling a library function, we loop over the threshold values of interest and calculate TP, TN, FP, and FN for each threshold. From these, we can directly calculate the FPR and TPR, which gives us the set of points we need to plot. The code to do this is straightforward:

```
def table(labels, probs, t):
    tp = tn = fp = fn = 0
    for i,l in enumerate(labels):
        c = 1 if (probs[i,1] >= t) else 0
        if (l == 0) and (c == 0):
            tn += 1
        if (l == 0) and (c == 1):
            fp += 1
        if (l == 1) and (c == 0):
            fn += 1
        if (l == 1) and (c == 1):
            tp += 1
    return [tp, tn, fp, fn]

def main():
    labels = np.load(sys.argv[1])
    probs = np.load(sys.argv[2])
    pname = sys.argv[3]

    th = [0.9, 0.8, 0.7, 0.6, 0.5, 0.4, 0.3, 0.2, 0.1]
    roc = []
    for t in th:
        tp, tn, fp, fn = table(labels, probs, t)
        tpr = tp / (tp + fn)
        fpr = fp / (tn + fp)
        roc.append([fpr, tpr])
    roc = np.array(roc)
```

```
xy = np.zeros((roc.shape[0]+2, roc.shape[1]))
xy[1:-1,:] = roc
xy[0,:] = [0,0]
xy[-1,:] = [1,1]
plt.plot(xy[:,0], xy[:,1], color='r', marker='o')
plt.plot([0,1],[0,1], color='k', linestyle=':')
plt.xlabel("FPR")
plt.ylabel("TPR")
plt.savefig(pname)
plt.show()
```

The main function loads the labels and probabilities. The loop over th applies the different threshold values, accumulating the ROC points in roc by calling the table function, which calculates the TP, TN, FP, and FN for the current threshold.

The table function loops over all the per class probabilities assigning a class label of 1 if the class 1 probability is greater than or equal to the current threshold value. This class assignment is then compared to the actual class label, and the appropriate tally counter is incremented.

Once the ROC points are calculated, the plot is made by adding the point (0,0) to the beginning of the point list and the point (1,1) to the end of the list. Doing this ensures that the plot extends the full range of FPR values. The points are plotted and saved to disk.

The Precision–Recall Curve

Before leaving this section, we should mention one other evaluation curve that you will run across from time to time in machine learning. This is the *precision-recall (PR) curve*. As the name suggests, it plots the PPV (precision) and TPR (recall, sensitivity) as the decision threshold varies, just like an ROC curve. A good PR curve moves toward the upper right instead of the upper left as a good ROC curve does. The points of this curve are easily generated in sklearn using the precision_recall_curve function in the metrics module.

We're not spending time with this curve because it does not take the true negatives into account. Consider the definition of the PPV and TPR to see that this is so. My bias against the PR curve stems from the same concern as my bias against the F1 score. By not taking the true negatives into account, the PR curve and F1 score give an incomplete picture of the quality of the classifier. The PR curve does have utility when the true positive class is rare or when the true negative performance is not essential. However, in general, for evaluating classifier performance, I claim it is best to stick to the ROC curve and the metrics we have defined.

Handling Multiple Classes

All of the metrics we've discussed so far apply to binary classifiers only. Of course, we know that many classifiers are multiclass: they output multiple labels, not just 0 or 1. To evaluate these models, we'll extend our idea of the confusion matrix to the multiclass case and see that we can also extend some of the metrics we're already familiar with as well.

We need some multiclass model results to work with. Thankfully, the MNIST data is already multiclass. Recall, we went to the trouble of recoding the labels to make the dataset binary. Here we'll train models with the same architectures, but this time we'll leave the labels as they are so that the model will output one of ten labels: the digit it assigned to the test input, the output of the predict method of the MLPClassifier class. We won't show the code as it's identical to the code in the previous section except that predict is called in place of predict_proba.

Extending the Confusion Matrix

The basis for our binary metrics was the 2×2 confusion matrix. The confusion matrix is readily extended to the multiclass case. To do that, we let the rows of the matrix represent the actual class labels, while the columns of the matrix represent the model's predictions. The matrix is square with as many rows and columns as there are classes in the dataset. For MNIST, then, we arrive at a 10×10 confusion matrix since there are 10 digits.

We calculate the confusion matrix from the actual known test labels and the predicted labels from the model. There is a function in the metrics module of sklearn, confusion_matrix, which we can use, but it's straightforward enough to calculate it ourselves:

```
def confusion_matrix(y_test, y_predict, n=10):
    cmat = np.zeros((n,n), dtype="uint32")
    for i,y in enumerate(y_test):
        cmat[y, y_predict[i]] += 1
    return cmat
```

Here n is the number of classes, fixed at 10 for MNIST. If needed, we could instead determine it from the supplied test labels.

The code is straightforward. The inputs are vectors of the actual labels (y_test) and the predicted labels (y_predict), and the confusion matrix (cmat) is filled in by incrementing each possible index formed from the actual label and the predicted label. For example, if the actual label is 3 and the predicted label is 8, then we add one to cmat[3,8].

Let's look at the confusion matrix for a model with one hidden layer of 100 nodes (Table 11-8).

Table 11-8: Confusion Matrix for the Model with a Single Hidden Layer of 100 Nodes

	0	1	2	3	4	5	6	7	8	9
0	943	0	6	9	0	10	7	1	4	0
1	0	1102	14	5	1	1	3	1	8	0
2	16	15	862	36	18	1	17	24	41	2
3	3	1	10	937	0	20	3	13	17	6
4	2	8	4	2	879	0	14	1	6	66
5	19	3	3	53	13	719	17	3	44	18
6	14	3	4	2	21	15	894	1	4	0
7	3	21	32	7	10	1	0	902	1	51
8	17	14	11	72	11	46	21	9	749	24
9	10	11	1	13	42	5	2	31	10	884

The rows represent the actual test sample label, $[0, 9]$. The columns are the label assigned by the model. If the model is perfect, there will be a one-to-one match between the actual label and the predicted label. This is the main diagonal of the confusion matrix. Therefore, a perfect model will have entries along the main diagonal, and all other elements will be 0. Table 11-8 is not perfect, but the largest counts are along the main diagonal.

Look at row 4 and column 4. The place where the row and column meet has the value 879. This means that there were 879 times when the actual class was 4 and the model correctly predicted "4" as the label. If we look along row 4, we see other numbers that are not zero. Each of these represents a case where an actual 4 was called another digit by the model. For example, there were 66 times when a 4 was called a "9" but only one case of a 4 being labeled a "7".

Column 4 represents the cases when the model called the input a "4". As we saw, it was correct 879 times. However, there were other digits that the model accidentally labeled as "4", like the 21 times a 6 was called a "4" or the one time a 1 was mistaken for a "4". There were no cases of a 3 being labeled a "4".

The confusion matrix tells us at a glance how well the model is doing on the test set. We can quickly see if the matrix is primarily diagonal. If it is, the model is doing a good job on the test set. If not, we need to take a closer look to see what classes are being confused with other classes. A simple adjustment to the matrix can help. Instead of the raw counts, which require us to remember how many examples of each class are in the test set, we can divide the values of each row by the sum of the row. Doing so converts the entries from counts to fractions. We can then multiply the entries by 100 to convert to percents. This transforms the confusion matrix into what we'll call an *accuracy matrix*. The conversion is straightforward:

```
acc = 100.0*(cmat / cmat.sum(axis=1))
```

Here cmat is the confusion matrix. This produces an accuracy matrix, Table 11-9.

Table 11-9: A Confusion Matrix Presented as per Class Accuracies

	0	1	2	3	4	5	6	7	8	9
0	**96.2**	0.	0.6	0.9	0.	1.1	0.7	0.1	0.4	0.
1	0.	**97.1**	1.4	0.5	0.1	0.1	0.3	0.1	0.8	0.
2	1.6	1.3	**83.5**	3.6	1.8	0.1	1.8	2.3	4.2	0.2
3	0.3	0.1	1.	**92.8**	0.	2.2	0.3	1.3	1.7	0.6
4	0.2	0.7	0.4	0.2	**89.5**	0.	1.5	0.1	0.6	6.5
5	1.9	0.3	0.3	5.2	1.3	**80.6**	1.8	0.3	4.5	1.8
6	1.4	0.3	0.4	0.2	2.1	1.7	**93.3**	0.1	0.4	0.
7	0.3	1.9	3.1	0.7	1.	0.1	0.	**87.7**	0.1	5.1
8	1.7	1.2	1.1	7.1	1.1	5.2	2.2	0.9	**76.9**	2.4
9	1.	1.	0.1	1.3	4.3	0.6	0.2	3.	1.	**87.6**

The diagonal shows the per class accuracies. The worst performing class is 8 with an accuracy of 76.9 percent, and the best performing class is 1 with an accuracy of 97.1 percent. The non-diagonal elements are the percentage of the actual class labeled as a different class by the model. For class 0, the model called a true zero class "5" 1.1 percent of the time. The row percentages sum to 100 percent (within rounding error).

Why did class 8 do so poorly? Looking across the row for class 8, we see that the model mistook 7.1 percent of the actual 8 instances for a "3" and 5.2 percent of the instances for a "5". Confusing an 8 with a "3" was the biggest single mistake the model made, though 6.5 percent of 4 instances were labeled "9" as well. A moment's reflection makes sense of the errors. How often do people confuse 8 and 3 or 4 and 9? This model is making errors similar to those humans make.

The confusion matrix can reveal pathological performance as well. Consider the MNIST model in Figure 11-3, with a single hidden layer of only two nodes. The accuracy matrix it produces is shown in Table 11-10.

We can immediately see that this is an inferior model. Column 5 is entirely zero, meaning the model never outputs "5" for any input. Much the same is true for output labels "8" and "9". On the other hand, the model likes to call inputs "0", "1", "2", or "3" as those columns are densely populated for all manner of input digits. Looking at the diagonal, we see that only 1 and 3 stand a reasonable chance of being correctly identified, though many of these will be called "7". Class 8 is rarely correctly labeled (1.3 percent). A poorly performing model will have a confusion matrix like this, with oddball outputs and large off-diagonal values.

Table 11-10: Accuracy Matrix for the Model with Only Two Nodes in Its Hidden Layer

	0	1	2	3	4	5	6	7	8	9
0	**51.0**	1.0	10.3	0.7	1.8	0.0	34.1	0.7	0.0	0.4
1	0.4	**88.3**	0.4	1.1	0.8	0.0	0.0	9.3	1.0	0.0
2	8.6	2.8	**75.2**	6.9	1.7	0.0	1.4	3.0	0.3	0.6
3	0.2	1.0	4.9	**79.4**	0.3	0.0	0.0	13.5	0.0	0.2
4	28.4	31.3	7.3	2.1	**9.7**	0.0	0.3	13.6	1.0	0.5
5	11.4	42.5	2.2	4.9	4.4	**0.0**	0.1	16.5	0.9	0.3
6	35.4	1.0	5.4	0.2	1.4	0.0	**55.0**	0.0	0.0	0.1
7	0.4	5.2	2.0	66.2	0.8	0.0	0.0	**25.5**	0.2	0.3
8	10.5	41.9	2.8	8.0	4.1	0.0	0.1	22.1	**1.3**	0.4
9	4.7	9.1	5.8	26.2	5.8	0.0	0.2	41.2	2.2	**3.1**

Calculating Weighted Accuracy

The diagonal elements of an accuracy matrix tell us the per class accuracies for the model. We can calculate an overall accuracy by averaging these values. However, this could be misleading if one or more classes is far more prevalent in the test data than the others. Instead of a simple average, we should use a weighted average. The weights are based on the total number of test samples from each class divided by the total number of test samples presented to the model. Say we have three classes and their frequency and per class accuracies in our test set are as in Table 11-11:

Table 11-11: Hypothetical per Class Accuracies for a Model with Three Classes

Class	Frequency	Accuracy
0	4,004	88.1
1	6,502	76.6
2	8,080	65.2

Here we have $N = 4,004 + 6,502 + 8,080 = 18586$ test samples. Then, the per class weights are shown in Table 11-12.

Table 11-12: Example per-class weights

Class	Weight
0	4,004 / 18,586 = 0.2154
1	6,502 / 18,586 = 0.3498
2	8,080 / 18,586 = 0.4347

The average accuracy can be calculated to be

$$\text{ACC} = 0.2154 \times 88.1 + 0.3498 \times 76.6 + 0.4347 \times 65.2 = 74.1$$

Philosophically, we should replace the weights with the actual per class prior probabilities, if we know them. These probabilities are the true likelihood of the class appearing in the wild. However, if we assume that the test set is fairly constructed, we're likely safe using only the per class frequencies. We claim that a properly built test set will represent the true prior class probabilities reasonably well.

In code, the weighted mean accuracy can be calculated succinctly from the confusion matrix:

```
def weighted_mean_acc(cmat):
    N = cmat.sum()
    C = cmat.sum(axis=1)
    return ((C/N)*(100*np.diag(cmat)/C)).sum()
```

N is the total number of samples that were tested, which is just the sum of the entries in the confusion matrix since every sample in the test set falls somewhere in the matrix, and C is a vector of the number of samples per class. This is just the sum of the rows of the confusion matrix. The per class accuracy, as a percentage, is calculated from the diagonal elements of the confusion matrix (`np.diag(cmat)`) divided by the number of times each class shows up in the test set, C. Multiply by 100 to make these percent accuracies.

If we summed these per class and divided by the number of classes, we would have the (potentially misleading) unweighted mean accuracy. Instead, we first multiply by C/N, the fraction of all test samples that were of each class (recall, C is a vector), and then sum to get the weighted accuracy. This code works for any size confusion matrix.

For the MNIST models of the previous section, we calculate weighted mean accuracies to be those in Table 11-13.

Table 11-13: Weighted Mean Accuracies for the MNIST Models

Architecture	Weighted mean accuracy
2	40.08%
100	88.71%
100 × 50	88.94%
500 × 250	89.63%

Table 11-13 shows the sort of diminishing returns we've seen previously as the model size increases. The single hidden layer of 100 nodes is virtually identical to the two hidden layer model with 100 and 50 nodes and only 1 percent worse than the much larger model with 500 nodes and 250 nodes in its hidden layers. The model with only two nodes in the hidden layer performs poorly. Since there are 10 classes, random guessing would tend to have an accuracy of $1/10 = 0.1 = 10$ percent, so even this very strange model that maps 784 input values (28×28 pixels) to only two and then to ten output nodes is still four times more accurate than random guessing. However, this is misleading on its own because, as we just saw in Table 11-10, the confusion matrix for this model is quite strange. We certainly would not want to use this model. Nothing beats careful consideration of the confusion matrix.

Multiclass Matthews Correlation Coefficient

The 2×2 confusion matrix led to many possible metrics. While it's possible to extend several of those metrics to the multiclass case, we'll consider only the main metric here: the Matthews correlation coefficient (MCC). For the binary case, we saw that the MCC was

$$\text{MCC} = \frac{\text{TP} \cdot \text{TN} - \text{FP} \cdot \text{FN}}{\sqrt{(\text{TP} + \text{FP})(\text{TP} + \text{FN})(\text{TN} + \text{FP})(\text{TN} + \text{FN})}}$$

This can be extended to the multiclass case by using terms from the confusion matrix like so

$$\text{MCC} = \frac{c \times s - \sum_k^K p_k \times t_k}{\sqrt{(s^2 - \sum_k^K p_k^2) \times (s^2 - \sum_k^K t_k^2)}}$$

where

$$t_k = \sum_i^K C_{ik}$$

$$p_k = \sum_i^K C_{ki}$$

$$c = \sum_k^K C_{kk}$$

$$s = \sum_i^K \sum_j^K C_{ij}$$

Here, K is the number of classes, and C is the confusion matrix. This notation is from the sklearn website's description of the MCC, giving us a direct view of how it's implemented. We don't need to follow the equations in detail; we need to know only that the MCC is built from the confusion matrix in the multiclass case as in the binary case. Intuitively, this makes sense. The binary MCC is a value in the range $[-1, +1]$. The multiclass case changes the lower bound based on the number of classes, but the upper bound remains 1.0, so the closer the MCC is to 1.0, the better the model is doing.

Calculating the MCC for the MNIST models, as we did for the weighted mean accuracy, gives Table 11-14.

Table 11-14: The MCC for the MNIST Models

Architecture	MCC
2	0.3440
100	0.8747
100 × 50	0.8773
500 × 250	0.8849

Again, this shows us that the smallest model is inferior while the other three models are all quite similar in terms of performance. The time to make predictions on the 10,000 test samples, however, varies quite a bit by model. The single hidden layer model with 100 nodes takes 0.052 seconds, while the largest model needs 0.283 seconds, over five times longer. If speed is essential, the smaller model might be preferable. Many factors come into play when deciding on a model to use. The metrics discussed in this chapter are guides, but they should not be followed blindly. In the end, only you know what makes sense for the problem you are trying to solve.

Summary

In this chapter, we learned why accuracy is not a sufficient measure of the performance of a model. We learned how to generate the 2×2 confusion matrix for a binary classifier, and what this matrix tells us about the model's performance on the held-out test set. We derived basic metrics from the 2×2 confusion matrix and used those basic metrics to derive more advanced metrics. We discussed the utility of the various metrics to build our intuition as to how and when to use them. We then learned about the receiver operating characteristics (ROC) curve, including what it illustrates about the model and how to interpret it to compare models against each other. Finally, we introduced the multiclass confusion matrix, giving examples of how to interpret it and how to extend some of the binary classifier metrics to the multiclass case.

In the next chapter, we'll reach the pinnacle of our machine learning models: convolutional neural networks (CNNs). The next chapter introduces the basic ideas behind the CNN; later chapters will conduct many experiments using this deep learning architecture.

12

INTRODUCTION TO CONVOLUTIONAL NEURAL NETWORKS

In this chapter, we'll introduce a new and potent approach to dealing with multidimensional information. In particular, we'll work through the theory and high-level operation of *convolutional neural networks* (CNNs), a cornerstone of modern deep learning.

We'll begin by presenting the motivations behind the development of CNNs. Convolutions are the heart of CNNs, so they'll come next. We'll discuss them in some detail, in particular how they're used by the CNN. We'll then introduce a basic CNN and work through its anatomy. We'll use this basic CNN architecture for the remainder of the chapter. After we dissect a CNN, we'll work through how convolutional layers work. Then come pooling layers. We'll see what they do, what benefit they offer, and what price they exact in return. To round out our discussion of the fundamental components of a CNN, we'll present the fully connected layers, which, in reality, are just the layers of a traditional, fully connected, feed-forward neural network like those of Chapter 8.

One topic will be conspicuously absent from this chapter: the mechanics of training a CNN. In part, we'll gloss over training because it's messy once convolutional layers are introduced, but primarily because we've already discussed backpropagation in Chapter 9, and we use the same algorithm to train a CNN. We calculate the weights and biases of all layers from the average loss over the training minibatch and use backprop to determine the derivatives we need to update the weights and biases for each stochastic gradient descent step.

Why Convolutional Neural Networks?

CNNs have several advantages over traditional neural networks. First, the convolutional layers of a CNN require vastly fewer parameters than fully connected neural networks, as we'll see later in the chapter. CNNs require fewer parameters because the convolution operation applies parameters in each layer to small subsets of the input instead of the entire input at once, as is done with a traditional neural network.

Second, CNNs introduce the idea of *spatial invariance*, the ability to detect a spatial relationship in the input regardless of where it appears. For example, if the input to a neural network is an image of a cat, a traditional neural network will take the image in as a single feature vector, meaning that if a cat appears in the upper-left corner of the image, the network will learn that cats can appear in the upper-left corners of the image but not that they can also appear in the lower-right corners (unless the training data contains examples with cats in the lower-right corners). For a CNN, however, the convolution operation can detect cats anywhere they appear.

While CNNs are usually used with two-dimensional inputs, they can also be used with one-dimensional inputs, like the feature vectors we have worked with up to now. However, the feature vectors we've worked with, like the iris measurements, don't reflect any sort of spatial relationship as the parts of an image of a cat do. There's nothing there for the convolution operation to take advantage of. This doesn't mean that a CNN won't work, but it does mean that it might not be the best sort of model to use. As always, we need to understand how various model types operate so we select the best model for the task at hand.

NOTE *Depending on who you ask, CNNs were either developed in 1980 by Fukushima to implement the Neocognitron model or in 1998 by LeCun et al. as presented in their famous paper "Gradient-Based Learning Applied to Document Recognition," which, as of this writing, has been referenced over 21,000 times. My take is that both deserve credit, though LeCun used the phrase* convolutional neural network *or* convnet *as they are still sometimes called, and what is described in the paper is what we will work with in this book. The Neocognitron reflected some of the ideas in a CNN, but not CNNs themselves.*

Convolution

Convolution involves sliding one thing over another. For us, this means sliding a *kernel*, a small 2D array, over the input, which might be the input image to the CNN or the output of a lower convolutional layer. There is a formal mathematical definition of convolution, but it really won't help us right now. Luckily, all our inputs are discrete, which means we can get away with a bit of a hand-waving. For simplicity, we'll focus on only the two-dimensional case.

Scanning with the Kernel

The *kernel* is the thing we are asking the convolutional layer to learn during training. It's a collection of small 2D arrays that we move over the input. Ultimately, the kernels become the weights of a convolutional layer in a CNN.

The essential operation of convolution is taking some small section of the input, the same size as the kernel, covering it with the kernel, performing some operation on the set of numbers to produce a single output number, and then repeating the process after moving the kernel to a new position in the input. Just how far the kernel is moved is known as the *stride*. Typically, the stride is 1, meaning the kernel slides over one element of the input.

Figure 12-1 shows the effect of convolution on part of an MNIST digit image.

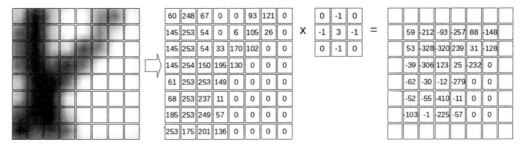

Figure 12-1: Convolving a kernel with an image

The image portion is on the left of Figure 12-1, where you can see part of a handwritten 8. The boxes correspond to pixel intensities, though for presentation purposes, we've expanded the original image so that many shades of gray are visible in each "pixel" box. The actual pixel values the convolution works with are given next, after the arrow.

Here, the kernel is

$$\begin{bmatrix} 0 & -1 & 0 \\ -1 & 3 & -1 \\ 0 & -1 & 0 \end{bmatrix}$$

This is the set of numbers we'll slide over the input pixels. This is a 3×3 matrix, so we need to cover a 3×3 region of the input image. The first 3×3 region, the upper-left corner, is

$$\begin{bmatrix} 60 & 248 & 67 \\ 145 & 253 & 54 \\ 145 & 253 & 54 \end{bmatrix}$$

We said that convolution performs an operation with the kernel and the covered region as the input. The operation is straightforward: multiply corresponding entries and sum them. Finding the first output value of the convolution begins with

$$\begin{bmatrix} 60 & 248 & 67 \\ 145 & 253 & 54 \\ 145 & 253 & 54 \end{bmatrix} \times \begin{bmatrix} 0 & -1 & 0 \\ -1 & 3 & -1 \\ 0 & -1 & 0 \end{bmatrix} = \begin{bmatrix} 0 & -248 & 0 \\ -145 & 759 & -54 \\ 0 & -253 & 0 \end{bmatrix}$$

When the preceding elements are summed, this gives the output value as

$$0 + (-248) + 0 + (-145) + 759 + (-54) + 0 + (-253) + 0 = 59$$

Okay, the output of the first convolution operation is 59. What do we do with that number? The kernel is 3×3, an odd number along each side. This means that there is a middle element, the one with the 3 in it. The place in the output array where the middle number is gets replaced with the output value, the 59. Figure 12-1 shows the full output of the convolution. Sure enough, the first element of the output is 59, located at the center of the kernel when the kernel is covering the upper-left corner.

The remaining output values are calculated in precisely the same way but by moving the kernel over 1 pixel each time. When the end of a row is reached, the kernel moves back to the left side but down 1 pixel. In this way, it slides over the entire input image to produce the output shown in Figure 12-1, just like the scan lines of an old analog television.

The next output value is

$$\begin{bmatrix} 248 & 67 & 0 \\ 253 & 54 & 0 \\ 253 & 54 & 33 \end{bmatrix} \times \begin{bmatrix} 0 & -1 & 0 \\ -1 & 3 & -1 \\ 0 & -1 & 0 \end{bmatrix} = \begin{bmatrix} 0 & -67 & 0 \\ -253 & 162 & 0 \\ 0 & -54 & 0 \end{bmatrix}$$

which sums to −212, as we see on the right side of Figure 12-1.

Repeating the convolution operation produces the output shown in Figure 12-1. Notice the empty boxes around the output. These values are empty because the middle of our 3×3 kernel does not cover the edge of the input array. Therefore, the output matrix of numbers is two smaller in each dimension than the input. If the kernel were 5×5, there would be a border 2 pixels wide instead of 1.

Implementations of 2D convolution need to make a decision about these border pixels. There are options, and most toolkits support several of them. One is to simply ignore these pixels and make the output smaller than the input, as we've shown in Figure 12-1. This approach is often known as *exact* or *valid* because we retain only values that are actually output by the operation.

Another approach is to imagine that a border of 0 values surrounds the input image. The border is as thick as is needed so that the kernel fits with its middle value matching the upper-left pixel of the input. For our example in Figure 12-1, this means a border of 1 pixel because the kernel is 3×3 and there is one element on either side of the kernel's center value. If the kernel were 5×5, the border would be 2 pixels since there are two values on either side of the kernel center. This is known as *zero-padding* and gives an output that is the same size as the input. Instead of convolving a 28×28 pixel MNIST digit image with a 3×3 kernel and getting a 26×26 pixel output as shown in Figure 12-1, we get an output that is also 28×28 pixels.

If we zero pad the example image in Figure 12-1, we can fill in the first empty output square like so

$$\begin{bmatrix} 0 & 0 & 0 \\ 0 & 60 & 248 \\ 0 & 145 & 253 \end{bmatrix} \times \begin{bmatrix} 0 & -1 & 0 \\ -1 & 3 & -1 \\ 0 & -1 & 0 \end{bmatrix} = \begin{bmatrix} 0 & 0 & 0 \\ 0 & 180 & -248 \\ 0 & -145 & 0 \end{bmatrix}$$

which sums to −213. This means that the upper-left corner of the output matrix in Figure 12-1, which currently has an empty box, could be replaced by −213. Similarly, the rest of the empty boxes would have values, and the output of the convolution operation would be 28×28 pixels.

Convolution for Image Processing

Convolution, when used in a neural network, is sometimes viewed as magical, a special operation that lets convolutional neural networks do the wonderful things that they can do. This is more or less true, but the convolution operation is certainly not anything new. Even if we ignore mathematics entirely and think only of the discrete convolution of 2D images, we see that image scientists were using convolution for image processing decades before convolution was applied to machine learning.

The convolution operation allows for all manner of image processing. For example, consider the images shown in Figure 12-2.

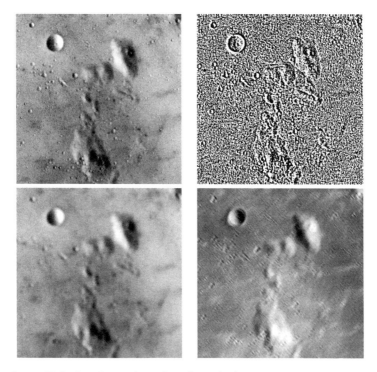

Figure 12-2: 5 × 5 convolution kernels applied to an image

The original moon image is on the upper left. The other three images are the output from convolving the moon image with different 5 × 5 kernels. Moving clockwise from the upper right, the kernels either emphasize edges, diagonal structures (upper left to lower right), or blur the input image. All of this is accomplished by changing the values in the kernel, but the convolution operation remains the same.

From a machine learning perspective, the power of a convolutional approach comes partially from the savings in terms of parameters. If a model can learn a set of kernels, that is a smaller set of numbers to learn than the weights for a fully connected model. This is a good thing on its own. The fact that a convolution can pull out other information about an image, such as its slowly changing components (the blur of Figure 12-2), its rapidly changing components (the edges of Figure 12-2), or even components along a specific direction (the diagonals of Figure 12-2), means that the model gains insight as to what is in the input. And, since we move the kernel over the image, we're not dependent upon *where* in the image these structures occur.

Anatomy of a Convolutional Neural Network

Medical students learn about anatomy by dissecting a cadaver to see the parts and how they relate to each other. In similar, though less challenging, fashion, we'll start with the body of a CNN, an illustration of its basic architecture, and then pull it apart to learn what each component is and what it does.

Figure 12-3 shows us our body. This is the default example CNN used by the Keras toolkit to train a model that classifies MNIST digits. We'll use it as our standard for the remainder of this chapter.

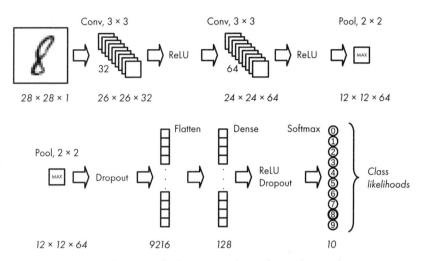

Figure 12-3: The architecture of a basic convolutional neural network

How do we interpret this figure? Like a traditional neural network, a CNN has an input and an output. In this case, the input is the digit image on the upper left. The network then flows left to right, following the arrows. At the end of the top row, the network continues on the following row. Note, we've duplicated the layer at the end of the top row and placed it at the beginning of the next row for presentation purposes.

The flow continues along the bottom row, again left to right, until the output is reached. The output here is a softmax layer to give us the likelihoods of each of the possible digits, just as we saw for the traditional neural networks of Chapter 10.

Different Types of Layers

Between each arrow is a layer of the network. The first thing we notice is that, unlike a traditional neural network, a CNN has many kinds of layers. Let's list them here. We'll discuss each in turn:

- Convolutional (*Conv*)
- ReLU
- Pooling (*Pool*)
- Dropout
- Flatten
- Dense

We should note that we're using the Keras names for the layers. For instance, Keras uses *Dense* for what many other toolkits call *fully connected* or even *InnerProduct* layers.

Several of these layers should already be familiar. We know a ReLU layer implements a rectified linear unit that takes each of its inputs and asks if it is greater than or less than 0. If the input is less than 0, the output is 0; otherwise, the output is the input. We can express this mathematically as

$$\mathrm{ReLU}(x) = \max(0, x)$$

where the *max* function returns the largest of its two arguments.

Likewise, we mentioned dropout in Chapter 9. Dropout selects a percentage of its outputs at random during training and sets them to 0. This provides a powerful form of regularization to help the network learn meaningful representations of the input data. There are two dropout layers in our basic CNN. The first uses a probability of 25 percent, meaning during any minibatch pass while training, some 25 percent of the outputs will be set to 0. The second dropout layer uses a probability of 50 percent.

The *Flatten* and *Dense* layers are old friends, though we know them by another name and not as independent entities. Our traditional feedforward neural network uses fully connected layers to process a one-dimensional vector. Here, Flatten and Dense work together to implement a fully connected layer. The Flatten layer takes its input—usually a four-dimensional array (we'll see why later)—and turns it into a vector. It does something similar to what we did to construct the vector form of the MNIST dataset, where we put the pixels of each row end-to-end to unravel the two-dimensional image. The Dense layer implements a traditional neural network layer, where each input value is mapped to each node of the Dense layer. Typically, the output of the Dense layer is passed to another Dense layer or a softmax layer to let the network make predictions.

Internally, many layers of a CNN expect four-dimensional arrays as inputs and produce four-dimensional arrays as outputs. The first dimension is the number of inputs in the minibatch. So, if we have a minibatch of 24, the first dimension of the 4D array will be 24.

The second and third dimensions are called the *height* and *width*. If the input to a layer is the input to the model (say, an image), then these dimensions are truly the height and width dimensions of the image. If the input is really the output of some other layer, say a (yet to be described) convolutional layer, the *height* and *width* refer to the output from applying a convolutional kernel to some input. For example, the output in Figure 12-1 has height and width of 26.

The last dimension is the number of channels, if an input image; or the number of *feature maps*, if the output of a convolutional or pooling layer. The number of channels in an image is simply the number of bands, where a grayscale image has a single band and a color image typically has three bands, one each for red, green, and blue. Some color images also have an alpha channel used to specify how transparent a pixel is, but these are typically dropped before passing the image through a CNN.

The output in Figure 12-1 is called a *feature map* because it is the response from convolving a kernel over an input. As we saw in Figure 12-2, convolving a kernel over an image can pull out features in the image, so the outputs of the kernels used by a convolutional layer are called *feature maps*.

This leaves two layers to investigate: *Convolutional* and *Pooling*. These layers are new.

In our basic CNN, the convolutions operate on sets of two-dimensional inputs where by *set* I mean a stack of two-dimensional arrays, where the third dimension is the number of channels or feature maps. This means that unlike every other model we've looked at in this book, the input here really is the full image, not a vector created from the image. In terms of CNNs, however, the convolutions need not operate on only two-dimensional inputs. Three-dimensional convolutions exist, as do one-dimensional, though both are seldom used compared to two-dimensional convolutions.

A pooling layer is used to reduce the spatial dimension of its input by combining input values according to some rule. The most common rule is *max*, where the largest value in the small block moved over the input is kept; the other values are discarded. Again, we'll cover pooling layers at length in this chapter.

Many other layer types can be used by modern networks, and many of these are directly supported in Keras already, though it's possible to add your own layers. This flexibility is one reason Keras often quickly supports new deep learning developments. As with a traditional neural network, for a layer to have weights that can be learned, the layer needs to be differentiable in a mathematical sense so that the chain rule can continue, and the partial derivatives can be calculated to learn how to adjust the weights during gradient descent. If the previous sentence is not clear, it's time to review the backprop section of Chapter 9.

Passing Data Through the CNN

Let's look again at Figure 12-3. A lot is happening here beyond just the order and names of the layers. Many layers have numbers in italics running along the bottom. These numbers represent the dimensions of the output of the layer, the height, width, and number of feature maps. If the layer has only a single number, it outputs a vector with that many elements.

The input to the CNN is a $28 \times 28 \times 1$ image. The output of a convolutional layer is a set of feature maps. Thus the output of the first convolutional layer is $26 \times 26 \times 32$, meaning there are 32 feature maps, each a 26×26 image calculated from the single $28 \times 28 \times 1$ input image. Similarly, the output of the second convolutional layer is $24 \times 24 \times 64$, a set of 64 feature maps derived from the $26 \times 26 \times 32$ input, which was itself the output of the first convolutional layer.

We see that the pooling layer at the end of the first row takes its $24 \times 24 \times 64$ input and reduces it to $12 \times 12 \times 64$. The "max" label tells us what the pooling is doing; it takes a 2×2 region of the input and returns the largest value. Since the input is 2×2 and it returns only one value, this reduces each 24×24 input to a 12×12 output. This process is applied to each feature map so that the output is $12 \times 12 \times 64$.

Looking at the bottom row of Figure 12-3 shows us that the Flatten layer takes the $12 \times 12 \times 64$ output of the pooling layer and turns it into a vector of 9,216 elements. Why 9,216? Because $12 \times 12 \times 64 = 9,216$. Next, the Dense layer has 128 nodes, and, finally, our output softmax has 10 nodes because there are 10 classes, the digits 0 through 9.

In Figure 12-3, the ReLU and Dropout layers have no numbers below them. These layers do not alter the shape of their inputs. They simply perform some operation on each of the elements regardless of the shape.

The convolutional layers of our basic CNN have other numbers associated with them: "3×3" and "32" or "64". The 3×3 tells us the size of the convolutional kernel, and the 32 or 64 tells us the number of feature maps.

We already alluded to the 2×2 part of the pooling layer. This represents the size of the pooling kernel, which, much like a convolutional kernel, slides over the input, feature map by feature map (or channel by channel), to reduce the size of the input. Working with a 2×2 pooling kernel implies that, typically, the output will be one-half the size of the input in each of the row and column dimensions.

Figure 12-3 has familiar parts, but the presentation is new to us, and we have these mysterious new layers to think about, like convolutional and pooling layers, so we are sure to be somewhat nebulous in our understanding right now. That is perfectly fine. We have new ideas and some visual indications of how they link together to make a CNN. For now, this is all we need. The remainder of this chapter will, I hope, be a series of "aha!" moments for you as you think back to this figure and its parts. When you understand what each is doing, you'll start to see why they are where they are in the processing chain, leading from image input to output softmax predictions.

Convolutional Layers

If our discussion of convolution ended with the preceding sections, we'd understand the essential operation but still be in the dark about exactly *how* a convolutional layer in a CNN works. Bearing this in mind, let's look at how the convolution idea generalizes across the inputs and outputs of a CNN's convolutional layer.

How a Convolution Layer Works

The input and output of a convolutional layer can both be thought of as stacks of 2D arrays (or matrices). The operation of the convolutional layer is best illustrated with a simple example showing how to map the input stack of arrays to the output stack.

Before we present our example, we need to introduce some terminology. We previously described the convolution operation in terms of applying a kernel to an input, both of which are 2D. We'll continue to use the term *kernel* for this single, 2D matrix. When implementing a convolutional layer, however, we'll soon see that we need stacks of kernels, which are typically referred to in machine learning as *filters*. A filter is a stack of kernels. The filter, via its kernels, is applied over the input stack to produce the output stack. Since during training the model is learning kernels, it is fair to say that the model is also learning filters.

For our example, the input is a stack of two 5×5 arrays, the kernel size is 3×3, and we want an output stack that is three deep. Why three? Because, as the designer of the CNN architecture, we believe that learning three outputs will help the network learn the task at hand. The convolution operation determines the width and height of each output array; we select the depth. We'll use valid convolution, losing a border of thickness one on the output, meaning our input will drop two in width and height. Therefore, a 5×5 input convolved with a 3×3 kernel will create a 3×3 output.

That accounts for the change in dimension, but how do we go from a stack of two arrays to a stack of three? The key to mapping the $5 \times 5 \times 2$ input to the desired $3 \times 3 \times 3$ output is the set of kernels, the filter, learned during training. Let's see how the filter gives us the mapping we want.

We'll assume we already know the filters at this point, each of which is a $3 \times 3 \times 2$ stack of kernels. In general, if there are M arrays in the input stack and we want N arrays in the output stack using a kernel that is $K \times K$, then we need a set of N filters, each one of which is a stack of $K \times K$ kernels M deep. Let's explore why.

If we break up the stack so we can see each element clearly, our input stack looks like this:

$$0: \begin{bmatrix} -1 & 2 & 2 & -2 & -2 \\ -1 & 0 & 2 & 0 & 2 \\ 1 & 2 & 2 & 1 & -2 \\ -1 & 2 & 2 & 2 & 2 \\ 1 & -1 & 1 & 0 & -1 \end{bmatrix}$$

$$1: \begin{bmatrix} 2 & -2 & -1 & -2 & -2 \\ 1 & 1 & 2 & 1 & -2 \\ 2 & 2 & -1 & -1 & 0 \\ -1 & -1 & 2 & -2 & 2 \\ -1 & -2 & 0 & -2 & 0 \end{bmatrix}$$

We have two 5×5 matrices labeled 0 and 1. The values were selected at random.

To get an output stack of three, we need a set of three filters. The stack of kernels in each filter is two deep, to mirror the number of arrays in the input stack. The kernels themselves are 3×3, so we have three $3 \times 3 \times 2$ filters, where we convolve each kernel in the filter with the corresponding input array. The three filters are

$$\begin{array}{cccc} & k_0 & k_1 & k_2 \\ 0: & \begin{bmatrix} 1 & -1 & 1 \\ 1 & -1 & 0 \\ -1 & -1 & 1 \end{bmatrix} & \begin{bmatrix} 0 & -1 & 0 \\ -1 & 1 & -1 \\ -1 & 1 & 0 \end{bmatrix} & \begin{bmatrix} 1 & 0 & 0 \\ -1 & 0 & 0 \\ 0 & -1 & 0 \end{bmatrix} \\ \\ 1: & \begin{bmatrix} -1 & 0 & 0 \\ 1 & 1 & -1 \\ 0 & 0 & 1 \end{bmatrix} & \begin{bmatrix} 0 & 1 & 0 \\ 0 & 1 & 1 \\ 0 & 0 & 0 \end{bmatrix} & \begin{bmatrix} -1 & 1 & 1 \\ 1 & 0 & 1 \\ -1 & 0 & 0 \end{bmatrix} \end{array}$$

where we've added 0 and 1 labels to show which kernels are applied to which input stack arrays. We also have a bias vector, as we did for the traditional neural network layers. This is a vector, one value for each kernel stack, that we add in at the end to help align the output of the convolutional layer to the data, just as we did for the traditional neural network layers. The bias adds one more degree of freedom to the layer—one more thing that can be learned to help the layer learn the most it can from the data. For our example, the bias vector is $b = \{1, 0, 2\}$, selected at random.

To get the output stack, we convolve each kernel of each filter with the corresponding input array, sum the elements of the resulting output, and add the bias value. For filter k_0, we convolve the first input array with the first kernel to get

$$
\begin{bmatrix}
-1 & 2 & 2 & -2 & -2 \\
-1 & 0 & 2 & 0 & 2 \\
1 & 2 & 2 & 1 & -2 \\
-1 & 2 & 2 & 2 & 2 \\
1 & -1 & 1 & 0 & -1
\end{bmatrix}
*
\begin{bmatrix}
1 & -1 & 1 \\
1 & -1 & 0 \\
-1 & -1 & 1
\end{bmatrix}
=
\begin{bmatrix}
-3 & -7 & -1 \\
1 & -4 & 3 \\
-1 & 1 & -3
\end{bmatrix}
$$

Note we're using $*$ to mean the full convolution operation, which is fairly standard. We repeat this operation for the second kernel in k_0, applying it to the second array of the input:

$$
\begin{bmatrix}
2 & -2 & -1 & -2 & -2 \\
1 & 1 & 2 & 1 & -2 \\
2 & 2 & -1 & -1 & 0 \\
-1 & -1 & 2 & -2 & 2 \\
-1 & -2 & 0 & -2 & 0
\end{bmatrix}
*
\begin{bmatrix}
-1 & 0 & 0 \\
1 & 1 & -1 \\
0 & 0 & 1
\end{bmatrix}
=
\begin{bmatrix}
-3 & 3 & 6 \\
6 & -1 & -2 \\
-6 & -1 & -1
\end{bmatrix}
$$

Finally, we sum the two convolution outputs and add in the bias value:

$$
\begin{bmatrix}
-3 & -7 & -1 \\
1 & -4 & 3 \\
-1 & 1 & -3
\end{bmatrix}
+
\begin{bmatrix}
-3 & 3 & 6 \\
6 & -1 & -2 \\
-6 & -1 & -1
\end{bmatrix}
=
\begin{bmatrix}
-6 & -4 & 5 \\
7 & -5 & 1 \\
-7 & 0 & -4
\end{bmatrix}
+ 1 =
\begin{bmatrix}
-5 & -3 & 6 \\
8 & -4 & 2 \\
-6 & 1 & -3
\end{bmatrix}
$$

This gives us the first output array, the application of filter k_0 to the input stack.

We repeat this process for filters k_1 and k_2 to get their outputs so that the final convolutional layer output for the given input is

$$
\begin{bmatrix}
-5 & -3 & 6 \\
8 & -4 & 2 \\
-6 & 1 & -3
\end{bmatrix}
\begin{bmatrix}
-1 & 2 & -6 \\
4 & -3 & 1 \\
0 & -3 & -5
\end{bmatrix}
\begin{bmatrix}
-5 & 0 & -3 \\
0 & 0 & -5 \\
7 & -3 & 4
\end{bmatrix}
$$

where we have written the stacked arrays side by side, a $3 \times 3 \times 3$ output, as desired.

Our convolutional layer example mapped a $5 \times 5 \times 2$ input to a $3 \times 3 \times 3$ output. If we naïvely used a fully connected layer instead, we would need a weight matrix that has $50 \times 27 = 1350$ weights that need to be learned. In contrast, the convolutional layer used only $3 \times 3 \times 2$ weights per filter and three filters for a total of 54 weights, excluding bias values. This is a significant reduction.

Using a Convolutional Layer

The preceding example showed us how a convolutional layer works. Now let's see the effect of one. Imagine that we've trained the network shown in Figure 12-3, so we have the weights and biases we need to run unknown images through the network. (You'll see how to train a CNN in Chapter Summary.)

The first layer of the network in Figure 12-3 is a convolutional layer that maps a $28 \times 28 \times 1$ input, the single-channel grayscale digit image, to a $26 \times 26 \times 32$ output using a filter with 32 3×3 kernels. Therefore, we know that the weights between the input image and output fit in an array that is $3 \times 3 \times 1 \times 32$: 3×3 for the kernel size, 1 for the number of input channels, and 32 for the number of kernels in the filter.

After training, what do the 32 3×3 kernels of the filter actually look like? We can extract them from the trained model and print them as a set of 32 3×3 matrices. Here are the first two:

$$\begin{bmatrix} 0.022 & 0.163 & 0.152 \\ 0.032 & 0.104 & 0.290 \\ -0.322 & -0.345 & -0.221 \end{bmatrix} \begin{bmatrix} 0.141 & 0.239 & 0.311 \\ 0.005 & -0.026 & 0.215 \\ -0.158 & -0.370 & -0.207 \end{bmatrix}$$

This is nice, but not particularly helpful for building intuition about what the kernels do.

We can also visualize the kernels of a filter by converting the matrices to images. To get the kernels as images, we first note that all the kernel values happen to fit in the range $[-0.5, +0.5]$, so if we add 0.5 to each kernel value, we've mapped the range to $[0, 1]$. After this, multiplication by 255 converts the kernel values to byte values, the same values a grayscale image uses. Additionally, a value of 0 is now 127, which is a middle gray value.

After this conversion, the kernels can be shown as grayscale images, where negative kernel values are closer to black, and positive kernel values are closer to white. A final step is needed, however, because the mapped kernels are still only 3×3 pixels. The last step is to upscale the 3×3 images to 64×64 pixels. We'll upscale in two different ways. The first uses nearest-neighbor sampling to show the kernel in blocks. The second uses a Lanczos filter, which smooths the image, making it easier to see the orientation of the kernel. Figure 12-4 shows the kernel images with the block versions on top and the smoothed versions on the bottom.

*Figure 12-4: The 32 learned kernels of the first convolutional layer (top).
Smoothed versions to show the orientations more clearly (bottom).*

These images represent the 32 kernels learned by the first convolutional layer of the model in Figure 12-3. There is just enough detail in the images to hint that the kernels are selecting for structure in specific directions, just like the kernel that produced the image on the lower right of Figure 12-2, which emphasized diagonal structures.

Let's turn our attention now to the effect of the kernels. What do the kernels do to an input MNIST image? We can run a sample MNIST image through the kernels by convolving each kernel with the sample, here a "3", and following a process similar to the one that produced the preceding kernel images. The result is a set of 32 26 × 26 images, which we again upscale to 64 × 64 before displaying them. Figure 12-5 shows the result.

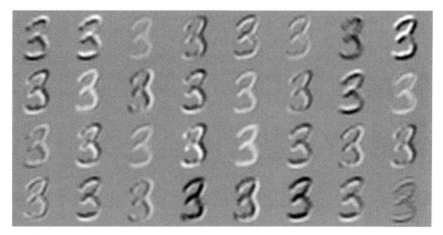

Figure 12-5: The 32 kernels applied to a sample MNIST input

The order of the kernels shown in Figure 12-4 matches the images in Figure 12-5. For example, the top-right image of Figure 12-4 shows a kernel that is light on the upper left and dark on the lower right, meaning it will detect structures along the diagonal from lower left to upper right. The output from applying this kernel to the sample is the upper-right image of Figure 12-5. We see that the kernel enhanced parts of the three that are primarily diagonal from the lower left to the upper right. Note, this example is easy to interpret because the input is a grayscale image with a single channel. This means that there is no summing of kernel outputs across channels as we previously saw for the more general operation.

Typically, the first convolutional layer of a CNN learns kernels that select for specific orientations, textures, or, if the input image is RGB, colors. For the grayscale MNIST images, orientation is most important. The kernels learned at higher convolutional layers in the CNN are also selecting for things, but the interpretation of *what* the kernel is selecting becomes more and more abstract and difficult to understand. It is worth noting that the kernels learned by a CNN's first convolutional layer are very similar to the first layer of visual processing in the mammalian brain. This is the primary visual cortex or V1 layer that detects lines and edges. Additionally, always keep in mind that the set of convolutional and pooling layers are there to learn a new feature representation: a new representation of the input image. This new representation does a better job of separating classes so that the fully connected layers can more easily distinguish between them.

Multiple Convolutional Layers

Most CNNs have more than one convolutional layer. One reason for this is to build up features that are influenced by larger portions of the input as one goes deeper into the network. This introduces the ideas of *receptive field* and *effective receptive field*. The two concepts are similar and often confused. We can explain both by looking at Figure 12-6.

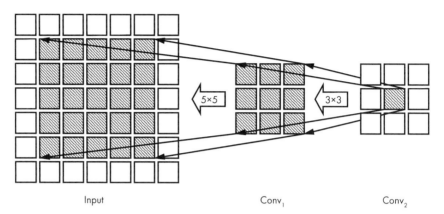

Figure 12-6: Receptive fields

The figure shows the *output* of two convolutional layers and the input to the model. We're showing only the relevant parts of the output, using a 3×3 kernel. We're also ignoring the depth of the filters since the receptive fields (defined next) are the same across the depth of the convolutional layer outputs.

Figure 12-6 should be read right to left as the arrows indicate. This is the opposite direction to the flow of data through the network. Here, we are looking back to earlier layers to see what has influenced the output value at a higher layer. The squares are output values. The rightmost shaded square is one of the outputs of $Conv_2$. This is our starting point for looking back to see what influences this value. The arrows point to the outputs of $Conv_1$ that influence the shaded value in $Conv_2$. The value in $Conv_2$ then has a 3×3 *receptive field* as it is directly influenced by the 3×3 shaded outputs of $Conv_1$. This is how we'll define *receptive field*: the set of outputs from the layer immediately before that directly influence the output of the current layer.

If we look at the set of input values that directly influence the 3×3 shaded region of $Conv_1$, we see a 5×5 region. This makes sense: each shaded output of $Conv_1$ has a receptive field that is a 3×3 region of the input. The receptive field is 3×3 because the kernels of $Conv_1$ are 3×3 kernels. They overlap so that the shaded 5×5 input region is what all the shaded $Conv_1$ outputs are influenced by.

Look again at the rightmost shaded output value. If we trace back to the input all the values that can influence it, we see that the shaded 5×5 region of the input can affect its value. This region of the input is the *effective receptive field* for the rightmost shaded output of Conv$_2$. This output value responds, ultimately, to what is happening in the input image in the leftmost shaded region. As the CNN gets deeper, with additional convolutional layers, we can see how the effective receptive field can change so that deeper convolutional layers are working with values ultimately derived from larger and larger portions of the input to the model.

Initializing a Convolutional Layer

In Chapter 9, we saw that the performance of a traditional neural network was strongly influenced by the type of random initialization used for the learned weights and biases. The same is true for CNNs. Recall that the weights of a convolutional layer are the values of the kernels. They are learned during backprop, just like the weights of a traditional neural network. We need an intelligent way to initialize these values when we set up the network. Fortunately, the best initialization approaches for a traditional neural network apply directly to convolutional layers as well. For example, Keras defaults to Glorot initialization, which, as we saw in Chapter 9, is sometimes called Xavier initialization in other toolkits.

Let's move on now from convolutional layers to pooling layers. These are simpler but perform an important, if somewhat controversial, function.

Pooling Layers

Our favorite figure, Figure 12-3, shows a pooling layer after the first two convolutional layers. This pooling layer takes an input stack of $24 \times 24 \times 64$ and produces an output stack of $12 \times 12 \times 64$. The pooling part is marked as "2×2". What's going on here?

The key is the "2×2". This means, for each of the 64 24×24 inputs, we move a 2×2 sliding window over the input and perform an operation similar to convolution. Not explicitly called out in Figure 12-3 is that the stride is also 2 so that the sliding 2×2 window jumps by two to avoid overlapping itself. This is typically the case, but doesn't need to be. Since the pooling operation is per input in the stack, the output leaves the stack size unchanged. This is contrary to what a convolutional layer often does.

Let's look at the pooling operation applied to a single input in the stack, a 24×24 matrix. Figure 12-7 shows us what's going on.

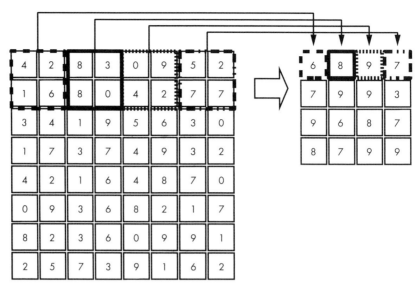

Figure 12-7: Applying 2 × 2 max pooling to an 8 × 8 input

The first 2 × 2 values are mapped to the first output value. Then we move over two and map the next 2 × 2 region to the output and so on until the entire input is mapped. The operation performed on each 2 × 2 region is up to the architect of the CNN. The most common operation is "select the largest value," or *max pooling*, which is what we show in Figure 12-7. This is also the operation the model in Figure 12-3 is performing. Another fairly common pooling operation is to average the values.

We can see from Figure 12-7 that the 8 × 8 input matrix is mapped to a 4 × 4 output matrix. This explains why the output of the pooling layer in Figure 12-3 is 12 × 12; each dimension is half the size of the input.

The pooling operation is straightforward but throws information away. So why do it at all? The primary motivation for pooling is to reduce the number of values in the network. Typically, as depth increases, the number of filters used by convolutional layers increases, by design. We see this for even the simple network of Figure 12-3, where the first convolutional layer has 32 filters, while the second has 64. Therefore, the second convolutional layer outputs 24 × 24 × 64 = 36,864 values, but after 2 × 2 pooling, there are only 12 × 12 × 64 = 9,216 values to work with, a 75 percent reduction. It's important to note that we're talking about the number of values present as we move data through the network, not the number of learned parameters in the layers. The second convolutional layer in Figure 12-3 has 3 × 3 × 32 × 64 = 18,432 learned parameters (ignoring bias values), while the pooling layer has no learned parameters.

This reduction in the number of values in the output, which is our representation of the input, speeds up computation and acts as a regularizer to guard against overfitting. The regularization techniques and rationales of Chapter 9 are equally valid for CNNs. However, since pooling throws information away and selects proxies to represent entire regions of the representation (the convolutional layer outputs), it alters the spatial relationship between parts of the input. This loss of spatial relationships might be critical for some applications and has motivated people like Geoffrey Hinton to eliminate pooling by introducing other types of networks (search for "capsule networks").

Specifically, Hinton said the following regarding pooling layers in response to a question on Reddit asking for his most controversial opinion on machine learning:

> The pooling operation used in convolutional neural networks is a big mistake and the fact that it works so well is a disaster. If the pools do not overlap, pooling loses valuable information about where things are. We need this information to detect precise relationships between the parts of an object.

He elaborates further in the answer, pointing out that allowing pooling operations to overlap does preserve some of the spatial relationships in a crude way. An overlapping pooling operation might be to use a 2×2 window as we used in Figure 12-7, but use a stride of 1 instead of 2.

Concerns aside, pooling layers are an essential part of CNNs as presently implemented, but be careful when adding them to a model. Let's move on now to the top layers of a CNN, the fully connected layers.

Fully Connected Layers

In the second row of Figure 12-3, all the layers starting with *Flatten* form the fully connected layer of the model. The figure uses Keras terminology; many people call the *Dense* layer the fully connected layer and assume there is a Flatten operation as part of it along with the activation (ReLU) and optional dropout before the softmax layer. Therefore, the model in Figure 12-3 has only one fully connected layer.

We previously stated that the net effect of the convolutional and pooling layers is to change the representation of the input feature (the image, say) into one that makes it easier for a model to reason about. During training, we are asking the network to learn a different, often more compact, representation of the input to help the model perform better on unseen inputs. For the model in Figure 12-3, all the layers up to and including the pooling layer (and the dropout layer after it for training) are there to learn a new representation of the input image. In this case, the fully connected layer is the model: it will take that new representation and ultimately make a classification based on it.

Fully connected layers are just that, fully connected. The weights between the flattened final pooling layer of 9,216 elements for Figure 12-3 ($12 \times 12 \times 64 = 9,216$) and the Dense layer of 128 elements are the same as if we were building a traditional neural network. This means that there are $9,216 \times 128 = 1,179,648$ weights plus an additional 128 bias values that need to be learned during training. Therefore, of the 1,199,882 parameters (weights and biases) in the model of Figure 12-3, 98.3 percent of them are in the transition between the final pooling layer and the fully connected layer. This illustrates an important point: fully connected layers are *expensive* in terms of parameters that need to be learned, just as they are for traditional neural networks. Ideally, if the feature learning layers, the convolutional and pooling layers, are doing their job well, we might expect to need only one or two fully connected layers.

Fully connected layers have another disadvantage, besides memory use, that can impact their utility. To see what this disadvantage is, consider the following scenario: you want to be able to locate digits in grayscale images. Assume for simplicity that the background is black. If you use the model of Figure 12-3 trained on MNIST digits, you will have a model that is very good at identifying digits centered in 28×28 pixel images, but what if the input images are large and you do not know where the digits are in the image, let alone how many digits there are? Then things get a little more interesting. The model of Figure 12-3 expects input images that are 28×28 pixels in size and only that size. In Chapter 13, we will work through this problem in detail as an experiment, but for now, let's discuss fully convolutional layers, a possible solution to this disadvantage of using fully connected layers in CNNs.

Fully Convolutional Layers

In the last section, I said that the model of Figure 12-3 expects input images that are 28×28 pixels in size and only that size. Let's see why.

There are many kinds of layers in this model. Some, like the ReLU and dropout layers, have no impact on the dimensionality of the data flowing through the network. The same cannot be said of the convolutional, pooling, and fully connected layers. Let's look at these layers one by one to see how they are tied to the dimensionality of the input image.

The convolutional layers implement convolutions. By definition, a convolution involves moving a fixed-size kernel over some input image (thinking purely 2D here). Nothing in that operation specifies the size of the input image. The output of the first convolutional layer in Figure 12-3 is $26 \times 26 \times 32$. The 32 comes from the number of filters selected by the architecture. The 26×26 comes from using a 3×3 convolution kernel on a 28×28 input with no padding. If the input image were instead 64×64 pixels, the output of this layer would be $62 \times 62 \times 32$, and we wouldn't need to do anything to alter the architecture of the network. The convolutional layers of a CNN are agnostic to the spatial dimensions of their inputs.

The pooling layer in Figure 12-3 takes a $24 \times 24 \times 64$ input and produces a $12 \times 12 \times 64$ output. As we previously saw, the pooling operation is much like the convolution operation: it slides a fixed size window over the input, spatially, and produces an output; in this case, the output is half the dimensionality of the input while leaving the depth the same. Again, nothing in this operation fixes the spatial dimensions of the input stack. If the input stack were $32 \times 32 \times 64$, the output of this max pooling operation would be $16 \times 16 \times 64$ without a change needed to the architecture.

Finally, we have the fully connected layer that maps the $12 \times 12 \times 64 = 9{,}216$ pooling output to a 128 element fully connected (Dense) layer. As we saw in Chapter 8, fully connected neural networks use matrices of weights between layers in their implementation. There are 9,216 elements in the output of the pooling layer and a fixed 128 in the dense layer, so we need a matrix that is 9,216 × 128 elements. This size *is* fixed. If we use the network with a larger, say 32 × 32, input image, by the time we get through the pooling layer, the output size will be 14 × 14 × 64 = 12,544, which would require an existing 12,544 × 128 weight matrix to map to the fully connected layer. Of course, this won't work; we trained a network that uses a 9,216 × 128 matrix. The fully connected layers of a CNN fix the input size of the CNN. If we could get around this, we could apply inputs of any size to the CNN, assuming memory allows.

We could, naïvely, simply slide a 28 × 28 window over the larger input image, run each 28×28 pixel image through the model as we trained it, and output a larger map, where each pixel now has a probability of that digit being present. There are 10 digits, so we would have 10 output maps. This sliding window approach certainly works, but it's very computationally expensive, as many simplistic implementations of algorithms often are.

Fortunately for us, we can do better by converting the fully connected layer into an equivalent convolutional layer to make the model a *fully convolutional network*. In a fully convolutional network, there are no fully connected layers, and we're not restricted to using a fixed input size. The relationship between input size and the output of the network when it is fully convolutional is something we will see in Chapter 13, but the essential operation is to look at the size of the last standard convolutional or pooling layer and replace the fully connected layer that follows with a convolutional layer using a kernel of the same size.

In Figure 12-3, the output of the pooling layer is 12 × 12 × 64. Therefore, instead of the 128-element fully connected layer that we saw fixes our input size, we can mathematically get the same calculation by changing the fully connected layer into a 12 × 12 × 128 convolutional layer. Convolving a 12 × 12 kernel over a 12 × 12 input produces a single number. Therefore, the output of the 12 × 12 × 128 convolutional layer will be a 1 × 1 × 128 array, which is functionally the same as the 128 outputs of the fully connected layer that we originally used. Additionally, the convolution operation between a 12 × 12 kernel and a 12 × 12 input is to simply multiply the kernel values by the input values, element by element, and sum them. This is what a fully connected layer does for each of its nodes.

We do not save anything in terms of the number of parameters when using a convolutional layer this way. We can see this from Figure 12-3. The 9,216 elements of the pooling layer output times the 128 nodes of the fully connected layer means we have 9,216 × 128 = 1,179,648 weights + 128 bias terms needed for both the fully connected and fully convolutional layers. When moving to the 12 × 12 × 128 convolutional layer, we have 12 × 12 × 64 × 128 = 1,179,648 weights to learn, the same as before. However, now we also have the freedom to change the input size, as the 12 × 12 × 128 convolutional layer will automatically convolve over any larger input, giving us outputs that represent the application of the network to 28 × 28 regions of the input with a stride determined by the specific architecture of the network.

Fully convolutional networks stem from the 2014 paper by Long, Shelhamer, and Darrell, "Fully Convolutional Networks for Semantic Segmentation," which has been referenced over 19,000 times as of this writing. The phrase *semantic segmentation* refers to assigning a class label to each pixel of the input image. Currently, the go-to architecture for semantic segmentation is the U-Net (see "U-Net: Convolutional Networks for Biomedical Image Segmentation" by Ronneberger, Fischer, and Brox, 2015) which has seen widespread success, especially in medical domains.

We've discussed the primary CNN layers, those found in Figure 12-3. There are many more that we could cover, but they are generally beyond what we want to present at this level, with one exception, batch normalization, which we'll experiment with in Chapter 15. New layer types are being added all the time in response to active research projects. However, in the end, the core includes the layers we have discussed in this chapter. Let's move on now and see how a trained CNN processes unknown inputs.

Step by Step

In the previous sections, we discussed the architecture and layers of our sample CNN, Figure 12-3. In this section, we will illustrate the operation of the network to see how it responds to two new inputs, one a "4" and the other a "6". We assume the network is fully trained; we'll train for real it in Chapter 13.

The input image is passed through the model layer by layer

$$\text{input} \rightarrow \text{conv}_0 \rightarrow \text{conv}_1 \rightarrow \text{pool} \rightarrow \text{dense} \rightarrow \text{softmax}$$

using the trained weights and biases to calculate outputs for each layer. We will refer to these as the *activations*. The output of the first convolutional layer is a stack of 32 26×26 images, the response of the input image to each of the 32 kernels. This stack then passes to the second convolutional layer to produce 64 24×24 outputs. Note, between the two convolutional layers is a ReLU operation that clips the output so that anything that would have been negative is now 0. Doing this adds a nonlinearity to the data as it flows through the network. Without this nonlinearity, the net effect of the two convolutional layers is to act like a single convolutional layer. With the nonlinearity imposed by the ReLU, we enable the two convolutional layers to learn different things about the data.

The second ReLU operation makes the stack of 64 24×24 outputs 0 or positive. Next, a 2×2 max pooling operation reduces the 64 outputs to 12×12 in size. After this, a standard fully connected layer produces 128 output values as a vector from the 9,216 values in the stack of 12×12 activations. From this, a set of 10 outputs, one for each digit, is calculated via a softmax. These are the output values of the network representing the network's confidence as to which class label should be assigned to the input image.

We can illustrate the activations by displaying the output images: either 26×26 for the first convolutional layer, 24×24 for the second convolutional layer, or 12×12 for the pooling layer. To show the activations from the fully connected layer, we can make an image of 128 bars, where the intensity of each bar represents the vector value. Figure 12-8 shows the activations for our two sample digits.

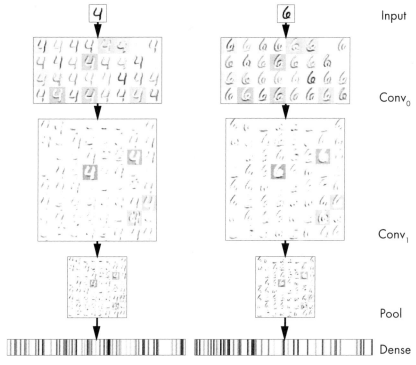

Figure 12-8: Model activations per layer. The output is inverted: darker implies stronger activation.

Note that the images are inverted so that darker corresponds to stronger activation values. We are not showing the softmax outputs. These values are

	0	1	2	3	4	5	6	7	8	9
4	0.00	0.00	0.00	0.00	0.99	0.00	0.00	0.00	0.00	0.00
6	0.00	0.00	0.00	0.00	0.00	0.00	0.99	0.00	0.00	0.00

indicating that in both cases, the model is very confident of the class label that should be assigned and that it was, in fact, correct.

Looking back at Figure 12-8, we see that the output of the first convolutional layer is simply the response of the single input image (grayscale) and the kernels of the layer. This hearkens back to Figure 12-2, where we saw that convolution could be used to highlight aspects of the input image. After the ReLU operation, the responses of the 64 filters of the second convolutional layer, each a stack of 32 kernels, seems to be picking out different portions or strokes in the input images. These can be thought of as a set of smaller components from which the input is constructed. The second

ReLU and pooling operation preserve much of the structure of the second convolutional layer outputs, but reduce the size to one quarter what it was previously. Finally, the output of the fully connected layer shows the pattern derived from the input image, the new representation that we expect to be easier to classify than the raw image input.

The dense layer outputs of Figure 12-8 are different from each other. This begs the question: what do these outputs look like for several instances of four and six digits? Is there something in common that we can see, even in these values? We might expect that there is because we know this network has been trained and has achieved a very high accuracy of over 99 percent on the test set. Let's take a look at running ten "4" and ten "6" images from the test set through the network and compare the dense layer activations. This gives us Figure 12-9.

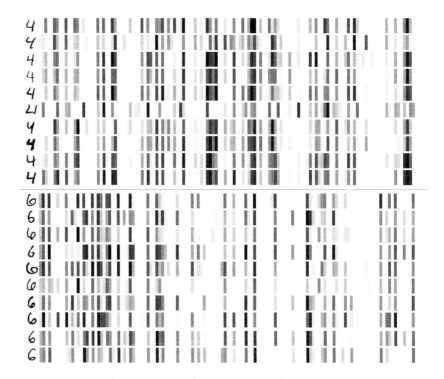

Figure 12-9: Dense layer activations for ten instances of 4 and 6. The output is inverted: darker implies stronger activation.

On the left, we see the actual input to the model. On the right is the representation of the 128 outputs in the fully connected layer, the one that feeds into the softmax. Each digit has a particular pattern that is common to each one of the digits. However, there are also variations. The middle "4" has a very short stem, and we see that its representation in the fully connected layer is also different from all the other examples. Still, this digit was successfully called a "4" by the model with a certainty of 0.999936.

Figure 12-9 provides evidence that the model learned what we wanted it to learn in terms of representation of the input. The softmax layer maps the 128 elements of the dense layer to 10, the output nodes from which the softmax probabilities are calculated. This is, in effect, a simple traditional neural network with no hidden layers. This simpler model succeeds in correctly labeling the images because the new representation of the inputs does a much better job of separating the classes so that even a simple model can make solid predictions. It also succeeds because the training process jointly optimizes both the weights of this top layer model and the weights of the lower layers that generate the input to the model at the same time, so they reinforce each other. Sometimes you will see this referred to in the literature at *end-to-end* training.

We can demonstrate the claim that the features are better separated by looking at a plot of the dense layer activations for the MNIST test data. Of course, we can't look at the actual plot, as I have no idea how to visualize a plot in 128 dimensions, but all is not lost. The machine learning community has created a powerful visualization tool called *t-SNE*, which, fortunately for us, is part of sklearn. This algorithm intelligently maps high-dimensional spaces to lower-dimensional spaces, including 2D. If we run a thousand randomly selected MNIST test images through the model and then run the resulting 128-dimension dense layer activations through t-SNE, we can produce a 2D plot where the separation between classes reflects the actual separation in the 128-dimensional space. Figure 12-10 is the result.

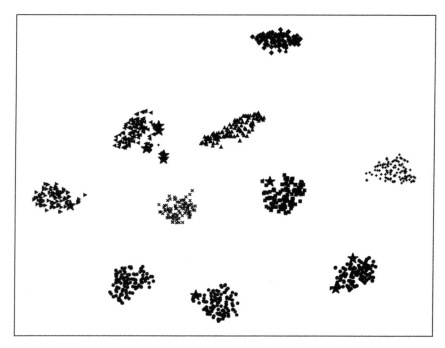

Figure 12-10: How well the model separates test samples by class (t-SNE plot)

In this plot, each class uses a different plot symbol. If the model did not correctly classify the sample, it is shown as a larger star. In this case, only a handful of samples were misclassified. The separation by class type is very evident; the model has learned a representation that makes it straightforward to decide on the correct class label in most cases. We can readily count 10 different blobs in the t-SNE plot.

Summary

In this chapter, we introduced the major components of convolutional neural networks. These are workhorse networks for modern deep learning, especially for vision tasks because of their ability to learn from spatial relationships. We worked through a model to classify MNIST digits and detailed new processing layers, including convolutional layers and pooling layers. We then learned that the fully connected layers of a CNN are analogs of the traditional neural networks we learned about in earlier chapters.

Next, we saw how to modify the fully connected layers to enable operation on larger inputs. Finally, we looked at the activations generated by the network when a sample image was passed through and saw how the convolution and pooling layers worked together to produce a new representation of the input, one that helped to separate the classes in the feature space, thereby enabling high accuracy.

In the next chapter, we'll continue our look at CNNs, but instead of theory, we'll work with actual examples to see how the various parameters of the network, and the hyperparameters used during training, affect model performance. This will help us build intuition about how to work with CNNs in the future.

13

EXPERIMENTS WITH KERAS AND MNIST

In the last chapter, we covered the essential components and functionality of a CNN. In this chapter, we'll work with our test model from Chapter 12. We'll first learn how to implement and train it in Keras. After that, we'll conduct a set of experiments that will build our intuition for how different architectures and learning parameter choices affect the model.

From there, we'll move beyond classification of simple input images and expand the network by converting it into a fully convolutional model capable of processing arbitrary inputs and locating digits wherever they occur in the input.

After fully convolutional networks, we'll wander a little deeper into the pool of deep learning and fulfill a promise made in Chapter 7: we'll explore how well CNNs perform on the scrambled MNIST digit experiment. We saw in Chapter 10 that scrambling the pixels of the digits made it virtually impossible for us to see what the digit was but had little to no effect on how well a traditional neural network was able to interpret the digits. Is the same true with a CNN? We'll find out.

Building CNNs in Keras

The model from Figure 12-3 is straightforward to implement in Python using the keras library. We'll list the code first, explain it, and then run it to see what sort of output it produces. The code naturally falls into three sections. The first loads the MNIST data and configures it for Keras; the second builds the model; and the third trains the model and applies it to the test data.

Loading the MNIST Data

Listing 13-1 has the first part of our code.

```
import keras
from keras.datasets import mnist
from keras.models import Sequential
from keras.layers import Dense, Dropout, Flatten
from keras.layers import Conv2D, MaxPooling2D
from keras import backend as K

batch_size = 128
num_classes = 10
epochs = 12
img_rows, img_cols = 28, 28
```

❶ `(x_train, y_train), (x_test, y_test) = mnist.load_data()`

❷
```
if K.image_data_format() == 'channels_first':
    x_train = x_train.reshape(x_train.shape[0], 1, img_rows, img_cols)
    x_test = x_test.reshape(x_test.shape[0], 1, img_rows, img_cols)
    input_shape = (1, img_rows, img_cols)
else:
    x_train = x_train.reshape(x_train.shape[0], img_rows, img_cols, 1)
    x_test = x_test.reshape(x_test.shape[0], img_rows, img_cols, 1)
    input_shape = (img_rows, img_cols, 1)
```

❸
```
x_train = x_train.astype('float32')
x_test = x_test.astype('float32')
x_train /= 255
x_test /= 255
```

❹
```
y_train = keras.utils.to_categorical(y_train, num_classes)
y_test = keras.utils.to_categorical(y_test, num_classes)
```

Listing 13-1: Loading and data preprocessing

Keras is a rather large toolkit consisting of many modules. We import the library first and then specific functions from it. The mnist module gives us access to the MNIST data from within Keras; the Sequential model type is for implementing a CNN. Our CNN will need some specific layers, the ones we saw used in Figure 12-3: Dense, Dropout, Flatten, Conv2D, and Max-Pool2D, all of which we import. Keras supports a plethora of other layers; I encourage you to spend some quality time with their documentation pages: *https://keras.io/*.

Next, we set the learning parameters, including the number of epochs, classes, and minibatch size. There are 10 classes, and the images are 28×28 pixel grayscale. Like sklearn, in Keras, you specify the number of epochs (full passes through the training set), not the number of minibatches that should be processed. Keras automatically processes the entire training set per epoch in sets of the minibatch size—here 128 samples at a time. Recall that MNIST's training set consists of 60,000 samples, so there are at least $60,000/128 = 468$ minibatches per epoch using integer division. There will be 469 if Keras uses the remainder, the samples that do not build a complete minibatch. Remember that each minibatch process results in a gradient descent step: an update of the parameters of the network.

After loading the MNIST train and test data ❶ come a few lines of code that may seem somewhat mysterious at first ❷. Keras is a higher-level toolkit that uses potentially different lower-level backends. In our case, the backend is TensorFlow, which we installed in Chapter 1. Different backends expect the model input in different forms. The image_data_format function returns a string indicating where the underlying toolkit expects to see the number of channels or filters for convolutional layers. The TensorFlow backend returns channels_last, meaning it expects an image to be represented as a 3D array of H × W × C, where H is the image height, W is the image width, and C is the number of channels. For a grayscale image like MNIST, the number of channels is 1. The code in ❷ reformats the input images to match what Keras is expecting to see.

The next block of code converts the byte image values to floating-point numbers in the range [0, 1] ❸. This is the only scaling done to the input data, and this type of scaling is typical of CNNs that work with images.

Finally, the to_categorical function is used to map the class labels in y_test to one-hot vector representations ❹, which is how Keras wants to see the labels. As we'll see, the model has 10 outputs, so the mapping is to a vector of 10 elements; each element is 0 except for the element whose index corresponds to the label in y_test. That element is set to 1. For example, y_test[333] is of class 6 (a "6" digit). After the call to to_categorical, y_test[333] becomes

```
array([0.,0.,0.,0.,0.,0.,1.,0.,0.,0.], dtype=float32)
```

where all entries are 0 except index 6, which is 1.

Building Our Model

With the dataset preprocessed, we can build our model. The code shown in Listing 13-2 builds the exact model we defined with pictures in Figure 12-3.

```
model = Sequential()
model.add(Conv2D(32, kernel_size=(3, 3),
                 activation='relu',
                 input_shape=input_shape))
model.add(Conv2D(64, (3, 3), activation='relu'))
model.add(MaxPooling2D(pool_size=(2, 2)))
model.add(Dropout(0.25))
model.add(Flatten())
model.add(Dense(128, activation='relu'))
model.add(Dropout(0.5))
model.add(Dense(num_classes, activation='softmax'))

model.compile(loss=keras.losses.categorical_crossentropy,
              optimizer=keras.optimizers.Adadelta(),
              metrics=['accuracy'])

print("Model parameters = %d" % model.count_params())
print(model.summary())
```

Listing 13-2: Building the MNIST model

Keras defines the model as an instance of the Sequential class. The model is built by adding layers to that instance, hence all the calls to the add method. The argument to add is the new layer. The layers are added from the input side to the output side, so the first layer we need to add is the 2D convolutional layer that uses a 3 × 3 kernel on the input image. Note, we are not specifying the number of images nor the minibatch size; Keras will handle that for us when the model is put together and trained. Right now, we are defining the architecture.

Using the architecture defined in Figure 12-3, the first layer is a Conv2D layer. The first argument is the number of filters; here, 32. The kernel size is given as a tuple, (3,3). Kernels don't need to be square, hence the kernel width and height. It's possible that the spatial relationship of the parts of your input might be better detected with a non-square kernel. If so, Keras lets you use one. That said, almost all kernels in practical use are square. After the kernel, we define an activation function to apply to the output of the convolutional layer, here a ReLU. The shape of the input to this layer is explicitly defined via input_shape, and we saw that earlier for our MNIST model using a TensorFlow backend, the shape is a tuple, (28,28,1).

Next, we add the second convolutional layer. This one has 64 filters, also using a 3 × 3 kernel and a ReLU activation on the output. Note, we do not need to specify the shape here: Keras knows the input shape because it knows the shape of the previous convolutional layer's output.

Max pooling comes next. We explicitly state that the pooling size is 2×2, with an implied stride of 2. If we wanted to use average pooling here, we would replace `MaxPooling2D` with `AveragePooling2D`.

After pooling comes our first dropout layer, which uses a 25 percent probability of dropping an output, here the output of the max-pooling layer.

We discussed earlier how Keras separates the operations of a fully connected layer into Flatten and Dense layers. This allows more fine-grained control of the architecture. We add a `Flatten` layer to map the pooling output to a vector and then pass this vector to a `Dense` layer to implement the classic fully connected layer. The dense layer has 128 nodes and uses a ReLU for the activation function. If we want dropout on the output of the dense layer, we need to add it explicitly, so we add one with a probability of 50 percent.

The final dense layer has 10 nodes, one for each possible class label. The activation is set to `softmax` to get a softmax output on the inputs to this layer. Since this is the last layer we define, the output of this layer, the softmax probabilities for membership in each of the 10 classes, is the output of the entire model.

To configure the model for training, we need to call the `compile` method. This sets the loss function used during training (`loss`) and the specific optimization algorithm to use (`optimizer`). The `metrics` keyword is used to define which metrics to report during training. For our example, we are using the categorical cross-entropy loss, which is the multiclass version of the binary cross-entropy loss. We described this loss function in Chapter 9; it is the go-to loss function for many CNNs.

We will need to discuss the optimizer keyword more thoroughly. In Chapter 9, we presented gradient descent and the more common version, stochastic gradient descent. As you might expect, the machine learning community has not been content to simply use this algorithm as is; much research has been done to see if it can be improved upon for training neural networks. This has led to the development of multiple variations on gradient descent, many of which Keras supports.

If we want, we can use classic stochastic gradient descent here. The example, however, is using a variant called *Adadelta*. This is itself a variant of the Adagrad algorithm that seeks to change the learning rate (step size) intelligently during training. For practical purposes, we should consider Adadelta an improved version of stochastic gradient descent. Keras also supports other optimization approaches that we do not intend to cover here, but you can read about in the Keras documentation, particularly Adam and RMSprop.

After the call to `compile`, our model is defined. The convenience methods `count_params` and `summary` produce output characterizing the model itself. When we run the code, we'll see the sort of output they produce.

Training and Evaluating the Model

Finally, with both data and model defined, we can train and then evaluate the model on the test data. The code for this is in Listing 13-3.

```
history = model.fit(x_train, y_train,
        batch_size=batch_size,
        epochs=epochs,
        verbose=1,
        validation_data=(x_test, y_test))
score = model.evaluate(x_test, y_test, verbose=0)
print('Test loss:', score[0])
print('Test accuracy:', score[1])
model.save("mnist_cnn_model.h5")
```

Listing 13-3: Training and testing the MNIST model

The fit method trains the network using the supplied training samples (x_train) and a one-hot vector version of the associated class label (y_test). We also pass in the number of epochs and the minibatch size. Setting verbose to 1 will produce the output shown in Listing 13-4. Lastly, we have validation _data. For this example, we're being a bit sloppy and passing in all the test data instead of holding some back for final testing. (This is just a simple example, after all.) Normally, we'd hold some test data back to use after the final model has been trained. This ensures that results on this held-out test data represent what we might encounter when using the model in the wild.

Notice that the fit method returns something. This is a History object, and its history property holds a per epoch summary of the training and validation loss and accuracy values. We can use these to make summary plots if we wish.

Once the model is trained, we can get a score, similar to the score of sklearn, by calling the evaluate method and passing in the test data. The method returns a list with the loss and accuracy of the model on the supplied data, which we simply print.

We can use the save method to write the model itself to disk for future use. Notice the file extension. Keras dumps the model in an HDF5 file. *HDF5* is a generic hierarchical data format widely used in scientific circles. In this case, the file contains all the weights and biases of the model and the layer structure.

Running this code produces the output shown in Listing 13-4:

```
Using TensorFlow backend.
Model parameters = 1199882

Layer (type)                    Output Shape              Param #
=================================================================
conv2d_1 (Conv2D)               (None, 26, 26, 32)        320
conv2d_2 (Conv2D)               (None, 24, 24, 64)        18496
max_pooling2d_1 (MaxPooling2    (None, 12, 12, 64)        0
dropout_1 (Dropout)             (None, 12, 12, 64)        0
flatten_1 (Flatten)             (None, 9216)              0
dense_1 (Dense)                 (None, 128)               1179776
dropout_2 (Dropout)             (None, 128)               0
dense_2 (Dense)                 (None, 10)                1290
=================================================================
Total params: 1,199,882
Trainable params: 1,199,882
Non-trainable params: 0

Train on 60000 samples, validate on 10000 samples
Epoch  1/12-loss:0.2800 acc:0.9147 val_loss:0.0624 val_acc:0.9794
Epoch  2/12-loss:0.1003 acc:0.9695 val_loss:0.0422 val_acc:0.9854
Epoch  3/12-loss:0.0697 acc:0.9789 val_loss:0.0356 val_acc:0.9880
Epoch  4/12-loss:0.0573 acc:0.9827 val_loss:0.0282 val_acc:0.9910
Epoch  5/12-loss:0.0478 acc:0.9854 val_loss:0.0311 val_acc:0.9901
Epoch  6/12-loss:0.0419 acc:0.9871 val_loss:0.0279 val_acc:0.9908
Epoch  7/12-loss:0.0397 acc:0.9883 val_loss:0.0250 val_acc:0.9914
Epoch  8/12-loss:0.0344 acc:0.9891 val_loss:0.0288 val_acc:0.9910
Epoch  9/12-loss:0.0329 acc:0.9895 val_loss:0.0273 val_acc:0.9916
Epoch 10/12-loss:0.0305 acc:0.9909 val_loss:0.0296 val_acc:0.9904
Epoch 11/12-loss:0.0291 acc:0.9911 val_loss:0.0275 val_acc:0.9920
Epoch 12/12-loss:0.0274 acc:0.9916 val_loss:0.0245 val_acc:0.9916
Test loss: 0.02452171179684301
Test accuracy: 0.9916
```

Listing 13-4: MNIST training output

We've excluded some informational and warning messages from the lower-level TensorFlow toolkit and condensed the output to make it easier to follow in the text.

At the start of the run, Keras informs us that TensorFlow is our backend. It also shows us the shape of the training data, the now familiar 60,000 samples with a shape of 28 × 28 × 1 (×1 since the images are grayscale). We have the usual 10,000 test samples as well.

Next comes a report on the model. This report shows the layer type, shape of the output from the layer, and the number of parameters in the layer. For example, the first convolutional layer uses 32 filters and 3 × 3 kernels, so the output with a 28 × 28 input will be 26 × 26 × 32. The None listed for each layer is in the place where the number of elements in the minibatch normally is. The printout is showing only the relationship between the layers; because nothing in the architecture changes the number of elements in the minibatch, there's no need to explicitly mention the minibatch elements (hence the None). The parameters are 3 × 3 × 32 for the filters plus an additional 32 bias terms for the 320 parameters listed.

As mentioned in Chapter 12, the lion's share of the parameters in the model are between the Flatten layer and the Dense layer. The layer named dense_2 is the softmax layer mapping the 128 elements of the Dense layer to the 10 elements of the softmax: 128 × 10 + 10 = 1290, where the additional 10 are the bias terms. Note that the Dropout and Pooling layers have no parameters because there is nothing to learn in those layers.

After the report on the model's structure, we have the verbose output of the training call to fit. We asked for 12 epochs—12 full passes through the training data—using a minibatch of 128 samples. The output lists the stats for each pass. We see that the loss goes down as we train, which is expected if the model is learning, and that the accuracy (acc) on the training data goes up. The validation data is used during training to test the model, but this data is not used to update the model's weights and biases. The loss on the validation data is also going down with each epoch, but more slowly. What we don't want to see here is the validation loss going up, though it will jump around somewhat, especially if the validation set is not very big. We see an opposite effect with the validation accuracy (val_acc). It is going up for each epoch of training. If the model were to start overfitting, we'd see this accuracy go down after some point. This is the value of validation data: to tell us when to stop training.

The final two lines of output are the loss and accuracy of the model on the test samples passed to the evaluate method. Since the validation and test sets are the same in this example, these lines match the output for epoch 12. The final accuracy of this model is 99.16 percent—certainly a very good accuracy to see.

Plotting the Error

We can use the saved history to plot the loss or error (1 – accuracy) as a function of the training epoch. The plots are similar in shape, so we show only the error plot in Figure 13-1.

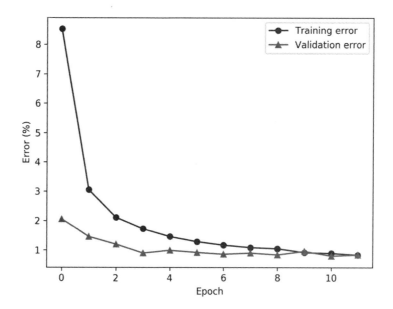

Figure 13-1: The MNIST training and validation errors as a function of epoch

The error on the training data falls off quickly and, as we've seen before, tends toward 0 as training continues. In this case, the validation error falls slightly and then levels off at a value similar to the training error. At this point in the book, you might have alarm bells going off in your head when you look at Figure 13-1. The initial training error is *greater than* the initial validation error!

The full cause of this is hard to pin down, but one component is using dropout in the network. Dropout is applicable only during training, and because of the dropping of nodes in layers, dropout is in effect training many models at once, which, initially, causes a large error before the model "settles down" and the error drops per epoch. We can see that this might be the case here because if we simply comment out the Dropout layers in Listing 13-4 and retrain, we get a new error plot, Figure 13-2.

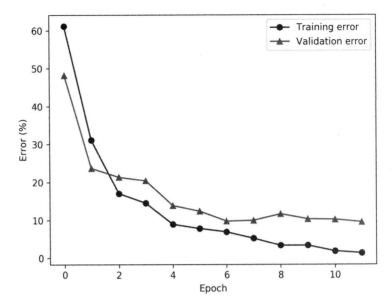

Figure 13-2: The MNIST training and validation errors as a function of epoch when no Dropout layers are present

In Figure 13-2, we see that the validation error quickly becomes greater than the training error, as we would expect. Additionally, we see that the final validation error is much greater than the final validation error for Figure 13-1, about 10 percent versus 1 percent. This is also something we expect if dropout is actually a sensible thing to use, which it is. Note also that by the 12th epoch, the training set error is roughly the same regardless of the presence of Dropout layers.

Finally, some of what we see in Figures 13-1 and 13-2 is due to the way Keras reports training and validation accuracies. The reported training accuracy (and loss) at the end of an epoch is the average over the epoch, but, of course, this is changing as the model learns and tends to increase. However, the validation accuracy reported is for the model as it is at the end of the epoch, so at times is it possible for the training accuracy to be reported as less than the validation accuracy.

Now that we've seen how to build a simple CNN and run it on a dataset, we are in a position to start experimenting with CNNs. Of course, there are an infinite number of experiments we could perform—just look at the rate at which new papers on deep learning appear on sites like *arxiv.org* or the explosion of attendance at machine learning conferences—so we need to restrict ourselves to some basic explorations. Hopefully, these will motivate you to explore more on your own.

Basic Experiments

We did a bit of experimentation already when we removed the Dropout layer. All our experiments follow the same general pattern: make a slightly different version of the model, train it, and evaluate it against the test set. We will try three different types of experiments. The first type modifies the architecture of the model; removing Dropout layers falls into this category. The second type explores the interplay between training set size, minibatch size, and epochs. The last type alters the optimizer used during training.

In all three cases, to avoid excessive code listings, we'll simply comment on the variation to the code in the previous section with the understanding that the remaining code is the same from experiment to experiment. We'll number the experiments, and you can match the results with the number to find the actual Python source code for the experiment. The code is available from the website associated with this book: *https://nostarch.com/practical-deep-learning-python/*.

In the previous section, we used the entire training set of 60,000 samples for training and the whole test set of 10,000 samples for both validation and as the final test set. Here, we'll restrict ourselves to using the first 1,000 or 1,024 training samples as the entire training set. Additionally, we'll use the first 1,000 samples of the test set as the validation set and reserve the last 9,000 samples for the final test set we'll use when training is complete. We'll report the accuracy of these 9,000 images that were unseen during training. The results will include the baseline model accuracy and number of parameters, for comparison purposes.

Bear in mind that unless stated otherwise, the accuracies we present represent a single training session for each experiment. You should get slightly different results if you run these experiments yourself, but those slight differences shouldn't outweigh the larger differences in accuracy that will result from changing the model and/or training process.

Finally, the models in this section are multiclass, so we could examine the confusion matrices to see how the models are making their mistakes. However, it would be exceedingly tedious to do this for each experiment. Instead, we will use the overall accuracy as our metric, trusting that it is a sufficient measure in this case.

Architecture Experiments

Architecture modifications imply removing or adding new layers or altering the parameters of a layer. We've made a number of architecture modifications and compiled the resulting accuracies in Table 13-1.

Table 13-1: Results from Modifying the Model Architecture

Exp.	Modification	Test accuracy	Parameters
0	Baseline	92.70%	1,199,882
1	Add Conv3, 3 × 3 × 64 before Pooling	94.30%	2,076,554
2	Duplicate Conv2, Pooling layer	94.11%	261,962
3	Conv1, 3 × 3 × 32 to 5 × 5 × 32	93.56%	1,011,978
4	Dense layer to 1,024 nodes	92.76%	9,467,274
5	Conv1, Conv2, halve number of filters	92.38%	596,042
6	Second Dense layer with 128 nodes	91.90%	1,216,394
7	Dense layer to 32 nodes	91.43%	314,090
8	Remove Pooling layer	90.68%	4,738,826
9	No ReLU after conv layers	90.48%	1,199,882
10	Remove Conv2	89.39%	693,962

In Table 13-1, the baseline results and model size are given first, followed by the various experiments from most accurate to least accurate. Let's look at the table and interpret the results.

First, we see that adding a third convolutional layer after the second convolutional layer (Experiment 1) improves the performance of the model but also adds 876,672 parameters. Increasing the depth of the network seems to improve the performance of the model but at the expense of increasing the number of parameters.

However, in Experiment 2 we also increase the depth of the network by duplicating the second convolutional layer and the following pooling layer, but because of the second pooling layer, the total number of parameters in the network goes down by 937,920. This is a substantial saving for virtually the same performance. This indicates that depth is good, but so is the judicious use of pooling layers to keep the number of parameters small. For this dataset, Experiment 2 is a solid architecture to use.

Next, we see that an adjustment to the kernel size of the first convolutional layer, Experiment 3, leads to an improvement relative to the baseline. There are more parameters in the first convolutional layer (832 versus 320), but because of the edge effects when using an exact convolution, by the time we get to the output of the Flatten layer, there are now only 7744 values versus 9216 for the baseline model. This means that the large matrix between the Flatten and Dense layers goes from 1,179,776 down to 991,360 parameters with a net result that the model overall has 187,904 fewer parameters.

This is good: better performance and fewer parameters to learn. Is there a downside to the change of Experiment 3? Not really. Instead, one might argue that adjusting the kernel size for the first convolutional layer has made the model more appropriate for the spatial information in the digit images, thereby making the new representation learned by the convolutional and pooling layers that much better at separating the classes. In general, there seems to be a best kernel size for the first convolutional layer, the layer that deals with the input to the model. That kernel size is related to the spatial structure of the inputs: some sizes will be better at detecting input features that are better for separating the classes. This general rule does not appear to hold for higher convolutional layers, and there the prevailing wisdom is to use 3 × 3 kernels for most convolutional layers except the first.

Can we combine Experiment 3 and Experiment 2? Certainly. We simply make the first convolutional layer of Experiment 2 use a 5 × 5 kernel instead of a 3 × 3 kernel. If we do this, we get a model with an overall accuracy of 94.23 percent that needs only 188,746 parameters. With this trivial change, we've achieved the performance of Experiment 10 by using only 9 percent of the parameters.

You might be tempted to simply increase the size of the Dense layer, the layer that can be thought of as using the new feature representation discovered by the convolutional and pooling layers below it. However, doing so (Experiment 4) results in no real improvement in overall accuracy, but with a substantial increase in the number of parameters. We know the cause: the 9,216 × 128 weight matrix between the Flatten and Dense layers is now a 9,216 × 1,024 matrix. Clearly, for CNNs, we want to create the best feature representation so that a simpler top layer can be used.

With Experiment 5, we see that we can make the model significantly smaller, a reduction of 603,840 parameters, while still achieving the same overall accuracy by simply halving the number of filters learned in each of the convolutional layers: 32 → 16 for Conv1 and 64 → 32 for Conv2. Again, this is a good optimization provided the slight (perhaps in this case meaningless) difference in accuracy is acceptable. If we look again at Figure 12-8, we can see that, especially for the second convolutional layer with 64 filters, the responses are very similar for many filters. This implies that there are redundant filters that are not adding much to the new feature representation presented to the Dense layers. Despite halving the number of filters learned, there are still filters that learn to capture the important aspects of the input data used to separate the classes.

Experiment 7 plays with the Dense layer nodes, and Experiment 6 adds a second Dense layer. Neither offers a real benefit. For Experiment 7, the change in the number of model parameters is significant due to the 9,216 × 128 matrix weight becoming a 9,216 × 32 matrix. However, 32 nodes does not seem to be the ideal number to make use of the new feature representation. The second Dense layer of Experiment 6 isn't too awful in terms of increasing the number of parameters to learn, but it isn't buying us much, either. If we use a larger training set, we might get some improvement, but we'll leave that as an exercise for the reader.

In the previous chapter, we read about the criticisms levied against pooling layers. What if we remove the pooling layer entirely (Experiment 8)? First, we see that accuracy drops relative to the baseline model. Worse, we see that the size of the network has increased dramatically, from 1,199,882 parameters to 4,738,826, by a factor of nearly four. This is due to the increase in the number of elements in the output of the Flatten layer, which has gone from 9,216 to 36,864, resulting in a weight matrix of $36,864 \times 128 + 128 = 4,718,720$ elements. This example demonstrates why we use pooling layers even with the price they bring in terms of the loss of information about the relative position of object parts.

Each of the convolutional layers in the baseline model uses ReLU on its outputs. Removing these ReLU operations, Experiment 9, leads to a 2 percent reduction in accuracy on the test set. Clearly, the ReLU is helping somewhat. What might it be doing? The ReLU leaves positive values unchanged and sets negative values to 0. When used with the output of a convolutional layer, the ReLU is keeping more strongly activated responses to the filters, positive responses, while suppressing negative responses. This seems to be helping the entire process of learning a new representation of the input.

Finally, Experiment 10 removed Conv2 entirely. This has the greatest effect on the overall accuracy because the features passed to the Dense layer are then based solely on the output of the first convolutional layer filters. There was no opportunity for the model to learn from these outputs and develop filter responses based on the larger effective receptive field seen by the second convolutional layer.

However, given what we saw in the results of Experiment 3, which increased the kernel size used by the first convolutional layer, we might wonder whether this change from 3×3 to 5×5 kernels might somewhat compensate for the loss of the second convolutional layer. Fortunately, this is very easy to test. We simply change the 3×3 kernel parameter of Conv1 to a 5×5 and train again. Doing this validates our intuition: the resulting overall accuracy increases to 92.39 percent, virtually the same as the baseline model. Also, this 5×5 model has only 592,074 parameters, making the change inexpensive in terms of the number of model parameters.

From all of these results, do we have a winner, an architecture that is lean but highly effective? We do—it is Experiment 2 with a 5×5 kernel for the first convolutional layer. In Keras, to build this architecture, we need the code in Listing 13-5.

```
model = Sequential()
model.add(Conv2D(32, kernel_size=(5, 5),
                 activation='relu',
                 input_shape=input_shape))
model.add(Conv2D(64, (3, 3), activation='relu'))
model.add(MaxPooling2D(pool_size=(2, 2)))
model.add(Dropout(0.25))

model.add(Conv2D(64, (3, 3), activation='relu'))
model.add(MaxPooling2D(pool_size=(2, 2)))
model.add(Dropout(0.25))
```

```
model.add(Flatten())
model.add(Dense(128, activation='relu'))
model.add(Dropout(0.5))
model.add(Dense(num_classes, activation='softmax'))
```

Listing 13-5: Building the architecture for Experiment 2

We've simply duplicated the Conv2D, MaxPooling2D, and Dropout layers and used (5,5) for the kernel size of the first layer.

If we train this model using all 60,000 samples of the MNIST training set, we get a final held-out test set accuracy of 99.51 percent for an error of 0.49 percent. This is using all 10,000 samples. According to *benchmarks.ai*, a website that tracks current bests on different machine learning datasets, the state-of-the-art MNIST error is 0.21 percent, so we are not state of the art, but we are better than the 99.16 percent accuracy we saw in Listing 13-4 for the default architecture.

Training Set Size, Minibatches, and Epochs

These experiments examine the interplay between training set size, minibatch size, and number of epochs. Our model will be the default model we were using previously, Experiment 0, but this time we'll use 1,024 samples for the training set. We'll be using powers of two as the minibatch sizes; this is a convenient size, as all of our minibatch sizes divide it evenly.

Recall, Keras, like sklearn, runs through a given number of epochs, or full passes through the training set. Additionally, the minibatch size (batch _size) specifies the number of samples used in each iteration, after which the average error (the cross-entropy loss) is used to update the parameters. Therefore, each processed minibatch leads to a single gradient descent step, and the training set size divided by the minibatch size is the number of gradient descent steps taken per epoch.

For our experiments, we'll use the following minibatch sizes:

```
1, 2, 4, 8, 16, 32, 64, 128, 256, 512, 1024
```

For a training set of 1,024 samples (approximately 100 for each digit), the number of gradient descent steps per epoch is the reverse of this list: 1,024 for a batch size of 1, down to 1 for a batch size of 1,024.

Let's generate two plots. The first will plot the final test set accuracy for the two cases: a fixed number of gradient descent steps regardless of minibatch size, and a fixed number of epochs irrespective of minibatch size. The second plot will show us the clock time to train the model for each case. The code leading to the plots is in Experiments 26 through 31 (fixed number of gradient descent steps) and Experiments 32 through 42 (fixed number of epochs).

The test set accuracy as a function of minibatch size is given as the mean of five runs in Figure 13-3, and the standard error of the mean given by the error bars. Let's look at the fixed number of gradient descent steps regardless of minibatch size (triangles). In some toolkits, this is referred to as using a fixed number of iterations, where *iteration* means a single update leading to a gradient descent step.

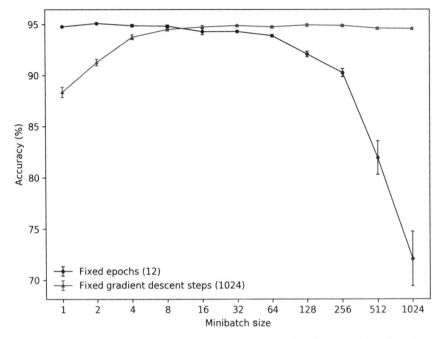

Figure 13-3: MNIST test set accuracy as a function of minibatch size and fixed gradient descent steps or fixed epochs

The number of gradient descent steps was fixed at 1,024. This means that we need to change the number of epochs, depending on how many minibatches are in the training set. For the case of a single sample used per update (`batch_size=1`), we get the required 1,024 steps in a single epoch, so we set the number of epochs to 1. For a minibatch size of two, we get 512 steps per epoch, so we set the number of epochs in the code to 2 to get 1,024 steps overall. The pattern continues: to get the 1,024 gradient descent steps for each minibatch size, we need to set the number of epochs to the minibatch size.

We see that except for the smallest minibatch sizes, when we fix the number of gradient descent steps, we get very consistent overall accuracies. After minibatch sizes of about 16, things do not change too much. The general rule for CNNs is to use smaller batch sizes. This seems to help with model generalization for datasets that are not as simple as MNIST, and, as we'll soon see, decreases training time significantly.

The second curve of Figure 13-3 shows the accuracy for a fixed number of epochs (circles). If we change the minibatch size but do not increase the number of training epochs to make the number of gradient descent steps remain constant, we'll be using larger and better estimates of the gradient, but we'll also be taking fewer steps. We see that doing this quickly results in a substantial decrease in accuracy. We should not be surprised. With a minibatch size of one, training for 12 epochs gives us a model that took $12 \times 1,024 = 12,288$ gradient descent steps. Granted, the gradient estimate was particularly noisy in this case since we use only one training sample to estimate it, but with lots of steps, we arrived at a well-performing model all the same. By the time we get to a minibatch of 1,024 samples, the size of our training set, we see that we took only 12 gradient descent steps before calling it a day. No wonder the results are so poor.

The second plot of this section is Figure 13-4.

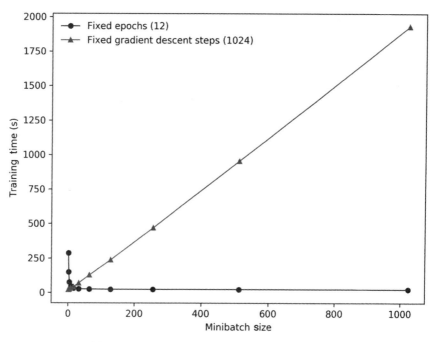

Figure 13-4: Model training time as a function of minibatch size and fixed gradient descent steps or fixed epochs

As before, let's start with the fixed number of gradient descent steps (triangles). We see immediately that the training time is linearly proportional to the minibatch size. This is reasonable since we just saw that we need to increase the number of epochs to keep the number of gradient descent steps constant while increasing the minibatch size. Therefore, the amount of data passed through the network is increasing proportionally, so the time required for the forward and backward training passes will increase proportionally as well. From this, we see that large minibatch sizes cost clock time.

For a fixed number of epochs, we see a different story. For tiny minibatch sizes, training time goes up due to the number of forward and backward passes. For the case of a minibatch of one, we need 12,288 such passes, as we just saw. However, by the time we get to minibatches of even 32 samples at a time, we have only $1024/32 = 32$ passes per epoch for a total of 384 for the entire training session. This is far fewer than for the smallest minibatch size, so we might expect the training time for minibatches this size or larger to be roughly constant in time, as we see in Figure 13-4.

What can we glean from these two plots? The following: to balance run time and accuracy, we want to use minibatch sizes that are large enough to give us a reasonable estimate of the gradient but small enough that, for a fixed number of model updates (gradient descent steps), we can train quickly. This argues for minibatch sizes in the 16 to 128 range, in general. Indeed, a review of the deep learning literature sees minibatches in this range almost exclusively for most applications. For this example, minibatch sizes above 16, based on Figure 13-3 (triangles), result in models that are all basically the same in terms of accuracy, but the training time for a model using a minibatch size of 16, according to Figure 13-4 (triangles), compared to one of size 1,024, is a few seconds versus approximately 30 minutes.

Optimizers

So far, all of our experiments have used the same gradient descent algorithm, or optimizer: Adadelta. Let's take a look at how our MNIST model does if we change the optimizer but leave everything else fixed. Our model is Experiment 0, the model we've been using all along in this chapter. We'll continue to use 1,000 test samples for validation and 9,000 to determine our final accuracy. However, instead of using the first 1,000 or 1,024 training samples, we'll increase the number to the first 16,384 samples. We fix the minibatch size at 128 and the number of epochs to 12, as before. We'll report the results as mean and standard error over five runs.

Keras currently supports the following optimizers: stochastic gradient descent (SGD), RMSprop, Adagrad, Adadelta, and Adam. We'll train using each of these in turn. For Adagrad, Adadelta, and Adam, we leave the parameters at their default settings, as recommended by the Keras documentation. For RMSprop, the only parameter the Keras documentation recommends adjusting is the learning rate (lr), which we set to 0.01, a typical value. For SGD, we set the learning rate to 0.01 as well and set standard momentum to 0.9, also a very typical value. The code is found in Experiments 43 through 47.

Figure 13-5 shows the test set accuracy (top) and training time (bottom) for each of the optimizers.

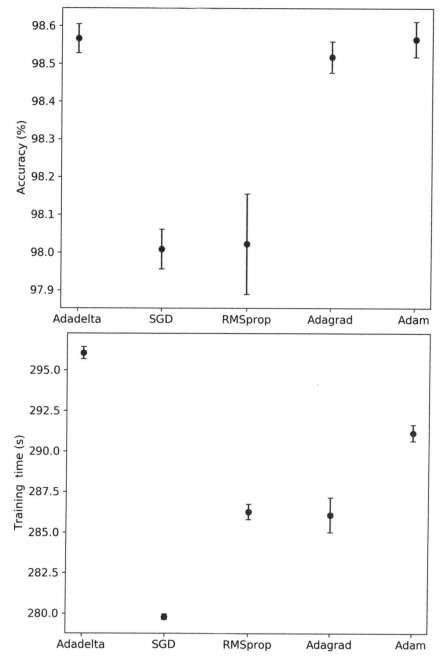

Figure 13-5: Test set accuracy (top) and training time (bottom) by optimization algorithm

First, notice that there is not too much difference between the results produced by each optimizer. This is good news. However, by looking at the error bars, it seems clear that Adadelta, Adagrad, and Adam all perform slightly better than SGD or RMSprop. This is borne out in the deep learning literature as well, though each dataset should be looked at independently.

In terms of training time, the different optimizers are also roughly equivalent, though SGD is fastest and consistently so. This performance difference might be important for a very large dataset. Adam is also consistently faster than Adadelta for basically the same performance. Again, these results are evident in the literature where both SGD and Adam are widely used.

This section has been thorough in terms of minute details associated with changing model architectures and training parameters. Hopefully, it has helped you develop intuition about how to configure a CNN and how to train it. Rules of thumb are hard to present in this area, but I have given some general guidance. Exceptions to these rules abound, however, and you have to simply try things, observe the results, and adapt when presented with a new dataset.

Let's move on now from classifying simple inputs to answering the question of how to make a model that can locate targets in arbitrary images.

Fully Convolutional Networks

We introduced fully convolutional networks in Chapter 12. Let's take our basic MNIST CNN model and convert it to a fully convolutional version and see how we can use it to locate digits in larger images. Our basic approach is to train the model using fully connected layers, as before, and then to create a fully convolutional version and update the weights with those from the fully connected model. We can then apply the new model to arbitrary size inputs to locate digits (hopefully).

Building and Training the Model

First, we train our base model on the full MNIST dataset. The only change we'll make is to train for 24 epochs instead of just 12. The output of this process is an HDF5 file that contains the trained weights and biases. All we then need to do is create the fully convolutional version by changing the fully connected layer and copy the weights and biases from the old model to the new. The code for this is straightforward, as shown in Listing 13-6.

```
from keras.models import Sequential, load_model
from kcras.layers import Dense, Dropout, Flatten
from keras.layers import Conv2D, MaxPooling2D
```

```
❶ weights = load_model('mnist_cnn_base_model.h5').get_weights()

   model = Sequential()
   model.add(Conv2D(32, kernel_size=(3, 3),
                   activation='relu',
           ❷ input_shape=(None,None,1)))
   model.add(Conv2D(64, (3, 3), activation='relu'))
   model.add(MaxPooling2D(pool_size=(2, 2)))
   model.add(Dropout(0.25))

❸ model.add(Conv2D(128, (12,12), activation='relu'))
   model.add(Dropout(0.5))

❹ model.add(Conv2D(10, (1,1), activation='softmax'))

❺ model.layers[0].set_weights([weights[0], weights[1]])
   model.layers[1].set_weights([weights[2], weights[3]])
   model.layers[4].set_weights([weights[4].reshape([12,12,64,128]), weights[5]])
   model.layers[6].set_weights([weights[6].reshape([1,1,128,10]), weights[7]])

   model.save('mnist_cnn_fcn_model.h5')
```

Listing 13-6: Creating the trained fully connected model

After importing the necessary Keras modules, we load the trained weights from the fully connected model ❶. Then, we construct the fully convolutional version much as we did for the fully connected version. However, there are some key differences. The first has to do with the input convolutional layer ❷. In the fully connected model, we specified the input image size here, 28×28 pixels with one channel (grayscale). For the fully convolutional case, we do not know the size of the input, so we use None instead for the width and height. We do know that the input will be a single channel image, so we leave the 1.

Since the Dense layers are the reason we have to use fixed size inputs, we replace them with equivalent convolutional layers ❸. We replace

```
model.add(Flatten())
model.add(Dense(128, activation='relu'))
```

with

```
model.add(Conv2D(128, (12,12), activation='relu'))
```

The (12,12) is the output size of the max-pooling layer above, and the 128 is the number of filters to learn that stand in for the 128 nodes we had before. Again, the critical point here is that the output of this convolutional layer is $1 \times 1 \times 128$ because convolving a 12×12 input with a 12×12 kernel produces a single output value. The difference is that the convolutional layer is not tied to any fixed input size as the combination of Flatten and Dense was.

The final softmax layer also needs to be made fully convolutional ❹. There are ten outputs, one per digit, and the activation remains the same. The kernel size, however, is 1×1. The input to this layer is $1 \times 1 \times 128$, so the kernel size to cover it is 1×1. Again, if we were to work through the math, we'd see that a $1 \times 1 \times 128$ input to a $1 \times 1 \times 10$ convolutional layer matches that of a fully connected layer of 128 nodes mapped to 10 nodes in the next layer. The difference here is that if the input is larger than 1×1, we can still convolve over it.

Now that we've constructed the fully convolutional version of our model, we need to copy the weights from the trained fully connected model to it ❺. We loaded the trained weights into weights. This is a list of NumPy arrays for the weights and biases, layer by layer. So, weights[0] refers to the weights of the first Conv2D layer, and weights[1] are the biases. Similarly, weights[2] and weights[3] are the weights and bias values for the second convolutional layer. We set them in the new fully convolutional model by updating the proper layers via the set_weights method. Layers 0 and 1 are the two convolutional layers.

Layer 4 is the new Conv2D layer that replaced the Flatten and Dense layers of the original model. Here when we set the weights, we need to reshape them to match the form of a convolutional layer: $12 \times 12 \times 64 \times 128$. This is for a 12×12 kernel mapped over 64 inputs leading to 128 outputs. The 64 is the number of 12×12 outputs from the pooling layer above.

Finally, we set the output layer weights. Again, we need to reshape them to $1 \times 1 \times 128 \times 10$ for the $1 \times 1 \times 128$ input and 10 outputs. The biases for the two new Conv2D layers are in weights[5] and weights[7], so we add them as well.

The fully convolutional model is now defined and completely populated with the weights and biases from the fully connected model. Figure 13-6 shows the mapping between models, with the original architecture on the left and the fully convolutional architecture on the right. The boxes represent layers, with the top set of numbers being the input and the bottom the output. For the fully convolutional model, input height and width are arbitrary and marked with "--".

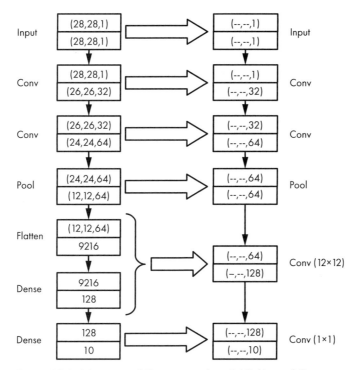

Figure 13-6: Mapping a fully connected model (left) to a fully convolutional model (right)

All that is left to do is write the new fully convolutional model to disk, and it's ready to use. Let's see how.

Making the Test Images

To test the fully convolutional model, we first need images with digits. Unlike our training images, which were small and had a single digit in the center, we want larger test images that contain many digits in arbitrary locations. The MNIST dataset consists of shades of gray on a black background; therefore, our test images should have a black background also. This will make the test images come from the same "domain" as the training images, which, as we've emphasized before, is critical. Making models adapt to different data domains is an active research area. Search for *domain adaptation*.

Making the test images by using Python and the digits from the MNIST test set is straightforward. We didn't use the test set images for training, so using them to make our larger test images isn't cheating. The code is shown in Listing 13-7.

```
import os
import sys
import numpy as np
import random
from PIL import Image

os.system("rm -rf images; mkdir images")

if (len(sys.argv) > 1):
    N = int(sys.argv[1])
else:
    N = 10

x_test = np.load("data/mnist/mnist_test_images.npy")

for i in range(N):
❶   r,c = random.randint(6,12), random.randint(6,12)
    g = np.zeros(r*c)
❷   for j in range(r*c):
        if (random.random() < 0.15):
            g[j] = 1
    g = g.reshape((r,c))
    g[:,0] = g[0,:] = g[:,-1] = g[-1,:] = 0

❸   img = np.zeros((28*r,28*c), dtype="uint8")
    for x in range(r):
        for y in range(c):
            if (g[x,y] == 1):
❹               n = random.randint(0, x_test.shape[0])
                im = x_test[n]
                img[28*x:(28*x+28), 28*y:(28*y+28)] = im

    Image.fromarray(img).save("images/image_%04d.png" % i)
```

Listing 13-7: Building large MNIST test set images

We're making use of the MNIST test set file we created in Chapter 5. We could just as quickly have loaded the test images through Keras, as we did earlier for our basic CNN experiments. The code itself creates an output directory, *images*, and gets the number of images to build from the command line, if given (N).

The images are of random sizes ❶. Here, r and c are the number of rows and columns in the large image in terms of the number of 28×28 MNIST digits. To decide where to place our digits so they don't overlap, we create a grid, g, with either a 0 or a 1 in each possible digit position (r*c of them) ❷. There is a 15 percent chance that any grid position will contain a 1. We then reshape the grid into an actual 2D array and set the border positions of the grid to 0 to ensure that no digits appear on the edge of the image.

The actual output image is then defined ❸ as the number of rows and columns are multiplied by 28, the width and height of the MNIST digit. We loop over each digit position (x and y), and if the grid value at that row and column is 1, then we select a digit at random and copy it to the current row and column digit position in the output image (img) ❹. When every grid position has been examined, the image is written to disk so that we can use it with our fully convolutional network.

Testing the Model

Let's test the model—first on single MNIST digits and then on the randomly generated large digit images. The fully convolutional model should work as well with single MNIST digits as the fully connected model did. The code to test this assertion is in Listing 13-8.

```
import numpy as np
from keras.models import load_model

x_test = np.load("data/mnist/mnist_test_images.npy")/255.0
y_test = np.load("data/mnist/mnist_test_labels.npy")
model = load_model("mnist_cnn_fcn_model.h5")

N = y_test.shape[0]
nc = nw = 0.0
for i in range(N):
 ❶ p = model.predict(x_test[i][np.newaxis,:,:,np.newaxis])
    c = np.argmax(p)
    if (c == y_test[i]):
        nc += 1
    else:
        nw += 1
print("Single MNIST digits, n=%d, accuracy = %0.2f%%" % (N, 100*nc/N))
```

Listing 13-8: Verifying that the fully convolutional model works with single MNIST digits

We load the MNIST test images and labels, along with the fully convolutional model, and then loop over each test image and ask the model to make a prediction ❶. Note, the image is 2D, but we must pass a 4D array to the predict method, hence using np.newaxis to create the missing axes. The prediction for the digit is stored in p as a vector of per class probabilities. The label associated with the largest of these probabilities is the label assigned to the input digit by the model c. If c matches the actual test label, we increment the number of correct predictions (nc); otherwise, we increment the number of wrong predictions (nw). Once all 10,000 test images have been processed, we can output the overall accuracy, which is 99.25 percent for my training of the fully convolutional model.

Okay, the fully convolutional model is highly accurate, but so what? We passed single-digit images to it as inputs and got a single output value. We had this capability before with the fully connected model. To expose the utility of the fully convolutional model, let's now pass the large MNIST digit images as input. In code, we do this as shown in Listing 13-9.

```
import os
import numpy as np
from keras.models import load_model
from PIL import Image

model = load_model("mnist_cnn_fcn_model.h5")

os.system("rm -rf results; mkdir results")
n = len(os.listdir("images"))

for i in range(n):
    f = "images/image_%04d.png" % i
❶   im = np.array(Image.open(f))/255.0
    p = model.predict(im[np.newaxis,:,:,np.newaxis])
    np.save("results/results_%04d.npy" % i, p[0,:,:,:])
```

Listing 13-9: Running the fully convolutional model over large test images

We import the necessary modules and then load the fully convolutional model. We then create a new output directory, *results*, and find the number of large digit images (n). Next, we loop over each of the large digit images.

After loading the image from disk, being careful to make a NumPy array from it and scaling it by 255 since the training data was also scaled by 255 ❶, we make a prediction and store the model output in p. Notice, we make a 4D input to predict, just as we did for the single digits earlier, but this time, im is larger than 28×28 and contains multiple digits. Because the model is fully convolutional, this isn't an issue; we will not get an error. Instead, p is a 4D array with the first dimension of one, the number of input images, and a final dimension of ten, the number of digits. The middle two dimensions of p are a function of the size of the input passed to the predict method. Since the input was larger than 28×28 pixels, the entire model convolved over the input image as though the model was a convolutional layer with a kernel of 28×28. Specifically, the output of this convolution has height and width of

$$h = \frac{H - 28}{2} + 1, \; w = \frac{W - 28}{2} + 1$$

where H, W are the height and width of the input image and h, w are the height and width of the output array from predict. The 28 in the formula is the size of the inputs we initially trained on, 28×28 digit images. Where did the mysterious 2 come from in the denominator? This is the stride of the 28×28 kernel over the input image. It is 2 because that is the factor the input image is changed by when it gets down to the fully convolutional output layers. The input was 28×28, but, after the two convolutional layers and the pooling layer, the input is mapped to 12×12 and $\lfloor 28/12 \rfloor = 2$.

We stated that the array in p is 4D; now we know we get a specific-size output based on convolving a 28 × 28 region over the input image using a stride of 2. What do we get at each of the h, w output array positions? The last element of the 4D output has size 10; these are the per class predictions at the specific h, w output position that corresponds to the 28 × 28 kernel.

Let's make this abstract description more concrete. The upper-left corner of Figure 13-7 shows one of the large input images where we've inverted it to make it black on a white background and added a border so you can see the full size of the image.

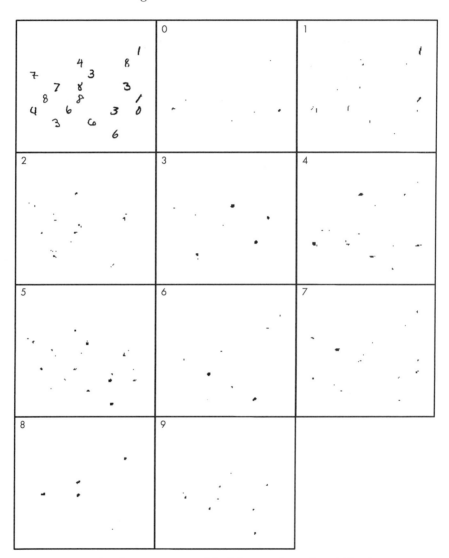

Figure 13-7: Per digit heatmap output of the fully convolutional model for the input image on the upper left. The model was trained on the standard MNIST dataset.

The image in the top left of Figure 13-7 is 336 pixels wide and 308 pixels tall, meaning the output from passing this image to the model will be an array that is $1 \times 141 \times 155 \times 10$, exactly what we expect from the equations on page 334 for the output array dimensions. The output array represents the model's predictions at each of the 28×28 regions of the input image when using a stride of 2. There is one prediction for each digit. For example, if p is the 4D output of the predict method for the image on the left of Figure 13-7, then p[0,77,88,:] will return a 10-element vector representing the per class probabilities of each digit class for the 28×28 input region of the image that maps to 77×88. In this case, we get the following:

```
array([0.10930195, 0.12363277, 0.131005  , 0.10506018, 0.05257199,
       0.07958104, 0.0947836 , 0.11399861, 0.08733559, 0.10272926],
      dtype=float32)
```

This tells us that there is no strong likelihood, according to the model, that any particular digit is present at this location. We know this because all the output probabilities are much lower than even the minimum cutoff threshold of 0.5. The output of predict can be thought of as a probability map, typically called a *heatmap*, giving us the probability that there is a digit in that location. The model output can be thought of as 10 heatmaps, one for each digit.

The remaining images of Figure 13-7 show the heatmaps for each of the 10 digits, again inverted so that higher probabilities are darker. The heatmaps were thresholded at 0.98, meaning any probability value less than 0.98 was set to 0. This removes the weak outputs like the ones we just saw. We are interested only in the model's strongest responses per digit. To make the heat maps, we double the size of the output from the model and set the output image locations with an offset to account for the position of the convolutional output. This is akin to what we saw in Figure 12-1, where the convolution operation returns an output that is smaller than the input when no zero padding is used. Specifically, the code that produces the digit heatmaps is in Listing 13-10.

```
import os
import sys
import numpy as np
from PIL import Image

❶ threshold = float(sys.argv[1])
  iname = sys.argv[2]
  rname = sys.argv[3]
  outdir= sys.argv[4]
  os.system("rm -rf %s; mkdir %s" % (outdir, outdir))

❷ img = Image.open(iname)
  c,r = img.size
  hmap = np.zeros((r,c,10))
```

```
    res = np.load(rname)
    x,y,_ = res.shape
    xoff = (r - 2*x) // 2
    yoff = (c - 2*y) // 2

❸ for j in range(10):
        h = np.array(Image.fromarray(res[:,:,j]).resize((2*y,2*x)))
        hmap[xoff:(xoff+x*2), yoff:(yoff+y*2),j] = h
    np.save("%s/graymaps.npy" % outdir, hmap)
❹ hmap[np.where(hmap < threshold)] = 0.0
    for j in range(10):
        img = np.zeros((r,c), dtype="uint8")
        for x in range(r):
            for y in range(c):
                ❺ img[x,y] = int(255.0*hmap[x,y,j])
        img = 255-img
        Image.fromarray(img).save("%s/graymap_digit_%d.png" % (outdir, j))
```

Listing 13-10: Building heatmap images

Here we're calling the output images *graymaps* because they're grayscale images representing the response of the model to different locations in the input image. We first pass in the threshold value, the source image name, the response of the model to that source image, and an output directory where the graymaps will be written ❶. This directory is overwritten each time. Next, the source image is loaded to get its dimensions ❷. These are used to create the output heatmaps (hmap). We also load the associated model responses (res) and calculate the offsets. Note that hmap is the same size as the image. We then fill in each digit graymap of hmap with the resized model response ❸ and store the full set of graymaps in the output directory.

To make the output grayscale images like those shown in Figure 13-7, we first threshold the heatmaps, setting any value less than the supplied cutoff to 0 ❹. Then, for each digit, we create an output image and simply scale the remaining heatmap values by 255 since they are probabilities in the range [0, 1) ❺. Then, before writing the image to disk, we invert by subtracting from 255. This makes stronger activations dark and weaker activations lighter. Because of the strong threshold applied (0.98), our output graymaps are effectively binary; this is what we want to indicate where the model is most certain of a digit being located.

Let's look back at Figure 13-7 and see if we can interpret these responses. The source image has one 0 on the lower right. If we look at the graymap for digit 0, we see a single dark blob in that location. This means the model has indicated a strong response that there is a 0 digit at that location. So far, so good. However, we also see another strong response from the model near the 4 on the left side of the input image. The model has made a mistake. The input has two 4s in it. If we look at the graymaps for digit 4, we see two dark blobs corresponding to these digits, but we also see many other small areas of strong activation near other digits that are not 4s. The model we trained was over 99 percent accurate on single MNIST test digits, so why are the responses of the fully convolutional model so noisy? Just look at all the small strong responses for 2s when the input does not contain any 2s. Sometimes, the model is doing well, as for 8s where the graymap shows strong responses for all the 8s in the input, but then it does poorly for other digits like 7s. And, there are no 5s at all, but the model is returning many hits.

Here is an opportunity for us to expand our thinking and intuition. We trained the model on the standard MNIST digit dataset. All of the digits in this dataset are well centered in the images. However, when the model is convolved over the large input image, there will be many times when the input to the model is not a well-centered digit but only part of a digit. The model has never seen partial digits, and since it must give an answer, it sometimes offers answers that are meaningless—the part of a digit it sees may be part of a 6, for example, but the model "thinks" it is a 5.

One possible solution is to teach the model about partial MNIST digits. We can do this by augmenting the standard MNIST dataset with shifted versions of its digits. Imagine a 4 shifted to the lower right so that only part of it is visible. It will still be labeled a 4, so the model will have an opportunity to learn what a shifted 4 digit looks like. The code to make this shifted dataset is in the file *make_shifted_mnist_dataset.py*, but we'll show only the function that makes a shifted copy of an input MNIST digit here. This function is called four times for each training and test image (to create a shifted test dataset). We keep the original centered digit and four randomly shifted copies of it to make a dataset that is five times as large as the original. The random shift function is.

```
def shifted(im):
    r,c = im.shape
    x = random.randint(-r//4, r//4)
    y = random.randint(-c//4, c//4)
    img = np.zeros((2*r,2*c), dtype="uint8")
    xoff = r//2 + x
    yoff = c//2 + y
    img[xoff:(xoff+r), yoff:(yoff+c)] = im
    img = img[r//2:(r//2+r),c//2:(c//2+c)]
    return img
```

with im being the input image supplied as a NumPy array. Based on the input size, we pick random x and y shifts that can be positive or negative and up to one-quarter of the image size. Varying this limit to, say, one-third or one-half would be worth the experiment. A new image is created (img), which is twice the size of the original. The original is then put into the larger image at an offset based on the shift positions, and the center portion of the larger image, matching the input image dimensions, is returned as the offset version of the input.

To use the augmented dataset, we need first to retrain the fully connected MNIST model, then rebuild the fully convolutional model using the new weights and biases, and, finally, run the large test images through the model as before. Doing all of this leads to new graymaps (Figure 13-8).

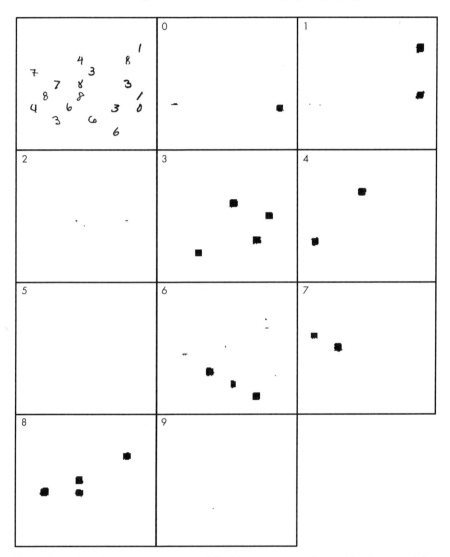

Figure 13-8: Per digit heatmap output of the fully convolutional model for the upper-left input image. The model was trained on the MNIST dataset augmented by shifting the digits.

We see a vast improvement, so we have impressive evidence that our intuition was correct: the initial model was unable to deal effectively with partial digits, but when we trained it with partial digits included, the resulting responses were robust over the actual digits and very weak to nonexistent for other digits. We really should not be surprised by these results. Our first model did not represent the space of inputs that the model would see when used in the wild. It knew nothing about partial MNIST digits. The second model was trained on a dataset that is a better representation of the space of possible inputs, so it performs significantly better.

Using fully convolutional networks in this way has been superseded in recent years by other, more advanced techniques that we do not have space nor computing power to work with in this book. Many models that localize objects in images output not a heatmap, but a bounding box covering the image. For example, the YOLO model (*https://pjreddie.com/darknet/yolo/*) is capable of real-time object detection in images, and it uses bounding boxes around the objects with their label. In Chapter 12, we mentioned semantic segmentation and U-Nets as current state-of-the-art models that assign a class label to each pixel of the input. Both of these approaches are useful and are, in a sense, extensions of the fully convolutional model approach we just demonstrated here.

Scrambled MNIST Digits

In Chapter 10, we showed that scrambling the order of the pixels in an MNIST digit (Figure 7-3), provided the remapping of pixels is deterministically applied to each image, poses no problem for a traditional neural network. It is still able to train well and assign class labels just as effectively as with unscrambled digits. See Figure 10-9.

Let's see if this still holds with CNNs. We made the scrambled MNIST digit dataset in Chapter 5. All we need to do here is substitute it for the standard MNIST dataset in our baseline CNN model, the one we started the chapter with. If we train this model with the scrambled data, and do so repeatedly to get some error bars, we get Figure 13-9.

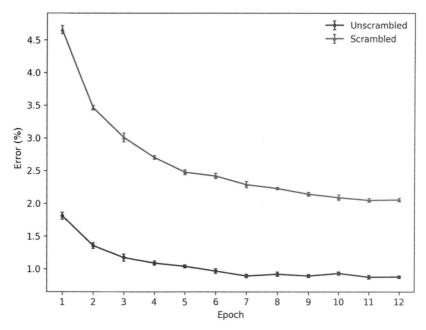

Figure 13-9: Test set error per epoch for a model trained on unscrambled and scrambled MNIST digits. Mean and SE over six training sessions.

Here we see that unlike the traditional neural network, the CNN does have some trouble: the test error for the scrambled digits is higher than for the unscrambled digits. Why? Recall, the CNN uses convolution and learns kernels that help create a new representation of the input, one that a simple model, the top layers, can readily use to distinguish between classes.

Convolution generates responses that are spatially dependent. In the case of the scrambled digits, that spatial dependence is mostly eliminated; it is only by considering the digit image as a whole, like a traditional neural network, that a class determination can be made. This means there is little for the lower layers of the CNN to learn. Of course, the CNN is still learning and does a better job with the scrambled digits than the traditional model in the end, about 2 percent error versus 4.4 percent, but the distinction between scrambled and unscrambled is more significant.

Summary

In this chapter, we built our intuition around CNNs by working with the MNIST dataset. We explored the effect of basic architecture changes; learned about the interplay among training set size, minibatch size, and number of training epochs; and explored the effect of the optimization algorithm.

We saw how to convert a model using fully connected layers into a fully convolutional model. We then learned how to apply that model to search for digits in arbitrarily sized input images. We also learned that we needed to increase the expressiveness of our dataset to do a better job of representing the distribution of inputs the model sees when used.

Finally, we saw via an experiment with the scrambled MNIST digits that the strength of CNNs—their ability to learn spatial relationships within data— can sometimes be of little help when the spatial relationships are weak or nonexistent.

In the next chapter, we'll continue our exploration of basic CNNs with a new dataset, one of actual images: CIFAR-10.

14

EXPERIMENTS WITH CIFAR-10

In this chapter, we'll perform a series of experiments with the CIFAR-10 dataset we built in Chapter 5. First, we'll see how two models, one shallow, the other deeper, perform on the full dataset. After that, we'll work with grouped subsets of the entire dataset to see if we can tell the difference between animals and vehicles. Next, we'll answer the question of what's better for the CIFAR-10 dataset, a single multiclass model or a set of binary models, one per class.

We'll close the chapter by introducing transfer learning and fine-tuning. These are important concepts, often confounded, that are widely used in the machine learning community, so we should develop an intuitive feel for how they work.

A CIFAR-10 Refresher

Before we dive into the experiments, let's refamiliarize ourselves with the dataset we're working with. CIFAR-10 is a 10-class dataset from the Canadian Institute for Advanced Research (CIFAR). We built this dataset in

Chapter 5 but deferred its use until now. CIFAR-10 consists of 32×32-pixel RGB images of animals (six classes) and vehicles (four classes). Take a look at Figure 5-4 for some sample images. The training set has 50,000 images, 5,000 from each class, so it is a balanced dataset. The test set consists of 10,000 images, 1,000 from each class. CIFAR-10 is probably the second most widely used standard dataset in machine learning after MNIST. There is also a 100-class version, CIFAR-100, that we'll not work with in this book, but you'll see it pop up often in the literature.

As of this writing, the best performing model on unaugmented CIFAR-10 has achieved a 1 percent error on the test set (*benchmarks.ai*). The model that did this has 557 million parameters. Our models will be significantly smaller and have a much larger test error. However, this is a true image dataset, unlike MNIST, which is very clean and has a uniform black background for every digit. Because of the variation in natural images, especially in their backgrounds, we might expect models to have a harder time learning the CIFAR-10 classes compared to MNIST.

For reference throughout the chapter, here are CIFAR-10 classes:

Label	Class	Label	Class
0	airplane	5	dog
1	automobile	6	frog
2	bird	7	horse
3	cat	8	ship
4	deer	9	truck

Working with the Full CIFAR-10 Dataset

Let's train two different models on the entire CIFAR-10 dataset. The first model is the same one we used in Chapter 13 for the MNIST dataset. We'll refer to this model as our *shallow model* because it has only two convolutional layers. We'll need to adapt it a touch for the 32×32 RGB inputs, but that's straightforward enough to do. The second model, which we'll call our *deep model*, uses multiple convolutional layers before the pooling and fully connected layers.

Additionally, we'll experiment with both stochastic gradient descent and Adadelta as our optimization algorithms. We'll fix the minibatch size at 64 and train for 60 epochs for a total of 46,875 gradient descent steps. For SGD, we'll use a learning rate of 0.01 and a momentum of 0.9. Recall, Adadelta is adaptive and alters the learning rate on the fly. We can decrease the learning rate for SGD as training progresses, but 0.01 is relatively small, and we have a large number of gradient descent steps, so we'll just leave it a constant.

The shallow model has 1,626,442 parameters, while the deep model has only 1,139,338. The deep model is deep because it has more layers, but because each convolutional layer is using exact convolution, the output decreases by two each time (for a 3×3 kernel). Therefore, the flatten layer after the pooling layer has only 7,744 values compared to 12,544 for the shallow model. The weight matrix between the flatten layer and the dense layer of 128 nodes contains the vast majority of the parameters, $7,744 \times 128 = 991,232$ compared to $12,544 \times 128 = 1,605,632$. Thus, going deeper has actually reduced the number of parameters to learn. This slightly counterintuitive result reminds us of the large expense incurred by fully connected layers and some of the initial motivation for the creation of CNNs.

Building the Models

You'll find the code for the shallow model in *cifar10_cnn.py* (Adadelta) and *cifar10_cnn_SGD.py* (SGD). We'll work through the code in pieces. The shallow model starts in much the same way as for the MNIST dataset, as shown in Listing 14-1.

```
import keras
from keras.models import Sequential
from keras.layers import Dense, Dropout, Flatten
from keras.layers import Conv2D, MaxPooling2D
from keras import backend as K
import numpy as np

batch_size = 64
num_classes = 10
epochs = 60
img_rows, img_cols = 32, 32

x_train = np.load("cifar10_train_images.npy")
y_train = np.load("cifar10_train_labels.npy")
x_test = np.load("cifar10_test_images.npy")
y_test = np.load("cifar10_test_labels.npy")

if K.image_data_format() == 'channels_first':
    x_train = x_train.reshape(x_train.shape[0], 3, img_rows, img_cols)
    x_test = x_test.reshape(x_test.shape[0], 3, img_rows, img_cols)
    input_shape = (3, img_rows, img_cols)
else:
    x_train = x_train.reshape(x_train.shape[0], img_rows, img_cols, 3)
    x_test = x_test.reshape(x_test.shape[0], img_rows, img_cols, 3)
    input_shape = (img_rows, img_cols, 3)

x_train = x_train.astype('float32')
x_test = x_test.astype('float32')
```

```
x_train /= 255
x_test /= 255

y_train = keras.utils.to_categorical(y_train, num_classes)
y_test = keras.utils.to_categorical(y_test, num_classes)
```

Listing 14-1: Preparing the CIFAR-10 dataset

We import the necessary modules and load the CIFAR-10 dataset from the NumPy files we created in Chapter 5. Notice that the image dimensions are now 32×32, not 28×28, and that the number of channels is 3 (RGB) instead of 1 (grayscale). As before, we scale the inputs by 255 to map the images to $[0, 1]$ and convert the label numbers to one-hot vectors using to_categorical.

Next, we define the model architecture (Listing 14-2).

```
model = Sequential()
model.add(Conv2D(32, kernel_size=(3, 3),
                activation='relu',
                input_shape=input_shape))
model.add(Conv2D(64, (3, 3), activation='relu'))
model.add(MaxPooling2D(pool_size=(2, 2)))
model.add(Dropout(0.25))
model.add(Flatten())
model.add(Dense(128, activation='relu'))
model.add(Dropout(0.5))
model.add(Dense(num_classes, activation='softmax'))

model.compile(loss=keras.losses.categorical_crossentropy,
                optimizer=keras.optimizers.Adadelta(),
                metrics=['accuracy'])
```

Listing 14-2: Building the shallow CIFAR-10 model

This step is identical to the MNIST version for the shallow model (see Listing 13-1). For the deep model, we add more convolutional layers, as shown in Listing 14-3.

```
model = Sequential()
model.add(Conv2D(32, kernel_size=(3, 3),
                activation='relu',
                input_shape=input_shape))

model.add(Conv2D(64, (3,3), activation='relu'))
model.add(Conv2D(64, (3,3), activation='relu'))
model.add(Conv2D(64, (3,3), activation='relu'))
model.add(Conv2D(64, (3,3), activation='relu'))

model.add(MaxPooling2D(pool_size=(2,2)))
model.add(Dropout(0.25))
```

```
model.add(Flatten())
model.add(Dense(128, activation='relu'))
model.add(Dropout(0.5))
model.add(Dense(128, activation='relu'))
model.add(Dropout(0.5))
model.add(Dense(num_classes, activation='softmax'))

model.compile(loss=keras.losses.categorical_crossentropy,
              optimizer=keras.optimizers.Adadelta(),
              metrics=['accuracy'])
```

Listing 14-3: Building the deep CIFAR-10 model

The extra convolutional layers give the model the opportunity to learn a better representation of the input data, which for CIFAR-10 is more complex than the simple MNIST images. The representation might be better because a deeper network can learn more abstract representations that encompass larger structures in the inputs.

The code snippets in Listings 14-2 and 14-3 compile the model using Adadelta as the optimization algorithm. We also want a version of each that uses SGD. If we replace the reference to Adadelta() in the compile method with the following

```
optimizer=keras.optimizers.SGD(lr=0.01, momentum=0.9)
```

we'll use SGD with the learning rate and momentum values we indicated earlier. For completeness, the rest of the code for both shallow and deep models is shown in Listing 14-4.

```
print("Model parameters = %d" % model.count_params())
print(model.summary())

history = model.fit(x_train, y_train,
          batch_size=batch_size,
          epochs=epochs,
          verbose=1,
          validation_data=(x_test[:1000], y_test[:1000]))

score = model.evaluate(x_test[1000:], y_test[1000:], verbose=0)
print('Test loss:', score[0])
print('Test accuracy:', score[1])

model.save("cifar10_cnn_model.h5")
```

Listing 14-4: Training and testing the CIFAR-10 models

This code summarizes the model architecture and number of parameters, trains by calling the fit method using the first 1,000 test samples for validation, and then evaluates the trained model on the remaining 9,000 test samples by calling the evaluate method. We report the test loss and accuracy. Then we write the model to disk (save), and store the history showing the per epoch loss and accuracy during training. We'll use the history files to generate plots showing the loss and error (1 − accuracy) as a function of the training epoch.

Listing 14-4 gives us four files: shallow model + Adadelta, shallow model + SGD, deep model + Adadelta, and deep model + SGD. Let's run each of these to see our final test accuracy and then look at plots of the training process to see what we can learn.

Running the code trains and evaluates the models. This takes some time on our CPU-only system, about eight hours total. The random initialization Keras uses means that when you run the code yourself, you should see slightly different answers. When I ran the code, I got Table 14-1.

Table 14-1: Test Set Accuracies by Model Size and Optimizer

	Shallow	Deep
Adadelta	71.9%	74.8%
SGD	70.0%	72.8%

The table tells us that using Adadelta gave us a more accurate model for both shallow and deep models compared to SGD. We also see that the deep model outperforms the shallow model regardless of optimizer. Adaptive optimizers like Adadelta and Adam (also in Keras) are generally preferred to plain old SGD for this reason. However, I have seen claims that SGD is ultimately just as good or better once the learning rate is set up right and decreased as training proceeds. Of course, nothing prevents us from starting with an adaptive optimizer and then switching to SGD after some number of epochs. The idea here is that the adaptive optimizer "gets close" to a minimum of the loss function while SGD fine-tunes the process at that point.

Analyzing the Models

Let's look at how the loss changes during training. Figure 14-1 shows the loss per epoch for the shallow and deep models using Adadelta (top) and SGD (bottom).

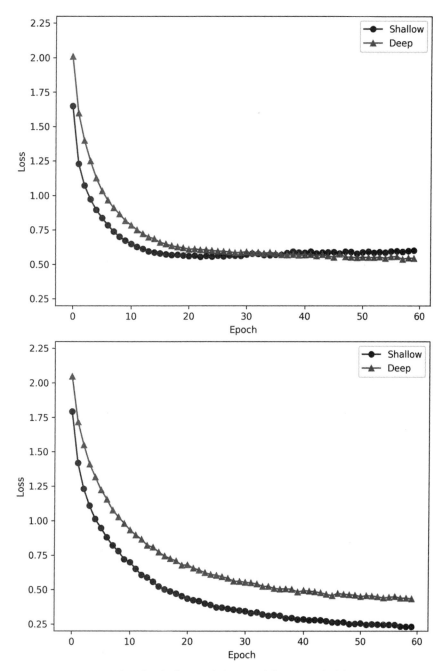

Figure 14-1: Training loss for shallow and deep models using Adadelta (top) and SGD (bottom)

Starting with the Adadelta loss plot, we see that compared to SGD, the loss is not as low. We also see that for the shallow model, the loss is increasing slightly per epoch. This is a counterintuitive result and seems to contradict conventional wisdom that the training loss should only decrease. There are reports of this happening with Adam, another adaptive optimizer, so it is likely an artifact of the adaptation algorithm. Regardless, as we saw in Table 14-1, Adadelta leads to higher accuracies for both shallow and deep models.

On the bottom of Figure 14-1, we see that SGD leads to a smaller loss for the shallow model compared to the deep model. This is typically interpreted as a hint for potential overfitting. The model is learning the details of the training set as the loss tends to 0. The shallow model using SGD was the least performant model according to Table 14-1. The deep model using SGD did not have such a small loss, at least up to 60 training epochs.

What about the validation set accuracy during training? Figure 14-2 plots the *error* by epoch. The error is easier to understand visually; it should tend toward 0 as accuracy increases. Again, the Adadelta models are on the top, and the SGD models are on the bottom.

As expected, regardless of optimizer, the deeper model performed better and had a lower validation set error during training. Note, the validation set error is not the final, held-out test set error, but instead the portion of the test set used during training, the first 1,000 samples in this case.

The SGD curves on the bottom of Figure 14-2 follow what our intuition should tell us: as the model trains, it gets better, leading to a smaller error. The deep model quickly overtakes the shallow model—again, an intuitive result. Also, the curves are relatively smooth as the model gets better and better.

The Adadelta error plots on the top of Figure 14-2 are a different story. There is an obvious decrease in the error after the first few epochs. However, after that, the validation set error jumps around somewhat chaotically though still following our intuition that the deep model should have a smaller error than the shallow model. This chaotic result is due to the adaptive nature of the Adadelta algorithm, which is adjusting the learning rate on the fly to search for a better minimum. From the results of Table 14-1, it's clear that Adadelta is finding better-performing models.

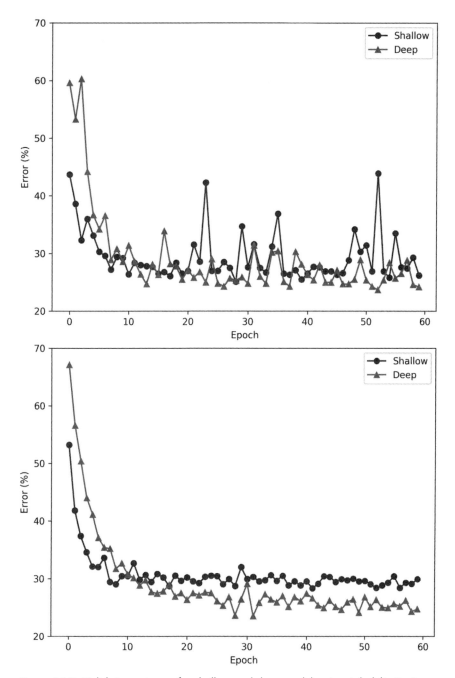

Figure 14-2: Validation set error for shallow and deep models using Adadelta (top) and SGD (bottom)

These experiments tell us that adaptive optimization algorithms and deeper networks (to a point) tend toward better-performing models. While recognizing the danger inherent in attempting to offer advice in this field, it seems safe to say that one should start with adaptive optimization and use a large enough model. To find out just what *large enough* means, I suggest starting with a modest model and, after training, making it deeper and seeing if that improves things. Eventually, the model will be too large for the training set, so there will be a cutoff point where increasing the size of the model no longer helps. In that case, get more training data, if possible.

Let's now shift our attention to working with subsets of CIFAR-10.

Animal or Vehicle?

Four of the ten classes in CIFAR-10 are vehicles; the remaining six are animals. Let's build a model to separate the two and see what we can learn from it. We already have the images; all we need do is recode the labels so that all the vehicles are marked as class 0 and all the animals as class 1. Doing this is straightforward, as shown in Listing 14-5.

```
import numpy as np
y_train = np.load("cifar10_train_labels.npy")
y_test  = np.load("cifar10_test_labels.npy")
for i in range(len(y_train)):
    if (y_train[i] in [0,1,8,9]):
        y_train[i] = 0
    else:
        y_train[i] = 1
for i in range(len(y_test)):
    if (y_test[i] in [0,1,8,9]):
        y_test[i] = 0
    else:
        y_test[i] = 1
np.save("cifar10_train_animal_vehicle_labels.npy", y_train)
np.save("cifar10_test_animal_vehicle_labels.npy", y_test)
```

Listing 14-5: Adjusting the labels of CIFAR-10 into vehicles (class 0) and animals (class 1)

We load the existing train and test label files, already matched in order with the train and test image files, and build new label vectors mapping the vehicle classes—classes 0, 1, 8, and 9—to 0 and all the others to 1.

The code in the previous section for building and training the model remains the same except for the definition of the model architecture and the particular file we load for the train and test labels. The number of classes (num_classes) is set to 2, the minibatch size is 128, and we'll train for 12 epochs. The training set isn't completely balanced—there are 20,000 vehicles and 30,000 animals—but the imbalance isn't severe, so we should be in good shape. Remember that when one class is scarce, it becomes difficult for the model to learn it well. We'll stick with Adadelta as the optimizer and use the first 1,000 test samples for validation and the remaining 9,000 for final test. We'll use the same shallow architecture used in the previous section.

Training this model on the CIFAR-10 images with the recoded labels gives us a final test accuracy of 93.6 percent. Let's be a little pedantic and calculate all the performance metrics from Chapter 11. To do this, we update the tally_predictions function defined in that chapter (Listing 11-1) to work with a Keras model. We'll also use basic_metrics (Listing 11-2) and advanced_metrics (Listing 11-3) from Chapter 11. The updated code for tally_predictions is shown in Listing 14-6.

```
def tally_predictions(model, x, y):
    pp = model.predict(x)
    p = np.zeros(pp.shape[0], dtype="uint8")
❶   for i in range(pp.shape[0]):
        p[i] = 0 if (pp[i,0] > pp[i,1]) else 1
    tp = tn = fp = fn = 0
    for i in range(len(y)):
        if (p[i] == 0) and (y[i] == 0):
            tn += 1
        elif (p[i] == 0) and (y[i] == 1):
            fn += 1
        elif (p[i] == 1) and (y[i] == 0):
            fp += 1
        else:
            tp += 1
    score = float(tp+tn) / float(tp+tn+fp+fn)
    return [tp, tn, fp, fn, score]
```

Listing 14-6: Calculating basic metrics for Keras models

We pass in the model, test samples (x), and test labels (y). Unlike the sklearn version of tally_predictions, here we first use the model to predict per class probabilities (pp). This returns a 2D array, one row for each sample in x, where the columns are the probabilities assigned per class. Here there are two columns because there are only two classes: vehicle or animal.

Before we can tally the true positives, true negatives, false positives (vehicle classified as animal), and false negatives (animal classified as vehicle), we need to assign a class label to each test sample. We do this by looping over the predictions, row by row, and asking whether the probability for class 0 is greater than class 1 or not ❶. Once we have assigned a predicted class label (p), we can calculate the tallies and return them along with the overall score (accuracy). We pass the list returned by tally_predictions to basic_metrics and then pass the output of both of these functions to advanced_metrics, as in Chapter 11.

The full set of binary classifier metrics gives us the following:

Metric	Result
TP	5,841
FP	4,80
TN	3,520
FN	159
TPR (sensitivity, recall)	0.9735
TNR (specificity)	0.8800
PPV (precision)	0.9241
NPV	0.9568
FPR	0.1200
FNR	0.0265
F1	0.9481
MCC	0.8671
κ	0.8651
Informedness	0.8535
Markedness	0.8808
Accuracy	0.9361

We see that this is a well-performing model although a specificity of 88 percent is a little on the low side. As argued in Chapter 11, the Matthews correlation coefficient (MCC) is possibly the best single number for characterizing a binary classifier. Here we have an MCC of 0.8671 out of 1.0, indicative of a good model.

Recall that the *sensitivity* is the probability that an animal is called an "animal" by this model, and the *specificity* is the probability that a vehicle is called a "vehicle." The *precision* is the probability that when the model assigns a label of "animal," it is correct, and the *NPV (negative predictive value)* is the probability of the model being correct when it assigns a label of "vehicle." Note also that the false positive rate (FPR) is 1 − specificity, and the false negative rate (FNR) is 1 − sensitivity.

A little more code will calculate the ROC curve and its area:

```
from sklearn.metrics import roc_auc_score, roc_curve
def roc_curve_area(model, x, y):
    pp = model.predict(x)
    p = np.zeros(pp.shape[0], dtype="uint8")
    for i in range(pp.shape[0]):
        p[i] = 0 if (pp[i,0] > pp[i,1]) else 1
    auc = roc_auc_score(y,p)
    roc = roc_curve(y,pp[:,1])
    return [auc, roc]
```

Again, we pass in the trained model, the test samples (x), and the animal or vehicle labels (y). We also convert the output probabilities to class predictions, as we did in Listing 14-6. The AUC is 0.9267, and Figure 14-3 shows the ROC curve (note the zoomed axes). This curve is steep and close to the upper-left corner of the plot—all good signs of a well-performing model.

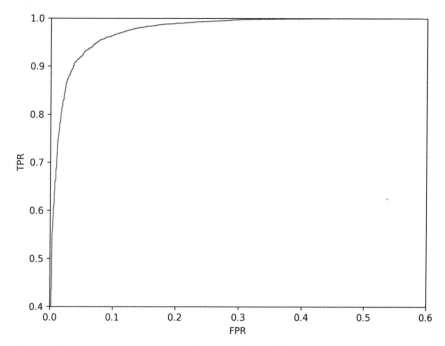

Figure 14-3: ROC curve for the animal or vehicle model

We grouped animals and vehicles and asked a single model to learn something about the difference between them. Clearly, some characteristics differentiate the two classes, and the model has learned to use them successfully. However, unlike most binary classifiers, we know finer label assignments for the test data. For example, we know which of the animals are birds or deer or frogs. Likewise, we know which samples are airplanes, ships, or trucks.

When the model makes a mistake, the mistake is either a false positive (calling a vehicle an animal) or a false negative (calling an animal a vehicle). We chose animals to be class 1, so false positives are cases where a vehicle was called an animal. The converse is true for false negatives. We can use the full class labels to tell us how many of the false positives are represented by which vehicle classes, and we can do the same for the false negatives to tell us which animal classes were assigned to the vehicle class. A few lines of code in Listing 14-7 give us what we are after.

```
import numpy as np
from keras.models import load_model
x_test = np.load("cifar10_test_images.npy")/255.0
y_label= np.load("cifar10_test_labels.npy")
y_test = np.load("cifar10_test_animal_vehicle_labels.npy")
model = load_model("cifar10_cnn_animal_vehicle_model.h5")
pp = model.predict(x_test)
p = np.zeros(pp.shape[0], dtype="uint8")
for i in range(pp.shape[0]):
    p[i] = 0 if (pp[i,0] > pp[i,1]) else 1
```

```
hp = []; hn = []
❶ for i in range(len(y_test)):
      if (p[i] == 0) and (y_test[i] == 1):
          hn.append(y_label[i])
      elif (p[i] == 1) and (y_test[i] == 0):
          hp.append(y_label[i])
hp = np.array(hp)
hn = np.array(hn)
a = np.histogram(hp, bins=10, range=[0,9])[0]
b = np.histogram(hn, bins=10, range=[0,9])[0]
print("vehicles as animals: %s" % np.array2string(a))
print("animals as vehicles: %s" % np.array2string(b))
```

Listing 14-7: Using the fine class labels to determine which classes account for false positives and false negatives

First, we load the test set images, actual labels (y_label), and animal or vehicle labels (y_test). Then, as before, we load the model and get the model predictions (p). We want to keep track of the actual class label for each false positive and false negative, the mistakes the classifier has made. We do this by looping over the predictions and comparing them to the animal or vehicle labels ❶. When there is an error, we keep the actual label of the sample, be it an FN (hn) or FP (hp). Note that this works because when we defined the animal or vehicle labels, we were careful to keep the order the same as the original label set.

Once we have the actual labels for all FP and FN cases, we use histogram to do the tallying for us. There are 10 actual class labels, so we tell histogram that we want to use 10 bins. We also need to specify the range for the bins (range=[0,9]). We want only the counts themselves, so we need to keep only the first array returned by histogram, hence the [0] at the end of the call. Finally, we print the arrays to get

```
vehicles as animals: [189  69   0   0   0   0   0   0 105 117]
animals as vehicles: [  0   0  64  34  23  11  12  15   0   0]
```

This means that of the vehicles the model called "animal," 189 of them were of class 0, airplane. The vehicle class least likely to be identified as an animal is class 1, automobile. Ships and trucks were similarly likely to be mistaken for an animal. Going the other way, we see that class 2, birds, were most likely to be mistaken for vehicles and class 5, dogs, were least likely to be misclassified, though frogs were a close second.

What to make of this? The most commonly misclassified vehicle is an airplane, while the most commonly misclassified animal is a bird. This makes sense: a picture of an airplane and a picture of a bird flying do look similar. I'll leave it to you to make connections among the other categories.

Binary or Multiclass?

Conventional wisdom in machine learning is that a multiclass model will generally outperform multiple binary models. While this is almost certainly true for large datasets, large models, and situations with many classes, like the ImageNet dataset of 1,000 classes, how does it pan out for small models like the ones we're working with in this chapter? Let's find out.

There are 5,000 instances of each class in the CIFAR-10 dataset and 10 classes. This means we can train 10 binary models where the target class (class 1) is one of the 10 classes, and the other class is everything else. This is known as a *one-vs-rest* approach. To classify an unknown sample, we run it through each of the 10 classifiers and assign the label of the model returning the most confident answer. The datasets are all imbalanced, 5,000 class 1 instances to 45,000 class 0, but, as we'll see, there is still enough data to learn the difference between classes.

We need some code to train 10 one-vs-rest models. We'll use the shallow architecture we've used before, with a minibatch size of 128, and we'll train for 12 epochs. Before we can train, however, we need to reassign the class labels for the train and test sets so that all instances of the target class are a 1 and everything else is a 0. To build the per class labels, we'll use Listing 14-8.

```
import sys
import numpy as np
❶ class1 = eval("["+sys.argv[1]+"]")
y_train = np.load("cifar10_train_labels.npy")
y_test  = np.load("cifar10_test_labels.npy")
for i in range(len(y_train)):
    if (y_train[i] in class1):
        y_train[i] = 1
    else:
        y_train[i] = 0
for i in range(len(y_test)):
    if (y_test[i] in class1):
        y_test[i] = 1
    else:
        y_test[i] = 0
np.save(sys.argv[2], y_train)
np.save(sys.argv[3], y_test)
```

Listing 14-8: Building the per class labels

This code makes use of the command line. To call it, use something like

```
$ python3 make_label_files.py 1 train_1.npy test_1.npy
```

The first argument is the desired target class label, here 1 for automobiles, and the next two arguments are the names in which to store the new label assignments for the train and test images. The code itself loops over the actual train and test labels, and if the label is the target class, the corresponding output label is 1; otherwise, it is 0.

This code is more flexible than mapping a single class. By using eval ❶, we can pass in a comma-separated string of all the CIFAR-10 labels we want to treat as the target class. For example, to use this code to make labels for the animal versus vehicle example of the previous section, we'd make the first argument 2,3,4,5,6,7.

Once we have new labels for each of the 10 classes, we can use them to train 10 models. All we need do is change num_classes to 2 and load each of the respective reassigned label files for y_train and y_test. At the bottom of the file, we need to change the call to model.save to store the per class models as well. We'll assume the models are in files named *cifar10_cnn_<X>_model.h5* where *<X>* is a digit, 0–9, representing a CIFAR-10 class label. Our multiclass model is the shallow architecture trained on the full CIFAR-10 dataset for 12 epochs (*cifar10_cnn_model.h5*). To train the binary models, use the train_single_models script. This script calls *cifar10_cnn_arbitrary.py* to train a model using a specified binary dataset.

To test the models, we need to first load them all from disk along with the test set data. Then we need to run all the data through the multiclass model and each of the individual class models keeping the predictions. From the predictions, we can assign class labels and build confusion matrices to see how well each approach does. First, let's load the test set and the models:

```
x_test = np.load("cifar10_test_images.npy")/255.0
y_test = np.load("cifar10_test_labels.npy")
mm = load_model("cifar10_cnn_model.h5")
m = []
for i in range(10):
    m.append(load_model("cifar10_cnn_%d_model.h5" % i))
```

Notice that we are scaling the test set by 255, as we did with the training data. We'll keep the multiclass model in mm and load the 10 single class models into the list, m.

Next, we apply the models to each test set sample:

```
mp = np.argmax(mm.predict(x_test), axis=1)
p = np.zeros((10,10000), dtype="float32")
for i in range(10):
    p[i,:] = m[i].predict(x_test)[:,1]
bp = np.argmax(p, axis=0)
```

Calling predict with the 10,000 test samples returns a 10,000 × 10 matrix for the multiclass model or 10,000 × 2 for the individual models. Each row corresponds to a test sample, and each column is the model's output for each class. For the multiclass case, we set mp to the maximum value across the columns (axis=1) to get a vector of 10,000 values, each of which is the predicted class label.

We loop over the individual models and call `predict`, keeping only the class 1 probabilities. These are placed into p, where the rows are the individual model outputs for that class label, and the columns are the specific class 1 prediction probabilities for each of the 10,000 test samples. If we return the maximum value across the rows by using `argmax` and `axis=0`, we'll get the class label of the model that had the highest predicted probability for each test sample. This is what is in bp.

With our predictions in hand, we can generate the confusion matrices:

```
cm = np.zeros((10,10), dtype="uint16")
cb = np.zeros((10,10), dtype="uint16")

for i in range(10000):
    cm[y_test[i],mp[i]] += 1
    cb[y_test[i],bp[i]] += 1

np.save("cifar10_multiclass_conf_mat.npy", cm)
np.save("cifar10_binary_conf_mat.npy", cb)
```

Here rows represent the true class label, and columns represent the model's predicted label. We also store the confusion matrices for future use.

We can display the confusion matrices with the code in Listing 14-9:

```
print("One-vs-rest confusion matrix (rows true, cols predicted):")
print("%s" % np.array2string(100*(cb/1000.0), precision=1))
print()
print("Multiclass confusion matrix:")
print("%s"  % np.array2string(100*(cm/1000.0), precision=1))
```

Listing 14-9: Displaying the confusion matrices. See cifar10_one_vs_many.py

We divide the counts in cb and cm by 1,000 because each class is represented by that many samples in the test set. This converts the confusion matrix entries to a fraction and then a percent when multiplied by 100.

So, how did we do? The multiple one-vs-rest classifiers produced

Class	0	1	2	3	4	5	6	7	8	9
0	**75.0**	2.8	3.4	2.1	1.7	0.4	2.3	0.2	4.1	8.0
1	0.8	**84.0**	0.2	0.9	0.3	0.3	1.1	0.0	1.2	11.2
2	6.5	1.6	**54.0**	6.3	9.5	5.3	9.1	2.3	0.8	4.6
3	1.6	3.6	3.8	**52.1**	7.1	12.9	10.6	2.2	0.9	5.2
4	1.8	0.8	3.6	6.5	**67.6**	2.3	8.6	5.3	1.3	2.2
5	1.4	1.4	3.5	16.9	4.7	**61.8**	4.0	2.6	0.5	3.2
6	0.8	0.7	1.4	3.4	2.8	1.0	**86.4**	0.2	0.3	3.0
7	1.5	1.3	1.7	4.9	5.2	5.2	1.5	**71.5**	0.1	7.1
8	5.3	4.4	0.1	1.1	0.5	0.6	1.1	0.5	**79.1**	7.3
9	1.7	4.0	0.2	0.8	0.1	0.4	0.5	0.3	0.8	**91.2**

And the multiclass classifier came up with

Class	0	1	2	3	4	5	6	7	8	9
0	**70.2**	1.6	6.0	2.6	3.3	0.5	1.8	0.9	9.8	3.3
1	2.0	**79.4**	1.0	1.3	0.5	0.5	1.3	0.4	2.8	10.8
2	5.2	0.6	**56.2**	6.6	13.5	6.1	7.3	2.6	1.4	0.5
3	1.2	1.1	7.2	**57.7**	10.2	11.5	7.3	1.7	1.2	0.9
4	1.9	0.2	5.2	4.6	**77.4**	1.6	4.8	2.7	1.5	0.1
5	1.0	0.2	6.4	20.7	7.7	**56.8**	2.7	3.5	0.8	0.2
6	0.3	0.1	4.5	5.2	5.7	1.5	**82.4**	0.0	0.0	0.3
7	1.4	0.2	4.0	6.3	10.1	4.1	0.9	**71.7**	0.1	1.2
8	4.7	3.0	0.8	2.0	1.3	0.6	1.0	0.6	**82.6**	3.4
9	2.4	6.1	0.7	2.6	1.2	0.7	1.2	1.6	3.2	**80.3**

The diagonals are the correct class assignments. Ideally, the matrix would be only diagonal elements. All other elements are mistakes, cases where the model or models chose the wrong label. Since each class is equally represented in the test set, we can calculate an overall accuracy for both models by using the unweighted average of the diagonals. If we do this, we get the following:

one-vs-rest: 72.3%
multiclass: 71.5%

The one-vs-rest classifiers have the slight edge in this case, though the difference is less than 1 percent. Of course, we needed to do 10 times the work to get the one-vs-rest confusion matrix—ten classifiers were used instead of just one. The multiclass model was about 10 percent better on class 4 (deer) than the one-vs-rest models, but it was approximately 11 percent worse on class 9 (trucks). These are the two most substantial per class differences in accuracy. The multiclass model is confusing trucks with class 8, ships (3.2 percent), and class 1, cars (6.1 percent), more often than the one-vs-rest models. We can see how this might happen. Trucks and cars have wheels, and trucks and ships are (especially at the low resolution of CIFAR-10) both box-like.

Did we arrive at a definitive answer regarding one-vs-rest or multiclass models? No, nor could we in general. However, we did, objectively, get slightly better performance by using the multiple models.

One argument given against using multiple models, besides the extra computation necessary, is that using a single model for multiple classes provides the model with the opportunity to see examples that are similar to a particular class but are not instances of that class. These hard negatives serve to regularize the model by forcing it to (indirectly) pay attention to features that are dissimilar between classes instead of features that might be strongly associated with a class but are also present in other classes. We first encountered hard negatives in Chapter 4.

However, in this case, it's difficult to say that the argument holds. For the multiclass model, class 9 (trucks) was more likely to be confused with class 1 (car, 6.1 percent) than one-vs-rest models (4.0 percent). One possible explanation might be that the multiclass model was forced, with limited training data, to try to learn the difference between trucks, cars, and other vehicles, while the one-vs-rest models were, individually, trying to learn only the difference between a truck and any other vehicle.

Transfer Learning

We'll use the term *transfer learning* to refer to taking a pretrained deep network and using it to produce new features for another machine learning model. Our transfer learning example will be a toy model meant to show the process, but many models have been built using features generated by large pretrained networks that used huge datasets. In particular, many models have been built using features generated by AlexNet and the various ResNet architectures, which were pretrained on the ImageNet dataset.

We'll use the pretrained model to turn input images into output feature vectors, which we'll then use to train classical machine learning models. When a model is used to turn an input into another feature representation, typically a new feature vector, the output is often called an *embedding*: we are using the pretrained network to embed the inputs we want to classify into another space—one that we hope will let us build a useful model. We can use transfer learning when the model we want to develop has too few training examples to make a good model on its own.

When using transfer learning, it is helpful to know or believe that both models were trained using similar data. If you read the literature, you'll find that this is true for many of the typical transfer learning examples. The inputs are natural images of some class, and the embedding models were trained on natural images. By natural image, I mean a photograph of something in the world as opposed to an x-ray or other medical image. Clearly, the CIFAR-10 images and the MNIST images are quite different from each other, so we shouldn't hope for too much success with transfer learning. We're using what we have on hand to demonstrate the technique.

We'll use a shallow CIFAR-10 model like the ones we just saw to generate the embedding vectors. This model was trained on the full CIFAR-10 dataset for 12 epochs. We'll embed the MNIST dataset by passing the MNIST digit images through the pretrained model, keeping the output of the Dense layer, the 128-node vectors used to generate the 10-class softmax predictions.

We need to consider a few things before making the embedding. First, the CIFAR-10 model was trained on 32×32 RGB images. Therefore, we need to make the MNIST digit images fit this input expectation. Second, even though there are 10 classes for both CIFAR-10 and MNIST, this is only a coincidence; in practice, the number of classes between the two datasets do not need to match.

How should we get the 28×28 MNIST images into a model that's expecting 32×32 RGB images? Typically, when working with image data and transfer learning, we'll resize the images to make them fit. Here, since the MNIST digits are smaller than the CIFAR-10 images, we can center the 28×28 digit image in the middle of a 32×32 input. Moreover, we can turn a grayscale image into an RGB image by setting each channel (red, green, and blue) to the single grayscale input.

The code for all of the following is in *transfer_learning.py*. Setting up the embedding process looks like this:

```
import numpy as np
from keras.models import load_model
from keras import backend as K
from keras.datasets import mnist

(x_train, y_train), (x_test, y_test) = mnist.load_data()
x_train = x_train/255.0
x_test = x_test/255.0
model = load_model("cifar10_cnn_model.h5")
```

We first load the modules we need from Keras. Then we load the Keras model file, *cifar10_cnn_model.h5*, which contains a shallow model from the first section of this chapter trained for 12 epochs on the full CIFAR-10 dataset.

Once we have the data loaded and scaled, we can pass each MNIST train and test image through the Keras model and extract the 128-node vector from the Dense layer. This turns each MNIST image into a 128-element vector; see Listing 14-10.

```
train = np.zeros((60000,128))
k = 0
for i in range(600):
    t = np.zeros((100,32,32,3))
❶   t[:,2:30,2:30,0] = x_train[k:(k+100)]
    t[:,2:30,2:30,1] = x_train[k:(k+100)]
    t[:,2:30,2:30,2] = x_train[k:(k+100)]
    _ = model.predict(t)
❷   out = [model.layers[5].output]
    func = K.function([model.input, K.learning_phase()], out)
```

```
    train[k:(k+100),:] = func([t, 1.])[0]
    k += 100
np.save("mnist_train_embedded.npy", train)

test = np.zeros((10000,128))
k = 0
for i in range(100):
    t = np.zeros((100,32,32,3))
    t[:,2:30,2:30,0] = x_test[k:(k+100)]
    t[:,2:30,2:30,1] = x_test[k:(k+100)]
    t[:,2:30,2:30,2] = x_test[k:(k+100)]
    _ = model.predict(t)
    out = [model.layers[5].output]
    func = K.function([model.input, K.learning_phase()], out)
    test[k:(k+100),:] = func([t, 1.])[0]
    k += 100
np.save("mnist_test_embedded.npy", test)
```

Listing 14-10: Running the MNIST images through the pretrained CIFAR-10 model

There are 60,000 MNIST training images. We pass each through the Keras model in blocks of 100 to be more efficient than processing each image individually; this means we need to process 600 sets of 100. We do the same for the test images, of which there are 10,000, so we process 100 sets of 100. We'll store the output vectors in train and test.

The processing loop for both the train and test images first creates a temporary array, t, to hold the current set of 100 images. To use the Keras model predict method, we need a four-dimensional input: the number of images, height, width, and number of channels. We load t by copying the current set of 100 train or test images, indexed by k, to t; we do that three times, once for each channel ❶. With t loaded, we call the predict method of the model. We throw the output away, since we're after the values output by the Dense layer of the Keras model. This is layer 5 for the shallow architecture ❷. The output of func is the 100 output vectors of the Dense layer we get after passing the inputs through the network. We assign these to the current block of 100 in train and move to the next set of 100. When we've processed the entire MNIST dataset, we keep the embedded vectors in a NumPy file. Then we repeat every step we used to process the training set for the test set.

At this point, we have our embedded vectors, so it's natural to ask whether or not the embedding is helping separate the classes. We can see if this is true by using a t-SNE plot of the vectors by class label (Figure 14-4).

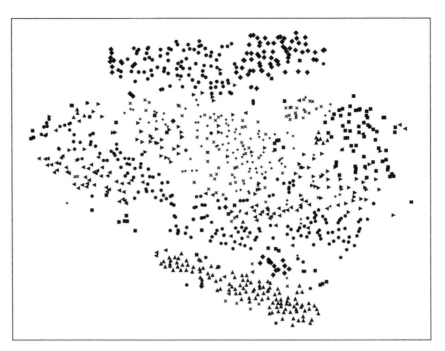

Figure 14-4: t-SNE plot showing the separation by class for the embedded MNIST digit vectors

Compare this figure with Figure 12-10, which shows the separation for a model trained explicitly on MNIST digits. That model shows a clear, unambiguous separation of the classes, but Figure 14-4 is far less clear. However, even though there is overlap, there are concentrations of the classes in different parts of the plot, so we have some reason to hope that a model might be able to learn how to classify digits using these vectors.

Let's train some models using the embedded vectors. For this, we'll head back into the world of classical machine learning. We'll train some of the models we trained in Chapter 7 by using the vector form of the MNIST digits images.

The code to train and test the models is straightforward. We'll train a Nearest Centroid, 3-Nearest Neighbor, Random Forest with 50 trees, and a linear SVM with $C = 0.1$, as shown in Listing 14-11.

```
from sklearn.neighbors import KNeighborsClassifier
from sklearn.ensemble import RandomForestClassifier
from sklearn.neighbors import NearestCentroid
from sklearn.svm import LinearSVC

clf0 = NearestCentroid()
clf0.fit(train, y_train)
nscore = clf0.score(test, y_test)

clf1 = KNeighborsClassifier(n_neighbors=3)
clf1.fit(train, y_train)
```

```
kscore = clf1.score(test, y_test)

clf2 = RandomForestClassifier(n_estimators=50)
clf2.fit(train, y_train)
rscore = clf2.score(test, y_test)

clf3 = LinearSVC(C=0.1)
clf3.fit(train, y_train)
sscore = clf3.score(test, y_test)

print("Nearest Centroid    : %0.2f" % nscore)
print("3-NN                : %0.2f" % kscore)
print("Random Forest       : %0.2f" % rscore)
print("SVM                 : %0.2f" % sscore)
```

Listing 14-11: Training classical models using the MNIST embedded vectors

We load the relevant sklearn modules, create the specific model instances, and call fit, passing in the 128-element training vectors and the associated class labels. The score method returns the overall accuracy of the now trained model on the test set.

Running this code gives us scores of

Model	Score
Nearest Centroid	0.6799
3-Nearest Neighbors	0.9010
Random Forest (50)	0.8837
SVM (C=0.1)	0.8983

which we can compare to the scaled scores for same models in Table 7-10:

Model	Score
Nearest Centroid	0.8203
3-Nearest Neighbors	0.9705
Random Forest (50)	0.9661
SVM (C=0.1)	0.9181

Clearly, in this case, our embedding is not giving us a head start over the raw data. We should not be surprised by this: we knew our two datasets were fairly distinct, and the t-SNE plot showed that the pretrained CIFAR-10 model was not ideally suited to separating the MNIST images in the embedding space. The poor separation of the classes in Figure 14-4 explains the poor performance of the Nearest Centroid model: 68 percent accuracy versus 82 percent when trained on the digit images themselves. Moreover, by their very nature, digit images are already distinct from each other, especially on a uniform background, since the digits were intended by humans to be easily distinguished by sight.

A bit of code gives us the confusion matrix for any of these models:

```
def conf_mat(clf,x,y):
    p = clf.predict(x)
    c = np.zeros((10,10))
    for i in range(p.shape[0]):
        c[y[i],p[i]] += 1
    return c
cs = conf_mat(clf, test, y_test)
cs = 100.0*cs / cs.sum(axis=1)
np.set_printoptions(suppress=True)
print(np.array2string(cs, precision=1, floatmode="fixed"))
```

Here clf is any of the models, test is the embedded test set, and y_test is the labels. We return the confusion matrix with counts in each element, so we divide by the sum of the rows, since the row represents the true label, and multiply by 100 to get percents. Then we print the array using NumPy commands to get a single digit of accuracy and no scientific notation.

We know already why the Nearest Centroid result is so poor. What about the Random Forest and SVM? The confusion matrix for the Random Forest model is shown here:

Class	0	1	2	3	4	5	6	7	8	9
0	96.7	0.0	0.5	0.5	0.4	0.2	0.9	0.0	0.4	0.3
1	0.0	98.6	0.5	0.0	0.4	0.1	0.4	0.0	0.1	0.1
2	1.8	0.2	87.0	2.5	1.0	1.0	1.7	0.8	4.1	0.6
3	1.1	0.1	2.5	**80.8**	0.2	**6.7**	0.9	1.1	**6.0**	1.6
4	0.3	0.4	1.3	0.0	88.3	0.1	1.9	1.7	0.6	5.2
5	0.6	0.8	0.7	9.8	1.6	**78.8**	**1.8**	1.1	1.6	0.8
6	3.0	0.4	0.6	0.0	0.7	1.0	93.5	0.2	0.4	0.0
7	0.2	1.0	2.9	0.1	2.7	0.4	0.0	87.7	0.7	4.4
8	1.4	0.1	2.7	5.0	1.5	1.6	0.6	0.8	84.0	2.0
9	2.2	0.2	1.3	1.6	2.9	0.6	0.3	3.4	1.5	86.2

We've highlighted the two lowest-performing classes, 3 and 5, along with the two digits they are most often confused with. We see that the model is confusing 3's with 5's and 8's. The SVM confusion matrix shows the same effect. If we take Figure 14-4 and show only classes 3, 5, and 8, then we get Figure 14-5. Considerable mixing between the classes is plain to see.

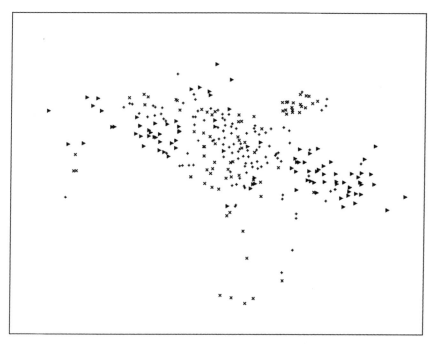

Figure 14-5: t-SNE plot showing class 3 (plus), class 5 (cross), and class 8 (triangle right)

The purpose of this section was to introduce the idea of transfer learning through an example that used the datasets we had on hand. As you can see, this experiment was not a success. The datasets we used were very different from each other, so we might have expected this to be the case, but it was useful to verify for ourselves. In the next section, we'll see how we can go one step beyond transfer learning.

Fine-Tuning a Model

In the previous section, we defined transfer learning as using weights from a model trained on one dataset with data from a (hopefully very similar) dataset. We used the weights to map the inputs to a new space and trained models on the mapped data. In this section, we'll do something similar, but instead of leaving the weights as they are, we'll let the weights vary while we continue training the model with a new, smaller dataset. We are calling this *fine-tuning*.

In fine-tuning, we are training a neural network, but instead of initializing the weights to random values, selected according to an intelligent initialization scheme, we start with the weights from a model trained on a similar but different dataset. We might use fine-tuning when we do not have a lot of training data, but we believe our data comes from a distribution that's very similar to one for which we have either a lot of data or a trained model. For example, we might have access to the weights of a large model trained with a large dataset, like the ImageNet dataset we've mentioned previously. It is quite simple to download such a pretrained model. Additionally, we might have a small dataset of images for classes that are not in ImageNet; say, photographs of guppies, angelfish, and tetras. These are popular freshwater aquarium fish not in ImageNet. We can start with a larger model pretrained on ImageNet and fine-tune using the smaller fish dataset. That way, we can take advantage of the fact that the model is already well adapted to inputs of this kind and, hopefully, get a good model with a small dataset.

Our experiment will use CIFAR-10. Our goal is to train a model to differentiate between images of dogs and cats using the deep architecture from the first section of this chapter. However, our dataset is small; we have approximately 500 images of each class to work with. We also have a larger dataset, all the vehicles from CIFAR-10.

Therefore, we'll train the following models with this data:

1. The shallow architecture using the small dog and cat dataset.

2. The deep architecture using the small dog and cat dataset.

3. The deep architecture pretrained on the vehicle data and fine-tuned on the small dog and cat dataset.

For the last case, we'll train several variations using different combinations of frozen weights.

Building Our Datasets

Before we get to fine-tuning, we need to build our datasets. We'll use unaugmented CIFAR-10 to construct the small dog and cat dataset. We'll use *augmented* CIFAR-10 to construct the vehicle dataset. We augmented CIFAR-10 in Chapter 5.

Building the small dog and cat dataset is straightforward, as shown in Listing 14-12.

```
x_train = np.load("cifar10_train_images.npy")[:,2:30,2:30,:]
y_train = np.load("cifar10_train_labels.npy")
x_test = np.load("cifar10_test_images.npy")[:,2:30,2:30,:]
y_test = np.load("cifar10_test_labels.npy")
xtrn = []; ytrn = []
xtst = []; ytst = []

for i in range(y_train.shape[0]):
    if (y_train[i]==3):
```

```
        xtrn.append(x_train[i])
        ytrn.append(0)
    if (y_train[i]==5):
        xtrn.append(x_train[i])
        ytrn.append(1)
for i in range(y_test.shape[0]):
    if (y_test[i]==3):
        xtst.append(x_test[i])
        ytst.append(0)
    if (y_test[i]==5):
        xtst.append(x_test[i])
        ytst.append(1)

np.save("cifar10_train_cat_dog_small_images.npy", np.array(xtrn)[:1000])
np.save("cifar10_train_cat_dog_small_labels.npy", np.array(ytrn)[:1000])
np.save("cifar10_test_cat_dog_small_images.npy", np.array(xtst)[:1000])
np.save("cifar10_test_cat_dog_small_labels.npy", np.array(ytst)[:1000])
```

Listing 14-12: Building the small dog and cat dataset

We load the full CIFAR-10 data, train and test, and then loop over each sample. If the class is 3, cat, or 5, dog, we add the image and label to our lists, making sure to recode the class label so that 0 is cat and 1 is dog. When all the samples have been added, we keep the first 1,000 and write them to disk to be our small dog and cat training and test sets. Keeping the first 1,000 samples gives us a dataset that is close to split 50/50 between classes.

Notice that immediately after loading the CIFAR-10 images, we subscript them with [:,2:30,2:30,:]. Recall, the augmented version of the dataset includes small shifts of the image, so when we built it in Chapter 5, we reduced the size from 32×32 to 28×8. Therefore, when we build our vehicle dataset, we'll be working with images that are 28×28 pixels. The subscript extracts the center 28×28 region of each image. The first dimension is the number of images in the train or test set. The last dimension is the number of channels—three since these are RGB images.

Building the vehicle dataset is equally straightforward (Listing 14-13).

```
x_train = np.load("cifar10_aug_train_images.npy")
y_train = np.load("cifar10_aug_train_labels.npy")
x_test = np.load("cifar10_aug_test_images.npy")
y_test = np.load("cifar10_test_labels.npy")

vehicles= [0,1,8,9]
xv_train = []; xv_test = []
yv_train = []; yv_test = []

for i in range(y_train.shape[0]):
    if (y_train[i] in vehicles):
        xv_train.append(x_train[i])
        yv_train.append(vehicles.index(y_train[i]))
```

```
for i in range(y_test.shape[0]):
    if (y_test[i] in vehicles):
        xv_test.append(x_test[i])
        yv_test.append(vehicles.index(y_test[i]))

np.save("cifar10_train_vehicles_images.npy", np.array(xv_train))
np.save("cifar10_train_vehicles_labels.npy", np.array(yv_train))
np.save("cifar10_test_vehicles_images.npy", np.array(xv_test))
np.save("cifar10_test_vehicles_labels.npy", np.array(yv_test))
```

Listing 14-13: Building the vehicle dataset

Here we work with the augmented versions. The augmented test set is 28×28 pixels per image using the central region of the original test set. Also, as we loop through the train and test sets looking for samples that are in one of the vehicle classes, we can do our recoding of the class label by asking for the index into the vehicles list of the element matching the current sample's class label, hence using index on vehicles. The vehicle dataset has 200,000 samples in the training set, 50,000 from each of the four classes.

To proceed then, we need to (1) train the deep model on the vehicle dataset; (2) adapt the model to the dog and cat dataset; and (3) train the deep model initialized with the weights from the vehicle model. We'll also train the shallow and deep models from scratch, using the dog and cat dataset for comparison purposes.

We gave the code for the deep model in the first section of this chapter so we won't reproduce it here. In particular, see Listing 14-3. The code itself is in the file *cifar10_cnn_vehicles.py*. The relevant changes for the vehicle model are shown here:

```
batch_size = 64
num_classes = 4
epochs = 12
img_rows, img_cols = 28,28

x_train = np.load("cifar10_train_vehicles_images.npy")
y_train = np.load("cifar10_train_vehicles_labels.npy")
x_test = np.load("cifar10_test_vehicles_images.npy")
y_test = np.load("cifar10_test_vehicles_labels.npy")
```

We use a minibatch size of 64. There are four classes (airplane, automobile, ship, truck), and we'll train for 12 epochs. When we're done training, we'll store the model in *cifar10_cnn_vehicles_model.h5* so we can use its weights and biases for fine-tuning the dog and cat model. Training this model takes several hours on our CPU system. The final test accuracy is 88.2 percent, so it is performing well enough for our purposes.

Adapting Our Model for Fine-Tuning

Now we need to adapt the vehicle model for the dog and cat dataset and fine-tuning. Specifically, we need to replace the top softmax layer that expects four classes with one that expects two. We also need to decide which layer's weights we'll freeze and which we'll update during training. This step is essential, and we'll see how our choices affect the fine-tuning results.

When fine-tuning, it's standard practice to freeze lower-level weights; they are not updated at all when training. The idea here is that if our new data is similar to the data used for the pretraining step, the lower levels of the model are already adapted, and we should not change them. We allow only the higher-level layers to change as these are the ones that need to learn about the representation of the new data. Which layers we freeze and which we allow to train depends on the size of the model and the data itself. Experimentation is required. Note that the transfer learning of the previous section can be considered fine-tuning with all the weights frozen.

Note that if we're using SGD with fine-tuning, we typically reduce the learning rate by a factor of, say, 10. The rationale is the same as for freezing the lower-level weights: the model is already "close" to a desired minimum of the error function, so we don't need big steps to find it. Our experiment will use Adadelta, which will adjust the learning rate step size for us.

The deep model has multiple convolutional layers. We'll experiment with freezing the first two; these are the lowest and are most likely already tuned to the low-level features of the CIFAR-10 dataset, at least the vehicles. Of course, since our dog and cat images come from CIFAR-10 as well, we know that they are from the same parent distribution or domain as the vehicle images. We'll also experiment with a model that freezes all the convolutional layers and allows only the dense layers to be adapted during training. Doing this is reminiscent of transfer learning, though we'll allow the dense layers to update their weights.

Let's create the code for fine-tuning by using the vehicle model that we trained earlier (Listing 14-14).

```
import keras
from keras.models import load_model
from keras.layers import Dense
from keras import backend as K
import numpy as np

batch_size = 64
num_classes = 2
epochs = 36
img_rows, img_cols = 28,28

x_train = np.load("cifar10_train_cat_dog_small_images.npy")
```

```
y_train = np.load("cifar10_train_cat_dog_small_labels.npy")
x_test = np.load("cifar10_test_cat_dog_small_images.npy")
y_test = np.load("cifar10_test_cat_dog_small_labels.npy")

if K.image_data_format() == 'channels_first':
    x_train = x_train.reshape(x_train.shape[0], 3, img_rows, img_cols)
    x_test = x_test.reshape(x_test.shape[0], 3, img_rows, img_cols)
    input_shape = (3, img_rows, img_cols)
else:
    x_train = x_train.reshape(x_train.shape[0], img_rows, img_cols, 3)
    x_test = x_test.reshape(x_test.shape[0], img_rows, img_cols, 3)
    input_shape = (img_rows, img_cols, 3)

x_train = x_train.astype('float32')
x_test = x_test.astype('float32')
x_train /= 255
x_test /= 255

y_train = keras.utils.to_categorical(y_train, num_classes)
y_test = keras.utils.to_categorical(y_test, num_classes)
```

Listing 14-14: Fine-tuning the vehicle model. See cifar10_cnn_cat_dog_fine_tune_3.py.

These lines should be familiar by now. First we load and preprocess the small dog and cat dataset. Note that we are using a minibatch size of 64, two classes (0 = cat, 1 = dog), and 36 epochs.

Next, we need to load the vehicle model, strip off its top layer, and replace it with a two-class softmax (Listing 14-15). This is also where we will freeze some combination of the first two convolutional layers.

```
model = load_model("cifar10_cnn_vehicles_model.h5")

❶ model.layers.pop()
❷ model.outputs = [model.layers[-1].output]
  model.layers[-1].outbound_nodes = []
❸ model.add(Dense(num_classes, name="softmax", activation='softmax'))

❹ model.layers[0].trainable = False
  model.layers[1].trainable = False

model.compile(loss=keras.losses.categorical_crossentropy,
              optimizer=keras.optimizers.Adadelta(),
              metrics=['accuracy'])
```

Listing 14-15: Adjusting the vehicle model for dogs and cats

After we load the model, we use Keras to remove the top layer ❶. We need to patch the model to make the next-to-top layer look like the top layer; this allows the add method to work correctly ❷. Then, we add a new softmax layer for two classes ❸. This example is set to freeze the weights of the first two convolutional layers ❹. We'll test each possible combination involving the first two convolutional layers. Finally, we compile the updated model and specify the Adadelta optimizer.

We train the model by calling the `fit` method, as before as shown in Listing 14-16.

```
score = model.evaluate(x_test[100:], y_test[100:], verbose=0)
print('Initial test loss:', score[0])
print('Initial test accuracy:', score[1])

history = model.fit(x_train, y_train,
          batch_size=batch_size,
          epochs=epochs,
          verbose=0,
          validation_data=(x_test[:100], y_test[:100]))

score = model.evaluate(x_test[100:], y_test[100:], verbose=0)
print('Test loss:', score[0])
print('Test accuracy:', score[1])

model.save("cifar10_cnn_cat_dog_fine_tune_3_model.h5")
```

Listing 14-16: Training and testing the dog and cat model

We are calling evaluate using the last 90 percent of the test data, *before* calling `fit`. This will give us an indication of how well the dog and cat model does when using the vehicle weights as they are. Then we call `fit` and evaluate a second time. Finally, we save the model and the training history. This model froze both of the first two convolutional layers. Other models will freeze or unfreeze these layers for the remaining three possibilities.

We mentioned earlier that we'd also train a model by freezing all of the convolutional layers. In essence, this is saying that we want to preserve whatever new representation the vehicle model learned and apply it directly to the dog and cat model , allowing only the top fully connected layers to adjust themselves. This is almost the same as the transfer learning approach of the previous section. To freeze all the convolutional layers, we replace the direct assignments to specific layers' trainable property with a loop over all the layers:

```
for i in range(5):
    model.layers[i].trainable = False
```

Testing Our Model

Let's run the fine-tuning tests. We'll train each possible combination six times so we can get statistics on the mean accuracies. This accounts for the stochastic nature of the initialization process. Although we initialized the model with pretrained weights, we added a new top softmax layer with two outputs. The output of the dense layer below it has 128 nodes, so each model needs to randomly initialize $128 \times 2 + 2 = 258$ weights and biases for the new layer. This is the source of the difference.

Without training, the initial model accuracy hovers around 50 to 51 percent, with each model slightly different because of the initialization we just mentioned. This is a two-class model, so this means that without any training, it is randomly guessing between dog and cat.

After we have trained all of the models and tallied all of the per model accuracies, we get Table 14-2, where we present accuracy as mean $\pm$ standard error.

Table 14-2: Dog and Cat Test Set Accuracies for the Shallow, Deep, and Fine-Tuned Deep Models

Model	Freeze $Conv_0$	Freeze $Conv_1$	Accuracy (%)
Shallow	–	–	64.375 ± 0.388
Deep	–	–	61.142 ± 0.509
Fine-tune 0	False	False	62.683 ± 3.689
Fine-tune 1	True	False	69.142 ± 0.934
Fine-tune 2	False	True	68.842 ± 0.715
Fine-tune 3	True	True	70.050 ± 0.297
Freeze all	–	–	57.042 ± 0.518

What to make of these results? First, we see that training the deep architecture from scratch with the small dog and cat dataset is not particularly effective: only about 61 percent accurate. Training the shallow architecture from scratch does better, with an accuracy of around 64 percent. These are our baselines. Will fine-tuning a model trained on different data help? From looking at the fine-tune results, the answer is "yes," but clearly, not all the fine-tuning options are equally effective: two are even worse than the best from-scratch result ("Fine-tune 0" and "Freeze all"). So, we do not want to freeze all the convolutional layers, nor do we want to be free to update all of them.

This leaves fine-tune models 1, 2, and 3 to consider. The "Fine-tune 3" model performed best, though the differences between these models are not statistically significant. Let's go with freezing the first two convolutional layers, then. What might be happening to make this approach better than the other models? By freezing these lowest layers, we are fixing them and preventing them from being changed by training. These layers were trained on a much larger vehicle dataset that included standard augmentations like shifts and rotates. And, as we already saw in Figure 12-4, the kernels learned by these lower layers are edge and texture detectors. They have been conditioned to learn about the sorts of structures present in CIFAR-10 images, and, since our dog and cat dataset is also from CIFAR-10, it is reasonable to believe that the same kernels will be useful with those images as well.

However, when we froze all the convolutional layers of the deep architecture, we saw a significant decrease in performance. This implies that higher-level convolutional layers are not well-adapted to the dog and cat structures, which, again, makes perfect sense. Because of their effective receptive fields, higher layers are learning about larger structures in the input images; these are also the larger structures that distinguish dogs from cats. If we cannot modify these layers, there is no opportunity for them to be conditioned on the very things that we need them to learn.

This fine-tuning example shows the power of the technique when it is applicable. However, like most things in machine learning, there is only intuition as to why and when it's successful. Recent work has shown that sometimes, fine-tuning a large model trained on a dataset that is not very close to the intended dataset can lead to performance that is no better than training a shallower model, provided enough data is present. For example, see "Transfusion: Understanding Transfer Learning for Medical Imaging" by Maithra Raghu et al. This paper uses transfer learning/fine-tuning between pretrained ImageNet models and medical images and shows that shallow models trained from scratch are often just as good.

Summary

This chapter explored convolutional neural networks applied to the CIFAR-10 dataset. We started by training two architectures, one shallow, the other deep, on the full dataset. We then asked whether or not we can train a model to distinguish between animals and vehicles. Next, we answered the question of whether or not a single multiclass model or multiple binary models performed better for CIFAR-10. After this, we introduced two fundamental techniques, transfer learning and fine-tuning, and showed how to implement them in Keras. These techniques should be understood and in your deep learning bag of tricks going forward.

In the next chapter, we'll present a case study with a dataset we have not yet worked with. We'll assume the role of data scientists tasked with making a model for this dataset and work our way through, from initial data processing to model exploration and final model construction.

15

A CASE STUDY: CLASSIFYING AUDIO SAMPLES

Let's bring together everything that we've learned throughout the book. We'll be looking at a single case study. The scenario is this: we are data scientists, and our boss has tasked us with building a classifier for audio samples stored as *.wav* files. We'll begin with the data itself. We first want to build some basic intuition for how it's structured. From there, we'll build augmented datasets we can use for training models. The first dataset uses the sound samples themselves, a one-dimensional dataset. We'll see that this approach isn't as successful as we would like it to be.

We'll then turn the audio data into images to allow us to explore two-dimensional CNNs. This change of representation will lead to a big improvement in model performance. Finally, we'll combine multiple models in ensembles to see how to leverage the relative strengths and weaknesses of the individual models to boost overall performance still more.

Building the Dataset

There are 10 classes in our dataset, which consists of 400 samples total, 40 samples per class, each 5 seconds long. We'll assume we cannot get any more data because it's time-consuming and expensive to record the samples and label them. We must work with the data we are given and no more.

Throughout this book, we have consistently preached about the necessity of having a good dataset. We'll assume that the dataset we have been handed is complete in the sense that our system will encounter only types of sound samples in the dataset; there will be no unknown class or classes. Additionally, we'll also assume that the balanced nature of the dataset is real, and all classes are indeed equally likely.

The audio dataset we'll use is called ESC-10. For a complete description, see "ESC: Dataset for Environmental Sound Classification" by Karol J. Piczal (2015). The dataset is available at *https://github.com/karoldvl/ESC-50/*. But it needs to be extracted from the larger ESC-50 dataset, which doesn't have a license we can use. The ESC-10 subset does.

Let's do some preprocessing to extract the ESC-10 *.wav* files from the larger ESC-50 dataset. Download the single ZIP-file version of the dataset from the preceding URL and expand it. This will create a directory called *ESC-50-master*. Then, use the code in Listing 15-1 to build the ESC-10 dataset from it.

```
import sys
import os
import shutil

classes = {
    "rain":0,
    "rooster":1,
    "crying_baby":2,
    "sea_waves":3,
    "clock_tick":4,
    "sneezing":5,
    "dog":6,
    "crackling_fire":7,
    "helicopter":8,
    "chainsaw":9,
}

with open("ESC-50-master/meta/esc50.csv") as f:
    lines = [i[:-1] for i in f.readlines()]
lines = lines[1:]

os.system("rm -rf ESC-10")
os.system("mkdir ESC-10")
os.system("mkdir ESC-10/audio")
```

```
meta = []
for line in lines:
    t = line.split(",")
    if (t[-3] == 'True'):
        meta.append("ESC-10/audio/%s %d" % (t[0],classes[t[3]]))
        src = "ESC-50-master/audio/"+t[0]
        dst = "ESC-10/audio/"+t[0]
        shutil.copy(src,dst)

with open("ESC-10/filelist.txt","w") as f:
    for m in meta:
        f.write(m+"\n")
```

Listing 15-1: Building the ESC-10 dataset

The code uses the ESC-50 metadata to identify the sound samples that belong to the 10 classes of the ESC-10 dataset and then copies them to the *ESC-10/audio* directory. It also writes a list of the audio files to *filelist.txt*. After running this code, we'll use only the ESC-10 files.

If all is well, we should now have 400 five-second *.wav* files, 40 from each of the 10 classes: rain, rooster, crying baby, sea waves, clock tick, sneezing, dog, crackling fire, helicopter, and chainsaw. We'll politely refrain from asking our boss exactly why she wants to discriminate between these particular classes of sound.

Augmenting the Dataset

Our first instinct should be that our dataset is too small. After all, we have only 40 examples of each sound, and we know that some of those will need to be held back for testing, leaving even fewer per class for training.

We could resort to *k*-fold validation, but in this case, we'll instead opt for data augmentation. So, how do we augment audio data?

Recall, the goal of data augmentation is to create new data samples that could plausibly come from the classes in the dataset. With images, we can make obvious changes like shifting, flipping left and right, and so on. With continuous vectors, we've seen how to use PCA to augment the data (see Chapter 5). To augment the audio files, we need to think of things we can do that will produce new files that still sound like the original class. Four thoughts come to mind.

First, we can shift the sample in time, much as we can shift an image to the left or right a few pixels. Second, we can simulate a noisy environment by adding a small amount of random noise to the sound itself. Third, we can shift the pitch of the sound, and make it higher or lower by some small amount. Not surprisingly, this is known as *pitch shifting*. Finally, we can lengthen or compress the sound in time. This is known as *time shifting*.

Doing all of this sounds complicated, especially if we haven't worked with audio data before. I should point out that in practice, being presented with unfamiliar data is a very real possibility; we don't all get to choose what we need to work with.

Fortunately for us, we're working in Python, and the Python community is vast and talented. It turns out that adding one library to our system will allow us to easily do time stretching and pitch shifting. Let's install the librosa library. This should do the trick for us:

```
$ sudo pip3 install librosa
```

With the necessary library installed, we can augment the ESC-10 dataset with the code in Listing 15-2.

```
import os
import random
import numpy as np
from scipy.io.wavfile import read, write
import librosa as rosa
N = 8
os.system("rm -rf augmented; mkdir augmented")
os.system("mkdir augmented/train augmented/test")
❶ src_list = [i[:-1] for i in open("ESC-10/filelist.txt")]
z = [[] for i in range(10)]
for s in src_list:
    _,c = s.split()
    z[int(c)].append(s)
❷ train = []
test = []
for i in range(10):
    p = z[i]
    random.shuffle(p)
    test += p[:8]
    train += p[8:]
random.shuffle(train)
random.shuffle(test)
augment_audio(train, "train")
augment_audio(test, "test")
```

Listing 15-2: Augmenting the ESC-10 dataset, part 1

This code loads the necessary modules, including the librosa module, which we'll just call rosa, and two functions from the SciPy wavfile module that let us read and write NumPy arrays as *.wav* files.

We set the number of samples per class that we'll hold back for testing (N=8) and create the output directory where the augmented sound files will reside (augmented). Then we read the file list we created with Listing 15-1 ❶. Next, we create a nested list (z) to hold the names of the audio files associated with each of the 10 classes.

Using the list of files per class, we pull it apart and create train and test file lists ❷. Notice that we randomly shuffle the list of files per class and the final train and test lists. This code follows the convention we discussed in Chapter 4 of separating train and test first, then augmenting.

We can augment the train and test files by calling `augment_audio`. This function is in Listing 15-3.

```
def augment_audio(src_list, typ):
    flist = []
    for i,s in enumerate(src_list):
        f,c = s.split()
❶     wav = read(f) # (sample rate, data)
        base = os.path.abspath("augmented/%s/%s" %
                                (typ, os.path.basename(f)[:-4]))
        fname = base+".wav"
❷     write(fname, wav[0], wav[1])
        flist.append("%s %s" % (fname,c))
        for j in range(19):
            d = augment(wav)
            fname = base+("_%04d.wav" % j)
❸         write(fname, wav[0], d.astype(wav[1].dtype))
            flist.append("%s %s" % (fname,c))

    random.shuffle(flist)
    with open("augmented_%s_filelist.txt" % typ,"w") as f:
        for z in flist:
            f.write("%s\n" % z)
```

Listing 15-3: Augmenting the ESC-10 dataset, part 2

The function loops over all the filenames in the given list (`src_list`), which will be either train or test. The filename is separated from the class label, and then the file is read from disk ❶. As indicated in the comment, `wav` is a list of two elements. The first is the sampling rate in Hz (cycles per second). This is how often the analog waveform was digitized to produce the *.wav* file. For ESC-10, the sampling rate is always 44,100 Hz, which is the standard rate for a compact disc. The second element is a NumPy array containing the actual digitized sound samples. These are the values we'll augment to produce new data files.

After setting up some output pathnames, we write the original sound sample to the augmented directory ❷. Then, we start a loop to generate 19 more augmented versions of the current sound sample. The augmented dataset, as a whole, will be 20 times larger, for a total of 8,000 sound files, 6,400 for training and 1,600 for testing. Note, the sound samples for an augmented source file are assigned to `d`. The new sound file is written to disk using the sample rate of 44,100 Hz and the augmented data matching the datatype of the source ❸.

As we create the augmented sound files, we also keep track of the filename and class and write them to a new file list. Here `typ` is a string indicating train or test.

This function calls yet another function, `augment`. This is the function that generates an augmented version of a single sound file by randomly applying some subset of the four augmentation strategies mentioned previously: shifting, noise, pitch shifting, or time-shifting. Some or all of these might be used for any call to augment. The augment function itself is shown in Listing 15-4.

```
def augment(wav):
    sr = wav[0]
    d = wav[1].astype("float32")
❶  if (random.random() < 0.5):
        s = int(sr/4.0*(np.random.random()-0.5))
        d = np.roll(d,s)
        if (s < 0):
            d[s:] = 0
        else:
            d[:s] = 0
❷  if (random.random() < 0.5):
        d += 0.1*(d.max()-d.min())*np.random.random(d.shape[0])
❸  if (random.random() < 0.5):
        pf = 20.0*(np.random.random()-0.5)
        d = rosa.effects.pitch_shift(d, sr, pf)
❹  if (random.random() < 0.5):
        rate = 1.0 + (np.random.random()-0.5)
        d = rosa.effects.time_stretch(d,rate)
        if (d.shape[0] > wav[1].shape[0]):
            d = d[:wav[1].shape[0]]
        else:
            w = np.zeros(wav[1].shape[0], dtype="float32")
            w[:d.shape[0]] = d
            d = w.copy()
    return d
```

Listing 15-4: Augmenting the ESC-10 dataset, part 3

This function separates the samples (d) from the sample rate (sr) and makes sure the samples are floating-point numbers. For ESC-10, the source samples are all of type int16 (signed 16-bit integers). Next come four if statements. Each one asks for a single random float, and if that float is less than 0.5, we execute the body of the if. This means that we apply each possible augmentation with a probability of 50 percent.

The first if shifts the sound samples in time ❶ by rolling the NumPy array, a vector, by some number of samples, s. This value amounts to at most an eighth of a second, sr/4.0. Note that the shift can be positive or negative. The quantity sr/4.0 is the number of samples in a quarter of a second. However, the random float is in the range [−0.5, +0.5], so the ultimate shift is at most an eighth of a second. If the shift is negative, we need to zero samples at the end of the data; otherwise, we zero samples at the start.

Random noise is added by literally adding a random value of up to one-tenth of the range of the audio signal back in ❷. When played, this adds hiss, as you might hear on an old cassette tape.

Next comes shifting the pitch of the sample by using librosa. The pitch shift is expressed in musical steps, or fractions thereof. We randomly pick a float in the range [−10, +10] (pf) and pass it along with the data (d) and sampling rate (sr) to the librosa pitch_shift effect function ❸.

The last augmentation uses the librosa function to stretch or compress time (time_stretch) ❹. We adjust using an amount of time (rate) that is in the range [−0.5, +0.5]. If time was stretched, we need to chop off the extra samples to ensure that the sample length remains constant. If time was compressed, we need to add zero samples at the end.

Lastly, we return the new, augmented samples.

Running the code in Listing 15-2 creates a new *augmented* data directory with subdirectories *train* and *test*. These are the raw sound files that we'll work with going forward. I encourage you to listen to some of them to understand what the augmentations have done. The filenames should help you quickly tell the originals from the augmentations.

Preprocessing Our Data

Are we ready to start building models? Not yet. Our experience told us that the dataset was too small, and we augmented accordingly. However, we haven't yet turned the raw data into something we can pass to a model.

A first thought is to use the raw sound samples. These are already vectors representing the audio signal, with the time between the samples set by the sampling rate of 44,100 Hz. But we don't want to use them as they are. The samples are all exactly five seconds long. At 44,100 samples per second, that means each sample is a vector of $44,100 \times 5 = 220,500$ samples. That's too long for us to work with effectively.

With a bit more thought, we might be able to convince ourselves that distinguishing between a crying baby and a barking dog might not need such a high sampling rate. What if instead of keeping all the samples, we kept only every 100th sample? Moreover, do we really need five seconds' worth of data to identify the sounds? What if we kept only the first two seconds worth?

Let's keep only the first two seconds of each sound file; that's 88,200 samples. And let's keep only every 100th sample, so each sound file now becomes a vector of 882 elements. That's hardly more than an unraveled MNIST digit image, and we know we can work with those.

Listing 15-5 has the code to build the actual initial version of the dataset we'll use to build the models.

```
import os
import random
import numpy as np
from scipy.io.wavfile import read
sr = 44100 # Hz
N = 2*sr   # number of samples to keep
w = 100    # every 100
```

```
afiles = [i[:-1] for i in open("augmented_train_filelist.txt")]
trn = np.zeros((len(afiles),N//w,1), dtype="int16")
lbl = np.zeros(len(afiles), dtype="uint8")
for i,t in enumerate(afiles):
❶   f,c = t.split()
    trn[i,:,0] = read(f)[1][:N:w]
    lbl[i] = int(c)
np.save("esc10_raw_train_audio.npy", trn)
np.save("esc10_raw_train_labels.npy", lbl)

afiles = [i[:-1] for i in open("augmented_test_filelist.txt")]
tst = np.zeros((len(afiles),N//w,1), dtype="int16")
lbl = np.zeros(len(afiles), dtype="uint8")
for i,t in enumerate(afiles):
    f,c = t.split()
    tst[i,:,0] = read(f)[1][:N:w]
    lbl[i] = int(c)
np.save("esc10_raw_test_audio.npy", tst)
np.save("esc10_raw_test_labels.npy", lbl)
```

Listing 15-5: Building reduced samples dataset

This code builds train and test NumPy files containing the raw data. The data is from the augmented sound files we built in Listing 15-2. The file list contains the file location and class label ❶. We load each file in the list and put it into an array, either the train or test array.

We have a one-dimensional feature vector and a number of train or test files, so we might expect we need a two-dimensional array to store our data, either 6400 × 882 for the training set or 1600 × 882 for the test set. However, we know we'll ultimately be working with Keras, and we know that Keras wants a dimension for the number of channels, so we define the arrays to be 6400 × 882 × 1 and 1600 × 882 × 1 instead. The most substantial line in this code is the following:

```
trn[i,:,0] = read(f)[1][:N:w]
```

It reads the current sound file, keeps only the sound samples (`[1]`), and from the sound samples keeps only the first two seconds, worth at every 100th sample, `[:N:w]`. Spend a little time with this code. If you're confused, I'd suggest experimenting with NumPy at the interactive Python prompt to understand what it's doing.

In the end, we have train and test files for the 882 element vectors and associated labels. We'll build our first models with these. Figure 15-1 shows the resulting vector for a crying baby.

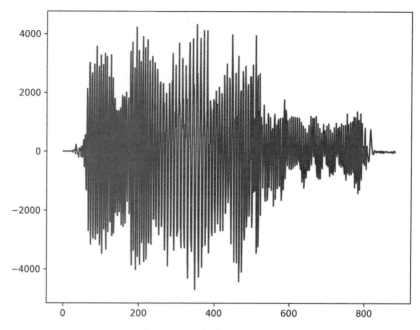

Figure 15-1: Feature vector for a crying baby

The x-axis is sample number (think "time"), and the y-axis is the sample value.

Classifying the Audio Features

We have our training and test sets. Let's build some models and see how they do. Since we have feature vectors, we can start quickly with classical models. After those, we can build some one-dimensional convolutional networks and see if they perform any better.

Using Classical Models

We can test the same suite of classical models we used in Chapter 7 with the breast cancer dataset. Listing 15-6 has the setup code.

```
import numpy as np
from sklearn.neighbors import NearestCentroid
from sklearn.neighbors import KNeighborsClassifier
from sklearn.naive_bayes import GaussianNB
from sklearn.ensemble import RandomForestClassifier
from sklearn.svm import LinearSVC

x_train = np.load("esc10_raw_train_audio.npy")[:,:,0]
y_train = np.load("esc10_raw_train_labels.npy")
```

```
x_test  = np.load("esc10_raw_test_audio.npy")[:,:,0]
y_test  = np.load("esc10_raw_test_labels.npy")

❶ x_train = (x_train.astype('float32') + 32768) / 65536
x_test = (x_test.astype('float32') + 32768) / 65536

train(x_train, y_train, x_test, y_test)
```

Listing 15-6: Classifying the audio features with classical models, part 1

Here we import the necessary model types, load the dataset, scale it, and then call a train function that we'll introduce shortly.

Scaling is crucial here. Consider the y-axis range for Figure 15-1. It goes from about −4000 to 4000. We need to scale the data so that the range is smaller and the values are closer to being centered around 0. Recall, for the MNIST and CIFAR-10 datasets, we divided by the maximum value to scale to [0, 1].

The sound samples are 16-bit signed integers. This means the full range of values they can take on covers $[−32,768, +32,767]$. If we make the samples floats, add 32,768, and then divide by 65,536 (twice the lower value) ❶, we'll get samples in the range $[0, 1)$, which is what we want.

Training and evaluating the classical models is straightforward, as shown in Listing 15-7.

```
def run(x_train, y_train, x_test, y_test, clf):
    clf.fit(x_train, y_train)
    score = 100.0*clf.score(x_test, y_test)
    print("score = %0.2f%%" % score)

def train(x_train, y_train, x_test, y_test):
    print("Nearest Centroid        : ", end='')
    run(x_train, y_train, x_test, y_test, NearestCentroid())
    print("k-NN classifier (k=3)   : ", end='')
    run(x_train, y_train, x_test, y_test, KNeighborsClassifier(n_neighbors=3))
    print("k-NN classifier (k=7)   : ", end='')
    run(x_train, y_train, x_test, y_test, KNeighborsClassifier(n_neighbors=7))
    print("Naive Bayes (Gaussian)  : ", end='')
    run(x_train, y_train, x_test, y_test, GaussianNB())
    print("Random Forest (trees=  5) : ", end='')
    run(x_train, y_train, x_test, y_test,
        RandomForestClassifier(n_estimators=5))
    print("Random Forest (trees= 50) : ", end='')
    run(x_train, y_train, x_test, y_test,
        RandomForestClassifier(n_estimators=50))
    print("Random Forest (trees=500) : ", end='')
    run(x_train, y_train, x_test, y_test,
        RandomForestClassifier(n_estimators=500))
    print("Random Forest (trees=1000): ", end='')
    run(x_train, y_train, x_test, y_test,
```

```
                RandomForestClassifier(n_estimators=1000))
    print("LinearSVM (C=0.01)        : ", end='')
    run(x_train, y_train, x_test, y_test, LinearSVC(C=0.01))
    print("LinearSVM (C=0.1)         : ", end='')
    run(x_train, y_train, x_test, y_test, LinearSVC(C=0.1))
    print("LinearSVM (C=1.0)         : ", end='')
    run(x_train, y_train, x_test, y_test, LinearSVC(C=1.0))
    print("LinearSVM (C=10.0)        : ", end='')
    run(x_train, y_train, x_test, y_test, LinearSVC(C=10.0))
```

Listing 15-7: Classifying the audio features with classical models, part 2

The train function creates the particular model instances and then calls run. We saw this same code structure in Chapter 7. The run function uses fit to train the model and score to score the model on the test set. For the time being, we'll evaluate the models based solely on their overall accuracy (the score). Running this code produces output like this:

```
Nearest Centroid            : score = 11.9%
k-NN classifier (k=3)       : score = 12.1%
k-NN classifier (k=7)       : score = 10.5%
Naive Bayes (Gaussian)      : score = 28.1%
Random Forest (trees=  5)   : score = 22.6%
Random Forest (trees= 50)   : score = 30.8%
Random Forest (trees=500)   : score = 32.8%
Random Forest (trees=1000)  : score = 34.4%
LinearSVM (C=0.01)          : score = 16.5%
LinearSVM (C=0.1)           : score = 17.5%
LinearSVM (C=1.0)           : score = 13.4%
LinearSVM (C=10.0)          : score = 10.2%
```

We can see very quickly that the classical models have performed terribly. Many of them are essentially guessing the class label. There are 10 classes, so random chance guessing should have an accuracy around 10 percent. The best-performing classical model is a Random Forest with 1,000 trees, but even that is performing at only 34.44 percent—far too low an overall accuracy to make the model one we'd care to use in most cases. The dataset is not a simple one, at least not for old-school approaches. Somewhat surprisingly, the Gaussian Naïve Bayes model is right 28 percent of the time. Recall that the Gaussian Naïve Bayes expects the samples to be independent from one another. Here the independence assumption between the sound samples for a particular test input is not valid. The feature vector, in this case, represents a signal evolving in time, not a collection of features that are independent of each other.

The models that failed the most are Nearest Centroid, *k*-NN, and the linear SVMs. We have a reasonably high-dimensional input, 882 elements, but only 6,400 of them in the training set. That is likely too few samples for the nearest neighbor classifiers to make use of—the feature space is too sparsely populated. Once again, the curse of dimensionality is rearing its ugly head.

The linear SVM fails because the features seem not to be linearly separable. We did not try an RBF (Gaussian kernel) SVM, but we'll leave that as an exercise for the reader. If you do try it, remember that there are now two hyperparameters to tune: C and γ.

Using a Traditional Neural Network

We haven't yet tried a traditional neural network. We could use the sklearn MLPClassifier class as we did before, but this is a good time to show how to implement a traditional network in Keras. Listing 15-8 has the code.

```
import keras
from keras.models import Sequential
from keras.layers import Dense, Dropout, Flatten
from keras import backend as K
import numpy as np

batch_size = 32
num_classes = 10
epochs = 16
nsamp = (882,1)
x_train = np.load("esc10_raw_train_audio.npy")
y_train = np.load("esc10_raw_train_labels.npy")
x_test  = np.load("esc10_raw_test_audio.npy")
y_test  = np.load("esc10_raw_test_labels.npy")
x_train = (x_train.astype('float32') + 32768) / 65536
x_test = (x_test.astype('float32') + 32768) / 65536
y_train = keras.utils.to_categorical(y_train, num_classes)
y_test = keras.utils.to_categorical(y_test, num_classes)

model = Sequential()
model.add(Dense(1024, activation='relu', input_shape=nsamp))
model.add(Dropout(0.5))
model.add(Dense(512, activation='relu'))
model.add(Dropout(0.5))
model.add(Flatten())
model.add(Dense(num_classes, activation='softmax'))

model.compile(loss=keras.losses.categorical_crossentropy,
              optimizer=keras.optimizers.Adam(),
              metrics=['accuracy'])
model.fit(x_train, y_train,
          batch_size=batch_size,
          epochs=epochs,
          verbose=0,
          validation_data=(x_test, y_test))
```

```
score = model.evaluate(x_test, y_test, verbose=0)
print('Test accuracy:', score[1])
```

Listing 15-8: A traditional neural network in Keras

After loading the necessary modules, we load the data itself and scale it as we did for the classical models. Next, we build the model architecture. We need only Dense layers and Dropout layers. We do put in a Flatten layer to eliminate the extra dimension (note the shape of nsamp) before the final softmax output. Unfortunately, this model does not improve things for us: we achieve an accuracy of only 27.6 percent.

Using a Convolutional Neural Network

Classical models and the traditional neural network don't cut it. We should not be too surprised, but it was easy to give them a try. Let's move on and apply a one-dimensional convolutional neural network to this dataset to see if it performs any better.

We haven't worked with one-dimensional CNNs yet. Besides the structure of the input data, the only difference is that we replace calls to Conv2D and MaxPooling2D with calls to Conv1D and MaxPooling1D.

The code for the first model we'll try is shown in Listing 15-9.

```
import keras
from keras.models import Sequential
from keras.layers import Dense, Dropout, Flatten
from keras.layers import Conv1D, MaxPooling1D
import numpy as np

batch_size = 32
num_classes = 10
epochs = 16
nsamp = (882,1)
x_train = np.load("esc10_raw_train_audio.npy")
y_train = np.load("esc10_raw_train_labels.npy")
x_test  = np.load("esc10_raw_test_audio.npy")
y_test  = np.load("esc10_raw_test_labels.npy")
x_train = (x_train.astype('float32') + 32768) / 65536
x_test = (x_test.astype('float32') + 32768) / 65536
y_train = keras.utils.to_categorical(y_train, num_classes)
y_test = keras.utils.to_categorical(y_test, num_classes)
model = Sequential()
model.add(Conv1D(32, kernel_size=3, activation='relu',
                 input_shape=nsamp))
model.add(MaxPooling1D(pool_size=3))
model.add(Dropout(0.25))
model.add(Flatten())
model.add(Dense(512, activation='relu'))
model.add(Dropout(0.5))
```

```
model.add(Dense(num_classes, activation='softmax'))
model.compile(loss=keras.losses.categorical_crossentropy,
              optimizer=keras.optimizers.Adam(),
              metrics=['accuracy'])
history = model.fit(x_train, y_train,
        batch_size=batch_size,
        epochs=epochs,
        verbose=1,
        validation_data=(x_test[:160], y_test[:160]))
score = model.evaluate(x_test[160:], y_test[160:], verbose=0)
print('Test accuracy:', score[1])
```

Listing 15-9: A 1D CNN in Keras

This model loads and preprocesses the dataset as before. This architecture, which we'll call the *shallow* architecture, has a single convolutional layer of 32 filters with a kernel size of 3. We'll vary this kernel size in the same way we tried different 2D kernel sizes for the MNIST models. Following the Conv1D layer is a single max-pooling layer with a pool kernel size of 3. Dropout and Flatten layers come next before a single Dense layer of 512 nodes with dropout. A softmax layer completes the architecture.

We'll train for 16 epochs using a batch size of 32. We'll keep the training history so we can examine the losses and validation performance as a function of epoch. There are 1,600 test samples. We'll use 10 percent for the training validation and the remaining 90 percent for the overall accuracy. Finally, we'll vary the Conv1D kernel size from 3 to 33 in an attempt to find one that works well with the training data.

Let's define four other architectures. We'll refer to them as *medium*, *deep0*, *deep1*, and *deep2*. With no prior experience working with this data, it makes sense to try multiple architectures. At present, there's no way to know ahead of time what the best architecture is for a new dataset. All we have is our previous experience.

Listing 15-10 lists the specific architectures, separated by comments.

```
# medium
model = Sequential()
model.add(Conv1D(32, kernel_size=3, activation='relu',
                input_shape=nsamp))
model.add(Conv1D(64, kernel_size=3, activation='relu'))
model.add(Conv1D(64, kernel_size=3, activation='relu'))
model.add(MaxPooling1D(pool_size=3))
model.add(Dropout(0.25))
model.add(Flatten())
model.add(Dense(512, activation='relu'))
model.add(Dropout(0.5))
model.add(Dense(num_classes, activation='softmax'))

# deep0
model = Sequential()
```

```python
model.add(Conv1D(32, kernel_size=3, activation='relu',
                 input_shape=nsamp))
model.add(Conv1D(64, kernel_size=3, activation='relu'))
model.add(Conv1D(64, kernel_size=3, activation='relu'))
model.add(MaxPooling1D(pool_size=3))
model.add(Dropout(0.25))
model.add(Conv1D(64, kernel_size=3, activation='relu'))
model.add(Conv1D(64, kernel_size=3, activation='relu'))
model.add(MaxPooling1D(pool_size=3))
model.add(Dropout(0.25))
model.add(Flatten())
model.add(Dense(512, activation='relu'))
model.add(Dropout(0.5))
model.add(Dense(num_classes, activation='softmax'))

# deep1
model = Sequential()
model.add(Conv1D(32, kernel_size=3, activation='relu',
                 input_shape=nsamp))
model.add(Conv1D(64, kernel_size=3, activation='relu'))
model.add(Conv1D(64, kernel_size=3, activation='relu'))
model.add(MaxPooling1D(pool_size=3))
model.add(Dropout(0.25))
model.add(Conv1D(64, kernel_size=3, activation='relu'))
model.add(Conv1D(64, kernel_size=3, activation='relu'))
model.add(MaxPooling1D(pool_size=3))
model.add(Dropout(0.25))
model.add(Conv1D(64, kernel_size=3, activation='relu'))
model.add(Conv1D(64, kernel_size=3, activation='relu'))
model.add(MaxPooling1D(pool_size=3))
model.add(Dropout(0.25))
model.add(Flatten())
model.add(Dense(512, activation='relu'))
model.add(Dropout(0.5))
model.add(Dense(num_classes, activation='softmax'))

# deep2
model = Sequential()
model.add(Conv1D(32, kernel_size=3, activation='relu',
                 input_shape=nsamp))
model.add(Conv1D(64, kernel_size=3, activation='relu'))
model.add(Conv1D(64, kernel_size=3, activation='relu'))
model.add(MaxPooling1D(pool_size=3))
model.add(Dropout(0.25))
model.add(Conv1D(64, kernel_size=3, activation='relu'))
model.add(Conv1D(64, kernel_size=3, activation='relu'))
model.add(MaxPooling1D(pool_size=3))
```

```
model.add(Dropout(0.25))
model.add(Conv1D(64, kernel_size=3, activation='relu'))
model.add(Conv1D(64, kernel_size=3, activation='relu'))
model.add(MaxPooling1D(pool_size=3))
model.add(Dropout(0.25))
model.add(Conv1D(64, kernel_size=3, activation='relu'))
model.add(Conv1D(64, kernel_size=3, activation='relu'))
model.add(MaxPooling1D(pool_size=3))
model.add(Dropout(0.25))
model.add(Flatten())
model.add(Dense(512, activation='relu'))
model.add(Dropout(0.5))
model.add(Dense(num_classes, activation='softmax'))
```

Listing 15-10: Different 1D CNN architectures

If we train multiple models, varying the first Conv1D kernel size each time, we get the results in Table 15-1. We've highlighted the best-performing model for each architecture.

Table 15-1: Test Set Accuracies by Convolutional Kernel Size and Model Architecture

Kernel size	Shallow	Medium	Deep0	Deep1	Deep2
3	**44.51**	41.39	**48.75**	54.03	9.93
5	43.47	41.74	44.72	53.96	48.47
7	38.47	40.97	46.18	52.64	49.31
9	41.46	**43.06**	46.88	48.96	9.72
11	39.65	40.21	45.21	52.99	10.07
13	42.71	41.67	46.53	50.56	**52.57**
15	40.00	42.78	46.53	50.14	47.08
33	27.57	42.22	41.39	48.75	9.86

Looking at Table 15-1, we see a general trend of accuracy improving as the model depth increases. However, at the deep2 model, things start to fall apart. Some of the models fail to converge, showing an accuracy equivalent to random guessing. The deep1 model is the best performing for all kernel sizes. When looking across by kernel size, the kernel with width 3 is the best performing for three of the five architectures. All of this implies that the best combination for the 1D CNNs is to use an initial kernel of width 3 and the deep1 architecture.

We trained this architecture for only 16 epochs. Will things improve if we train for more? Let's train the deep1 model for 60 epochs and plot the training and validation loss and error to see how they converge (or don't). Doing this produces Figure 15-2, where we see the training and validation loss (top) and error (bottom) as a function of epoch.

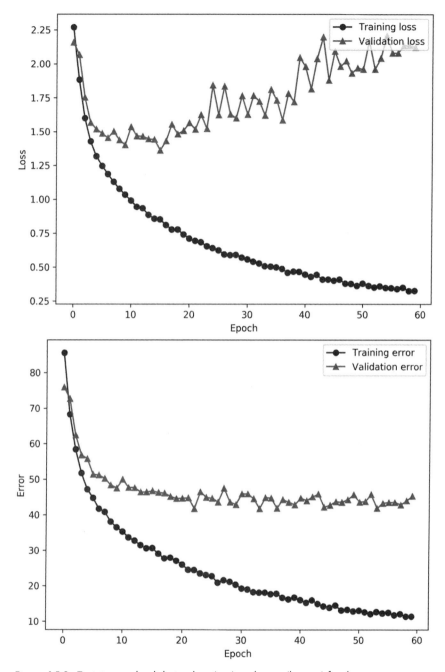

Figure 15-2: Training and validation loss (top) and error (bottom) for the deep1 architecture

Immediately, we should pick up on the explosion of the loss for the validation set. The training loss is continually decreasing until after about epoch 18 or so; then the validation loss goes up and becomes oscillatory. This is a clear example of overfitting. The likely source of this overfitting is our limited training set size, only 6,400 samples, even after data augmentation. The validation error remains more or less constant after initially decreasing. The conclusion is that we cannot expect to do much better than an overall accuracy of about 54 percent for this dataset using one-dimensional vectors.

If we want to improve, we need to be more expressive with our dataset. Fortunately for us, we have another preprocessing trick up our sleeves.

Spectrograms

Let's return to our augmented set of audio files. To build the dataset, we took the sound samples, keeping only two seconds' worth and only every 100th sample. The best we could do is an accuracy of a little more than 50 percent.

However, if we work with a small set of sound samples from an input audio file, say 200 milliseconds worth, we can use the vector of samples to calculate the *Fourier transform*. The Fourier transform of a signal measured at regular intervals tells us the frequencies that went into building the signal. Any signal can be thought of as the sum of many different sine and cosine waves. If the signal is composed of only a few waves, like the sound you might get from an instrument like the ocarina, then the Fourier transform will have essentially a few peaks at those frequencies. If the signal is complex, like speech or music, then the Fourier transform will have many different frequencies, leading to many different peaks.

The Fourier transform itself is complex-valued: each element has both a real and an imaginary component. You can write it as $a + bi$, where a and b are real numbers and $i = \sqrt{-1}$. If we use the absolute value of these quantities, we'll get a real number representing the energy of a particular frequency. This is called the *power spectrum* of the signal. A simple tone might have energy in only a few frequencies, while something like a cymbal crash or white noise will have energy more or less evenly distributed among all frequencies. Figure 15-3 shows two power spectra.

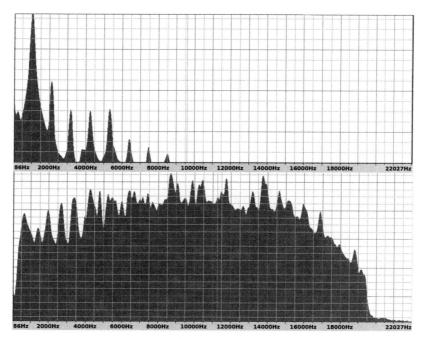

Figure 15-3: Power spectrum of an ocarina (top) and cymbal (bottom)

On the top is the spectrum of an ocarina, and on the bottom is a cymbal crash. As expected, the ocarina has energy in only a few frequencies, while the cymbal uses all the frequencies. The important point for us is that *visually* the spectra are quite different from each other. (The spectra were made with Audacity, an excellent open source audio processing tool.)

We could use these power spectra as feature vectors, but they represent only the spectra of tiny slices of time. The sound samples are five seconds long. Instead of using a spectrum, we will use a *spectrogram*. The spectrogram is an image made up of columns that represent individual spectra. This means that the x-axis represents time and the y-axis represents frequency. The color of a pixel is proportional to the energy in that frequency at that time.

In other words, a spectrogram is what we get if we orient the power spectra vertically and use color to represent intensity at a given frequency. With this approach, we can turn an entire sound sample into an image. For example, Figure 15-4 shows the spectrogram of a crying baby. Compare this to the feature vector of Figure 15-1.

Figure 15-4: Spectrogram of a crying baby

To create spectrograms of the augmented audio files, we need a new tool and a bit of code. The tool we need is called sox. It's not a Python library, but a command line tool. Odds are that it is already installed if you are using our canonical Ubuntu Linux distribution. If not, you can install it:

```
$ sudo apt-get install sox
```

We'll use sox from inside a Python script to produce the spectrogram images we want. Each sound file becomes a new spectrogram image.

The source code to process the training images is in Listing 15-11.

```
import os
import numpy as np
from PIL import Image

rows = 100
cols = 160
❶ flist = [i[:-1] for i in open("augmented_train_filelist.txt")]
N = len(flist)
img = np.zeros((N,rows,cols,3), dtype="uint8")
lbl = np.zeros(N, dtype="uint8")
p = []

for i,f in enumerate(flist):
    src, c = f.split()
  ❷ os.system("sox %s -n spectrogram" % src)
    im = np.array(Image.open("spectrogram.png").convert("RGB"))
  ❸ im = im[42:542,58:858,:]
    im = Image.fromarray(im).resize((cols,rows))
    img[i,:,:,:] = np.array(im)
```

```
        lbl[i] = int(c)
        p.append(os.path.abspath(src))

    os.system("rm -rf spectrogram.png")
    p = np.array(p)
❹ idx = np.argsort(np.random.random(N))
    img = img[idx]
    lbl = lbl[idx]
    p = p[idx]
    np.save("esc10_spect_train_images.npy", img)
    np.save("esc10_spect_train_labels.npy", lbl)
    np.save("esc10_spect_train_paths.npy", p)
```

Listing 15-11: Building the spectrograms

We start by defining the size of the spectrogram. This is the input to our model, and we don't want it to be too big because we're limited in the size of the inputs we can process. We'll settle for 100×160 pixels. We then load the training file list ❶ and create NumPy arrays to hold the spectrogram images and associated labels. The list p will hold the pathname of the source for each spectrogram in case we want to get back to the original sound file at some point. In general, it's a good idea to preserve information to get back to the source of derived datasets.

Then we loop over the file list. We get the filename and class label and then call sox, passing in the source sound filename ❷. The sox application is sophisticated. The syntax here turns the given sound file into a spectrogram image with the name *spectrogram.png*. We immediately load the output spectrogram into im, making sure it's an RGB file with no transparency layer (hence the call to convert("RGB")).

The spectrogram created by sox has a border with frequency and time information. We want only the spectrogram image portion, so we subset the image ❸. We determined the indices we're using empirically. It's possible, but somewhat unlikely, that a newer version of sox will require tweaking these to avoid including any border pixels.

Next, we resize the spectrogram so that it fits in our 100×160 pixel array. This is downsampling, true, but hopefully enough characteristic information is still present to allow a model to learn the difference between classes. We keep the downsampled spectrogram and the associated class label and sound file path.

When we've generated all the spectrograms, the loop ends, and we remove the final extraneous spectrogram PNG file. We convert the list of sound file paths to a NumPy array so we can store it in the same manner as the images and labels. Finally, we randomize the order of the images as a precaution against any implicit sorting that might group classes ❹. This is so that minibatches extracted sequentially are representative of the mix of classes as a whole. To conclude, we write the images, labels, and pathnames to disk. We repeat this entire process for the test set.

Are we able to visually tell the difference between the spectrograms of different classes? If we can do that easily, then we have a good shot of getting a model to tell the difference, too. Figure 15-5 shows 10 spectrograms of the same class in each row.

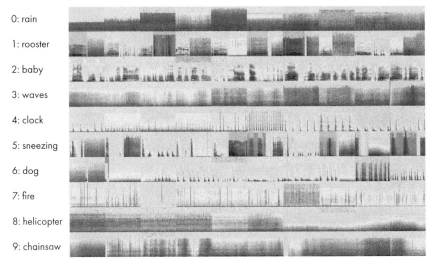

Figure 15-5: Sample spectrograms for each class in ESC-10. Each row shows 10 examples from the same class.

Visually, we can usually tell the spectra apart, which is encouraging. With our spectrograms in hand, we are ready to try some 2D CNNs to see if they do better than the 1D CNNs.

Classifying Spectrograms

To work with the spectrogram dataset, we need 2D CNNs. A possible starting point is to convert the shallow 1D CNN architecture to 2D by changing Conv1D to Conv2D, and MaxPooling1D to MaxPooling2D. However, if we do this, the resulting model has 30.7 million parameters, which is many more than we want to work with. Instead, let's opt for a deeper architecture that has fewer parameters and then explore the effect of different first convolutional layer kernel sizes. The code is in Listing 15-12.

```
import keras
from keras.models import Sequential
from keras.layers import Dense, Dropout, Flatten
from keras.layers import Conv2D, MaxPooling2D
```

```
import numpy as np

batch_size = 16
num_classes = 10
epochs = 16
img_rows, img_cols = 100, 160
input_shape = (img_rows, img_cols, 3)
x_train = np.load("esc10_spect_train_images.npy")
y_train = np.load("esc10_spect_train_labels.npy")
x_test = np.load("esc10_spect_test_images.npy")
y_test = np.load("esc10_spect_test_labels.npy")
x_train = x_train.astype('float32') / 255
x_test = x_test.astype('float32') / 255
y_train = keras.utils.to_categorical(y_train, num_classes)
y_test = keras.utils.to_categorical(y_test, num_classes)

model = Sequential()
model.add(Conv2D(32, kernel_size=(3,3), activation='relu',
                 input_shape=input_shape))
model.add(Conv2D(64, (3, 3), activation='relu'))
model.add(MaxPooling2D(pool_size=(2, 2)))
model.add(Dropout(0.25))
model.add(Conv2D(64, (3, 3), activation='relu'))
model.add(MaxPooling2D(pool_size=(2, 2)))
model.add(Dropout(0.25))
model.add(Flatten())
model.add(Dense(128, activation='relu'))
model.add(Dropout(0.5))
model.add(Dense(num_classes, activation='softmax'))

model.compile(loss=keras.losses.categorical_crossentropy,
              optimizer=keras.optimizers.Adam(),
              metrics=['accuracy'])
history = model.fit(x_train, y_train,
          batch_size=batch_size, epochs=epochs,
          verbose=0, validation_data=(x_test, y_test))
score = model.evaluate(x_test, y_test, verbose=0)
print('Test accuracy:', score[1])
model.save("esc10_cnn_deep_3x3_model.h5")
```

Listing 15-12: Classifying spectrograms

Here we are using a minibatch size of 16 for 16 epochs along with the Adam optimizer. The model architecture has two convolutional layers, a max-pooling layer with dropout, another convolutional layer, and a second max-pooling layer with dropout. There is a single dense layer of 128 nodes before the softmax output.

We'll test two kernel sizes for the first convolutional layer: 3×3 and 7×7. The 3×3 configuration is shown in Listing 15-12. Replace (3,3) with (7,7) to alter the size. All the initial 1D convolutional runs used a single training of the model for evaluation. We know that because of random initialization, we'll get slightly different results from training to training, even if nothing else changes. For the 2D CNNs, let's train each model six times and present the overall accuracy as a mean ± standard error of the mean. Doing just this gives us the following overall accuracies:

Kernel size	Score
3×3	78.78 ± 0.60%
7×7	78.44 ± 0.72%

This indicates that there is no meaningful difference between using a 3×3 initial convolutional layer kernel size or a 7×7. Therefore, we'll stick with 3×3 going forward.

Figure 15-6 shows the training and validation loss (top) and error (bottom) for one run of the 2D CNN trained on the spectrograms. As we saw in the 1D CNN case, after only a few epochs, the validation error starts to increase.

The 2D CNN performs significantly better than the 1D CNN did: 79 percent accuracy versus only 54 percent. This level of accuracy is still not particularly useful for many applications, but for others, it might be completely acceptable. Nevertheless, we'd like to do better if we can. It's worth noting that we have a few limitations in our data and, for that matter, our hardware, since we are restricting ourselves to a CPU-only approach, which limits the amount of time we are willing to wait for models to train. Here is where the some 25-fold increase in performance possible with GPUs would be helpful, assuming our use case allows for using GPUs. If we're planning to run the model on an embedded system, for example, we might not have a GPU available, so we'd want to stick with a smaller model anyway.

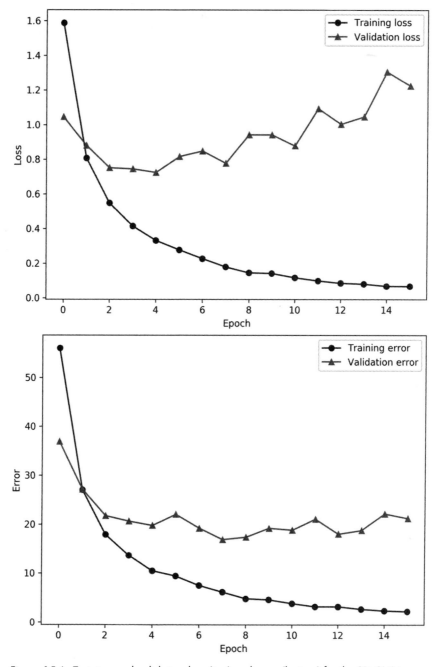

Figure 15-6: Training and validation loss (top) and error (bottom) for the 2D CNN architecture

Initialization, Regularization, and Batch Normalization

The literature tells us that there are other things we can try. We already augmented the dataset, a powerful technique, and we are using dropout, another powerful technique. We can try using a new initialization strategy, He initialization, which has been shown to often work better than Glorot initialization, the Keras default. We can also try applying L2 regularization, which Keras implements as weight decay per layer. See Chapter 10 for a refresher on these techniques.

To set the layer initialization algorithm, we need to add the following keyword to the Conv2D and first Dense layer:

```
kernel_initializer="he_normal"
```

To add L2 regularization, we add the following keyword to the Conv2D and first Dense layer:

```
kernel_regularizer=keras.regularizers.l2(0.001)
```

Here $\lambda = 0.001$. Recall, λ is the L2 regularization scale factor.

We could test these together, but instead we've tested them individually to see what effect, if any, they have for this dataset. Training six models as before gives the following overall accuracies:

Regularizer	Score
He initialization	$78.5 \pm 0.5\%$
L2 regularization	$78.3 \pm 0.4\%$

This is no different, statistically, from the previous results. In this case, these approaches are neither beneficial nor detrimental.

Batch normalization is another well-tested, go-to technique widely used by the machine learning community. We mentioned batch normalization briefly in Chapter 12. Batch normalization does just what its name suggests: it normalizes the inputs to a layer of the network, subtracting per feature means and dividing by the per feature standard deviations. The output of the layer multiplies the normalized input by a constant and adds an offset. The net effect is the input values are mapped to new output values by a two-step process: normalize the input and then apply a linear transform to get the output. The parameters of the linear transform are learned during backprop. At inference time, means and standard deviations learned from the dataset are applied to unknown inputs.

Batch normalization has shown itself time and again to be effective, especially in speeding up training. Machine learning researchers are still debating the exact reasons *why* it works as it does. To use it in Keras, you simply insert batch normalization after the convolutional and dense layers of the network (and after any activation function like ReLU used by those layers). Batch normalization is known to not work well with dropout, so we'll also remove the Dropout layers. The relevant architecture portion of the model code is shown in Listing 15-13.

```
from keras.layers import BatchNormalization

model = Sequential()
model.add(Conv2D(32, kernel_size=(3, 3),
                 activation='relu', input_shape=input_shape))
model.add(BatchNormalization())

model.add(Conv2D(64, (3, 3), activation='relu'))
model.add(BatchNormalization())
model.add(MaxPooling2D(pool_size=(2, 2)))

model.add(Conv2D(64, (3, 3), activation='relu'))
model.add(BatchNormalization())
model.add(MaxPooling2D(pool_size=(2, 2)))

model.add(Flatten())
model.add(Dense(128, activation='relu'))
model.add(BatchNormalization())
model.add(Dense(num_classes, activation='softmax'))
```

Listing 15-13: Adding in batch normalization

If we repeat our training process, six models with mean and standard error reporting of the overall accuracy, we get

$$\text{Batch normalization} \quad 75.56 \pm 0.59\%$$

which is significantly less than the mean accuracy found without batch normalization but including dropout.

Examining the Confusion Matrix

We've seen in this section that our dataset is a tough one. Augmentation and dropout have been effective, but other things like ReLU-specific initialization, L2 regularization (weight decay), and even batch normalization have not improved things for us. That doesn't mean these techniques are ineffective, just that they are not effective for this particular small dataset.

Let's take a quick look at the confusion matrix generated by one of the models using our chosen architecture. We've seen previously how to calculate the matrix; we'll show it here for discussion and for comparison with the confusion matrices we'll make in the next section. Table 15-2 shows the matrix; as always, rows are the true class label, and columns are the model-assigned label.

Table 15-2: Confusion Matrix for the Spectrogram Model

Class	0	1	2	3	4	5	6	7	8	9
0	**85.6**	0.0	0.0	5.6	0.0	0.0	0.0	5.0	0.6	3.1
1	0.0	**97.5**	1.2	0.0	0.6	0.6	0.0	0.0	0.0	0.0
2	0.0	13.8	**72.5**	0.6	0.6	3.8	6.2	0.0	0.6	1.9
3	25.0	0.0	0.0	**68.1**	0.0	2.5	0.6	0.0	2.5	1.2
4	0.6	0.0	0.0	0.0	**84.4**	6.2	5.0	3.8	0.0	0.0
5	0.0	0.0	0.6	0.0	0.0	**94.4**	4.4	0.6	0.0	0.0
6	0.0	0.0	1.2	0.0	0.0	10.6	**88.1**	0.0	0.0	0.0
7	9.4	0.0	0.6	0.0	15.6	1.9	0.0	**63.8**	7.5	1.2
8	18.1	1.9	0.0	5.6	0.0	1.2	2.5	6.9	**55.6**	8.1
9	7.5	0.0	8.1	0.6	0.0	0.6	0.0	1.9	10.0	**71.2**

The three worst-performing classes are helicopter (8), fire (7), and waves (3). Both waves and helicopter are most often confused with rain (0), while fire is most often confused with clock (4) and rain. The best performing classes are rooster (1) and sneezing (5). These results make sense. A rooster's crow and a person sneezing are distinct sounds; nothing really sounds like them. However, it is easy to see how waves and a helicopter could be confused with rain, or the crackle of a fire with the tick of a clock.

Does this mean we're stuck at 78.8 percent accuracy? No, we have one more trick to try. We've been training and evaluating the performance of single models. Nothing is stopping us from training multiple models and combining their results. This is *ensembling*. We presented ensembles briefly in Chapter 6 and again in Chapter 9 when discussing dropout. Now, let's use the idea directly to see if we can improve our sound sample classifier.

Ensembles

The core idea of an ensemble is to take the output of multiple models trained on the same, or extremely similar, dataset(s) and combine them. It embodies the "wisdom of the crowds" concept: one model might be better at certain classes or types of inputs for a particular class than another, so it makes sense that if they work together, they might arrive at a final result better than either one could do on its own.

Here, we'll use the same machine learning architecture we used in the previous section. Our different models will be separate trainings of this architecture using the spectrograms as input. This is a weaker form of ensembling. Typically, the models in the ensemble are quite different from each other, either different architectures of neural networks, or completely different types of models like Random Forests and *k*-Nearest Neighbors. The variation between models here is due to the random initialization of the networks and the different parts of the loss landscape the network finds itself in when training stops.

Our approach works like this:

1. Train multiple models ($n = 6$) using the spectrogram dataset.
2. Combine the softmax output of these models on the test set in some manner.
3. Use the resulting output from the combination to predict the assigned class label.

We hope that the set of class labels assigned after combining the individual model outputs is superior to the set assigned by the model architecture used alone. Intuitively, we feel that this approach should buy us something. It makes sense.

However, a question immediately arises: how do we best combine the outputs of the individual networks? We have total freedom in the answer to that question. What we are looking for is an $f()$ such that

$$y_{predict} = f(y_0, y_1, y_2, \ldots, y_n)$$

where y_i, $i = 0, 1, \ldots, n$ are the outputs of the n models in the ensemble and $f()$ is some function, operation, or algorithm that best combines them into a single new prediction, $y_{predict}$.

Some combination approaches come readily to mind: we could average the outputs and select the largest, keep maximum per class output across the ensemble and then choose the largest of those, or use voting to decide which class label should be assigned. We'll try all three of these.

Let's start with the first three approaches. We already have the six ensemble models: they're the models we trained in the previous section to give us the mean accuracy on the test set. This model architecture uses dropout, but no alternate initialization, L2 regularization, or batch normalization.

It's straightforward enough to run the test set through each of the models trained in the previous section (Listing 15-14):

```
import sys
import numpy as np
from keras.models import load_model

model = load_model(sys.argv[1])
x_test = np.load("esc10_spect_test_images.npy")/255.0
y_test = np.load("esc10_spect_test_labels.npy")
❶ prob = model.predict(x_test)
❷ p = np.argmax(prob, axis=1)

cc = np.zeros((10,10))
for i in range(len(y_test)):
    cc[y_test[i],p[i]] += 1

❸ print(np.array2string(cc.astype("uint32")))
cp = 100.0 * cc / cc.sum(axis=1)
```

```
❹ print(np.array2string(cp, precision=1))
  print("Overall accuracy = %0.2f%%" % (100.0*np.diag(cc).sum()/cc.sum(),))
  np.save(sys.argv[2], prob)
```

Listing 15-14: Applying multiple models to the test set

This code expects the name of the trained model file as the first argument and the name of an output file to store the model predictions as the
second argument. Then, it loads the model and spectrogram test data, applies the model to the test data ❶, and predicts class labels by selecting the
highest output value ❷.

The code also calculates the confusion matrix and displays it twice, first
as actual counts ❸ and again as a percentage of the actual class ❹. Finally,
it displays the overall accuracy and writes the probabilities to the disk. With
this code, we can store the predictions of each of the six models.

Now that we have the predictions, let's combine them in the first of the
three ways mentioned previously. To calculate the average of the model predictions, we first load each model's predictions, and then average and select
the maximum per sample as shown in Listing 15-15.

```
p0 = np.load("prob_run0.npy")
p1 = np.load("prob_run1.npy")
p2 = np.load("prob_run2.npy")
p3 = np.load("prob_run3.npy")
p4 = np.load("prob_run4.npy")
p5 = np.load("prob_run5.npy")
y_test = np.load("esc10_spect_test_labels.npy")
prob = (p0+p1+p2+p3+p4+p5)/6.0
p = np.argmax(prob, axis=1)
```

Listing 15-15: Averaging the test set results

The resulting percentage confusion matrix is

Class	0	1	2	3	4	5	6	7	8	9
0	**83.8**	0.0	0.0	7.5	0.0	0.0	0.0	4.4	0.0	4.4
1	0.0	**97.5**	1.9	0.0	0.0	0.6	0.0	0.0	0.0	0.0
2	0.0	10.0	**78.1**	0.0	0.0	3.1	6.2	0.0	0.0	2.5
3	9.4	0.0	0.0	**86.2**	0.0	3.1	0.6	0.0	0.0	0.6
4	0.6	0.0	0.0	0.0	**83.1**	5.6	5.0	5.6	0.0	0.0
5	0.0	0.0	0.0	0.0	0.6	**93.8**	5.6	0.0	0.0	0.0
6	0.0	0.0	0.6	0.0	0.0	8.8	**90.6**	0.0	0.0	0.0
7	8.1	0.0	0.0	0.0	17.5	1.9	0.0	**64.4**	7.5	0.6
8	6.2	0.0	0.0	7.5	0.0	1.9	4.4	8.8	**66.2**	5.0
9	5.0	0.0	5.0	1.2	0.0	0.6	0.0	1.9	10.6	**75.6**

with an overall accuracy of 82.0 percent.

This approach is helpful: we went from 79 percent to 82 percent in overall accuracy. The most significant improvements were in class 3 (waves) and class 8 (helicopter).

Our next approach, shown in Listing 15-16, keeps the maximum probability across the six models for each class and then selects the largest to assign the class label.

```
p = np.zeros(len(y_test), dtype="uint8")
for i in range(len(y_test)):
    t = np.array([p0[i],p1[i],p2[i],p3[i],p4[i],p5[i]])
    p[i] = np.argmax(t.reshape(60)) % 10
```

Listing 15-16: Keeping the test set maximum

This code defines a vector, p, of the same length as the vector of actual labels, y_test. Then, for each test sample, we form t, a concatenation of all six models' predictions for each class. We reshape t so that it is a one-dimensional vector of 60 elements. Why 60? We have 10 class predictions times 6 models. The maximum of this vector is the largest value, the index of which is returned by argmax. We really don't want this index; instead, we want the class label this index maps to. Therefore, if we take this index modulo 10, we will get the proper class label, which we assign to p. With p and y_test, we can calculate the confusion matrix:

Class	0	1	2	3	4	5	6	7	8	9
0	82.5	0.0	0.0	9.4	0.0	0.0	0.0	4.4	0.6	3.1
1	0.0	95.0	4.4	0.0	0.0	0.0	0.0	0.6	0.0	0.0
2	0.0	10.0	78.8	0.0	0.0	3.1	5.6	0.0	0.0	2.5
3	5.0	0.0	0.0	90.6	0.0	2.5	0.6	0.0	0.6	0.6
4	1.2	0.0	0.0	0.0	81.2	6.2	5.0	6.2	0.0	0.0
5	0.0	0.0	0.0	0.0	0.6	93.8	5.6	0.0	0.0	0.0
6	0.0	0.0	0.6	0.0	0.6	8.8	90.0	0.0	0.0	0.0
7	8.8	0.0	0.0	0.0	16.2	2.5	0.0	65.0	6.9	0.6
8	8.1	0.0	0.0	6.2	0.0	1.9	4.4	9.4	63.1	6.9
9	3.8	0.0	4.4	3.1	0.0	0.0	0.0	1.9	10.6	76.2

This gives us an overall accuracy of 81.6 percent.

Voting is the typical approach used to combine outputs from several models. To implement voting in this case, we'll use Listing 15-17.

```
t = np.zeros((6,len(y_test)), dtype="uint32")
❶ t[0,:] = np.argmax(p0, axis=1)
t[1,:] = np.argmax(p1, axis=1)
t[2,:] = np.argmax(p2, axis=1)
t[3,:] = np.argmax(p3, axis=1)
t[4,:] = np.argmax(p4, axis=1)
t[5,:] = np.argmax(p5, axis=1)
```

```
p = np.zeros(len(y_test), dtype="uint8")
for i in range(len(y_test)):
    q = np.bincount(t[:,i])
    p[i] = np.argmax(q)
```

Listing 15-17: Voting to select the best class label

We first apply argmax across the six model predictions to get the associated labels ❶, storing them in a combined matrix, t. We then define p as before to hold the final assigned class label. We loop over each of the test samples, where we use a new NumPy function, bincount, to give us the number of times each class label occurs for the current test sample. The largest such count is the most often selected label, so we use argmax again to assign the proper output label to p. Note, this code works because our class labels are integers running consecutively from 0 through 9. This alone is a good enough reason to use such simple and ordered class labels.

Here is the confusion matrix produced by this voting procedure:

Class	0	1	2	3	4	5	6	7	8	9
0	**86.2**	0.0	0.0	8.8	0.0	0.0	0.0	3.8	0.0	1.2
1	0.0	**98.1**	1.2	0.0	0.0	0.6	0.0	0.0	0.0	0.0
2	0.0	10.6	**78.1**	0.0	0.0	3.1	5.6	0.0	0.0	2.5
3	14.4	0.0	0.0	**81.2**	0.0	3.1	0.6	0.0	0.0	0.6
4	0.6	0.0	0.0	0.0	**83.8**	5.6	5.0	5.0	0.0	0.0
5	0.0	0.0	0.0	0.0	0.6	**94.4**	5.0	0.0	0.0	0.0
6	0.0	0.0	1.2	0.0	0.6	9.4	**88.8**	0.0	0.0	0.0
7	8.8	0.0	0.0	0.0	18.1	1.9	0.0	**65.6**	5.0	0.6
8	7.5	0.0	0.0	6.9	0.0	3.1	3.8	8.8	**67.5**	2.5
9	5.6	0.0	6.2	1.2	0.0	0.6	0.0	1.9	11.2	**73.1**

This gives us an overall accuracy of 81.7 percent.

Each of these three ensemble approaches improved our results, almost identically. A simple combination of the model outputs gave us, essentially, an accuracy boost of 3 percent over the base model alone, thereby demonstrating the utility of ensemble techniques.

Summary

This chapter presented a case study, a new dataset, and the steps we need to take to work through building a useful model. We started by working with the dataset as given to us, as raw sound samples, which we were able to augment successfully. We noticed that we had a feature vector and attempted to use classical models. From there, we moved on to 1D convolutional neural networks. Neither of these approaches was particularly successful.

Fortunately for us, our dataset allowed for a new representation, one that illustrated more effectively what composed the data and, especially important for us, introduced spatial elements so that we could work with 2D convolutional networks. With these networks, we improved quite a bit on the best 1D results, but we were still not at a level that was likely to be useful.

After exhausting our bag of CNN training tricks, we moved to ensembles of classifiers. With these, we discovered a modest improvement by using simple approaches to combining the base model outputs (for example, averaging).

We can show the progression of models and their overall accuracies to see how our case study evolved:

Model	Data source	Accuracy
Gaussian Naïve Bayes	1D sound sample	28.1%
Random Forest (1,000 trees)	1D sound sample	34.4%
1D CNN	1D sound sample	54.0%
2D CNN	Spectrogram	78.8%
Ensemble (average)	Spectrogram	82.0%

This table shows the power of modern deep learning and the utility of combining it with well-proven classical approaches like ensembles.

This chapter concludes our exploration of machine learning. We started at the beginning, with data and datasets. We moved on to the classical machine learning models, and then dove into traditional neural networks so that we would have a solid foundation from which to understand modern convolutional neural networks. We explored CNNs in detail and concluded with a case study as an illustration of how you might approach a new dataset to build a successful model. Along the way, we learned about how to evaluate models. We became familiar with the metrics used by the community so that we can understand what people are talking about and presenting in their papers.

Of course, this entire book has been an introduction, and we have barely scratched the surface of the ever-expanding world that is machine learning. Our final chapter will serve as a jumping-off point—a guide to where you may want to wander next to expand your machine learning knowledge beyond the tight bounds we've been required to set for ourselves here.

16

GOING FURTHER

You now have what I feel is a good introduction to modern machine learning. We
have covered building datasets, classical
models, model evaluation, and introductory
deep learning, from traditional neural networks to
convolutional neural networks. This short chapter is
intended to help you go further.

We'll look at both short-term "what's next" sorts of things as well as
longer-term forks in the road you may wish to explore. We'll also include
online resources where you will find the latest and greatest (always cognizant
that anything online is ephemeral). After that comes a necessarily subjective
list of conferences you may wish to attend. We'll close the chapter and book
with a thank you and a goodbye.

Going Further with CNNs

Even after four chapters' worth of material, we've barely scratched the surface of what convolutional neural networks can do. In part, we limited ourselves so you could grasp the fundamentals. And, in part, we were limited
because we made a conscious decision not to require a GPU. Training complex models with a GPU is, in general, 20 to 25 times faster than using a

CPU. With a GPU in your system, preferably designed for deep learning applications, the possibilities increase dramatically.

The models we developed were small, reminiscent of the original LeNet models LeCun developed in the 1990s. They get the point across, but they will not go too far in many cases. Modern CNNs come in a variety of flavors and now "standard" architectures. With a GPU, you can explore these larger architectures.

These architectures should be on your list of what to look at next:

- ResNet
- U-Net
- VGG
- DenseNet
- Inception
- AlexNet
- YOLO

Fortunately, the Keras toolkit we introduced (but also barely explored) supports all of these architectures. The two that seem especially useful to me are ResNet and U-Net. The latter is for semantic segmentation of inputs and has been widely successful, especially in medical imaging. To successfully train any of these architectures before your computer's power supply or hard drive has failed, to say nothing of your heart, you do need a GPU. Medium to higher-end gaming GPUs (from NVIDIA, for example) will support new enough versions of CUDA that you can get going with a card for under 500 USD. The real trick is ensuring that your computer will support the card. The power requirements are high, typically requiring a power supply of 600W or more, and a slot that supports a double-wide PCIe card. Go for RAM over performance; the more RAM the GPU has, the larger a model it will support.

Even if you don't upgrade your system with a GPU, it's worth your time to study the aforementioned architectures to see what makes them special and to understand how additional layers work. Check out the Keras documentation for more details: *keras.io*.

Reinforcement Learning and Unsupervised Learning

This book has dealt exclusively with supervised learning. Of the three main branches of machine learning, supervised learning is probably the most widely used. Recalling the Marx brothers, supervised learning is like Groucho, the one everyone remembers. That isn't an insult to the memory of Harpo and Chico, nor is it an insult to the other two branches of machine learning: reinforcement learning and unsupervised learning.

Reinforcement learning is goal-oriented; it encourages models to learn how to behave and act to maximize a reward. Instead of learning how to take an input and map it to a specific output class, as in supervised learning, reinforcement learning learns how to act in the current situation to maximize an overall goal, like winning a game. Many of the impressive news stories related to machine learning have involved reinforcement learning. These include the first Atari 2600 game-playing systems capable of beating the best humans, as well as the fall of the world Go champion to AlphaGo, and the even more impressive achievement of AlphaGo Zero, which mastered Go from scratch without learning from millions of games played by humans. Any self-driving car system is likely extremely complex, but it's a sure bet that reinforcement learning is a key part of that system.

Unsupervised learning refers to systems that learn on their own from unlabeled input data. Historically, this meant clustering, algorithms like *k*-means that take unlabeled feature vectors and attempt to group them by some similarity metric. Currently, one might argue that unsupervised learning is viewed as somewhat unimportant, given the insane amount of work being done with supervised learning and reinforcement learning. This is only half true; a lot of supervised learning is attempting to use unlabeled data (search for *domain adaptation*). How much of our own learning is unsupervised? An autonomous system set loose on an alien world will likely be more successful if it can learn things its creators didn't know it would need to know. This suggests the importance of unsupervised learning.

Generative Adversarial Networks

Generative adversarial networks (GANs) burst on the scene in 2014, the brainchild of deep learning researcher Ian Goodfellow. GANs were quickly heralded as the most significant advance in machine learning in 20 years (Yann LeCun, spoken at NIPS 2016, Barcelona).

Recent news about models that can generate an infinite number of photo-quality human faces use GANs. So do models that create simulated scenes and convert images of one style (say, a painting) to another (like a photograph). GANs wed a network that generates outputs, often based on some random setting of its input, to a discriminative network that tries to learn how to tell the difference between real inputs and inputs that came from the generative part. The two networks are trained together so that the generative network gets better and better at fooling the discriminative network. In contrast, the discriminative network gets better and better at learning how to tell the difference. The result is a generative network that is pretty good at outputting what you want it to output.

A proper study of GANs would require a book, but they are well worth a look and some of your time, at least to develop an intuitive sense of what is going on. A good place to start is with the particularly popular GAN architecture, CycleGAN, which has, in turn, spawned a small army of similar models.

Recurrent Neural Networks

A major topic entirely ignored by this book is *recurrent neural networks (RNNs)*. These are networks with feedback loops, and they work well for processing sequences like a time series of measurements—think sound samples or video frames. The most common form is the LSTM, the long short-term memory network. Recurrent networks are widely used in neural translation models like Google Translate that have made it possible to do real-time translation between dozens of languages.

Online Resources

The online resources for machine learning are legion and growing daily. Here are a few places that I find helpful and that are likely to stand the test of time. In no particular order:

Reddit Machine Learning (*www.reddit.com/r/MachineLearning/***)**
Look here for up-to-the-minute news and discussions of the latest papers and research.

Arxiv (*https://arxiv.org/***)** Machine learning progresses too quickly for most papers to go through the lengthy peer-review process print journals require. Instead, almost without exception, researchers and many conferences place all their papers on this preprint server, providing free access to the very latest in machine learning research. It can be daunting to sift through. Personally, I use the Arxiv app for my phone and several times a week peruse the following categories: Computer Vision and Pattern Recognition, Artificial Intelligence, Neural and Evolutionary Computing, and Machine Learning. The number of papers appearing in just these categories per week is impressive and a good indication of how active this field really is. To address the insane quantity of papers, deep learning researcher Andrej Karpathy created the useful Arxiv Sanity site at *http://www.arxiv-sanity.com/*.

GitHub (*https://github.com/***)** This is a place where people can host software projects. Go to the site directly and search for machine learning projects or use a standard search engine and add the keyword *github* to the search. With the explosion of machine learning projects, a beautiful thing has happened. The vast majority of the projects are freely available, even for commercial use. This typically includes full source code and datasets. If you read about something in a paper on Arxiv, you'll likely find an implementation of it on Github.

Coursera (*https://www.coursera.org/***)** Coursera is a premier site for online courses, the vast majority of which can be audited for free. There are other sites, but Coursera was co-founded by Andrew Ng, and his machine learning course is very popular.

YouTube (*www.youtube.com*)   YouTube is a force of nature at this point, but it is chock-full of machine learning videos. Let the viewer beware, but with some digging and judicious selection, you'll find a lot here, including demonstrations of the latest and greatest. Search for "Neural Networks for Machine Learning" taught by Geoffrey Hinton.

Kaggle (*https://www.kaggle.com/*)   Kaggle hosts machine learning competitions and is a good resource for datasets. Winners detail their models and training processes, providing ample opportunity to learn the art.

Conferences

One of the best ways to learn a new language is to immerse yourself in a culture that speaks the language. The same is true for machine learning. The way to immerse yourself in the culture of machine learning is to attend conferences. This can be expensive, but many schools and companies view it as important, so you might be able to get support for attending.

The massive explosion of interest in machine learning has caused a new phenomenon, one that I haven't seen happen in other academic disciplines: conferences selling out. This is true of the biggest conferences, but it might be happening to other conferences as well. If you want to attend, be aware that timing matters. Again, in no particular order, and missing many good but smaller conferences, consider the following:

NeurIPS (formerly NIPS)   Short for *Neural Information Processing Systems*, this is likely the biggest machine learning conference. At this academic conference, you can expect to see the latest research presented. NeurIPS has sold out quickly in recent years, in under 12 minutes in 2018 (!), and has now switched to a lottery system, so unless you are a presenter of some kind, getting the golden ticket email allowing you to register is not assured. It's usually held in Canada.

ICML   Short for *International Conference on Machine Learning*, this is perhaps the second largest annual conference. This academic conference has several tracks and workshops and is typically held in Europe or North America.

ICLR   The International Conference on Learning Representations is a deep learning–focused academic conference. If you want in-the-weeds technical presentations on deep learning, this is the place to be.

CVPR   Computer Vision and Pattern Recognition is another large conference that's perhaps slightly less academic than ICLR. CVPR is popular and not exclusively machine learning–oriented.

GTC   The GPU Technology Conference, sponsored by NVIDIA, is a technical conference as opposed to an academic conference. The annual presentation of new NVIDIA hardware happens here, along with a large expo, in San Jose, California.

The Book

Saying there are a few machine learning books out there is like saying there are a few fish in the sea. However, as far as deep learning is concerned, one stands head-and-shoulders above the rest: *Deep Learning* by Ian Goodfellow, Yoshua Bengio, and Aaron Courville (MIT Press, 2016). See *http://www.deeplearningbook.org/*.

Deep Learning is the book you should go to if you want to get serious about being a machine learning researcher. Even if you don't, it covers the key topics in depth and with mathematical rigor. The book is not for those looking to get better at using one toolkit or another, but for those who want to see the theory behind machine learning and the math that goes with it. In essence, it's an advanced undergraduate—if not graduate-level text, but that shouldn't put you off. At some point, you will want to take a look at this book, so keep it in the back of your mind—or on your bookshelf.

So Long and Thanks for All the Fish

We've reached the end of the book. There's no monster here, only ourselves, and the knowledge and intuition we've gained by working through the preceding chapters. Thank you for persevering. It's been fun for me to write; I genuinely hope it's been fun for you to read and contemplate. Don't stop now—take what we've developed and run with it. If you're like me, you'll see applications for machine learning everywhere. Go forth and classify!

INDEX

curse of dimensionality, 55
curve fitting, 213

P

p-value, 8
parent distribution, 7, 60, 252
partial derivative, 201
Pasteur, Louis, 167
Piczal, Karol J., 378
Pillow, 3
    PIL, 48
    convert, 50
    fromarray, 49
    open, 49
    save, 49
    show, 49
    documentation, 50
Plato, 7, 60
pooling, 299
positive predictive value (PPV), 258
power spectrum, 394
Powers, David Martin, 262
precision, 258
precision-recall curve, 275
preprocessing, 83
primary visual cortex, 297
principal component analysis (PCA),
    95, 153, 158
    MNIST, 158
prior class probability, 60, 253
probability, 6
    Bayes' theorem, 114
    distribution, 7
    Gaussian distribution, 8
    joint probability, 115
    likelihood, 114
    normal distribution, 7, 8, 116
    notation
      uniform distribution, 8
    parent distribution, 7, 60
    posterior probability, 114
    prior class probability, 60
    prior probability, 114
    uniform distribution, 7
probability distribution, 7
probability map, 336
pseudorandom sequence, 140
Python
    blocks, 12
    bottom-tested loop, 22
    break, 22–23
    continue, 22–23
    control structures, 19
      for, 20
      if, 12, 19
      try, 24
      while, 22
      with, 23
    data structures, 13
    debugging, 24
    dictionaries, 13, 18
    documentation, 27
    dynamic typing, 14
    editor conventions, 13
    enumerate, 20
    essence, 11
    except, 24
    exceptions, 24
    exiting, 12
    False, 16
    floating-point numbers, 13
    for loops, 20
    function definition, 24
      defaults, 25
    if statement, 19
    intentation, 12
    interactive mode, 12
    librosa, 380
    list comprehensions, 21
    list operations, 15
    lists, 13, 15
      copying, 16
    lists in memory, 30
    module, 26
      copy, 17
      deepcopy, 17
      time, 26, 32
    namespaces, 26
    None, 16
    pass, 13
    pickle, 45, 184
    primitive data types, 15
    range, 20, 39
    statements, 12
    strings, 13, 14
      quotes, 15
    top-tested loop, 22
    True, 16
    try, 24
    tuple, 17
    variables, 13–14

tensor, 6
TensorFlow, 2
    documentation, 2
test data, 68
toolkit
    Apache MXNet, 2
    Caffe, 2
    Caffe2, 2
    HDF5, 3
    installation, 3
    Keras, 2
    NumPy, 2
    Pillow, 3
    PyTorch, 2
    scikit-learn, 2
    TensorFlow, 2
    versions, 3
training data, 68
training set, xxviii
transcendental functions, 173
transfer learning, 361
    embedding, 361
trigonometric functions, 173
true negative rate (TNR), 257
truc positive rate (TPR), 257

U

U-Net, 340
Ubuntu, 1
UCI Machine Learning Repository, 84
uniform distribution, 7
uniformly distributed, 211
unsupervised learning, xxviii, 412

V

validation data, 68
Vapnik, Vladimir, 124
variance, 7
vector, 4, 31
    column vector, 4
    dot product, 5
    inner product, 5
    multiplication, 5
    outer product, 5
    row vector, 4

W

weight decay, 216
weight initialization, 190, 211, 243
    Glorot, 212
    He, 212
    Xavier, 212
weight update, 193–194
weighted accuracy, 279
weights, 172
Williams, Ronald J., 200
Windows, 3

Y

YOLO, 340
Youden's *J* statistic, 262
YouTube, 415

Z

zero-padding, 287

COLOPHON

The fonts used in *Practical Deep Learning* are New Baskerville, Futura, The Sans Mono Condensed and Dogma. The book was typeset with LaTeX 2_ε package nostarch by Boris Veytsman *(2008/06/06 v1.3 Typesetting books for No Starch Press)*.

The book was printed and bound by Sheridan Books, Inc. in Chelsea, Michigan. The paper is 60# Finch Offset, which is certified by the Forest Stewardship Council (FSC).

The book uses layflat binding, in which the pages are bound together with a cold-set, flexible glue and the first and last pages of the resulting book block are attached to the cover. The cover is not actually glued to the book's spine, and when open, the book lies flat and the spine doesn't crack.

Never before has the world relied so heavily on the Internet to stay connected and informed. That makes the Electronic Frontier Foundation's mission—to ensure that technology supports freedom, justice, and innovation for all people—more urgent than ever.

For over 30 years, EFF has fought for tech users through activism, in the courts, and by developing software to overcome obstacles to your privacy, security, and free expression. This dedication empowers all of us through darkness. With your help we can navigate toward a brighter digital future.